The Inductive
Bible Study Companion
Unlock the Word

SHANNON BUCHBACH

DEDICATION

To my YWAM friends and family.
Special thanks go to the staff and students of Muizenberg's 2010 School of Biblical Studies where this project began.

CONTENTS

ACKNOWLEDGMENTS

I received tremendous help whilst preparing this book. There are too many people to thank in full here, but a few people must be mentioned by name.

First, my husband. You brought this to print through your encouragement.

Also, Sarah, James, Chris, Jenny, Leanne, Jaco and Christine. Without your championing I would not have made a start, let alone seen it through to the end.

Mothers are known for their endless support, and mine is no different; my father deserves a mention, too.

Michele, you worked tirelessly to edit this book for the Kingdom.
Lastly, my friend, Lucky. Thank you for using your God-given talents to illustrate this book.

FROM THE AUTHOR

Let me begin by sharing a part of my journey with you and the reason why I am passionate about the development of Biblical resources. I knew that the Bible was a book to be used. I tried to do Bible studies. I had even read through a number of the books, including a select few of the Old Testament, such as Genesis, Joshua and Job. Despite this I always felt a sense that I was missing out. It was like I had a treasure map and I had found the "X" where the treasure was hidden – I just didn't know how to unlock the treasure chest. In my longing for more, I had prayed to God for revelation, and He answered my prayers.

I was blessed to be able to take time out of my working life to become a student of the Bible. During this time, I found my key to the chest. I gained the basic understanding of history I needed to understand the books of the Bible and began my journey of exploration, which I still delight in. There is always more that we can learn from Scripture. The Bible has an endless supply of precious jewels contained within it and they are there waiting for us to discover them.

I believe that we need to find a way to unlock the chest of gems God has for each of us, within the pages of Scripture. Our Bibles were not made to sit on the shelf at home. They can teach, inspire, encourage, confront and heal. Hebrews 4:12 proclaims that: *"For the Word of God is living and active . . ."*

The Bible, read with the Holy Spirit, comes to life, and gives life. It is a treasure trove just waiting to be explored and I pray that you will find new jewels and weighty gold in its pages. However, many within the church are lacking the map required to find the treasure chest, and the keys they require to unlock it. It is my prayer that the Inductive Bible Study Companion (IBSC) will become a map and key for you, enabling you to find the wealth of treasures contained within the pages of Scripture.

To finish on the words of 2 Timothy 3:15-17: *". . . the sacred writings, which are able to make you wise for salvation through faith in Christ Jesus. All Scripture is breathed out by God and profitable for teaching, for reproof, for correction, and for training in righteousness, that the man of God may be competent, equipped for every good work."*

May you be blessed with many insights and discoveries on your journey through God's living Word.

With blessings,
Shannon Buchbach
Drakensberg, South Africa, 2015

INTRODUCTION TO THE COMPANION

The Inductive Bible Study Companion for individuals

To gain a broad overview of the Bible

Many of us start with the grand plan of "reading through the entire Bible". Our motives might be correct and we can make it through Genesis, or maybe even Exodus, but then Leviticus comes up and, whilst our intentions are in the right place, they do not lead to action.

For each book of the Bible, this Companion gives a brief introduction to the historical context in which it was written; remembering that the books of the Bible were written separately and the Bible that we have today was not compiled until recent times. This overview can make a whole book come to life and help your understanding of why it was originally written. Once you have an idea of what the original readers of the text were going through, you are then able to accurately interpret the Word, and finally bring it to a meaningful application for your own life.

To gain a broad overview of the Bible

Alternatively, you may wish to focus in on just one book of the Bible. The IBSC can help you keep the "big picture" of each book in mind. This is important because, without it, you can find yourself focusing on just one or two verses and end up with an entirely different (and wrong) interpretation of what those words meant.

Each book has insightful interpretation questions to help you dig deeper into the book. It also gives you an overview of important historical background, the reason why the book was written and key observations to make when reading through the text. The IBSC will help you to delve deeper into your chosen book.

For the "old hands"

For those of you who have been studying the Bible for many years, you will know that there are always more gems to find. I pray that for you, the IBSC may give a new angle of exploration and supply you with more questions to ponder on and pray about.

Not "an intellectual"?

Each of us has a unique way of learning and we can learn to nurture this in the study of God's Word. The IBSC has an extra section of interpretation giving alternative ways of studying the Bible, whilst not detracting from what you will learn of God's Truth.

The Inductive Bible Study Companion for small groups

The IBSC sets the scene on each book and follows through with interpretation questions and application ideas that will get discussions flowing. Use it to bring structure to a study, or for a reference point when teaching. The background information provided for each book will help your small group to dig deeper, and see beyond the surface of the text, thereby generating insightful discussions and life-changing applications.

GUIDE TO USING THE COMPANION

General bible study tips

Stay big picture

Reading the Bible in its entirety will help give you an overview of the "big picture" of the Bible. This is very necessary as the Bible tells a story; it is the story of God's plan for man's redemption and shows the unfailing love that He has for mankind, whom He created in His image. Once a strong foundational understanding is built, you will have plenty of time to go back and pore over smaller sections of Scripture, focus in on a particular theme, or concentrate on an individual book within the Bible.

It may seem like a great commitment, resolving to study each book of the Bible in quick succession, but it will give even greater rewards in the currency of understanding God's heart for man and the reason mankind needed a Saviour. To gain a "big picture" overview, trace the following themes from Genesis right through to Revelation: the character of God, the character of man, and God's plan for man's salvation.

Completing the studies

Each book of the Bible has been given its own chapter within the IBSC. The studies give you the information that you need to correctly interpret Scripture and gain insight into the character of God and nature of man. The lay-out will guide you to personal revelations. Do not be afraid to ask questions of God and questions of the text as you complete your studies. The purpose of each section of the studies is explained below.

During your first and second readings of a given book

This section of each chapter gives you keys that will unlock the text, so it is best to read it before the chosen book. Read the main study themes listed for that book as well as aspects of the text to pay attention to as you read your Bible. These will help you when it comes to interpreting the Bible text. They will help you to explore what it meant to those to whom it was originally written.

Themes

The themes highlight key topics within the books. They disclose the core message that the author was addressing by writing the book. Consider looking at a painting in a gallery. In appreciating the picture, we may zoom in on specific details – for example, the different brush stroke techniques utilised by the artist – but to become lost in details, and lose sight of the complete picture, means we are blind to the beauty of the grand design. Considering themes as you read the book will help you to remain focused on the larger picture that God, the artist, was painting.

Things to notice from the text

These sections give key observations to make when reading through the text, prior to commencing your interpretation, to answer the question: What do I need to see from this text? Highlight these key observations, so important observations stand out from the page; consider it as a way of making your page become interactive.

Marking these suggestions will help you during interpretation. This step of Bible study is known as observation. Below are some examples of how you may wish to highlight your observations in your Bible.

Examples

Genesis asks you to: "Highlight the actions of God throughout the book of Genesis to focus on the character of God."

- Genesis 1:1 *In the beginning, God created the heavens and the earth.*
- Genesis 12:17 *But the LORD afflicted Pharaoh and his house with great plagues because of Sarai, Abram's wife.*
- Genesis 31:24 *But God came to Laban the Aramean in a dream by night and said to him, "Be careful not to say anything to Jacob, either good or bad."*

Isaiah asks you to: "Mark re-occurring ideas and images (motifs): Righteousness."

- Isaiah 32:14-20 *For the palace is forsaken, the populous city deserted; the hill and the watchtower will become dens forever, a joy of wild donkeys, a pasture of flocks; until the Spirit is poured upon us from on high, and the wilderness becomes a fruitful field, and the fruitful field is deemed a forest. Then justice will dwell in the wilderness, and righteousness abide in the fruitful field. And the effect of righteousness will be peace, and the result of righteousness, quietness and trust forever. My people will abide in a peaceful habitation, in secure dwellings, and in quiet resting places. And it will hail when the forest falls down, and the city will be utterly laid low. Happy are you who sow beside all waters, who let the feet of the ox and the donkey range free.*

Matthew asks you to: "Mark the words "fulfil" and "sign", as well as Old Testament (O.T.) quotes."

- Matthew 3:2-4 "Repent, for the kingdom of heaven is at hand." For this is

O.T. { he who was spoken of by the prophet Isaiah when he said, "The voice of one crying in the wilderness: 'Prepare the way of the Lord; make his paths straight.'" Now John wore a garment of camel's hair and a leather belt around his waist, and his food was locusts and wild honey.

O.T. {
- Matthew 2:17-19 Then was |fulfilled| what was spoken by the prophet Jeremiah: "A voice was heard in Ramah, weeping and loud lamentation, Rachel weeping for her children; she refused to be comforted, because they are no more." But when Herod died, behold, an angel of the Lord appeared in a dream to Joseph in Egypt, ...
- Matthew 12:38 Then some of the scribes and Pharisees answered him, saying, "Teacher, we wish to see a sign from you."

2 Corinthians asks you to mark: "Important commands from Paul to the Corinthians."

- 2 Corinthians 6:14-15 *Do not be unequally yoked with unbelievers. For what partnership has righteousness with lawlessness? Or what fellowship has light with darkness? What accord has Christ with Belial? Or what portion does a believer share with an unbeliever?*
- 2 Corinthians 8:10-12 *And in this matter I give my judgement: this benefits you, who a year ago started not only to do this work but also to desire to do it. So now finish doing it as well, so that your readiness in desiring it may be matched by your completing it out of what you have. For if the readiness is there, it is acceptable according to what a person has, not according to what he does not have.*

[At this point, you will complete the first reading of the book. As you read, keep in mind the information that was given in this section. It is best to read the book out loud and with speed to absorb as much of the text, as fast as possible].

Chapter summaries

These are optional as they can be time consuming for the larger books. If you choose to do them, you will receive a much deeper appreciation of the book. By the end of The IBSC, you will have paraphrased the entire Bible! Go through each chapter and try to summarise it in one paragraph, using your own words; force yourself to stay big picture and capture the heart of each chapter.

After your initial readings of a given book

Whenever possible, try to read the Bible book out loud and in one sitting. Reading aloud helps to increase attention, and reading in one sitting helps to maintain the natural flow of a book. Most of the smaller books can be read in ten to twenty minutes. Do this before commencing the study. This will help you to keep the big picture in mind, and prevent you from becoming caught up in the details of a single verse. Reading the book as a whole helps to reveal the core message that the author was trying to get across to his audience.

Setting of the book

This information is gathered from clues within the text as well as knowledge of history. The setting of the book is important as it places the book in its historical context, and thereby assures accurate interpretation. The setting of the book is made up of the author, the date it was written, from where it was written and the original reader.

The original reader refers to the people or church to whom the text was originally written. For example, the book of 2 Corinthians was a letter written by Paul to the church in Corinth; he had a target audience and was addressing specific issues that existed within that church. A far better understanding of Paul's message will be gained by considering the situation in Corinth at the time the book was written.

In the books of the prophets, there are two additional sections for the book's setting. This is the original hearer and the time the prophecies were spoken. It is important to remember that the prophets both spoke their prophecies (to the original hearers) and recorded their prophecies (to the original readers). The original hearers and readers are not always the same group of people!

Reason written

Why was this book written? Each book of the Bible was written to fulfil a specific purpose at that time in history. For example, the first five books of the Bible, known as the Pentateuch, were written as a reminder of Israelite history, what God had done, the covenant He had established with them, and the Law, by which the Israelites were to live.

Big picture

The information contained within this section builds upon that given in *Setting of the book*, and further establishes the context of the book. It falls under the following subdivisions:

Historical background

To understand a book in its original context we need to know what that context was! Think of reading Shakespeare's "Romeo and Juliet" where he writes "I bite my thumb at you." Unless someone told you that, in Shakespeare's day, this was a great insult, then the action described makes little sense in today's culture. *Historical background* provides important cultural information to bring understanding to cultural references within the book.

Character portrayal

Put yourself "in the shoes" of the original reader so you can understand how they would have responded to the message. This is key to coming to an accurate interpretation of the text and its meaning. Each chapter of this Companion contains a portrayal of a fictional character, or event, to illustrate the cultural setting in which that book was written. This character portrayal will help you to gain a feel for who the original readers were, as well as the author, and the circumstances in which the book was written.

Book overview

Remaining focused on the big picture, prevents you from taking verses and passages of Scripture out of context and therefore also prevents developing wrong theology. The *Book overview* provides an overview of the book, laying out the main ideas and helping you to interpret the book in light of the author's overall message.

Help with difficult passages

Some passages in Scripture are the subject of much debate within the church. These passages are not salvation-related and should not unsettle believers; however, many will be interested in hearing some of the schools of thought that exist, so this subsection explains some of the main interpretations put forward by theologians.

Help with symbolism

This subsection is uniquely provided for the book of Revelation. Its purpose is to help bring clarity for main images and symbols used within the book.

Interpretation

Always consider what the passage would have meant to the original readers. Remember to keep the big picture of a book in mind, not becoming confused by the few verses that even theologians cannot agree on in interpretation. Reading with the big picture in mind helps you to accurately understand the meaning of a passage by studying it within its broader context.

Interpretation questions

The questions listed in this section give you guidance on how to study the book.

A few examples of what these questions stimulate you to think about include: the importance of a passage, what it shows of God's character, what it shows of man's character, what the author wanted to convey, and how the original readers would have felt as they heard the book read. These questions help us to approach study from different angles, which will help us to dig deeper into the text, discovering new treasures.

Creative interpretation

This section cuts straight to the heart of the author's message through small, often artistic, assignments. Not all of us are academic-minded and so this subsection provides an alternative ways of unlocking a book's message. The "Creative interpretation" subsection provides alternative ideas for studying the book, whilst not subtracting from the understanding you will gain of God and His Word.

Application inspiration

This section brings us to the heart of all Bible study. The end purpose of all Bible studies should be application within the life of the student. Knowledge without application is meaningless. As James wrote (James 1:23-25): *'For if anyone is a hearer of the word and not a doer, he is like a man who looks intently at his natural face in a mirror. For he looks at himself and goes away and at once forgets what he was like. But the one who looks into the perfect law, the law of liberty, and perseveres, being no hearer who forgets but a doer who acts, he will be blessed in his doing'.*

Can you imagine looking in the mirror in the morning, with your hair messy or toothpaste left around your mouth, and then leaving for work without fixing what you have seen? James feels the same way towards Scripture; it would be equally ridiculous, in his opinion, to read the Word of God and then not live out what it says to do. It is not always easy to think of ways we can apply Scripture to our lives and so this section offers a few suggestions on how you could apply a book's the message within your own life.

Suggested study and reading orders

The IBSC offers several lists to guide the order of your study. Two of these will give you a "big picture" overview of the Bible; they highlight the character of God, the nature of man, mankind's need for a Saviour, and the fulfilment of God's redemptive plan. A third order of study gives time frames for covering every study in the IBSC in two years.

Whilst the IBSC is a study resource, enabling Christians to dig deeper into the heart of God's Word, it can be used to give additional depth to those reading through the Bible. To this end, a fourth order of reading enables coverage of all of Scripture in one year.

Finally, two lists of themes are also given. The first lists the themes, with key books that look at that theme under each heading. The second lists the books, with the key themes of each book given underneath them.

A final word

Enjoy your study of Scripture! God has many treasures just waiting for you to discover in His Word. Treat your study like a grand treasure hunt, with the Holy Spirit trekking with you as your ultimate companion. Before you start each study session, make sure to pray; asking God to guide your study, thinking and discoveries. Happy hunting!

SUGGESTED STUDY AND READING ORDERS

Big picture overview of Scripture 1

The following sequence gives a big picture overview of Scripture as you study the books of the Bible. It starts with the New Testament and then goes back to the Old Testament. This is helpful when you want to gain a New Testament understanding first. It is also helpful if you want to begin with what is more familiar to you.

☐ Luke – Jesus, Saviour of all
☐ Acts of the Apostles - God's Holy Spirit and the unstoppable Gospel
☐ Galatians - Salvation in Christ alone
☐ Colossians - Christ is sufficient for salvation
☐ Ephesians - In Christ
☐ Philippians - Unity through humility
☐ Romans - United by righteousness under grace
☐ 1 Corinthians - Defining unity and love
☐ 2 Corinthians - Boast in the Lord
☐ Psalms - The Lord, worthy of praise!

Commence Psalms assignment. Try to complete 3-5 psalms as you study each book.

☐ Philemon - Appeal for Onesimus
☐ Titus - Godly living and sound doctrine
☐ 1 Timothy - Sound doctrine leads to godly living
☐ 2 Timothy - Paul's last letter, one of discipleship
☐ James - Faith in action
☐ Mark – Christ, the suffering Servant
☐ 1 Peter - Hope to endure persecution
☐ 1 Thessalonians - Stay strong in your faith
☐ 2 Thessalonians - Day of Christ's return

- ☐ 2 Peter - Be vigilant awaiting Christ's return
- ☐ Jude - False teachers and Christ's return
- ☐ John - Life in Christ
- ☐ Revelation - Christ victorious
- ☐ 1 John - Abide in His Love, knowing you are saved
- ☐ 2 John - Hospitality with caution
- ☐ 3 John - Hospitality in love
- ☐ Hebrews - Supremacy of Christ brings hope
- ☐ Genesis - The first book; "the Beginning"
- ☐ Exodus - A holy God building a holy nation
- ☐ Leviticus - Be holy for I am Holy
- ☐ Numbers - The wilderness years
- ☐ Deuteronomy – Remember, love and obey
- ☐ Joshua - God fights for His people
- ☐ Judges - Sin cycles
- ☐ Ruth - Faith amongst faithlessness
- ☐ 1 & 2 Samuel - Israel rejects God as their King
- ☐ 1 & 2 Kings - The reason for the exile
- ☐ 1 & 2 Chronicles - Temple from building to burning
- ☐ Proverbs - Wisdom = Walking in fear of the Lord

Read through Proverbs, highlighting themes. Study Proverbs 1-9. Commence Proverbs theme assignment, trying to complete one theme study from Proverbs with each book you study.

Prophets to Israel
- ☐ Hosea - Israel plays the whore
- ☐ Amos - Judged for injustice

Prophets to Assyria
- ☐ Jonah - Grace available to all people
- ☐ Nahum - Assyria judged

Prophets to Judah
- ☐ Joel - The coming day of the Lord
- ☐ Isaiah - Salvation through the suffering Servant
- ☐ Micah - Lord of justice
- ☐ Habakkuk - Questioning God amidst unrighteousness
- ☐ Zephaniah - The choice is yours!
- ☐ Jeremiah - Judgement falls on Judah
- ☐ Lamentations - Jeremiah weeps for Judah

Prophets to Edom
- ☐ Obadiah - Sins against a brother

In-exile prophets and leaders
- ☐ Ezekiel - So they will know that I am the Lord

☐ Daniel - Whatever comes, God is bigger. Full stop.

Post-exile prophets and leaders

    ☐ Esther - Courage amidst persecution

    ☐ Ezra - Temple rebuilt, but was the lesson learned?

    ☐ Haggai - "Build My house!"

    ☐ Nehemiah - Rebuilding and renewal

    ☐ Malachi - Here comes the great day!

    ☐ Zechariah - Coming King, coming kingdom

    ☐ Job - Do the righteous suffer?

    ☐ Ecclesiastes - The search for life's meaning

    ☐ Song of Songs - Love between man and woman

    ☐ Matthew – Jesus, the prophesied Redeemer

Big picture overview of Scripture 2

The following sequence gives a big picture overview of Scripture as you study the books of the Bible. It starts with the New Testament and then goes back to the Old Testament. This is helpful when you want to gain a New Testament understanding first. It is also helpful if you want to begin with what is more familiar to you.

- ☐ Luke – Jesus, Saviour of all
- ☐ Acts of the Apostles - God's Holy Spirit and the unstoppable Gospel
- ☐ Galatians - Salvation in Christ alone
- ☐ Colossians - Christ is sufficient for salvation
- ☐ Ephesians - In Christ
- ☐ Philippians - Unity through humility
- ☐ Romans - United by righteousness under grace
- ☐ 1 Corinthians - Defining unity and love
- ☐ 2 Corinthians - Boast in the Lord
- ☐ Psalms - The Lord, worthy of praise!

Commence Psalms assignment. Try to complete 3-5 psalms as you study each book.

- ☐ Philemon - Appeal for Onesimus
- ☐ Titus - Godly living and sound doctrine
- ☐ 1 Timothy - Sound doctrine leads to godly living
- ☐ 2 Timothy - Paul's last letter, one of discipleship
- ☐ James - Faith in action
- ☐ Mark – Christ, the suffering Servant
- ☐ 1 Peter - Hope to endure persecution
- ☐ 1 Thessalonians - Stay strong in your faith
- ☐ 2 Thessalonians - Day of Christ's return
- ☐ 2 Peter - Be vigilant awaiting Christ's return

☐ Jude - False teachers and Christ's return

☐ John - Life in Christ

☐ Revelation - Christ victorious

☐ 1 John - Abide in His Love, knowing you are saved

☐ 2 John - Hospitality with caution

☐ 3 John - Hospitality in love

☐ Hebrews - Supremacy of Christ brings hope

☐ Genesis - The first book; "the Beginning"

☐ Exodus - A holy God building a holy nation

☐ Leviticus - Be holy for I am Holy

☐ Numbers - The wilderness years

☐ Deuteronomy – Remember, love and obey

☐ Joshua - God fights for His people

☐ Judges - Sin cycles

☐ Ruth - Faith amongst faithlessness

☐ 1 & 2 Samuel - Israel rejects God as their King

☐ 1 & 2 Kings - The reason for the exile

☐ 1 & 2 Chronicles - Temple from building to burning

☐ Proverbs - Wisdom = Walking in fear of the Lord

Read through Proverbs, highlighting themes. Study Proverbs 1-9. Commence Proverbs theme assignment, trying to complete one theme study from Proverbs with each book you study.

Prophets to Israel

☐ Hosea - Israel plays the whore

☐ Amos - Judged for injustice

Prophets to Assyria

☐ Jonah - Grace available to all people

☐ Nahum - Assyria judged

Prophets to Judah

☐ Joel - The coming day of the Lord

☐ Isaiah - Salvation through the suffering Servant

☐ Micah - Lord of justice

☐ Habakkuk - Questioning God amidst unrighteousness

☐ Zephaniah - The choice is yours!

☐ Jeremiah - Judgement falls on Judah

☐ Lamentations - Jeremiah weeps for Judah

Prophets to Edom

☐ Obadiah - Sins against a brother

In-exile prophets and leaders

☐ Ezekiel - So they will know that I am the Lord

☐ Daniel - Whatever comes, God is bigger. Full stop.

Post-exile prophets and leaders

- ☐ Esther - Courage amidst persecution
- ☐ Ezra - Temple rebuilt, but was the lesson learned?
- ☐ Haggai - "Build My house!"
- ☐ Nehemiah - Rebuilding and renewal
- ☐ Malachi - Here comes the great day!
- ☐ Zechariah - Coming King, coming kingdom
- ☐ Job - Do the righteous suffer?
- ☐ Ecclesiastes - The search for life's meaning
- ☐ Song of Songs - Love between man and woman
- ☐ Matthew – Jesus, the prophesied Redeemer

The Bible in two years

Study your way through Scripture in two years

The following list provides a week by week study layout, which will see you study each book of the Bible over the course of two years. Two years may seem long; however, it will be hard to find a more worthy investment for your time!

☐ Week 1-3
Genesis
☐ Week 4-5
Exodus
☐ Week 6-7
Luke
Psalms 1-3
☐ Week 8-9
Leviticus
Psalms 4-7
☐ Week 10-11
Hebrews
Psalms 8-10
☐ Week 12-13
Numbers
Psalms 11-14
☐ Week 14-15
Deuteronomy
Psalms 15-18
☐ Week 16-17
Joshua
Psalms 19-22

☐ Week 18-19
Judges
Psalms 23-26
☐ Week 20
Ruth
Psalms 27-28
☐ Week 21-23
1 &2 Samuel
Psalms 29-34
☐ Week 24-26
1 & 2 Kings
Commence Kings and
Chronicles special
assignment
Psalms 35-38
☐ Week 27-29
1 & 2 Chronicles
Complete Kings and
Chronicles special
assignment
Psalms 39-42
☐ Week 30-31

Hosea
Psalms 43-46
☐ Week 32-33
Amos
Psalms 47-50
☐ Week 34
Jonah
Psalms 51-53
☐ Week 35
Nahum
Psalms 54-56
☐ Week 36
Joel
Psalms 57-59
☐ Week 37-39
Isaiah
Psalms 60-64
☐ Week 40-41
Micah
Psalms 65-68
☐ Week 42
Zephaniah
Psalms 69-72
☐ Week 43-44
Jeremiah
Psalms 73-77
☐ Week 45
Habakkuk
Psalms 78-79
☐ Week 46-47
Ezekiel
Psalms 80-85
☐ Week 48-49
Daniel
Psalms 86-89
☐ Week 50
Lamentations
Psalms 90-95
☐ Week 51
Obadiah
Psalms 96-101
☐ Week 52-53
Ezra

Psalms 102-105
☐ Week 54
Haggai
Psalms 106-109
☐ Week 55
Esther
Psalms 110-114
☐ Week 56-57
Nehemiah
Psalms 115-118
☐ Week 58
Malachi
Psalms 119
☐ Week 59-60
Zechariah
Psalms 120-125
☐ Week 61-62
Job
Psalms 126-130
☐ Week 63
Ecclesiastes
Psalms 131-133
☐ Week 64
Song of Songs
Psalms 134-136
☐ Week 65
Read Proverbs
Choose 1 Proverbs theme
☐ Week 66-68
Matthew
Psalms 137-142
☐ Week 69-71
Acts of the Apostles
Psalms 143-147
☐ Week 72-73
Galatians
Psalms 148-150
☐ Week 74-75
Ephesians
Choose 1 Proverbs theme
☐ Week 76-77
Colossians
Choose 1 Proverbs theme

☐ Week 78-79
Romans
☐ Week 80
Philippians
Choose 1 Proverbs theme
☐ Week 81-82
1 Corinthians
Choose 1 Proverbs theme
☐ Week 83-84
2 Corinthians
Choose 1 Proverbs theme
☐ Week 85
1 Timothy
Choose 1 Proverbs theme
☐ Week 86
Titus
Choose 2 Proverbs theme
☐ Week 87
Philemon
Choose 2 Proverbs theme
☐ Week 88
1 Thessalonians
Choose 1 Proverbs theme
☐ Week 89-90
Mark
Choose 1 Proverbs theme
☐ Week 91
1 Peter
Choose 1 Proverbs theme
☐ Week 92
2 Timothy
Choose 1 Proverbs theme
☐ Week 93
James
Choose 1 Proverbs theme
☐ Week 94
2 Thessalonians
Choose 1 Proverbs theme
☐ Week 95
2 Peter
☐ Week 96
Jude
☐ Week 97

2 John
3 John
☐ Week 98
John
☐ Week 99-100
John
☐ Week 101
1 John
Choose 1 Proverbs theme
☐ Week 102-104
Revelation

The Bible in one year

Read through all of Scripture in one year

The following list provides a week by week study layout for one year. This may seem like a lot of work; however, it will be hard to find a more worthy investment for your time and energy!

Please remember that the IBSC has been developed as a study guide. If your goal is to read through Scripture (as opposed to studying the books), it is recommended that you still at least read the partnering information in the IBSC for each book before reading the book; this will set the stage and ensure you understand its context.

Take note that some weeks require more reading than others; however, it is beneficial to read a book in a short span of time, so as not to lose track of the overall message of the book.

☐ Week 1
   Matthew
   Psalm 1-2

☐ Week 2-3
   Genesis
   Galatians
   Psalm 3-4

☐ Week 4
   Exodus
   Psalm 5-6

☐ Week 5
   Leviticus
   Psalm 7-8

☐ Week 6
   Hebrews
   Psalm 9-12

☐ Week 7
   Numbers
   Psalm 13-14

☐ Week 8
   Deuteronomy
   Psalm 15-16

☐ Week 9
   Joshua
   Psalm 17-20

☐ Week 10
   Judges
   Ruth
   Psalm 21-23

☐ Week 11
   Job
   Psalm 24-27

☐ Week 12-14
   1 Samuel
   2 Samuel
   Psalm 28-33

☐ Week 15-17
   1 Kings
   2 Kings
   Psalm 34-39

☐ Week 18
   Song of Songs
   Psalm 40-47
   Proverbs 1-9

☐ Week 19-21
   1 Chronicles
   2 Chronicles
   Psalm 48-53
   Proverbs 10

☐ Week 22
   Ecclesiastes
   Psalm 54-61
   Proverbs 11

☐ Week 23
   Hosea
   Amos
   Psalm 62-65
   Proverbs 12:1-13

☐ Week 24
   Jonah
   Nahum
   Psalm 66-67
   Proverbs 13:14-18

☐ Week 25
   Joel
   Micah
   Psalm 68-69
   Proverbs 13:1-12

☐ Week 26-27
   Isaiah
   Habakkuk
   Psalm 70-73
   Proverbs 13:13-25

☐ Week 28-29
   Jeremiah

Lamentations
Psalm 74-77
Proverbs 14

☐ Week 30-31
   Ezekiel
   Psalm 78-81
   Proverbs 15

☐ Week 32
   Obadiah
   Philemon
   Psalm 82-85
   Proverbs 16

☐ Week 33
   John
   Psalm 86-87
   Proverbs 17:1-16

☐ Week 34
   Daniel
   Psalm 88-90
   Proverbs 17:17-28

☐ Week 35
   Revelation
   Psalm 91-92
   Proverbs 18:1-13

☐ Week 36
   Esther
   James
   Psalm 93-96
   Proverbs 18:14-24

☐ Week 37
   Ezra
   Haggai
   Psalm 97-98
   Proverbs 19:1-17

☐ Week 38
   Nehemiah
   Malachi
   Psalm 99-101
   Proverbs 19:18-29

☐ Week 39
   Zechariah
   Psalm 102-107
   Proverbs 20

☐ Week 40
  Mark
  Psalm 108-110
  Proverbs 21:1-15
☐ Week 41
  Acts of the Apostles
  Psalm 111-113
  Proverbs 21:16-31
☐ Week 42
  Colossians
  Ephesians
  Psalm 114-116
  Proverbs 22:1-16
☐ Week 43
  1 Corinthians
  Psalm 117-120
  Proverbs 22:17-23:8
☐ Week 44
  2 Corinthians
  Psalm 121-124
  Proverbs 23:9-35
☐ Week 45
  Philippians
  Psalm 125-132
  Proverbs 24
☐ Week 46
  Romans
  Psalm 133-135
  Proverbs 25
☐ Week 47
  1 Thessalonians
  2 Thessalonians
  Psalm 136-139

Proverbs 26
☐ Week 48
  Titus
  1 Timothy
  2 Timothy
  Psalm 140-141
  Proverbs 27
☐ Week 49
  1 Peter
  Psalms 142-144
  Proverbs 28
☐ Week 50
  2 Peter
  Jude
  Psalm 145-146
  Proverbs 29
☐ Week 51
  1 John
  2 John
  3 John
  Psalm 147-148
  Proverbs 30
☐ Week 52
  Luke
  Psalm 149-150
  Proverbs 31

Studying by theme

Key topics within the book have been listed below and partnered with the books in which the topic is a key theme. Studying by theme can be useful for small groups, digging deeper into a topic of interest, or exploring a topic of current media focus. When looking at themes, remember not to look at individual verses or passages of Scripture in isolation; all Scripture needs to be viewed in light of its context within an individual book, and the entire Bible.

Abide (in God)
- 1 John

Atonement
- Leviticus

Adultery/ Adulterous nation
- Proverbs
- Hosea

Beauty (physical)
- Song of Songs

Beginnings
- Genesis

Belief
- Luke
- John

Believers
- Ephesians (received in Christ; identity in Christ)
- Colossians (Christ is sufficient)
- Hebrews (confidence in Christ)
- 1 John (Abide in God)

Book of Law
- Deuteronomy

Bold in Faith
- Joshua
- Acts of the Apostles

Call (fulfilling one's call)
- 2 Timothy

Character of God
- All books

Character of man
- All books
- Genesis
- Numbers
- Psalms

Characters/ leaders
- Moses (Exodus and Numbers)
- Joshua (Joshua)
- The judges (Judges)
- Leaders and Kings (1 & 2 Samuel, 1 & 2 Kings, 1 & 2 Chronicles, Psalms, Daniel)

- The prophets (1 & 2 Kings, books of the prophets)
- Ezra (Ezra)
- Nehemiah (Nehemiah)
- Mordecai and Esther (Esther)
- Shadrach, Meshach and Abednego (Daniel)
- Jesus (Matthew, Mark, Luke, John)
- Paul (Acts of the Apostles, Romans, 1 & 2 Corinthians, Galatians, Ephesians, Philippians, Colossians, 1 & 2 Thessalonians, 1 & 2 Timothy, Titus, Philemon)
- Timothy (1 Timothy)

Children of God
- Romans

Christ
- A New Testament theme
- Matthew (Messiah/ Holy One)
- Mark (Suffering Servant)
- Luke (compassion of Christ)
- John (divinity of Christ)
- Ephesians (authority of Christ; received in Christ; identity in Christ)
- Colossians (fullness of God; Christ is sufficient)
- Hebrews (superiority of Christ; confidence in Christ)
- 1 Peter (example of Christ)

Christian living
- See "righteous living"

Christians
- See "believers"

Cleansing
- See "purification"

Comfort
- Job

Confidence
- 1 John ("Know": who you are, what Christ has done, and that you are in Him)

Covenant
- Genesis
- Exodus
- Ruth
- 1 & 2 Samuel
- 1 & 2 Kings
- Nehemiah
- Jeremiah
- Malachi

Day of the Lord
- Joel
- Obadiah
- Zephaniah
- Malachi
- 1 Thessalonians
- 2 Thessalonians
- Jude

Discipleship
- Matthew
- Mark
- Luke
- John
- 2 Timothy
- 1 Peter (example of Christ)

Discipline of God
- Numbers
- Proverbs

Drunkenness
- Proverbs

Endurance
- Mark
- 2 Timothy
- Hebrews
- 1 Peter
- Revelation

Eternal life
- John

Eternal Perspective
- Mark
- 2 Timothy
- 1 Peter

Evangelism
- John

Faith
- Joshua
- Habakkuk
- John
- Acts of the Apostles
- Romans
- Galatians
- 1 Thessalonians
- James

Faithfulness
- Joshua
- Ruth
- Song of Songs
- Mark (faithfulness of Jesus)

Faithlessness
- Jeremiah
- Hosea

False prophets/ teachers
- 2 Corinthians
- Galatians
- 1 Timothy
- 2 Peter
- 2 John
- Jude

Family
- Proverbs

Fear of the Lord
- Proverbs
- Ecclesiastes

Folly
- Proverbs
- Ecclesiastes

Forgiveness
- See "reconciliation"

God's name (for the sake of)
- Ezekiel
- Malachi

God's salvation plan
- Genesis

Gospel
- Acts of the Apostles (spread of)
- Galatians
- 2 Timothy

Grace
- Romans
- Galatians

Great day of the Lord
- See "day of the Lord"

Greed
- Proverbs

Grief
- Lamentations

Guidance (from God)
- Acts of the Apostles

Hearts
- Song of Songs
- Isaiah
- Jeremiah
- Lamentations
- Hosea (God's heart for His people)
- Jonah (God's heart for the nations)
- Colossians (thankful heart)
- Holiness
- Leviticus

Holy Spirit
- Judges
- Psalms
- Books of the prophets
- Ezekiel
- Luke
- Acts of the Apostles (actions

and empowerment of)
- Galatians

Hope
- Psalms
- 1 Thessalonians

Hospitality
- 2 John
- 3 John

Humility
- See "pride"

Romans
- Philippians

Idolatry
- An Old Testament theme
- Amos

Israel (north and south kingdoms)
- Judges
- 1 & 2 Kings
- 1 & 2 Chronicles
- Ezra

Psalms
- Hosea
- Haggai

Jesus
- See "Christ" and "Messiah"

Joy
- Philippians

Judgement/ Justice
- Isaiah
- Ezekiel
- Joel
- Obadiah
- Micah
- Zephaniah
- Revelation

Kingdom of God
- Daniel
- Obadiah
- Matthew
- Luke
- Revelation

Labour
- Proverbs
- Ecclesiastes
- Amos (laziness)

Law
- Leviticus
- Deuteronomy
- 1 & 2 Chronicles
- Romans
- Galatians

Laziness
- Proverbs
- Amos

Leadership
- See "characters/ leaders"

Proverbs
- 1 Timothy
- 2 Timothy
- Titus

(The) least
- Luke

Life
- See "eternal life"
- Proverbs

Living under God
- Ecclesiastes
- 1 Corinthians

Love
- Deuteronomy (love and obedience)
- Judges
- Song of Songs (love of God)
- Hosea (love of God)
- Obadiah (unbrotherly love)
- Jonah (love thy enemy)
- 1 Corinthians
- 1 John
- 2 John
- 3 John

Loyalty
- Ruth

Leadership Principles
- 1 & 2 Kings

Messiah/ Messianic Visions
- Psalms
- Isaiah
- Micah
- Zephaniah
- Zechariah
- Matthew (fulfilment of prophecies)

Mercy (of God)
- Judges
- Revelation

Miraculous signs
- John

Ministry
- Jeremiah

Money
- Proverbs

Name
- See "God's name"

Obedience
- Deuteronomy
- Joshua
- Ruth
- 1 & 2 Kings
- 1 & 2 Chronicles
- Esther
- James
- 1 John

Opposition/ Persecution
- Ezra
- Nehemiah
- Esther
- Psalms
- Jeremiah
- Mark
- Acts of the Apostles
- Philippians
- 1 Thessalonians
- 2 Thessalonians
- Revelation

Oppression (of the poor)/ outcast
- Proverbs
- Psalms
- Amos
- Luke

People of God
- See "Israel"
- Romans

Persecution
- See "opposition"

Poor/ needy
- Psalms
- Proverbs
- Amos
- James

Praise
- See "worship"

Prayer
- Nehemiah
- Jonah
- Luke
- 2 Thessalonians

Pride (and humility)
- Proverbs
- Isaiah
- Daniel
- Amos
- Obadiah
- 3 John

Presence of God
- Jonah

Purification
- Zephaniah
- Zechariah

Questioning God
- Lamentations
- Habakkuk

Reconciliation
- Obadiah
- Philemon

Relationship with God
- Psalms

Remembrance
- Exodus
- Deuteronomy
- Joshua
- Nehemiah

Repentance
- Joel

Revival/ Renewal/ Restoration
- 1 & 2 Chronicles
- Nehemiah
- Isaiah
- Ezekiel
- Zechariah

Rich
- Proverbs
- James

Righteous/ness
- Psalms
- Proverbs
- Romans
- Galatians

Righteous living
- Proverbs
- Ecclesiastes
- Romans
- Galatians
- Colossians
- 1 Timothy
- 2 Timothy
- Titus
- Philemon (cost of)
- 1 Peter

Sacrifice
- Malachi (right sacrifices)

Saints
- See "righteous"
- Revelation

Salvation
- Isaiah

- Matthew
- Colossians (Christ is sufficient)

Second coming (of Christ)
- 1 Thessalonians
- 2 Thessalonians
- 2 Peter
- Jude

Sin / Broken Covenant
- Judges (sin cycles)
- 1 & 2 Kings
- 1 & 2 Chronicles
- Isaiah
- Jeremiah
- Micah

Social Injustice
- Proverbs
- Isaiah
- Amos
- Micah
- Habakkuk
- James

Sorrow
- See "grief"

Sound doctrine
- 1 Timothy
- Titus

Sovereignty of God/ King of kings
- Esther
- Job
- Jeremiah
- Daniel
- Jonah
- Hebrews (superiority of Christ)

Speech/ tongue
- Proverbs
- James

Spirit of God
- See "Holy Spirit"

Strength of God

- 2 Corinthians

Submission
- 1 Peter

Suffering
- Job
- Mark
- Philippians
- 1 Thessalonians
- 2 Thessalonians
- 2 Timothy
- Hebrews
- 1 Peter

Super apostles
- See "false prophets/ teachers"

Teaching
- Titus

Temple
- 1 & 2 Chronicles
- Ezra
- Haggai

Tithing
- Malachi

Toil
- See "labour"

Tongue
- See "speech"

Trust in the Lord
- Psalms
- Isaiah

Truth
- Galatians (true Gospel)
- 2 John
- 3 John

Weakness
- 2 Corinthians

Wicked
- Psalms
- Proverbs

Wisdom
- Proverbs

- Ecclesiastes
- 1 Corinthians
- James

Witness
- 1 Corinthians
- Philippians

Works
- Romans
- Galatians

Women
- Proverbs

Worship
- Exodus
- Psalms
- Revelation

Worthiness of the Lamb
- John
- Revelation

Wrath of God
- Nahum
- Revelation

Unbelief
- Isaiah

Unity
- Romans
- 1 Corinthians
- Ephesians
- Philippians

Unfaithfulness
- See "faithlessness"

Vanity/ meaningless
- Ecclesiastes

THEMES OF THE BOOKS

Repeated themes in the Old Testament:

- Character of God
- Sovereignty of God
- Grace
- Justice
- Compassion
- Love for the poor, foreigner
- Blessings for obedience (and curses for disobedience)
- Remember (what God has done)

Genesis

- God's salvation plan
- Covenants
- Character of God
- Character of man
- Beginnings

Exodus

- Character of God – He is the hero of Exodus!
- Worship
- The covenant
- Character of Moses
- Remembrance

Leviticus

- Holiness
- Atonement

Numbers

- Character and nature of man versus Character and nature of God
- Character of Moses
- Discipline of God

Deuteronomy

- Remembrance
- Book of Law
- Love and obey; the call to be faithful
- God's love for Israel

Joshua

- Memorials and remembrance
- Obedience versus disobedience
- God's faithfulness (and character)
- Joshua's character
- Be bold in faith

Judges

- Character of the judges: their strengths and weaknesses
- Character of God,

particularly His jealousy, love, faithfulness and mercy
- The people of Israel
- The cycles of sin

Ruth
- Obedience to the covenant
- Loyalty
- God's faithfulness

1 & 2 Samuel
- Character of God
- People's character
- Keeping the covenant

1 & 2 Kings
- Obedience/ disobedience to the covenant
- Character of God
- Character of the Prophets
- Leadership principles

1 & 2 Chronicles
- Treatment of the temple
- Obedience (to the Law) and revival
- God's character
- Divided, but still part of God's people

Ezra
- The temple
- The people
- Character of Ezra
- Opposition

Nehemiah
- Covenant renewal
- Spiritual revival of the nation
- Opposition and persecution
- Character of Nehemiah
- Prayer
- Remembrance

Esther
- God's sovereignty and protection
- Persecution
- Obedience
- Character of Mordecai and Esther

Job
- God's character and sovereignty
- Suffering, loss and illness
- Comforting friends during suffering

Psalms
- Character of God
- Character of man
- Worship
- Trust in the Lord (God is greater than man's problems)
- The righteous and the wicked

Proverbs
- Wisdom = Fear of the Lord

Ecclesiastes
- Vanity/ meaningless
- Living under God compared with not living under Him
- Wisdom and folly
- Labour/ toil

Song of Songs
- Faithfulness
- Physical beauty
- Awakening the heart

Isaiah
- Salvation
- Trust versus unbelief
- Pride and humility
- Sin/ judgement/ restoration
- Social injustice
- Messianic visions (foretelling the Christ)

Jeremiah
- Sovereign Lord/ King of the

nations
- Unfaithfulness of the people
- (Broken) covenant/ hearts
- Jeremiah and his ministry
- Opposition in ministry

Lamentations
- Grieving / Sorrow
- Questioning God
- Jeremiah's character

Ezekiel
- God's judgement
- For the sake of My name
- Spirit of God
- Restoration for the people of God
- Ezekiel and his character

Daniel
- Sovereignty of God
- Kingdom of God
- Character of Daniel
- Character of kings
- Character of Shadrach, Meshach and Abednego
- Pride and humility

Hosea
- Faithlessness/ adulterous nations
- God's heart for His people– and what true love does
- God's character (faithfulness/ love)

Joel
- Day of the Lord
- Great day of the Lord (final judgement, finished, the end).
- Judgement
- Repentance

Amos
- Social injustice
- Oppression of the poor

- Pride
- Laziness
- Idolatry

Obadiah
- Pride
- God's judgement upon pride
- Unbrotherly love
- Day of the Lord and Kingdom of God

Jonah
- God's heart for nations
- God's sovereignty over creation
- Presence of God
- Prayer
- Love thy enemy
- Jonah's character

Micah
- Social injustice
- Judgement and justice
- Sins of Judah
- Messianic visions

Nahum
- Character of God
- Wrath of God

Habakkuk
- Questioning God (Asking "Why, God? Why?")
- Answers
- Social justice/ Social conscious
- Faith

Zephaniah
- Day of the Lord
- Judgement
- Cleansing/ purification
- Messianic Predications

Haggai
- The temple
- The People

Zechariah

- Cleansing/ Restoration
- Christ/ Messianic Predictions
- God's character

Malachi
- Day of the Lord

New Testament

Matthew
- Fulfilment of prophecies
- The end of the story/ salvation revealed
- Jesus the Christ, Messiah, and Holy One of God
- Kingdom of God

Mark
- Suffering
- Christ the Suffering Servant
- Persecution
- Endurance
- Faithfulness of Jesus (to the will/ plan of God)

Luke
- The Kingdom of God
- Prayer
- The Holy Spirit
- The least

John
- Eternal life
- Jesus' divinity
- Miraculous signs
- Discipleship
- Faith/ belief/ evangelism

Acts of the Apostles
- Actions of the Holy Spirit
- Empowerment of the Holy Sprit
- Spread of the Gospel
- Declaration of Gospel amidst persecution
- Boldness of faith

- "My name"
- Character of God
- Right sacrifices
- Covenant

- Guidance from God

Romans
- Character of God
- Grace versus works
- Law versus faith
- Righteousness
- Unity and humility
- Who are the children of God?

1 Corinthians
- Unity
- Love
- Living as a witness
- What is wisdom?

2 Corinthians
- God's strength in human weakness
- Paul's defence
- Super apostles

Galatians
- Grace
- False teachings versus true Gospel
- Righteousness through faith, not works
- Law versus Spirit
- Life in Christ

Ephesians
- Authority of Christ
- Received in Christ
- Identity in Christ
- Unity/ oneness

Philippians

- Unity through humility
- Joy in suffering
- Witnessing through persecution

Colossians
- Christ is the fullness of God
- Christ is sufficient
- Serving God with thankfulness
- Christian living

1 Thessalonians
- Hope
- Faith
- Suffering/ persecution
- Second coming

2 Thessalonians
- Day of the Lord/ Christ's return
- Suffering and persecution
- Prayer for the persecuted

1 Timothy
- Sound doctrine
- False teaching
- Church leadership
- Godly living

2 Timothy
- Suffering for the Gospel/ Eternal perspective
- Preaching the Gospel
- Discipleship/ Godly leadership
- Fulfilling one's call

Titus
- Sound doctrine
- Teaching
- Leadership
- Godly living

Philemon
- Forgiveness
- Reconciliation within the church

- Cost of being a Christian

Hebrews
- Superiority of Christ
- Endurance in suffering
- Confidence in Christ

James
- Faith
- Obedience
- Tongue/ speech
- Rich/ poor
- Wisdom

1 Peter
Suffering and endurance
- Eternal perspective
- Submission/ lifestyle
- Example of Christ

2 Peter
- False prophets
- Christ's second coming

1 John
- Love
- Abide (in God)
- Obedience
- "Know" – who you are, what Christ has done, and that you are in Him.

2 John
- Hospitality
- Truth and Love
- False teaching

3 John
- Hospitality
- Truth and Love
- Pride

Jude
- False teachers
- Day of Christ's return

Revelation
- Worthiness of the Lamb
- God's judgement and mercy
- God's justice and wrath

- Kingdom of God
   triumphant and victorious
- Praise and worship
- Enduring persecution

INTRODUCTION TO THE OLD TESTAMENT

The Old Testament shows God's character and the nature of man in stark contrast to one another. It reveals God's perfect creation, how it went wrong, and why man needs a Saviour. Yet, right from the start, God had a plan of redemption that would restore mankind to a right relationship with Him. It was not something that God made up as He went along; His plan was intentional and was brought to fullness in the coming of the Promised Messiah, Jesus Christ.

God brought these things about through the nation of Israel. The Old Testament tells the story of how Israel became a nation and recounts its early history. The Israelites were never faithful to God for extensive time periods. They lacked a long memory of what God had done for them, they constantly lapsed into idolatry. Yet God showed Himself to be faithful time and time again. He showed that His standard equals holiness and so His people must also be holy, but He is also merciful and gracious, slow to anger, and abounding in love. These are the characteristics of God and man you will see repeated through the Old Testament books.

Keep the overall themes of the Old Testament in mind when studying individual books. These include:

- Character of God
- Sovereignty of God
- Grace
- Justice
- Compassion
- Love for the poor and foreigner
- Blessings for obedience (and curses for disobedience)
- Remember (what God has done)

Remember that everything was part of God's ultimate plan to redeem His people, and draw all men back into a right relationship with Him. The tabernacle, sacrificial system, and laws that God gave to His people were all to foreshadow Christ and the coming Kingdom of God.

Treat the Old Testament for what it is: the story of a nation, the telling of God's heart for man, man's need for redemption, and God's plan for salvation.

Several time periods can be defined within the Old Testament:

- 2091-1406 BC; the patriarchs to the Promised Land
- 1406-1043 BC; the judges
- 1403-931 BC; the United Kingdom under King Saul, David and Solomon.
- 931-722/ 586 BC; the Divided Kingdom. The kingdom of Israel split in to two nations after the death of King Solomon. The Northern Kingdom of Israel went into exile in 722 BC and their southern brethren, of Judah, followed in 586 BC.

Walk with the Israelites as you read of the historical events in the life of that nation. Do not judge them. Rather put yourself in their shoes. Allow yourself to feel with the Israelites as you watch them make mistakes, and fall over and over again into sin against God. Walk with them step by step. Rejoice and grumble with them through the ups and the downs as the Israelites leave Egypt (the Exodus), knowing excitement, anticipation, joy, hope, bitterness, despair and doubt. Experience the confusion of the people in the time of the Kings as their rulers lead them astray. Feel the grief of the prophets when the Israelites refused to be called back to God, ultimately resulting in their exile.

Do not be purely academic when studying the Old Testament. Feel with the people, feel with God and feel with God's chosen leaders. Be challenged by what you see of man's nature. Be strengthened and encouraged by what you learn of God's faithfulness, mercy, and love.

Enjoy the journey!

INTRODUCTION TO THE PENTATEUCH

The first five books of the Bible are known as the Pentateuch, which means "five books", or "five volumes". Keep in mind that the books of Genesis, Exodus, Leviticus, Numbers and Deuteronomy were originally composed as a single book, with authorship attributed to Moses.

The Pentateuch documents the fall of man, and God's heart to bring mankind back into relationship with Him. Primarily though, it was written by Moses to provide a record of the story of Israel. It tells of God's promise to Abraham, how God took the Israelites out of slavery (a people without land, religion, culture, or identity), and how God made them into a great nation, and His chosen people.

God called Abraham, an old man without children, to be the father of many nations. Abraham was the first to be given God's promise. God would make a great nation from his descendants and give them fertile land. God reaffirmed this promise with each of the patriarchs of the faith, Abraham's descendants.

The Israelites rose to status in Egypt after Joseph, one of Abraham's descendants, became the ruler of that land. He was second only to Pharaoh. However after Joseph has passed away and a new Pharaoh took the throne, the people of Egypt began to fear the growing numbers of the Israelites and the people of God were forced into slavery. It seemed that God had forgotten His people . . . but looks can be deceiving. God had not forgotten them!

Once God freed the Israelites from slavery, He needed to prepare them to become a nation. God started with a group of slaves, who only knew their family identity. In the wilderness years, He gave them their history, lineage, a religious system, the Law, governance, and taught them warfare. The Law did not only reflect on religious ceremonies, but was to be an instruction manual for all of life: from relationships, to business, education, and government.

God was faithful to His promises. He brought them into the Promised Land and set Himself up as God and King over His people. The book of Joshua follows on from the Pentateuch and details the events as God's people took the land of Canaan and became established in the Promised Land.

GENESIS

The first book; "the Beginning"

"And I will make of you a great nation, and I will bless you and make your name great, so that you will be a blessing. I will bless those who bless you, and him who dishonors you I will curse, and in you all the families of the earth shall be blessed." – Genesis 12:2-3

You have now embarked on a journey with the Israelites that will lead you through the entire Old Testament. Prepare to travel with them as they discover their history and learn about their God. Your journey will continue with them through their ups and downs, failures, and continuous receipt of God's redeeming mercy. In your travels, you will learn of the character of God and the character of man.

Tip: Genesis is one of the larger books. It is worth the investment of your time as it is fundamental to correctly interpreting the rest of the Bible.

During your first reading

Themes to track
- God's salvation plan
- Covenants
- Character of God
- Character of man
- Beginnings

During your second reading

Things to notice in the text
- Highlight the actions of God throughout the book of Genesis. This will help you to see the characteristics of God being revealed. For example:
    - "God said . . ."
    - "God came . . ."
    - "God in anger . . ."

- Covenants: look for the promises given by God ("I will . . ." statements) as well as conditional statements (if you do "x", then I will do "y").

Chapter summaries

These are optional as they can be time consuming for the larger books. If you choose to do them, you will receive a much deeper appreciation of the book. By the end of The IBSC, you will have paraphrased the entire Bible! Go through each chapter and try to summarise it in one paragraph, using your own words; force yourself to stay big picture and capture the heart of each chapter.

After your initial readings

Setting of Genesis
Author

Moses penned the book of Genesis, as directed by God. Moses is accepted as the author of the first five books of the Bible, which are known collectively as the Pentateuch and were originally one book.

Recipient

The Pentateuch was written for the Jews of the Exodus. They had just left Egypt and four hundred years of slavery.

Date and place of writing

Many scholars favour dating the Exodus from Egypt around 1446 BC. So if Moses is accepted as the author, then the book can be dated between 1440 and 1406 BC. This falls during the forty year period that the Israelites spent in the wilderness, between the lands of Egypt and Canaan.

Reason written

Remember that the original readers had very little knowledge of their ancestors or personal history. Genesis was written to reveal their history, their God and His character, and the beginning of God's plan to redeem mankind. It was written to give them God's promise and to show them their need for a Saviour.

Big picture
Historical background

At this point in the story, the Israelites were in the desert after the Exodus from Egypt. They were emerging from four hundred years of slavery. They had no national identity. They knew nothing more of their history than the tribe from which they had descended (one of the twelve tribes of Israel, which are traced back to Israel's twelve sons).

As just-freed, former slaves they would have been asking many questions, chief amongst them were:

    1. Who is God? Who is this God who has taken us out of the land of Egypt?;

    2. Who are we? What are our religious, national and family identities?; and

3. What is sin? What does it look like in our lives?

These questions are important to keep in mind when reading Genesis because they will help you to understand why the author included the information that he did. For example, consider the numerous genealogies. These were important to the Israelites because they showed them that they went back to Adam and Abraham. Kinship with Adam gave them identity and worth because they were formed in the image of God, whilst also pointing to the need for a Saviour. Kinship with Abraham made them descendants of the promise, as covenants were passed down through family lines.

Remember that the original readers of Genesis had:

- NO national history to define themselves. They only had their family history.
- NO established traditions, doctrines, religious calendar, or prophetic writings.
- NO priesthood.
- NO land. They had been semi-nomadic, meaning that they had domestic animals, but moved their flocks with them.
- NO temple, synagogue, or place to centrally worship. Having been enslaved in Egypt, many of the Israelites would have adopted the Egyptian gods.

Covenants are also important in the book of Genesis, giving insight into God's interaction with man, as well as His heart towards mankind. Be sure to take note of them as you study this book.

There were several common forms of legally-binding covenants that the Israelites and surrounding nations would have understood:

1. Parity covenant – a covenant made between equals.
2. Suzerain/ Vassal covenant – a covenant between a greater kingdom, or king, (the Suzerain), and a lesser kingdom, or king, (the Vassal). Vassals were usually in a position, which left them little choice whether or not they would enter into a covenant with the Suzerain; for example, following a defeat in battle.
3. Royal grant – a covenant sworn between two individuals. A king promised to do something for one of his servants without any action required on the part of the servant. It was an unconditional covenant as opposed to the Suzerain/ Vassal covenant, which was conditional.

Going deeper with the Suzerain/ Vassal covenant

Characteristics of a Suzerain-Vassal relationship:

- Above all else, a Suzerain demanded loyalty from their Vassal.
- The Vassal Nation was brought under the law of the Suzerain Nation. A historical prologue would be given at the beginning of these laws, recounting what the Suzerain had done for the Vassal. This provided the Vassal with motivation to obey the laws of their Suzerain.
- The Suzerain determined the land boundaries of the Vassal Nation.
- The Suzerain demanded taxes and tributes from their Vassal.

- The Vassal was not allowed to make a covenant with any other king.
- The Suzerain would fight for the Vassal Nation, offering the lesser kingdom protection from hostile neighbours.

Relating the Suzerain/ Vassal covenant to Genesis

Essentially, God became both the Suzerain (King) and God of the Israelites. The covenant God established with His people reflected a Suzerain-Vassal relationship. The original readers would have known the conditions implicated by such a covenant. Not only the Israelites, but also the Egyptians and the nations of Canaan and Mesopotamia, would have understood what God was doing. God was speaking in a way that the world could understand. God was using Israel to bring the eyes of the entire world on to Him.

Character portrayal – from Jacob to Israel [1]

Jacob was born struggling. He grasped at his brother's heel in determination to be first from the womb, but alas, he was not. However he later succeeded in taking the inheritance of the firstborn from his brother, Esau, for the price of a single meal. He then took away his brother's blessing through deceit. He was appropriately named Jacob, meaning "trickster" or "supplanter", being someone who took what was not his.

Receiving the inheritance and blessing belonging to the eldest son did not result in an easy life for Jacob. He had to flee from his father's land, fearing retaliation from his brother, and he kept on wrestling with God and running from man during his years in exile.

A time came when Jacob had to return to his father's land. Jacob was terrified, knowing he would have to face his brother. He once again began to scheme, seeking a way to appease his brother. Coming to a river, he sent servants ahead to Esau with a gift. He then took his wives, children and livestock over the river, before returning to the other side to spend the night on the safer bank. It was a night that changed his life . . .

Jacob feared the Lord, but he feared the impending meeting with his brother more. His heart was torn between obedience to God and fleeing back into exile. His mind raced as he tried to plot a means of escape. And then a man appeared.

Who was that man who had appeared beside the bank? Jacob wondered. He had not recognised him. Looking back in time, Jacob could not remember exactly how they had engaged in combat. Perhaps the man had said something he did not like, or perhaps he had needed an outlet for his over-fraught nerves. It did not matter now. The fact was that they had fought and found themselves to be an even match, or so Jacob had believed. They strove, wrestled, and dodged through the night hours.

As day began to break, Jacob's opponent said to him: "Let me go, for the day has broken."

Jacob replied: "I will not let you go unless you bless me."

"What is your name?"

"Jacob," he answered.

Then the man said: "Your name shall no longer be called Jacob, but Israel, for you have striven with God, and with men, and have prevailed."

Jacob asked the man his name, but his opponent would not tell him. After the man had left him, Jacob sat nursing an aching hip, which had been damaged during their long engagement. It ached deep within the joint, and he could feel the blood pulsating in the damaged region. Jacob's mind was strangely disengaged from his injury as he mulled on the words of his opponent: "Your name shall no longer be called Jacob, but Israel, for you have striven with God, and with men, and have prevailed."

What did they mean? he wondered. Who was that man? As he pondered, he came to realise that he had been wrong. He had not been evenly matched with his opponent. He had spent the night fighting with God and was lucky to be alive! He could do nothing in his own strength. As he stood up, he was forced to shift his weight on to his uninjured leg. God had wounded his hip and he was certain that he would walk with a limp for the rest of his life.

Still, despite pain and the contemplation of a permanent disability, a strange peace had settled over his heart. He had seen God face to face, and yet the Holy One had allowed him to walk away with his life. In addition, he had received a new name. He would carry both his new name and the limp humbly as a reminder of God's sovereignty.

Israel meant "let God rule" or "God rules" and Israel bore his new name with increased faith, trusting God to deliver him from his brother. The limp would remind him that he could not do it alone and his name would remind him that he did not have to do so.

Book overview

God is chiefly seen in this book to be Creator, King-over-all, and faithful to His promises. Genesis reveals God's plan for salvation, and shows that man cannot thwart the will of God. He is sovereign. Genesis documents four key events for mankind: creation, the fall, the flood and the tower of Babel.

Genesis also documents their national history. It introduces the Israelites to the four major patriarchs of the faith and links their line to the promise God gave to Abraham. Abraham, Isaac, Jacob and Joseph were their forefathers with whom the covenant had been made. Moses was showing the people that the twelve tribes of Israel had inherited this covenant. The Israelites were shown that they were children of the promise and bound to the covenant. God was to be their Suzerain, their King.

Interpreting the book of Genesis
Interpretation questions
1. Look at the covenants God made, who God made them with, and when they were fulfilled. Remember that the covenants may not be fulfilled in Genesis. For example:
    a. What were the conditionals of God's covenant with Adam in the Garden of Eden? What did Adam and Eve need to do in order to retain the gift of Eden?

b. What did God promise to Noah after the flood?

c. What promises did God give to Abraham? What did Abraham have to do in order for God to be held to His word?

d. What elements of a Suzerain-Vassal covenant do you see displayed in God's covenant with His people, the Israelites? How would knowledge of this covenant strengthen Moses' original readers as they left four hundred years of slavery behind them as they fled Egypt?

2. What does Genesis reveal about the character of man?

a. What do you learn of man from the book of Genesis?

b. What does Genesis teach about man's inherent value?

c. What was revealed of man's weaknesses?

3. What do you see of God's character?

a. What do you learn about the Trinity?

b. How does God chose to relate with man? Consider how he relates with each of the key figures in the Israelites' history.

c. What does the beginning, Genesis 1-2, convey of how God would like to relate with man?

4. Look at some of the main characters of the promise (Abraham, Isaac, Jacob and Joseph). Go back to the passages in Genesis that speak of each character, rather than making notes from memory. We can become biased in our views when looking at familiar personalities, such as Abraham, and fail to see what Scripture really tells us about them. Consider their character attributes:

a. What were their strengths? What were their weaknesses?

b. What were their struggles?

c. Did they grow in faith or character through their lives?

5. Read Romans 8:18-25, which says that all creation is groaning, waiting to be set free from its bondage to corruption. If this is the case, what do you think creation was like when "it was good"?

6. For the following questions, what answers would Genesis have given to the original readers?

a. Why did God chose to rescue us? (Hint: consider the promise to Abraham).

b. What must we do as God's people?

c. Who is God, this Creator-of-all-things? (Remember they were coming out of Egypt where many gods were worshipped).

7. What were the Israelites learning of their origins and national history?

8. How would Genesis have transformed their thinking from that of slaves to the people of God's chosen nation?

Creative interpretation

1. Sketch Genesis 1:1-31, the creation, in sequence. Consider the Creator and the works of His hands. What did creation reveal of the character of God?

2. Draw a family tree, including on it all the main characters in the book of

THE INDUCTIVE BIBLE STUDY COMPANION

Genesis from Adam down to the sons of Jacob (Israel) and Esau (Edom). Alternatively, make a family tree from Abraham (when God made the covenant) down to the sons of Jacob (Israel) and Esau (Edom).

3. Consider the four key events listed in chapters 1-11 and comment on their importance: Creation, the Fall, the Flood, and the Tower of Babel. Also note what each event reveals about God's character and the character of man.

4. Complete a character study on one of the four patriarchs of the faith: Abraham, Isaac, Jacob, or Joseph. Consider their interactions with God. Observe how they treat their family, as well as strangers. Think about their actions and what beliefs might have motivated them.

Application inspiration

- Go on a hike and see the world that the Lord has made.
- Genesis contains many testimonies of God's work in the lives of men. Testimonies are important. They testify to a living and loving God and set Christianity apart from every other religion.
  - o What is your testimony? Consider how you came to know God, or something He has recently done in your life.
  - o Aim to share part of your testimony with a friend this week as an encouragement to them.
- Which patriarch did you relate to most in Genesis?
  - o Why did you relate to them?
  - o What attributes do you share with them?
  - o Are these attributes revealing strengths, or weaknesses?
  - o Pray through your insights with God.

[1] Paraphrase of Genesis 25:23-32

EXODUS

A Holy God building a Holy nation

"I will dwell among the people of Israel and will be their God. And they shall know that I am the LORD their God, who brought them out of the land of Egypt that I might dwell among them. I am the LORD their God." – Exodus 29:45-46

During your first reading

Themes to track
- Character of God – He is the hero of Exodus!
- Worship
- The covenant
- Character of Moses
- Remembrance

During your second reading

Things to notice in the text
- Highlight actions of God. For example:
  - "God said . . ."
  - "God manifested . . ."
  - "Lord appeared . . ."
  - "Lord had struck . . ."
  - "Lord commanded . . ."
- Highlight passages that give insight into God's character. For example:
  - Exodus 13:1-2 – God is a jealous God and demands His due;
  - Exodus 15:1-21 – God the Warrior King.
- Highlight emotions. For example:
  - Exodus 1:17, 21 – Midwives feared God;

- o   Exodus 18:9 – Jethro rejoiced;
- o   Exodus 19:16 – People in the camp trembled.
- The structure of the book, which can be divided into:
    - o   The Exodus;
    - o   The Law; and
    - o   The tabernacle.

Chapter summaries

These are optional as they can be time consuming for the larger books. If you choose to do them, you will receive a much deeper appreciation of the book. By the end of The IBSC, you will have paraphrased the entire Bible! Go through each chapter and try to summarise it in one paragraph, using your own words; force yourself to stay big picture and capture the heart of each chapter.

After your initial readings

Setting of Exodus
Author

Moses penned the book of Exodus, as directed by God. Moses is accepted as the author of the first five books of the Bible, which are known collectively as the Pentateuch and were originally one book.

Recipient

The Pentateuch was written for the Jews of the Exodus. They had just left Egypt and four hundred years of slavery.

Date and place of writing

Many scholars favour dating the Exodus from Egypt around 1446 BC. So if Moses is accepted as the author, then the book can be dated between 1440 and 1406 BC. This falls during the forty year period that the Israelites spent in the wilderness, between the lands of Egypt and Canaan.

Reason written

God commanded Moses to write down events as a memorial for the next generation. It was to be a reminder of what God had done, the covenant He had established with them, and the Law by which they were to live.

Big picture
Historical background

Refer to the *historical background* given for Genesis for information regarding the Israelites' early history, as they became a nation.

Egypt at the Exodus

The Egyptian Empire was at the height of its power during the Eighteenth Dynasty. Egypt's territory spanned from modern day Sudan to modern day Iraq.

They owed a large part of their prosperity to the Nile River, which runs through their land, giving them rich, fertile soil.

The Egyptian people had thousands of gods, including Pharaoh, who was seen as a manifestation of the gods on earth. Egyptian gods of relevance to Exodus include:

- Hapi (the spirit of the Nile) and Hatmeyt (the fish goddess);
- Hekt (frog-headed goddess; frogs represented fertility);
- Seb (god of creeping things);
- Khephera (god of resurrection, and the fly god);
- Hathor (cow-headed, love goddess) and Hapis (sacred-bull god);
- Im-Hotep (god of healing) and Sekmet (goddess of healing);
- Nut (sky goddess) and Shu (god of atmosphere);
- Senehem (locust-headed god; protected them from the ravishes of pests);
- Amon-Ra (sun god; the principle deity and creator of all things);
- Pharaoh (considered to have been god-manifest) and his son (also considered to have been a god).

Israelites at the Exodus

The Israelites were held in slavery to the Egyptians for four hundred years. During this time the Egyptian Empire was at the height of its power. This made the Israelites a part of the prevailing kingdom. They had been slaves at the centre of the world, coming under the protection of the greatest world power. They worked hard each day, but evening saw them return to homes of comfort.

It is recorded that there were 600 thousand Israelite men during the Exodus from Egypt. This makes an estimated population of 2 to 3 million people when women and children are taken into the equation. It was not a small group that Moses had to lead through the desert!

Character portrayal – a mother ponders her unknown God

"Mummy, my feet hurt!" the little girl cried.

Sapir looked fearfully ahead at the immense cloud before bending down and allowing her daughter to scramble up onto her back. By doing so, mother and daughter fell behind a few places in the throng of bodies that engulfed them.

They had been walking for days and the crowd was growing restless. Who was this God who had saved them from the Egyptians only to make them traipse across the desert?, Sapir asked with a bitter heart. They had been without water for two days. Surely a God who had done the wonders they had seen in Egypt could provide them with water?

Sapir was unsettled in her heart and mind by the events that had transpired over the past weeks. She was also fearful of the intentions of this mighty God. She didn't understand why they had to leave. Why didn't He just give His people the land of Egypt? She wondered whether this God was more powerful than those of the Egyptians. The plagues seemed to indicate that He was, but perhaps His power had only been for a period of time, or perhaps He had no rights to the Egyptian land.

The Egyptian gods had limited power, but the God of Abraham was said to be supreme. Sapir had difficulty perceiving how one God could show Himself as both a cloud and a pillar of fire, as well as have control over water, animals and, seemingly, all forms of life.

Sapir feared God and her heart pulled away from Him. She followed Him in fear and uncertainty, looking to those around her for guidance. She knew little about gods and this One seemed particularly unpredictable. Sapir could only hope that the promises of this God would prove true and that He would bring them to a land of safety. However for the time being it seemed like uncertainty would be the staple of her life and that of her young daughter she now bore upon her back.

Book overview

God used the hardened heart of Pharaoh to reveal Himself to the world as the One True God. Through the plagues, He demonstrated that He was greater than any other god. He brought a mighty nation, the world power, to its knees. His mighty hand instilled reverent fear in the hearts of His people as He reaffirmed His covenant with them.

In the wilderness, God began to establish His people's system of religion and law. The Israelites were introduced to the idea of a holy priesthood and were given instructions to build the tabernacle, God's dwelling place with man. They were also given the Ten Commandments, the foundational laws. Furthermore God showed them the importance of remembrance in maintaining reverent lives. For example, the Passover meal was one of the physical reminders of His faithfulness, given to the people so that they would not forget what He had done for them.

God was shaping Israel into His people. He desired to dwell in relationship them and, to do this, He had to shape them into a holy nation. In summary: they must be holy for He is holy.

Interpreting the book of Exodus

Interpretation questions

 1. What do you learn of God's character from:
  a. The Exodus?
  b. The Law He gave to His people?
  c. The tabernacle and the directions given for its construction?
 2. What does Exodus reveal about God? Refer back to the actions of God that you highlighted in the text. Consider some of the following:
  a. God's interaction with creation;
  b. How God uses people, how He calls people, and who He calls;
  c. Different aspects and traits of God's character;
  d. The Lord's reactions to situations and people;
  e. His sovereignty; for example, over creation and the false gods of Egypt.
 3. How do the people in the book of Exodus respond to the works of God's hands and the presence of the Lord? For example:
  a. Did they worship, groan, or respond in fear?

      b. Were they obedient or disobedient to God's commands; for example, did they turn to other gods?

      c. What were their emotional responses?

4. Contemplate the life and actions of Moses:

      a. What was revealed about the character of Moses?

      b. How did he grow in faith throughout the book and what caused the change?

      c. How might the Israelites have viewed him?

      d. How do you think his brother Aaron would have viewed him?

      e. How would Pharaoh and the Egyptians likely have viewed him?

5. Read the following verses: Exodus 7:13-14, 22, 8:15, 19, 9:12; Romans 1:18-32; and Hebrews 3:7-13.

      a. Did Pharaoh harden his own heart, or was it hardened by God?

      b. Was this injustice on the part of God?

6. Take time to consider the people of Egypt:

      a. How would the Egyptians have felt towards Moses when he returned to Egypt from Midian?

      b. How would this have changed during the initial plagues?

      c. How would the Egyptians have felt towards Moses when the Israelites, their slaves, left Egypt?

      d. What would they have thought about God during the plagues and as He took His people from their lands?

7. Look at the covenant and create a table listing in one column the "I will" promises of God and in the other column the "you shall" commands He gave to the Israelites.

8. With the laws given in Exodus 20:22-23, consider:

      a. Which of the Ten Commandments apply?

      b. What godly values do you see?

      c. List one to three principles that you can find.

      d. Give an application for today based on your principle/s.

9. It will be beneficial to have a diagram of the tabernacle next to you as you study it (or sketch it for yourself!).

      a. Write down what was to be in each section of the tabernacle and the symbolic relevance or physical purpose of each item.

      b. Also consider the significance of the detail God gave to them for the tabernacle's construction. It was to be perfect and holy. It was the only place where His presence could dwell with man.

      c. Meditate upon 1Corinthians 3:17 and 1 Corinthians 6:19.

Creative interpretation

1. Write a summary on the plagues of Egypt.

    o Comment on what they revealed about God, His plan for His people, His desire for mankind, and His character.

    o You may find it helpful to compare the plagues to the Egyptian gods listed in the *historical background* given above.

o Use visual illustrations to help depict the plagues.
2. Using the details and descriptions given in Exodus, attempt to sketch one part of the tabernacle or its artefacts.
   o Why do you think God put great detail into these commands?
   o What did the tabernacle symbolise and what was its purpose?
3. In a table, list some of the emotions that the Israelites felt during the Exodus, by the Red Sea, and in the Wilderness. Take note of what event or circumstance triggered each emotion displayed.

Application inspiration

- Whilst interpreting the book, you looked at what the Exodus, the Law, and the tabernacle revealed about God's character and core principles of faith. For example, the Law:
  o What it reveals about God's character:
    - God is holy and therefore His people must be holy.
    - God cares about the health and everyday lives of His people.
  o Principles it reflects for the Christian faith:
    - Our identity should come from who we are in Him: holy and righteous. Refer to Colossians 3:12-13.
    - We live under grace, not law, but the Law teaches us what it means to be holy and what God desires from our lives. Consider Romans 6:23 and 7:6-7.
    - We are redeemed and therefore are called to live holy lives. See also 1 Peter 1:14-16.
- Learning from the Israelites:
  o Are there areas where you wilfully walk in disobedience to God? Can you think of a specific event, small or large?
  o Is there something for which you are longing or waiting that you complain to God about, as the Israelites did with food and water?
  o Are there idols in your life that you need to remove? What about your body, job, sport, career . . .? These things in themselves are not bad, but are you placing them before God?
  o Are you open to the advice of other believers, as Moses was with his father-in-law, Jethro? How do you respond when someone, lovingly or not, corrects you?
- Spend time in reflection:
  o What was your response to reading of God's power and sovereignty?
  o Spend time reflecting on the holiness of God.
  o Read Psalm 29.

LEVITICUS

Be Holy for I am Holy

"You shall be holy to me, for I the LORD am holy and have separated you from the peoples, that you should be mine." – Leviticus 20:26

Consider reading the book of Hebrews in conjunction with Leviticus. Hebrews shows how Christ is the fulfilment of the sacrificial system, given in Leviticus. The sacrificial system was only a shadow of what was to come in Jesus, our Saviour and the true Sacrificial Lamb.

During your first reading

Themes to track
- Holiness
- Costliness of sin
- God's desire for relationship
- Atonement

During your second reading

Things to notice in the text
- Highlight the repeated words "holy" and "holiness".
- Mark for whom the commands were given. Was God giving them to Aaron and his sons (the priests), or to the Israelites (the people)?
- Mark the type of offering demanded: burnt offering, grain offering, sin offering, guilt offering, or fellowship/ peace offering.
- You may wish to mark conditions of the laws: look for the words "if" and "then".
- Underline key words in the laws to make each topic easier to locate. For example, in Leviticus 11 you may underline the words "you may eat", then

in Leviticus 12:2 "gives birth to a son", and in Leviticus 12:5, "a daughter".

Chapter summaries

These are optional as they can be time consuming for the larger books. If you choose to do them, you will receive a much deeper appreciation of the book. By the end of The IBSC, you will have paraphrased the entire Bible! Go through each chapter and try to summarise it in one paragraph, using your own words; force yourself to stay big picture and capture the heart of each chapter.

After your initial readings

Setting of Leviticus
Author

Moses penned the book of Leviticus, as directed by God. Moses is accepted as the author of the first five books of the Bible, which are known collectively as the Pentateuch and were originally one book.

Recipient

The Pentateuch was written for the Jews of the Exodus. They had just left Egypt and four hundred years of slavery.

Date and place of writing

Many scholars favour dating the Exodus from Egypt around 1446 BC. So if Moses is accepted as the author, then the book can be dated between 1440 and 1406 BC. This falls during the forty year period that the Israelites spent in the wilderness, between the lands of Egypt and Canaan.

Reason written

Leviticus provided the Israelites with an understanding of what was required for them to be holy and live as God's chosen people. God sought to teach them that because He is holy and desires to dwell in relationship with them, they must be holy too. God gave them an identity as a nation of priests, set apart from the surrounding peoples. He was establishing His priesthood and giving instructions for the sacrificial system.

Big picture
Historical background

Refer to the *historical background* given for Genesis for information regarding the covenant God made with His people and further background of the Israelites' early history.

Refer to the *historical background* given for Exodus for information on Egypt and its gods.

In Leviticus, God establishes the priesthood of His nation and the worship practices for His people. The Laws that He gave show that He was interested in all aspects of their lives, not just in the temple and religious practices. God did not want His name to be judged wrongly because of the practices of His people. He called His people to be set apart as a nation of priests, reflecting His holiness. In order to accomplish this, they needed to be set apart as different from the surrounding nations and people.

Many of the Laws that God stipulated were specifically related to the practices within the land of Canaan (the Promised Land), which the Israelites were about to enter, as well as the practices that they witnessed in Egypt. When settling in a new land it was the culture to take on the gods of that land, who were seen to have provided for the previous inhabitants. It would have been culturally normal for the Israelites to have taken on the gods and religious practices of the Canaanites, either to the exclusion of Yah-weh, or merging him into the Canaanite pantheon. God was ensuring this didn't happen.

Religion in the land of Canaan

The land of Canaan was made up of a number of principalities, but all these people shared a similar culture and religion. The Canaanites were polytheistic, worshipping multiple gods. They made sense of the world by creating gods who had power over set elements of nature and the environment. Whilst each god had a specific role there was fluidity in these, with each god being able to take on the roles or attributes of the other gods. Their gods did not act morally and were cruel to the people. Their religion had no concept of relationship between man and the gods.

The aim of their religious practices was to appease and manipulate cruel gods in order to gain favour and blessings. They could be manipulated or influenced through worship, offering sacrifices, magic, and flattery. However, the gods were fickle (changed their minds) and capricious (unpredictable), which bred fear amidst the populace. There was no central place of worship.

Sex and prostitution were also part of religious worship, using procreative sympathetic magic. With procreative sympathetic magic, a priest or priestess was believed to momentarily take over the being of the god or goddess and control their actions. Temple prostitution as worship was seen to be the sexual union of god and goddess in order to assure the fertility of mankind, animals, and nature. Blood, semen, and corpses were central to religious rites and practices in Canaan as these were powerful – symbolic of life and death.

Main gods worshipped in Canaan:
- El (or Il): the first god, father of the other gods, and god of fertility. He was known for horrid sexual perversions. El went out of popular worship in Canaan as he was said to be distant from humanity. His sons and daughters were the gods who interacted with mankind.
- Ba'al: lord of storm and sky. He was known for his military strength. Ba'al was said to be very involved in human affairs and so many religious rituals were centred upon him. Because he eventually replaced El as the chief god of the region, a lot of characteristics attributed to El were passed on to Ba'al. He was also credited with controlling rain and fertility – fertility

in agriculture, beasts, and mankind.

- There were three primary goddesses: Anath, Astarte and Asherah. These goddesses give a prime example of the fluidity of role and identity existing in the Canaan pantheon. All three were patronesses of sex and war: sex mainly in its sensuous aspect as lust, and war in its aspects of violence and murder. Asherah was the wife of El, but became Ba'al's wife and had sex with her children. Anath was a combination of the sister and spouse of Ba'al. Astarte demanded human sacrifice and women, particularly virgins, were burned to appease her.

- Molech: god of fire. He was a wrathful god that demanded life. Human sacrifice was required to gain favour – in war, during times of famine and drought, and when pestilence came. Sacrifices were often children, young girls, firstborn sons, and the most beautiful in the household. The idol of Molech was a metal statue of a cow. A fire would be lit in the god's belly and then the child placed on the burning hot, outstretched hands of the god to be burnt alive. The child's parents had to be present to witness the act.

- Mot: god of death, drought, barrenness, sterility, and misfortune. He was seen to be able to overpower Ba'al's regenerative powers during autumn and winter.

Health care and the Law

In addition to protecting the people from falling into the religious habits of surrounding nations, you will see that many laws in Leviticus are focused on hygiene and healthcare. Remember that the Israelites did not have the same understanding or knowledge about disease and microorganisms that we do today. Take as an example the food laws.

The laws on leprosy are another example of health laws in Leviticus. It is important to note that the original hearers and readers had a different classification system of leprosy than that which is used today. It included a variety of skin disorders from psoriasis to true leprosy. Symptoms of leprosy thus ranged from white patches on the skin, to running sores, to loss of limbs.

Character portrayal – God's laws made the Israelites stand out amidst the nations

Anat looked down at the babe in her arms and smiled, joy leaping in her heart. Moses had declared that women did not have to present to the tabernacle with their new born boys until forty days after birth and this law brought her relief. She knew of the Canaanite practices of child sacrifice to Molech. The thought sickened her. What kind of god demanded one child's life for the blessing of many more? And what kind of mother would give their child to such a god?

Her heart had peace now that she knew her child's life would not be demanded as a blood sacrifice. God remained an unknown factor to her and many of her people, but she was learning of Him and, with the joyful birth of her son, she decided that she would serve this God with gratitude.

The above example compares the law from Leviticus 12:1-8 with the practice of child sacrifice to Molech, which was common throughout the land of Canaan, the Promised Land, at the time that the Israelites entered into it.

Book overview

God continued to reveal aspects of His nature and character to His people as they dwelt in the wilderness. He is holy and His people were called to be holy. He wanted His people to be (a) set apart from the surrounding nations, (b) set apart for Him and His purposes, and (c) set apart by their identity as His people. Man is not by nature holy and so a means of atonement had to be established. The priests also had to bring atoning sacrifices to the Lord. This reminded the people that not even their spiritual leaders, the priests, were holy by nature.

It is important to note the different types of law found in the Old Testament. There are three different types, listed below, all of which are found in Leviticus:

- Moral law: the Ten Commandments and those reflective of it. They are foundational laws for man's relationship with God and with man.
- Civil law: relating to social, public or national laws. These relate to relationships between man and man.
- Ceremonial law: these laws were to safe guard against idolatry, prevent syncretism (mixing of religions), and make possible a relationship between God and His people. These laws related to relationship between God and man.

The sacrificial system introduced was a shadow of what was to come through Christ. It showed that forgiveness can only be obtained through the sacrifice of blood. The sacrificial system also taught the people that sin is costly. They were required to give their best livestock to the Lord in order to make atonement for their sins. Ultimately, Christ is the One to whom the sacrificial system pointed. He was the Scapegoat and the Sacrificial Lamb. The book of Hebrews links closely to Leviticus.

Interpreting the book of Leviticus
Interpretation questions
1. For each type of offering (burnt, grain, sin, guilt and fellowship), make note of the following:
   a. Whether it was a freewill offering (not compulsory), or required for forgiveness (compulsory);
   b. Its purpose;
   c. The animal/ item offered;
   d. Actions required from the offerer;
   e. Actions of the priest;
   f. God's portion of the sacrifice;
   g. Priests' portion of the sacrifice;
   h. Offerer's portion of the sacrifice.
2. What does it mean that God is holy?
3. Why was God concerned that His people be seen as different to the

surrounding nations?

4. From chapters 8:1-10:20, write a brief summary (around three to four paragraphs) on the priesthood. Include:
    a.   What was required of the priests?
    b.   How did God provide for His priest?
    c.   Comment on why the priesthood was important.

5. In the laws by which to live holy there are the laws of cleanliness (chapters 11-15) and the miscellaneous laws (chapters 17-20). Choose at least one law from each chapter and consider the following questions, which are guidelines for interpreting Old Testament laws:
    a.   Is the command restated in the New Testament? If so, where?
    b.   Is the command revoked in the New Testament? If so, where?
    c.   Which of the Ten Commandments applies?
    d.   What is the principle behind the Old Testament command? Why was God giving the people the law? What was His reason to give that specific law?
    e.   What godly values do you see? What does the law show of God's heart?
    f.   Bring it through to a statement of principle that is still applicable for today and how that principle might be applied in your local community.

6. In chapters 11:1-12:8, God distinguishes between clean and unclean animals as well as the necessary purification processes following childbirth.
    a.   List some of the reasons you believe God may have given these laws.
    b.   Consider what it showed about His involvement in healthcare and family.

7. As former slaves the Hebrew people would have had little knowledge of the treatment of diseases and important hygiene practices. In light of this, comment on what role God is taking on in chapters 13:1-14:57?

8. Considering the *historical background* given about the land of Canaan, comment on the specifics of the laws God gave involving bodily discharges in chapters 15:1-33. You may also wish to comment on how this would have affected the health and hygiene practices of the nation.

9. Considering the laws, is there a difference between sin and being unclean? Justify your answer.

10. Read chapter 16:1-34 about the Day of Atonement in conjunction with Hebrews 7:11-10:18. The commands regarding this day were given after the death of Aaron's two sons for disobedience. What effect would this have had on the Israelites?

11. List the importance of each of the following feasts, given in chapter 23, and what they revealed about God:
    a.   Sabbath rest;
    b.   Lord's Passover and Feast of Unleavened Bread;
    c.   Feast of First Fruits;

    d. Feast of Weeks;

    e. Feast of Trumpets;

    f. Feast of Booths.

12. What did the Year of Jubilee, discussed in chapter 25, reveal about God and His people?

13. How did God provide for the poor and the alien? What does this reveal about Him?

14. What was God communicating to His people in chapter 26? What does this reveal about God's character and the character of man?

15. How would the Israelites in the desert by Mt Sinai have been feeling as they heard these laws related through Moses?

16. Why did God give His Law to His people before they entered into the Promised Land?

Creative interpretation

1. As an illustration, buy a packet of gummy bears and then:

    a. Write down your sins from last week on a piece of paper. Write down as many as you can remember in the space of three minutes. Imagine thinking "have I covered every sin?" Have you really covered everything?

    b. For each sin, remove a gummy bear from the packet and put it in the bin. Yes: throw it out!

    c. How many did you throw out of the packet compared to how many are left?

    d. Imagine the Israelites as they live in accordance to the sacrificial system. Imagine killing your family's livelihood to cover your sins. Remember that it was not any old animal they could sacrifice, but the best. No animal with a defect could be sacrificed. How does this change your view on the costliness of sin?

2. Write a summary on the holiness of God and why His people must be holy. Comment on:

    a. The priesthood;

    b. What is clean and unclean;

    c. The Day of Atonement;

    d. Laws relating to conduct;

    e. Priests and the feasts; and

    f. The listed blessing (given for obedience) and curses (for disobedience).

Application inspiration

Reflect on the following questions

- Think about what you have learnt about the character of God, the nature of man, the costliness of sin, and the call to be holy as God is holy.

- What does it mean that you are to be holy?

- What sins do you pass off as "okay"? Do you use grace as an excuse to sin? Read Romans 6. What is your current attitude towards sin in your life: whether pride, sexual impurity, haughtiness, unforgiveness, acting in anger, or envy. Sin can be outward, but it can also manifest itself inwardly in the attitudes of the heart.
- Be motivated to live a holy life for God and know that it is only through Christ and God's grace that you can do so. Thank God for the cross, Christ's resurrection, and freedom from sin.

Think about your nation
- What defined the nation of God?
- What did God want to define His nation?
- What defines your nation?
- How would foreigners describe your nation?
- What would make you stand out as different from the many other countries of the world?
- What should define God's church, His holy people?
- Pray for your nation and church.

NUMBERS

The Wilderness Years

"But as for you, your dead bodies shall fall in this wilderness. And your children shall be shepherds in the wilderness forty years and shall suffer for your faithlessness, until the last of your dead bodies lies in the wilderness." – Numbers 14:32-33

During your first reading

Themes to track

- Character and nature of man versus Character and nature of God
- Character of Moses
- Discipline of God
- Trust and obey

During your second reading

Themes to track

- Take note of the disobedience, grumblings and sins of the people.
- Observe how God responded, and Moses reacted, to the people.
- Highlight the actions of God; for example:
    - o "A wind went out from the Lord . . ."
    - o "The Lord heard . . ."
    - o "The Lord said . . ."
- Ask these questions as you read:
    - o Is God unchanging?
    - o Is man unchanging?
    - o Is God always good?

Chapter summaries

These are optional as they can be time consuming for the larger books. If you choose to do them, you will receive a much deeper appreciation of the book. By the end of The IBSC, you will have paraphrased the entire Bible! Go through each chapter and try to summarise it in one paragraph, using your own words; force yourself to stay big picture and capture the heart of each chapter.

After your initial readings

Setting of Numbers
Author

Moses penned the book of Numbers, as directed by God. Moses is accepted as the author of the first five books of the Bible, which are known collectively as the Pentateuch and were originally one book.

Recipient

The Pentateuch was written for the Jews of the Exodus. They had just left Egypt and four hundred years of slavery.

Date and place of writing

Many scholars favour dating the Exodus from Egypt around 1446 BC. So if Moses is accepted as the author, then the book can be dated between 1440 and 1406 BC. This falls during the forty year period that the Israelites spent in the wilderness, between the lands of Egypt and Canaan.

Reason written

Moses was calling the second generation to remember the sins of their fathers and not to commit the same mistake. It was written as a reminder to be faithful to God.

Big picture
Historical background

Refer to the *historical background* given for Genesis for information regarding the Israelites' early history.

Refer to the *historical background* given for Leviticus for further information regarding the practices of the land into which the Israelites were preparing to enter.

The title of the book, Numbers, means "in the wilderness" and reflects the setting of the events it records. Numbers clearly shows that the people were subjected to forty years in the wilderness as a result of their disobedience towards God. It was because of their sins that the first generation of Israelites from the Exodus lost the opportunity to enter into the Promised Land.

It should only have taken the Israelites days to cross the desert to the land of Canaan. Instead, the second generation had to wait and watch until the last of the first generation died in the wilderness, due to disobedience. As a consequence of sin, it was not those who left Egypt, but rather the second generation, who were to enter into the Promised Land.

Women and religion

The vows of women in the land of Canaan were seen as valueless. Women did not have the right to make a vow. In addition, the women of Canaan had no religious worth, except as temple prostitutes.

Character portrayal – dying in the wilderness

"It's not fair! Just because I was born in Egypt and he wasn't," Doron complained, and not for the first time. "The difference of two years. Two years! Why should I have to pay for my father's mistake?"

"Hush!" his mother exclaimed. She was sick of the bickering between her sons. Like her eldest, she would also die in this barren place. Like her eldest, she would also die having only manna to eat day after day, sand between her toes and in her ears, and a tent for a home. She wished now that she had never told them why they were stuck in the wilderness. Although it was not like they would have remained in ignorance if she hadn't explained it to them. It came up every day in nearly every conversation. Someone inevitably complained about their circumstance. What good would whinging do for them? It only served to depress the camp's mood, or anger God.

Book overview

God was preparing His people to enter the Promised Land. Unfortunately, the preparation time was extended from approximately forty days to forty years because of the disobedience of the first generation, the people of the Exodus.

However needless the years in the wilderness were, God did not waste them. He used the years to form their army and the priesthood; he established worship practices and a legal system; He taught them that disobedience has serious consequences; and He handed over the religious leadership from Aaron to Aaron's sons. During this time, the people were completely reliant on God and learnt what it was to trust Him. He was their sole provider of food and water, He was the instigator of discipline, and He determined when the camp went out and when it stopped and set up.

The book of Numbers heralded the change from one generation to the next, as they learnt the lesson of faithfulness and obedience – the obedient received blessings, whilst the disobedient received the discipline of the Lord.

Help with difficult passages

The Red Heifer; Numbers 19

This is a much debated passage amongst theologians so let's first look at what is certain. This is the only time in the Old Testament where the sacrifice of a heifer (female cow) was made, rather than a bull. Adding to the uniqueness of the sacrifice is the rarity of the type of heifer required. After this initial sacrifice, the birth of another red, spotless and blemish-free heifer was not recorded in Israel until 2002 AD. It was an extraordinarily rare and unique sacrifice.

So what did it mean? And, more importantly, why was it needed?

Do not forget where the Israelites were at this point in their history, or what was required by the Law in order to be made pure and holy. The Law stipulated that people became unclean (or unfit to be before their holy God) after coming into contact with a dead body. Not only those who had contact with the bodies were unclean, but anyone who touched a defiled person became defiled too.

Now consider the camp of the Israelites. They were in the wilderness awaiting the death of an entire generation. This means that approximately one million people died over a forty-year period or close to seventy people per day if you take the average. Needless to say, there would have been a lot of dead bodies. How was the camp ever to remain pure, or clean? An impossible situation? Perhaps, although not for a merciful God.

The Almighty had a plan up His sleeve and it involved the red heifer. It was a unique sacrifice for a unique situation. The heifer was God's provision for cleanliness even in the midst of the people's disobedience (remembering that the first generation were dying because of their disobedience). God's response was mercy.

Is there any significance to the New Testament, or was this a once-off sacrifice? If you go to Hebrews 9:11-14 you will see that Christ is the perfect, redeeming sacrifice. The heifer foreshadowed Christ. The book of Hebrews makes it clear that the heifer only purified the flesh, whereas Christ's sacrifice brought complete purity and freedom from the works of the Law. [1]

God met a unique situation with a unique sacrifice to cleanse His people. Today, it is Christ's blood that purifies the church.

Interpreting the book of Numbers
Interpretation questions

1. From reading Numbers, and gaining support elsewhere in Scripture where required, record your findings on the following questions:
   a. Is God unchanging?
   b. Is man unchanging?
   c. Is God always good?
2. What was the significance of the censuses that God commanded Moses to take?
   a. What did they show?
   b. What distinction was God making?
   c. Explain why the tribe of Levi was not included with the other tribes in the censuses.
3. Why was the camp to be arranged around the centre of the Tent of Meeting?
4. Considering the priests, read Exodus 12:21-32, 13:11-16, and 32:19-29.
   a. Why did God re-establish His claim on the Levites in Numbers 3 and 8:5-26?
   b. Why did God chose to take the Levites for His own, rather than the firstborn children of every tribe?
   c. What character did God seek in His priests?
5. Read Numbers 16, again observing the priests.

    a. Did this dispel the qualities for which the Levites were first chosen?

    b. What did it reveal about the character of man?

    c. What was the significance of recording the flaws of the priests? How would this have impacted the people's view of the priesthood through the generations as they read God's Law and their nation's history?

6. What was God emphasising about man's character by showing that not even the priests could have full access, or rights, within the tabernacle (due to issues of holiness)? See Numbers 4:15 for an example.

7. What do you believe was God's purpose for the laws recorded in chapter 5?

    a. What was the heart or principle behind them?

    b. What were they meant to achieve?

8. Why would someone take the vow of a Nazarene? Who was allowed to take this vow?

9. Consider the significance of the sacrifice of the red heifer in chapter 10.

    a. Why was it needed?

    b. What was its purpose?

    c. What was the significance of this sacrifice?

    d. What did it reveal of God's character?

    e. Read Hebrews 9:11-14 and comment on how the red heifer foreshadowed Christ.

10. Make a three-columned table to explore how the Israelites as a people reveal man's faithlessness to a holy God.

    a. In the first column, note the verse reference.

    b. In the second column, record the actions and emotions of the people. For example, did they choose fear of man over fear of God, or did they act in disobedience to a command of God?

    c. In the third column, add God's response. What did His discipline look like? How was His mercy revealed in His discipline? Seek what God's heart was behind His response to the people, including the purpose behind His discipline.

11. The desert years are often referred to as "a time of wandering in the wilderness". This can imply that the time was without purpose.

    a. Do you believe that God was aimlessly moving His people around?

    b. What was He trying to achieve during those years?

12. Reflect on the character of Balaam (Numbers 22-24). He was selling blessings and curses, yet at the same time he walked in the fear of the Lord and refused to say anything that the Lord has not commanded him to say. In the end, he was killed by the Israelites.

    a. Look up Joshua 13:22 and Deuteronomy 18:10-12.

    b. Look up Joshua 24:9-10, Deuteronomy 23:3-5 and Nehemiah 13:1-2.

    c. Look up 2 Peter 2:15-16 and Jude 1:11.

       d. Look up Revelation 2:14, Numbers 25:1-5 and Numbers 31:16.

       e. Bearing the above references in mind, was he a good guy or a bad guy?

       f. Should God have commanded the Israelites not to have killed him?

13. Make sure to note the transition that occurs within the book, between chapter 26 and 27, from the first generation of Israelites (those who partook of the Exodus from Egypt), to the second generation (who were born in the wilderness). Did the transition bring a change of focus, or atmosphere, in the writing?

Creative interpretation

1. Draw a diagram displaying the camp set up as God commanded in Numbers 2.

       a. Why do you believe He had the camp arranged this way?

       b. Why were the Levites to be in the centre with the tabernacle?

2. Note the interchange in the book between the narrative (displaying the character and nature of man), and the giving of the Law (revealing the character and nature of God). Replicate the table below and beside the verse references, list what they reveal about God and man.

Interchange in the book of Numbers	
Narrative Character and nature of man	**Law** Character and nature of God
Chapters: 1 7 9:15-23 10:11-14:45 15:32-36 16, 17 20-26:51 31-33:49	Chapters: 2-6 8:9:15 10:1-10 15:1-31 15:37-41 18-19 26:52-30:16 33:50-36:13
Reminders of Israel's failure. Offers proof that rebellious man was faithless to a holy God.	In contrast, the Law clearly shows the faithfulness of God, and His holy standards. Offers proof of the faithfulness of a holy God to rebellious man.

Application inspiration

- God values history and the lessons of history. He instructed Moses to write the book of Numbers so that the Israelites would remember why they had to spend the years in the wilderness. God desires that we learn from those who went before us and also pass down our experiences of His faithfulness to the next generation.

  - With who can you share an experience, or from whom can you seek stories, of God's faithful?
  - Could you talk to your children about a memory you have of God's provision at a time when you were in need?
  - As a youth group, could you interview some of the elders in the church and make a congregational book containing each of their testimonies?
  - Ask someone whose faith you admire to coffee and have them share stories of faith; it might be your aunty, godmother, friend, youth leader or minister.

A question to ponder: Is man unchanging?

- In the desert years, the Israelites had God's Presence and direction tangibly, every day. They had clear instruction about what they had to do. Yet they complained, rebelled and disobeyed.
  - Are you different to the first generation of Israelites from the Exodus or is your spirit one of complaint and rebellion?
  - Do you long for God's visible, tangible presence in your life and think that having it would make it easier to walk in faithfulness to His commands?
  - What do you desire as proof of God and His faithfulness?
  - Are you aware that you have this presence in the Holy Spirit, who dwells within believers?
- Moses wished that everyone would have the Spirit. What do believers have today? The Spirit.
  - Are you listening to His quiet whisperings?
  - Are you sensitising your spiritual ear to hear His voice?
- Man wants what he does not have. Man is not changing.
  - How did God use the time in the wilderness to teach the Israelites?
  - How is God transforming the church today? What should be the response of the church?
  - What is God teaching you?

[1] Hebrews 9:13-14

DEUTERONOMY

Remember – Love – Obey

"Know therefore that the LORD your God is God, the faithful God who keeps covenant and steadfast love with those who love him and keep his commandments, to a thousand generations, and repays to their face those who hate him, by destroying them. He will not be slack with one who hates him. He will repay him to his face. You shall therefore be careful to do the commandment and the statutes and the rules that I command you today." – Deuteronomy 7:9-11

During your first reading

Themes to track

- Remembrance
- Book of Law
- Love and obey, the call to be faithful
- God's love for Israel

During your second reading

Things to notice in the text

- Highlight the repeated words "remember" and "forget".
- Mark passages that call the people to remembrance.
- Highlight the repeated words "love" and "hearts".
- Mark passages that relate to the character of God.

Chapter summaries

These are optional as they can be time consuming for the larger books. If you choose to do them, you will receive a much deeper appreciation of the book. By the end of The IBSC, you will have paraphrased the entire Bible! Go through each chapter and try to summarise it in one paragraph, using your own words; force

yourself to stay big picture and capture the heart of each chapter.

After your initial readings

Setting of Deuteronomy
Author

Moses penned the book of Deuteronomy, as directed by God. Moses is accepted as the author of the first five books of the Bible, which are known collectively as the Pentateuch and were originally one book.

Recipient

The Pentateuch was written for the Jews of the Exodus. They had just left Egypt and four hundred years of slavery.

Date and place of writing

Many scholars favour dating the Exodus from Egypt around 1446 BC. So if Moses is accepted as the author, then the book can be dated between 1440 and 1406 BC. This falls during the forty year period that the Israelites spent in the wilderness, between the lands of Egypt and Canaan.

Reason written

God was re-establishing His covenant with the second generation of Israelites from the Exodus as the people of God once again stood at the edge of the Promised Land.

Big picture
Historical background

Refer to the *historical background* given for Genesis for information regarding the Israelites' early history.

By this time the original readers, the second generation of Israelites from the Exodus, had passed through lands with foreign gods and were not oblivious to the religious practices of these people. The Canaanites and surrounding nations were involved in all kinds of horrific sacrifices and worship rituals, including human sacrifice. The people of the surrounding nations put a low value on human life. Death and perversion were at the core of their belief systems. The people of Israel would have been exposed to such practices, as they moved towards the Promised Land.

Refer to the *historical background* given for Leviticus for further information regarding the practices of the land into which the Israelites were about to enter.

The mountains of Ebal and Gerizim (refer to Deuteronomy 27) formed a natural amphitheatre in the valley that lay between them. As the Levites proclaimed the blessings and curses from opposite mountains, the Israelites, who had remained below, would have heard them ring out clearly across the valley.

Character portrayal – thoughts of Joshua

"I don't think that I can do this. These people are stubborn and disobedient. If they wouldn't listen to Moses, God's own prophet, why would they listen to me?" Joshua thought.

"Be strong and courageous," [1] Moses had said to the people.

"Be strong and courageous," [2] Moses had commanded him.

What did that mean? Did it imply that he would need strength and courage for what he was about to go up against? Joshua felt daunted.

"Be strong and courageous, for you shall bring the people of Israel into the land that I swore to give them. I will be with you," [3] the Lord had commanded when commissioning him.

"Yes, Lord," Joshua prayed, "I choose to be strong and courageous, but I will need you. I will need you to be with me every single, small step of the way. I know that you can overcome the nations before us. I trust that you will fight for your nation, and I believe that you will conqueror. I know that you will keep your promises and we will inherit the land. I just ask that you will go before me. Only you can lead your people. I need you."

"Be strong and courageous, for you shall bring the people of Israel into the land that I swore to give them. I will be with you." [3] The words echoed in Joshua's mind.

Book overview

Deuteronomy is a book that reveals God's character. His signs and wonders were displayed to them and their ancestors so that the people might know that He is the Lord. See God as you study this book. He desires people to turn to Him from their wickedness and sin. He is a great and awesome God who is to be feared. He is terrifying to behold.

In Deuteronomy, the people were reminded that God chose Israel and now Israel must choose Him. As God reinstated His covenant with the new generation, Moses handed the national leadership over to Joshua. These were the children of those who left Egypt in the Exodus. They had taken their parents' place as the warriors and leaders of Israel and were about to inherit the Promised Land. The book of Deuteronomy reminded them of God's faithfulness and His promises, but they were also being warned to remember the disobedience of their fathers that caused them to live in the wilderness for forty years.

God promised to bless those who listen to Him, but would humble those who turned against His commands. He promised that He would fight for His people, but to worship anything other than Him would be an abomination. He alone is worthy to be praised. He called His people to remember and celebrate all that He had done for them.

Interpreting the book of Deuteronomy

Interpretation questions

    1. Why did Moses again recount their past history in Deuteronomy 1-4?

        a. What point was he making by recapping what their fathers had gone through?

    b. How would the original readers, the second generation, have felt as they once again heard the story of their fathers' unfaithfulness?

2. Moses had already recorded the history of their wanderings. Why was he repeating this? Note the change of Moses' intended audience from the first to the second generation.

3. The words "remember" and "do not forget" are used repeatedly.
    a. What was the significance of the repetition?
    b. What was Moses hoping to instil in their minds?

4. What was said of:
    a. Remembering God's faithfulness?
    b. Remembering why they were entering the Promised Land? and
    c. Remembering why they were in the Wilderness for forty years?

5. What did the general laws and commands, given in Numbers 5-11, reveal about:
    a. The character of God and what He desired from His people?
    b. What God expected from His people?
    c. The importance of the heart and one's motives in worship?
    d. What the original readers would face when they entered into the Promised Land?
    e. How would the Israelites have felt as they heard God's promises restated?
    f. What were the people warned against doing?
    g. What did Moses fear the Israelites would do?
    h. What were the consequences listed for disobedience?

6. In chapter 12, God commanded the people to worship only at the place that He would designate. Refer to the *historical background* given for Leviticus to learn of the practices within the land of Canaan if you need to before answering the following:
    a. Why did He want them to only worship at a set location?
    b. What was the significance of this?
    c. What would this have conveyed to the surrounding nations?

7. Chapters 12-26 list more specific laws that were to help form the Israelites into a nation. The laws relate to issues of economy, justice, family, agriculture, war, and church. Choose at least ten of the laws and think through the following questions:
    a. What did the law show about God, His character or His values?
    b. Who did the law benefit and how were they benefited?
    c. As relevant to the law, mention any historical background you think is relevant – either of the Israelites or Canaanites. Consider the Canaanite religious practices and how they contrasted with the laws of God.
    d. List any verses outside of Deuteronomy that are of relevance or give further insight to the significance of the law.
    e. Why impact would the Law make on the formation of Israel as a nation?

    f. Bring your observations and interpretation through to application. Consider how the principle of the law could be applied today. How would following the principle, derived from the law, affect the economy, justice system, agriculture, military, families, or church in your nation?

8. What do the following verses show about who the people of God were, and were to be?

    a. Deuteronomy 4:3-4; 4:20; 4:32-35; 7:6-8; 9:5-6; 10:20-22; 11:18-19; 14:1-2; 16:15; 16:18-20; 23:19; 26:18-19; 29:10-15; 30:19-20.

9. Consider the character of God:

    a. What do the following verses reveal about God? Deuteronomy 3:22; 4:1; 4:24; 4:31; 4:39; 6:13-15; 7:9; 7:21; 8:18; 10:14; 10:17-19; 20:1; 31:6.

    b. What is revealed in Deuteronomy about God's heart for the orphan, alien and widow?

    c. What does Deuteronomy show about His heart for justice?

10. Three festivals are highlighted in Deuteronomy: the Passover, the Festival of Weeks, and the Festival of Booths (tabernacle).

    a. Why did God emphasise that these festivals were to be celebrations?

    b. What does this show about God?

    c. Why did God make them compulsory for the entire nation?

11. For each of the festivals listed in question 10, think about:

    a. What was the feast remembering?

    b. What were the requirements of the feast?

    c. Were sacrifices required and, if so, what were they to be?

    d. For what was God getting the glory?

12. What was the significance of listing the treaty conditions at the end of the book in chapters 27-30?

    a. How would the original readers have been feeling as they heard the list of blessings that went with obedience?

    b. How would hearing the curses have affected them as they stood on the edge of the Promised Land?

    c. If you have time, read through the book of Jeremiah, where most of these curses can be seen as God finally loses patience with His people's disobedience and sin.

13. Prior to his death, Moses handed the leadership over to Joshua (Deuteronomy 31-34).

    a. Why was it important for Moses to formally give the mantle of leadership to Joshua?

    b. How would Joshua have been feeling as he received this mantle?

    c. What can be surmised of Joshua's character from the books of Exodus, Leviticus, Numbers and Deuteronomy?

14. Consider the song recorded in chapter 32.

    a. What was the purpose of giving the song to the Israelites?

b. What can be learnt of the Israelites from the song?

c. What was revealed about the surrounding nations?

d. What do you see of God's character through the song?

15. What is the significance of Moses starting and ending the blessing in chapter 33 with declaring God's character and His works? Why would this blessing have been important for them to remember in the wake of Moses' death and as they enter into the Promised Land?

Creative interpretation

16. Using the commands, laws, and instructions in Deuteronomy, comment on the link between worship, love, and obedience.

17. Refer back to the *historical background* given for Genesis for information on Suzerain-Vassal covenants, where elements of the Suzerain-Vassal relationship were introduced. Find examples within the Pentateuch where each of the following characteristics of the relationship were displayed between God and His people:

a. The Suzerain established the land boundaries of the Vassal Nation. For example, Genesis 15:17-21 and Exodus 6:24.

b. The Suzerain would fight for the Vassal Nation.

c. Above all else, the Suzerain demanded loyalty.

d. The Vassal Nation was brought under the law of the Suzerain.

e. A historical prologue was given as an introduction to the laws. It recounted what the Suzerain had done for them to motivate the Vassal to obey the laws.

f. The Suzerain demanded taxes from their Vassal.

g. The Vassal was not allowed to form a covenant with any other king.

Application inspiration

- Deuteronomy focuses on remembrance. It charged the people to remember what God had done for them and what promises He had given to them.
  o Take some time to write about God's past faithfulness in your life.
  o Think about a promise that you feel He has given to you, which is yet to be fulfilled.
  o Record God's past faithfulness and your hope for the fulfilment of His promise. Why not turn it into a song or poem for your journal.
- The surrounding nations were meant to be baffled as they looked at Israel following God's laws. The lives of the Israelites, walked in obedience to God's commands, were meant to draw foreigners into His nation.
  o Is His Law relevant today?
  o Imagine if the entire population of a modern nation did not commit adultery. How would it look different? Think of the effects on HIV/AIDs, families, trust in marriage, and divorce

rates.

- o What is something in your country that would be changed by following one of God's laws?

- What do you do in celebration of God in order to remember what He has done?
    - o How much time do you spend on remembering what God has done for you, or saying thank you to Him at Easter, Christmas, or when celebrating the Lord's Supper?
    - o When you get a pay check, do you thank God for His provision in your life?
    - o When you say grace over your meals at night, is your grace said with a thankful heart or has it become an automated routine?

- God cares about the state of our hearts. The laws He gave His people show that He desires obedience. Spend time reflecting on Psalm 51:17.

[1] Deuteronomy 31:6
[2] Deuteronomy 31:7
[3] Deuteronomy 31:23

JOSHUA

God fights for His people

So Joshua took the whole land, according to all that the LORD had spoken to Moses. And Joshua gave it for an inheritance to Israel according to their tribal allotments. And the land had rest from war. – Joshua 11:23

During your first reading

Themes to track

- Memorials and remembrance
- Obedience versus disobedience
- God's faithfulness and other character attributes
- Joshua's character
- Boldness of faith

During your second reading

Things to notice in the text

- Take note of the "whose" (names of individuals and tribes).
- Circle places (cities and lands).
- Underline commands.
- Mark conditional statements (if "x", then "y").

Chapter summaries

These are optional as they can be time consuming for the larger books. If you choose to do them, you will receive a much deeper appreciation of the book. By the end of The IBSC, you will have paraphrased the entire Bible! Go through each chapter and try to summarise it in one paragraph, using your own words; force yourself to stay big picture and capture the heart of each chapter.

After your initial readings

Setting of Joshua

<u>Author</u>

Joshua wrote the majority of the book, but final additions would have been made shortly after his death by an unknown eye witness to the events.

<u>Recipient</u>

Joshua was written for the generation who conquered the Promised Land, and their children. These were the second and third generations from the Exodus.

<u>Date and place of writing</u>

Many scholars favour dating the Exodus from Egypt around 1446 BC, placing the time the Israelites entered into the land Canaan around 1406 BC. The book would have been completed within a few years following Joshua's death, which is placed around 1375 BC, from within the Promised Land.

<u>Reason written</u>

The book of Joshua was written to encourage faith and obedience by documenting Israel's victories under Joshua's leadership. It also records the division of land between the tribes, which was to be maintained throughout all generations.

Big picture

<u>Historical background</u>

The land of Canaan was different to the lands of its neighbours, Egypt and Mesopotamia. These nations had only one ruler, whereas Canaan was made up of many little kingdoms. This made it a volatile place to live as these small kingdoms were constantly striving against one another. However, the land was also fertile making it one of the wealthiest places to dwell, with the economy established on agriculture. Major trade routes between the surrounding nations ran through the land of Canaan, further contributing to the land's wealth.

Refer to the *historical background* given for Leviticus for further information regarding the religious practices of the people of Canaan.

Politically, the nations within Canaan were well established with allies and connections to other kings of the land. In comparison, the Israelites had no connections or allies as they entered the land.

Also keep in mind that the Israelites had been raised in the wilderness and their parents before them had been slaves. They were not trained for war and had no knowledge of battle strategy or experience at warfare.

<u>Character portrayal – Caleb to his children</u>

"Be careful to do all that Joshua is commanding you from the Lord," Caleb admonished. "I have seen what happens to those who question Him. He is a mighty God and a jealous one. You must be careful to do all that is written in the books of the Law and pass on to your children the good works that He has done for us.

"Tell them how He parted the Red Sea. It was just as it was when He parted the waters of the Jordan for us to cross into the Promised Land. Describe to them how millions of their people passed between pillars of water held back by the hands of God.

"Tell them how you spent forty years wandering in the desert because their ancestors, the people who witnessed the miracles of Egypt, did not believe God could perform them once more in a new land. Make sure you give Him the glory for defeating the Canaanites. Make sure they know that it was God who fought for His people.

"I will be with you only a short while longer, enjoying this rest that God has given to us. You must make sure that you and your children continue to walk in obedience to God's Law in order to receive His blessings. Never forget that, just as there are blessings for obedience, there are curses for disobedience. Do not repeat the mistakes of my generation. Choose God. Choose life. Live long in the land!"

Book overview

The book of Joshua records the Israelites entering into the Promised Land, as God fulfilled the promise that He had made to their patriarchs. God showed that He is faithful to His promises and is mighty to accomplish them. He is shown to be greater than the gods of the foreign nations. God left no doubt in their minds as to who was responsible for the victories, and that He was there fighting for His people. Israel needed Him in order to conqueror the Promised Land.

The book of Joshua details twenty-five of the most significant years in their national history as they conquered and settled the Promised Land. It ends with the people entering into a time of rest, as they settled into a "land flowing with milk and honey".

Help with difficult passages
Commander of the army of the LORD; Joshua 5

"When Joshua was by Jericho, he lifted up his eyes and looked, and behold, a man was standing before him with his drawn sword in his hand. And Joshua went to him and said to him, "Are you for us, or for our adversaries?" [1]

"And he said, "No; but I am the commander of the army of the LORD. Now I have come." And Joshua fell on his face to the earth and worshiped and said to him, "What does my lord say to his servant?" [2]

"And the commander of the LORD's army said to Joshua, "Take off your sandals from your feet, for the place where you are standing is holy." And Joshua did so." [3]

Who was the Commander of the Lord's army? Was it a man, God or an angel? Can one be sure who it was? Scripture often gives less information than one would like, but not less than is needed. You will always have questions that you cannot answer because God is greater than the extent man understands. There are many debated passages in Scripture, but try not to get hung up on them. Stay big picture – ask what the passage would mean to the original reader, the reason the author felt it important to include, and its place in God's salvation plan.

This event would have given confidence to Joshua, as the leader, and to the

Israelites, as they prepared to enter the Promised Land. Remember that they had been in this situation before. Perhaps there were those in the camp who were coming under the fear of their fathers and God used this event to strengthen their hearts. God is clearly saying "this is my battle, not yours".

So who was the Commander of the Lord's army? In Revelation 22:8-9, John was commanded to get to his feet when he falls down before an angel of the Lord. In comparison, when Moses went before God he was told to take off his sandals for the ground he stood on was holy. In Joshua, the command to take off his shoes is again given.

Interpreting the book of Joshua
Interpretation questions
1. Who was Joshua? In addition to what you learn of him in this book, read:
   a. Exodus 32:17-20, 33:11;
   b. Numbers 11:21-30, 13:16-20, 14:6-9, 26:63-65; and
   c. Deuteronomy 1:38, 3:21-22, 28, 34:9.
2. Why did Joshua rise to leadership? Consider also:
   a. Exodus 17:9-14, 24:13, 33:11;
   b. Numbers 14:28-30, 27:15-28; and
   c. Deuteronomy 31:7-8, 23.
3. How would the response of Rahab have affected the camp of Israel before battle?
4. Why was it significant that Rahab was allowed into the people of God?
5. Compare the report of the spies in Joshua 2:22-24 to that of the spies in Numbers 13:25-14:4.
6. Why exterminate the Canaanites?
   a. Was Joshua justified in massacring the inhabitants of the land?
   b. How did this command relate to God's plan to form His people into a holy nation?
7. Think about the Israelites as they entered, captured, and settled the land.
   a. What could have been their struggles?
   b. What were their questions?
   c. Was there disunity amongst the tribes and did they covet prized land in their hearts?
   d. Did they struggle with leadership?
   e. Were they in need of encouragement through miracles?
   f. What were their feelings towards the people of Canaan?
8. What was revealed of God through their battles to take the land?
9. Circumcising the camp:
   a. Look back to Genesis 17 and consider the symbolic meaning of circumcision. See also Deuteronomy 10 and Romans 2:25-29.
   b. What was the importance of circumcising the people as they entered the land?
   c. Reading Joshua 15:1, how would the people have been feeling making themselves vulnerable whilst their enemies heard of their

approach?

    d. What was God teaching them through their vulnerability?

10. Consider Joshua 5:13-15:

    a. Based on your current understanding, who do you believe appeared? Was it a man, angel or God? How did you come to this conclusion?

    b. Why was this event important to the Israelites at that exact moment in their history?

11. What do you learn about the consequences of obedience and disobedience in the book of Joshua?

12. Consider Joshua's final actions:

    a. What was the significance of Joshua making the people declare their devotion to the Lord in chapter 24?

    b. As Joshua prepared for his death, what was the focal point of his message to the people?

    c. What was the one thing from his message that he wanted them to hold to after his death?

13. Looking ahead to a New Testament understanding, read Hebrews 4:1-11.

    a. What was the rest being talked of in Joshua?

    b. What is the rest hinted at in Hebrews?

Creative interpretation

1. On Map 1, at the end of this section, mark the main routes of the conquest. Mark:

    a. Central Campaign

    b. Southern Campaign

    c. Northern Campaign

2. On Map 2 provided below, mark the division of the land of Canaan according to the tribal allocation recorded in Joshua.

3. Choose two different coloured pens. On Map 3 below, mark the cities designated as cities of refuge in one colour, and the cities given to the Levities in the other.

4. Find a current-day map and compare which nations are now in the place of the Israelites' territory.

The Conquest of Canaan
* this map provides estimated locations as some places remain unknown in exact locality

Tyre

Mt Hermon

Kedesh

Hazor

? merom
? madon

Acco

Sea of Galilee

Mt Carmel

Achshaph

Lasharon

Yarmuk River

Dor

Goiim Shimron
Jokneam

Megiddo

Taanach

Hepher

Mt Ebal
Tirzah
Mt Gerizim
Shechem

Jordan River

Aphek

Tappuah

Shiloh

Jabbok River

Joppa

Bethel

Ai

Gilgal

Gezer

Gibeon

Jericho

Shittium

Aijalon

Jerusalem

Ashdod

Jarmuth

Gath

Adullam

Libnah

Ashkelon

Dead Sea

Gaza

Lachish

Hebron

Arnon River

? Makkedah

Eglon

Debir

Beersheba

Arad

Hormah

Zered River

Map 1: Conquest of Canaan.

Division of Land

*many of these cities have
been estimated as exact
locations remain unknown

Map 2: Tribal allotment of land.

Cities of Refuge
and
Levitical Cities

*many of these cities are estimates as exact locations remain unknown

**Unknown cities that are not on the map: Ain, Beeshterah, Dimnah and Kartah

Rehob
Abdon
Kedesh
Kishon River
Kartin
Sea of Galilee
Hammath
Golan
Ashtaroth
Jokneam
Yarmuk River
Taanach
Ibleam
En-gannim
Ramoth-gilead
Shechem
Jabbok River
Mahanaim
Yarkon River
Gath-rimmon
Kibzaim
Beth-horon
Gibeon
Geba
Jazer
Eltekeh
Gezer
Almon
Anathoth
Mephaath
Gibbethon
Aijalon
Jerusalem
Heshbon
Bezer
Beth-Shemesh
Kedemoth
Libnah
Dead Sea
Jahaz
Hebron
Arnon River
Debir
Juttah
Holon
Eastern Desert
Brook Besor
Wadi of Egypt
MOAB
Zered River
EDOM

Map 3: Conquest of Canaan and division of land.

Application inspiration

- Make a list of people who you think are successful. What are their attributes? Why do you see them as successful?
- How do you define success? Write out your own definition for the word.
- Read through Hebrews 3:15-4:16. Meditate on Hebrews 4:3, 8-9. How should believers live in light of this hope?
- What do you want to conquer in the next week, month, or year? Perhaps it is starting a family, finishing school, getting good grades at university, or keeping in touch with friends. Whatever it is, acknowledge God's sovereignty, and offer it into His hands in prayer.
- Is there something that you believe God is asking you to do? Maybe it is to step into a new role at church, to help out with your children's sports club, or to invite someone over for dinner to practice hospitality. Will you walk in obedience to God's call on your life?
- How do you treat the "Rahabs" who you know? Would you invite them, flaws and all, to attend your church? Will you invite them to a church luncheon or sports' day? Will you welcome them into your life and your family?

[1] Joshua 5:13
[2] Joshua 5:14
[3] Joshua 5:15

INTRODUCTION TO THE RULERSHIP OF ISRAEL

Time of the judges

God's desire was to be King over His people. He had given Israel laws of governance, land, social order, religion, and health. He had been the General of their armies. And now, as the Israelites settled the land, His desire was to rule as their King, blessing their lands with safety and abundance as they walked in obedience to His laws.

The people started reasonably well as declared: *"Israel served the Lord all the days of Joshua, and all the days of the elders who outlived Joshua and had known all the work that the LORD did for Israel"* [1]. However, with the death of Joshua, the people forgot what God had done for them.

When entering the land, the people had not obeyed God's command to rid it of its original inhabitants. This command was not given because God was bloodthirsty. God wanted to protect His people from being led astray by the unrighteous living and idolatrous practices of their neighbours. This came to pass. They turned their gaze upon the former inhabitants of the land, whom they had not driven out, and these people led the Israelites into sin against God, thus starting the "sin cycles" seen in the book of Judges.

The covenant God had made with His people demanded that He send curses upon them for disobedience, as declared in Deuteronomy 28, just as He had promised to bless them for obedience. Nevertheless, God, in His great mercy, faithfully sent rescuers to save His people each time they cried out to Him for help. These "saviours" came in the form of judges. The sin cycles can be depicted as follows:

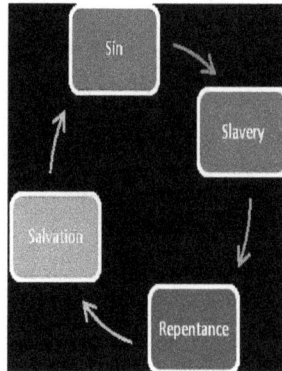

Illustration: Cycles of Sin recorded in Judges

Each cycle began with Israel sinning in the sight of God (*sin*). As a result, His wrath fell upon them and they would be taken into slavery or know defeat in war (*slavery*). The people would then cry out to the Lord in repentance, seeking His help (*supplication/repentance*), and their merciful God would send a saviour to deliver them from their enemies (*salvation*).

Thirteen judges are recorded in the book of Judges. The events of the book of Ruth also occurred during this period of Israel's history.

Time of the kings

The initial years in the land of Canaan saw God as the undisputed Ruler of His people. The judges had acted at His direction to save the nation, but He had been their King. However, after three hundred and sixty-three years in the land, Israel began to look askance at the rulers of the surrounding nations. They had already turned to worshipping the gods of these nations, now they wanted to have a human king over them in imitation of their neighbours. God had set Israel apart to be a light to the world. God's plan for His people was to make them a righteous nation that would draw other peoples into His kingdom. Instead, the people of God chose conformity, asking God to give them a human king.

God told Samuel to warn the people what life under a king would be like and then grant them their request. The people of God did not heed the warning and so God was rejected as their king. The first king of Israel, King Saul, was chosen by the people. He bore the physical attributes that they thought befitted a king. Saul turned from the Lord and ended his days seeking to kill David, the man anointed by God to be his successor.

Saul was the first king of what is known as the United Kingdom and was followed by David and Solomon. King David was a righteous king who sought the Lord. He knew what it was to fall short of God's perfect standard and yet he also knew of God's saving grace and unending love. King Solomon, son of David, began his rulership well, but he did not obey God's law, which commanded against taking foreigners as wives. Solomon married many foreign women who led him to worship idols and false gods.

During the reigns of Saul, David and Solomon, all the tribes stood united and the nation prospered as God blessed them. However, God's anger came upon Solomon and He declared that the kingdom would be torn from Solomon's line. This promise was fulfilled during the days of Solomon's son, Rehoboam. The kingdom was divided into north and south, forming two new nations. Only the southern tribes of Judah and Benjamin remained loyal to Rehoboam. This was in fulfilment of God's promise to David that there would always be someone from his line on the throne. They became the southern kingdom.

The Northern Kingdom became known as Israel and the southern kingdom, as Judah. The two kingdoms never reunited. The people continued to walk in sin and the kings perpetuated their transgressions, leading them further astray. The nation of Judah had a scattering of godly kings that led the nation into reform, yet it never lasted. Eventually, both kingdoms were sent into exile by God. Israel was sent into exile at the hands of the Assyrians in 722 BC, never to be re-established in their lands. Judah followed in 586 BC at the hands of the Babylonians.

Kings of Israel and Judah

Kings of Judah & Israel	Years of their Reign	Main Scripture References
Saul (United Kingdom)	1050/45 – 1011/10 BC	1 Samuel 9-31
David (United Kingdom)	1011/10 – 971/70 BC	1 Samuel 16-31; 2 Samuel; 1 Kings 1-2; 1 Chronicles
Solomon (United Kingdom)	971/70 – 931/30 BC	1 Kings 1-11; 2 Chronicles 1-9
Jeroboam (Israel)	931 – 909 BC	1 Kings 12:25-14:20
Rehoboam (Judah)	931 – 914 BC	1 Kings 14:21-31; 2 Chronicles 10-12
Abijam (Judah)	914 – 911 BC	1 Kings 15:1-8; 2 Chronicles 13
Asa (Judah)	911/10 – 870/69 BC	1 Kings 15:9-24; 2 Chronicles 14-16
Nadab (Israel)	909 – 908 BC	1 Kings 15:25-32
Baasha (Israel)	909/8 – 886/5 BC	1 Kings 15:33-16:7; 2 Chronicles 16:1-6
Elah (Israel)	886/5 – 885/4 BC	1 Kings 16:8-14
Zimri (Israel)	885/4 BC	1 Kings 16:11-20
Tibni (Israel)	885/4 BC	1 Kings 16:21-24
Omri (Israel)	885/4 – 874/3 BC	1 Kings 16:21-28
Ahab (Israel)	874/3 – 853 BC	1 Kings 16:29-22:40; 2 Chronicles 18
Jehoshaphat (Judah)	870/69 – 848 BC (coregent from 873/72)	1 Kings 22:(1)41-50 & 2 Kings 3:4-; 2 Chronicles 17-

		20
Ahaziah (Israel)	853 – 852 BC	1 Kings 22:51 – 2 Kings 1:18
Jehoram (Israel)	848 – 841 BC	2 Kings 3:1-27; 6:8-15; 8:28-9:26
Jehoram/ Joram (Judah)	848– 841 BC	2 Kings 8:16-24; 2 Chronicles 21
Ahaziah/ Jehoahaz (Judah)	841 BC	2 Kings 8:25-29; 2 Chronicles 22:1-9
Jehu (Israel)	841 – 814/13 BC	2 Kings 9:1-10:36 (see also 1 Kings 19:16-17; 2 Chronicles 22:7-9)
Athaliah (Judah)	841 – 835 BC	2 Kings 11:1-20; 2 Chronicles 22:10-23
Joash/ Jehoash (Judah)	835 – 796 BC	2 Kings 11:21-12:21; 2 Chronicles 22:10-25
Jehoahaz (Israel)	814/3 – 798 BC	2 Kings 13:1-9
Jehoash (Israel)	798 – 782/81 BC	2 Kings 13:10-14:16; 2 Chronicles 25:14-24
Amaziah (Judah)	796 – 767 BC	2 Kings 14:1-22; 2 Chronicles 25:1-26:1
Jeroboam II (Israel)	782/81 – 753 BC	2 Kings 14:23-29
Azariah/ Uzziah (Judah)	767 – 740/39 BC (coregent from 791/0)	2 Kings 15:1-7; 2 Chronicles 26
Zechariah (Israel)	753 – 752 BC	2 Kings 15:8-12
Shallum (Israel)	752 BC	2 Kings 15:13-16
Menahem (Israel)	752 – 742/1 BC	2 Kings 15:16-22
Pekahiah (Israel)	742/1 – 740/39 BC	2 Kings 15:23-26
Pekah (Israel)	740/39 – 732/1 BC	2 Kings 15:27-31; 2 Chronicles 28:6
Jotham (Judah)	740/39 – 732/1 BC (coregent from 750)	2 Kings 15:32-38; 2 Chronicles 27
Ahaz (Judah)	732/1 – 716/5 BC (coregent 744/3; senior partner 753)	2 Kings 16:1-20; 2 Chronicles 28
Hoshea (Israel)	732/1 – 723/2 BC	2 Kings 17
Hezekiah (Judah)	716/5 – 687/6 BC (coregent from 729)	2 Kings 18:1-20:21; 2 Chronicles 29-32
Manasseh (Judah)	687/6 – 642/1 BC (coregent from 696/5)	2 Kings 21:1-18; 2 Chronicles 33:1-20
Amon (Judah)	642/1 – 640/39 BC	2 Kings 21:19-26; 2 Chronicles 33:21-25
Josiah (Judah)	640/39 - 609 BC	2 Kings 22-23:30; 2 Chronicles 34-35

Jehoahaz (Judah)	609 BC	2 Kings 23:31-35; 2 Chronicles 36:1-4
Jehoiakim/ Eliakim (Judah)	609 – 597 BC	2 Kings 23:34-24:7; 2 Chronicles 36:4-8
Jehoiachin (Judah)	597 BC	2 Kings 24:8-17
Zedekiah/ Mattaniah (Judah)	597 – 587 BC	2 Kings 24:18-25:30

[1] Joshua 24:31

JUDGES

Sin Cycles

Then the LORD raised up judges, who saved them out of the hand of those who plundered them. Yet they did not listen to their judges, for they whored after other gods and bowed down to them. They soon turned aside from the way in which their fathers had walked, who had obeyed the commandments of the LORD, and they did not do so. – Judges 2:16-17

During your first reading

Themes to track
- Character of the judges, especially their strengths, and weaknesses.
- Character of God, particularly His jealousy, love, faithfulness, and mercy.
- The people of Israel.
- The cycles of sin (see diagram below):
  a. Israel does evil in the sight of God (*sin*), incurring His wrath and, as a result:
  b. The nation is taken into slavery (*slavery*), from where:
  c. They repent and cry out to Him (*supplication*), so
  d. God sends a saviour to His people and they are delivered from their enemies (*salvation*), but then:
  e. Israel again does evil in the sight of God (sin), incurring His wrath
  . . .

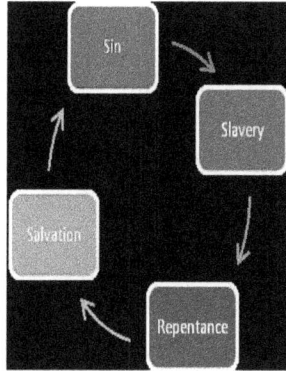

Illustration: Cycles of Sin recorded in Judges

During your second reading

Things to notice in the text
- Mark the start and end of each cycle of sin with a dividing line. A clue to find the start of a new cycle is the phrase "and the Israelites once again did evil in the sight of the Lord".
- Highlight God's responses. For example:
  - God delivered . . ."
  - "God heard . . ."
  - "the Lord replied . . ."
  - "He became . . ."
- Underline the repeated phrase "Israel had no king".
- Draw a line next to columns of the text that you feel reveal an aspect of a judge's character.

Chapter summaries

These are optional as they can be time consuming for the larger books. If you choose to do them, you will receive a much deeper appreciation of the book. By the end of The IBSC, you will have paraphrased the entire Bible! Go through each chapter and try to summarise it in one paragraph, using your own words; force yourself to stay big picture and capture the heart of each chapter.

After your initial readings

Setting of Judges
Author

There is no way of knowing for certain who wrote Judges. Most scholars agree that it would have had multiple authors, given the extended time frame of composition. Daniel, Nathan, Gad, and Samuel have all been suggested and Jewish tradition holds that Samuel was the author.

Recipient

The book of Judges was written for the people of Israel living during the reign of either King Saul, or King David – the first two kings of Israel.

Date and place of writing

Judges was probably completed at the end of the time of the judges, as the time of the kings began, with a broad dating between 1050 BC and 970 BC. A more specific dating suggestion for its completion is during the days of King David's persecution by King Saul. The book was written from an unknown location within Israel.

Reason written

The book gives a warning against idolatry, tribalism, and forgetting the Law; it called Israel back to relationship with God. The book may have been written to support King David's case over that of King Saul (during Saul's reign), by showing how the tribe of Benjamin (Saul's tribe) committed a horrific crime and came close to annihilation becoming a lost tribe – refer to Judges 19-21.

Big picture

Historical background

Time of the judges

The time of the judges is estimated to have spanned the years between 1200 and 1050 BC. However, take note that the book is not believed to have been written in chronological order. It is probable that at any one time there would have been multiple judges ruling throughout Israel, in different regions of the nation. When the book of Judges refers to the land being at rest, it was likely indicative of the part of land the specifically-mentioned judge was ruling over.

The nation of Israel during the time of the judges

Israel was a loose confederation of tribes without a human king. There was anarchy in the land with no organised government structure. Everyone was doing what was right in their own eyes. The people had moved away from the Levitical system of worship and sacrifice commanded by the Law. God's answer to the messes that His people got themselves into was to send His Spirit upon an individual, enabling that person to save the nation.

The judges

God is the ultimate Judge! Refer to Judges 11:27.

The judges of Israel led by charisma (by the Holy Spirit), not their own talents. They were used by God to rally His people to defeat the enemy. The judges were from diverse backgrounds and life situations. They usually had character flaws and weaknesses. Often the person chosen was a surprising choice, considering their culture. For example, being left-handed was seen as a curse and yet, in Judges 3:25, we learn that Ehud was a left-handed man.

Character portrayal – husband of an adulterous wife

"Contend! Contend with your mother, for she is not my wife, nor am I her husband. Let her therefore put away her fornications out of her sight, and her adulteries from between her breasts, lest I strip her naked and set her out as in the day that she was born; and lest I make her as the wilderness, and set her like a dry land, and slay her with thirst. And I will not have mercy on her sons, for they are the sons of adulteries. For their mother has prostituted herself." [1]

"And she shall follow after her lovers, but she shall not overtake them. She shall seek them, but shall not find them. Then she shall say, I will go and return to my first husband, for then it was better with me than now." [2]

"And now I will uncover her shamefulness in the sight of her lovers, and none shall deliver her out of my hand. I will also cause all her joy to cease, her feast days, her new moons, and her sabbaths, and all her appointed feasts." [3]

Would you extend grace to such a nation? Let's see how God ends the story:

"Therefore, behold, I will lure her and bring her into the wilderness, and speak comfortably to her. And I will give her vineyards to her from there, and the valley of Achor for a door of hope. And she shall sing there, as in the days of her youth, and as in the day when she came up out of the land of Egypt. And it shall be at that day, says Jehovah, you shall call Me, My Husband, and shall no more call Me, My Baal." [4]

"And I will betroth you to Me forever. Yea, I will betroth you to Me in righteousness, and in judgement, and in loving-kindness, and in mercies. I will even betroth you to Me in faithfulness. And you shall know Jehovah." [5]

During the period of the judges, just as in the time of Hosea, the people of God committed adultery against Him by turning to the surrounding nations and their ways, and yet when they repented, God showed them mercy.

Book overview

Throughout the book of Judges, God is proven to be faithful to His covenant and people, despite the unfaithfulness of Israel towards Him. Even some of the judges, who God raised up to deliver the people, turned from Him, sinning in some way. The Israelites were no longer living under the fear of the Lord. They did not remove all the people from the land of Canaan as commanded and the remnant of these people led the Israelites astray. The people were constantly caught up in the sin of idolatry, and had forgotten the Law of God.

In contrast, God did not forget His promises. The covenant He made with them did not just contain blessings. There were conditions in the contract, which included curses for disobedience. He was faithful in all of the conditions, including His promise to save them if they strayed, found themselves under His judgement, and then repented. When Israel abided by His Law, He protected them, fought for them, and blessed them in the land. When they turned from Him to idols, He handed them over into the hands of their enemies. And when they cried out in repentance, He had compassion. God remains faithful, despite man's disobedience.

His faithfulness goes further than that stipulated by the covenant. His love towards Israel is steadfast. Even when they cried out in anguish of circumstance, but not in true repentance, He responded by sending judges to save them. His mercy and compassion fuelled Him to help His people. God would not forget them or leave them on their own; He heard and responded to their groaning and pleas. God will never break His covenant with His people.

Interpreting the book of Judges
<u>Interpretation questions</u>

1. Note the change of focus from chapters 1-16 to chapters 17-21. The book's focus shifts from the judges to the state of the Levitical system and tribes.
2. What do you learn about the Holy Spirit through the book of Judges?
   a. What does Samson's life reveal about the Holy Spirit?
   b. What does his life show about what happens when one lightly esteems the Holy Spirit's presence in their life?
3. Write a brief summary on each of the judges, noting both their strengths and failings. What does this reveal about who God anoints to be leaders?
4. Review Leviticus 26.
   a. In light of this passage of Scripture, how do God's actions in Judges reveal His faithfulness?
   b. What else do you learn of God through His actions in this book?
5. When a judge died, the cycle of sin began again.
   a. Why do you think the people of Israel fell into this perpetuating cycle of sin?
   b. What was the cause of their continued unfaithfulness?
   c. What do the sin cycles reveal about the importance of leadership?
   d. What do the sin cycles reveal about the need for the Holy Spirit?
6. List some of the sins that you see the people walking into throughout the book. What do the actions of the people reveal about them and about the nature of man?
7. Remember that the people for whom this book was written were not the same as those in the stories. How would this have affected the people of Israel as they move from the period of the judges to having a physical king to rule over them?
8. There is a repeated phrase: "In those days there was no king in Israel. Everyone did what was right in his own eyes."
   a. What do you believe the author wished to imply by this phrase?
   b. How does it relate to the issue of obedience?
   c. What does it reveal about the importance of knowing Scripture and meditating upon God's Word? How does Scripture equip one in His ways? You may wish to refer to 2 Timothy 3:16-17 and 4:6-10 as New Testament references.
9. Some historians believe that Judges was written to plead King David's cause above that of King Saul. In light of this, consider how the book paints the tribe of Judah (to which David belonged), and the tribe of Benjamin (Saul's tribe).

<u>Creative interpretation</u>

1. Write a summary on how God is the true Hero of Judges.

2. Sketch a symbol, design or picture for each of the judges, to depict what you see as their main character attribute/s, and key event/s of their life. For example, for Samson you might chose to represent him by an illustration of long hair, strength, and a nagging woman.

Application inspiration

- Write out five lessons that you can learn from the book of Judges. For example, one might be that God can work through very frail, rough, and fallen people.

- Is there an aspect of God's character that you saw in this book with which you are struggling? Take it to God in prayer. It is okay to struggle with these things, but He wants you to bring them to Him.

- Wrestle with the tough questions. You have just been reading in Joshua and Judges about God's people going to war against their neighbours and each other. Should Christians go to war today and, if so, how should Christian soldiers act in war? Do not approach this question with pre-conceived ideas, but take it to God. Likewise, consider what it looks like to respond in love when other Christians have a different point of view to yours.

- Read Francine Rivers' book "Redeeming Love". It is based on the prophet Hosea who was told to marry a prostitute as a representation of God's heart towards His people. This book may help you gain perspective about how God felt about His people through the time of the judges.

- What area of sin has a hold on your life? Do you feel that you continually fall in one particular area; for example: pride, judgement, lust or deceit? Find scriptures that will help you when you are struggling. Pray for God to help you stop the cycle. Ask for a friend to pray for you in this area too.

[1] Hosea 2:2-4 (The Message)
[2] Hosea 2:7 (The Message)
[3] Hosea 2:10-11 (The Message)
[4] Hosea 2:14-16 (The Message)
[5] Hosea 2:19-20 (The Message)

RUTH

Faith amongst Faithlessness

Then the women said to Naomi, "Blessed be the LORD, who has not left you this day without a redeemer, and may his name be renowned in Israel! He shall be to you a restorer of life and a nourisher of your old age, for your daughter-in-law who loves you, who is more to you than seven sons, has given birth to him." – Ruth 4:14-15

During your first reading

Themes to track
- Obedience to the covenant
- Loyalty
- God's faithfulness

During your second reading

Things to notice in the text
- Characters: Boaz, Ruth, and Naomi.

Chapter summaries

These are optional as they can be time consuming for the larger books. If you choose to do them, you will receive a much deeper appreciation of the book. By the end of The IBSC, you will have paraphrased the entire Bible! Go through each chapter and try to summarise it in one paragraph, using your own words; force yourself to stay big picture and capture the heart of each chapter.

After your initial readings

Setting of Ruth

Author

The author of Ruth remains unknown. Some propose that the prophet, Samuel, wrote the book of Ruth. However, it is also proposed that the book was written to support King David's right to the throne. As Samuel died before the time of David's kingship, his authorship does not fit with this hypothesis, unless he was inspired by the Holy Spirit, ahead of need.

Recipient

The greatest level of support exists for the book being written to the Israelites during the time David reigned from Hebron, before he became crowned king over all of Israel.

Date and place of writing

Most scholars believe that the book was written during the reign of King David, due to the inclusion of his lineage, which would date the book between 1010 and 970 BC. The book of Ruth was probably written from within Judah, if it was written in support of David's rulership.

Reason written

Ruth was written to preserve the royal line and to show that King David had righteous ancestors. In addition, it would have motivated the Israelites to keep the covenant and to live a holy life. The author was bringing the people back to covenant faithfulness.

Big picture
Historical background

The story of Ruth and Naomi took place during the time of the judges. This was a dark time in Israel's history with the nation continually lapsing into the sin of idolatry. In the book of Ruth, Bethlehem was held forth as a shining example of faithfulness amidst national unfaithfulness.

The Moabites were despised neighbours of the Israelites and yet in this story, a daughter of the Moabites was given as an example of covenant loyalty. Ruth became the great-grandmother of David, and a member of Christ's lineage. It is likely that this book was also used to show that, whilst he came from humble beginnings, David was God's anointed king.

The kinsmen redeemer

What does it mean in Ruth 3:9, where it says: *"Spread your wings over your servant, for you are a redeemer"*? Culturally, this was an invitation, or proposition, for marriage. It seems that Ruth was asking for the protection of Boaz's house, name, and income.

Refer to the *historical background* given for Judges to gain an understanding of the atmosphere throughout Israel at this time.

Refer to 2 Samuel 1-5 for background surrounding David's rise to kingship.

Character portrayal – news gets around

Who was this Moabite? Boaz wondered. Everywhere he went, he heard the story. The young Moabite woman was constantly appearing as the topic of conversation.

What would cause her to give up everything and follow a woman without prospects, who could not give her hope for a second marriage? Normally the Moabites were hated or at least considered in distrust and dislike. Israel did not have a good history with their neighbours. So how had she won the regard of his fellow tribesmen?

Boaz was curious to meet the young woman. He was sure that she was strong, confident, fiercely loyal, and loving. That her fame had spread far and wide gave testimony to her character and the love she had for her mother-in-law. For whatever reason, he knew a longing to meet this woman, and perhaps even to protect and care for her. He prayed that his loving and mighty God would give her a future of hope and provision as reward for her love and faithfulness.

Book overview

Ruth is a story of faithful individuals during a time of widespread national disobedience to the covenant. The story began with a famine, but ended with provision. It began with death, but ended with the celebration of life. It started with mourning and tragedy, but finished with rejoicing, triumph, and victory. It showed that God is a faithful provider and blesses those who trust in Him. God brings redemption for His people and is faithful towards those who kept His covenant.

Ruth also foreshadowed Gentile inclusion amongst the people of God. Israel had a weakness, viewing themselves as superior to their neighbours. They forgot that they were called by God to be a blessing to all nations. They were not called because they were a holier nation, but to be an example and attract others to God; they were to call others into the Kingdom of God. The book of Ruth shows that Gentiles could enter into God's chosen people.

Today, the story acts as a reminder that God is Provider, Protector, Restorer, and Redeemer.

Help with difficult passages
Uncovering of the feet; Ruth 3:7

The Hebrew word for feet can mean feet, or place of the feet. The phrase "place of the feet" was also used as a euphemism for one's private parts (see also Deuteronomy 28:57).

What can one infer from this passage?

Several options include:

1. Ruth literally uncovered Boaz and lay down;
2. Ruth literally uncovered Boaz to request he play the role of kinsmen redeemer;
3. Ruth uncovered Boaz from waist down, inviting him to become the Levirate husband;
4. Ruth uncovered his feet, allowing the cool breeze to wake him up from drunkenness, and thus enable her to talk to him.

During the harvest, workers would sleep at the threshing floor to protect the crop. Prostitutes would find them there. By being careful that she was not seen, Boaz was protecting her from rape and her reputation from harm.

Consider what you know of Ruth and Boaz when interpreting these verses. Boaz was a man of God who knew the Law. Boaz called Ruth a righteous woman. There was one kinsman of closer relation to Ruth's late husband than Boaz, who Boaz promised to talk to before accepting Ruth's request. Given these facts, which of the above-listed options do you believe was most likely?

Interpreting the book of Ruth
<u>Interpretation questions</u>
1. The choice to stay or go:
    a. What comparison was drawn between Orpah and Ruth?
    b. Why was it significant that Ruth was given a choice between going home and staying with Naomi?
    c. Why was this included by the author?
    d. How might Ruth have felt as she chose to follow Naomi?
    e. What effect do you think her choice would have had on her mother-in-law?
2. At the beginning of chapter 2, Boaz was reaping his harvest in the midst of a drought and he allowed Ruth to take the left over sheafs.
    a. Consider Deuteronomy 24:19 and 28:9-11. Read Psalm 68:5.
    b. What do Boaz's actions reveal about his character?
    c. What do these laws reveal about God?
3. During chapter 3, consider:
    a. How might Ruth have felt going to Boaz in the evening?
    b. What risk was she taking?
    c. What do you believe happened when she "uncovered his feet and lay down"?
    d. Why does Boaz give Ruth barley to take back to her mother-in-law?
4. Who is a kinsman redeemer and what is their role? Laws you may wish to revise include the land rights in Leviticus 25, and the law of delivered marriage in Deuteronomy 25:5-10.
5. Look at the events which occurred as Boaz met the kinsman redeemer.
    a. Why did Boaz chose to meet the kinsman redeemer before witnesses (the townsmen)?
    b. What was the significance of the events that unfolded?
    c. Notice that it was the next day that Boaz went before the men. What does this reveal about Boaz's character?
    d. Why do you think that the other kinsman redeemer chose not to take his right of redemption? Is this of significance?
6. Consider the passage Ruth 4:13-17.
    a. What was revealed about God, Naomi, and Ruth?
    b. How had Naomi's heart changed with the birth of Obed?
7. In Matthew 1:15, Ruth was listed in the lineage of Christ. What was the significance of having a woman and a foreigner in His line?
8. What do you learn about loyalty from the story of Ruth?
9. How would the story of a faithful Moabite have affected the people of

Israel as they listened to it, especially knowing that it was during a time of their own unfaithfulness?

<u>Creative interpretation</u>
1. Complete a character study on each of the main characters: Naomi, Ruth, and Boaz. As you go through the book, list the attributes you see each display, and then write a brief overall summary.
   For example: For Ruth, you may think that she showed great loyalty. Ruth showed loyalty to Naomi by sacrificing everything: culture, family, home, and gods. News of Ruth's loyalty was told to Boaz and it led her to the blessing of marriage. It also made the townsmen acceptant of her marriage into their nation because they knew she was a woman of worth, loyal to the Lord and His Law.
2. Look at how the characters of Ruth compare to the judges as recorded in the book of Judges.
   a. Are there similarities?
   b. What were their differences?
   c. What does this show about how God is able to work with individuals?

Application inspiration

- How loyal are you to God? Are you willing to give up everything and anything for God? Will you go faithfully wherever He sends you?
- One needs to know the Law in order to be faithful to it.
   o How well do you know Scripture?
   o Do you make time to study it?
   o Do you look at Scripture alone and with others?
   o Are there people with whom you discuss the Bible?
   o How do you seek to apply the Word of God in your life?
   o Do you find it easy to find applications from Scripture for your life?
- Faithfulness in action is important. In chapter 2, Boaz was seen to have heard of Ruth's actions and judged her according to them. Think on Mark 9:50. How are you living as salt? Are there environments in which you tend to lose your saltiness?

1 & 2 SAMUEL

Israel rejects God as their King

But the thing displeased Samuel when they said, "Give us a king to judge us." And Samuel prayed to the LORD. And the LORD said to Samuel, "Obey the voice of the people in all that they say to you, for they have not rejected you, but they have rejected me from being king over them. – 1 Samuel 8:6-7

When studying these books, keep in mind that they were originally one book, which has been divided in order to make it easier to read.

During your first reading

Themes to track
- Character of God
- People's character
- Keeping the covenant
- Leadership
- Family

During your second reading

Things to notice in the text
- Fathers and sons
- Submission, humility, and non-retaliation
- Friendships, relationships, and discipleship
- Abuse of power
- Characters who think they are above the covenant.

Chapter summaries
These are optional as they can be time consuming for the larger books. If you

choose to do them, you will receive a much deeper appreciation of the book. By the end of The IBSC, you will have paraphrased the entire Bible! Go through each chapter and try to summarise it in one paragraph, using your own words; force yourself to stay big picture and capture the heart of each chapter.

After your initial readings

Setting of 1 & 2 Samuel
Author

The book is a compilation of writings, primarily attributed to Samuel, Nathan, and Gad. Editors added further details as the writings were assimilated into a book. Some also credit Abithar, the priest, as a contributing author.

Recipient

The books of 1 & 2 Samuel were written to the people of Israel during the period of the kings.

Date and place of writing

The compilation of the books of 1 & 2 Samuel would have been completed during the era of the kings, which spanned from 1050 BC to 586 BC. Given the primary authors, the writings would have been finished after 965 BC, placing it after the end of David's reign in 970 BC. No clearer date range can be determined. As 1 & 2 Samuel were compiled gradually, they would have been written at various places throughout the land of Israel.

Reason written

Samuel records the historic transition from the time of judges to that of the kings. The people were reminded that, whilst the era of the judges did not end well, the time of the kings was their choice, and one that they were stuck with. 1 & 2 Samuel called them to stop complaining about their king and live according to the covenant in righteousness.

Big picture
Historical background

Refer to the *historical background* given for Genesis for information about the Suzerain-Vassal relationship God established with His people. God was to be their King and they were to have no god except for Him.

The nations surrounding Israel were ruled by kings. Observing their neighbours, the people of God determined that they would be better off with a physical king than with God, the King of kings. The Israelites rejected God as their King, demanding they be given an earthly king. The book of Samuel records the transition of rulership from judges to kings. This brought the nation from a time of loose tribal organisation to an era of structured national government.

The Ark of God had been going with the people wherever they went, but eventually, in 2 Samuel, it came to rest in the City of David. The City of David became the nation's capital.

Notes about the battle with Goliath

A battle of champions was a normal thing at this time and in their culture, but the use of a slinger in such a battle was not common, being a tool of shepherds.

A slinger was a powerful weapon! Slingers were used to send a stone beyond a flock to bring straying sheep back into the herd, much like sheep dogs are used to herd sheep today. The stone could attain a distance of four hundred meters, and reach a speed of one hundred miles per hour. It was also highly accurate, with a skilled shepherd able to shoot a stone through a small ring. Different to a sling shot, the slinger was swung around to launch the stone, rather than pulled back and released.

The javelin was the only long range weapon Goliath had, indicating that he expected close range combat. Goliath did not pull out his sword in preparation as he advanced upon David. He did not consider what instrument David may have brought against him. Such actions suggest that he did not take David's challenge seriously.

The original readers

Remember that those in these stories are different people to those who first read the book of Samuel. As seen above, the time of writing was after the reign of both Saul and David. The original readers were living in a time when the kings frequently led the entire nation into sin and idolatry against God. The book of Samuel would have reminded them that it was their choice to have a king appointed over them.

<u>Character portrayal – Samuel's prayer when the people asked for a king</u>

Then all the elders of Israel gathered together and came to Samuel at Ramah and said to him, "Behold, you are old and your sons do not walk in your ways. Now appoint for us a king to judge us like all the nations." But the thing displeased Samuel when they said, "Give us a king to judge us." And Samuel prayed to the LORD:

"Am I alone in my devotion to you? Does nobody read the Law any more, or walk in your commands? My sons have turned to the ways of wickedness; they do not delight in your ways or follow your commandments. Have I not been faithful all of my days and have I not sought to hear your voice? How is it that I am to be rewarded by faithless sons and a disobedient nation?

"You have heard their cry for a king; they are not content with you ruling over them. This thing that they have asked for is not good. It shall only lead to further waywardness from the people. They seek nothing more than to be like the nations surrounding them. And yet, God, I fear their response if I am to deny them. Will they murder me? I do not put it beyond them. What is your will, Lord God?

And the LORD said to Samuel, "Obey the voice of the people in all that they say to you, for they have not rejected you, but they have rejected me from being king over them. According to all the deeds that they have done, from the day I brought them up out of Egypt even to this day, forsaking me and serving other gods, so they are also doing to you. Now then, obey their voice; only you shall solemnly warn them and show them the ways of the king who shall reign over them."[1]

Book overview

God alone is King! He is the One that causes nations and individuals to rise up and He can bring them crashing down. The book of Samuel testified to the fact that the Israelite kings were still subject to the Law of the True King. The covenant was held forth as the guideline to godly living, and the developer of righteous character.

Despite David being a main character and a mighty warrior, the events of his life were not the author's focus. The author was concerned about the character of people and how this character is developed. Character in the Old Testament was seen as developed through your obedience to the Law. It was about what one does and not what one says. The covenant held one standard for all people and provided a clear guide for godly character.

The author develops the characters of the book through:

- Indirect characterisation through comparison and contrast. For example, the Spirit falls on David as an evil spirit falls on Saul – see 1 Samuel 16:13-14.
- The actions of one character comment on another, such as Jonathan's actions in battle forming a contrast against those of his father, King Saul.

Help with difficult passages

Saul goes to a medium; 1 Samuel 28

Why would Saul cast out all the mediums from the land and then go out and consult one?

Saul went to a medium because God was not talking to him. The Spirit of the Lord had left him, but neither did he return to God and seek His wisdom. Saul put the voice of Samuel in the place of God, which is idolatry.

Was it really Samuel?

There are a few options debated amongst scholars:

1. It was demonic. A demon gave a false prophecy that Saul later self-fulfilled;
2. It was the medium using trickery and imitating Samuel. This is unlikely given her response, which was surprise;
3. It really was Samuel. If this is the case, God did extraordinary because when believers pass from this earth they enter into the presence of God.

Consider the woman's response. She was said to be a medium and she went about the process as usual; however, she was not expecting Samuel to actually show up! This reveals that something else was happening.

So did God step in and allow Samuel to go to Saul? It is not clear, but what is clear is that the root of Saul's act was *wrong*! Deuteronomy 18:10-11 lists the punishment for mediums as death. 1 Chronicles 10:13-14 reveals that Saul died because he consulted the medium, thus rebelling against God.

Do not wrestle with whether it can happen, *but rather* look at what Scripture clearly says: His people are not supposed to communicate with the dead. TALK TO GOD!

David takes a census; 2 Samuel 24 and 1 Chronicles 21

Is the act of taking a census a sin? No, because God commands it elsewhere in Scripture. In this case, it appeared to be an issue of motive. David was the one pushing for the census so that he would know the population number of Israel. What could the sin be that was involved? What is the outcome of knowing the size of your empire? Perhaps pride, or to analyse the military strength of the nation before battle, thus no longer trusting God to succeed despite numbers.

David was given three options to choose from for punishment; two would have greatly affected the people, and the other would have affected David. It is interesting to note that whilst David generally takes personal responsibility for his wrongs, in this case he allowed judgement to fall on the nation. Notice also that 2 Samuel 24:1 shows God to be angry at the whole nation; it seems that God was intending to bring judgement against the whole nation for their sins.

Another interesting observation to note is that Samuel says that God incited David whereas Chronicles says it was Satan. Why the radical difference? Consider the context of the story. What aspect of the event is recorded in the different books? Think of what motives the author of Samuel would have to say that God incited David and why the author of Chronicles would say that Satan incited him.

Interpreting the books of 1 & 2 Samuel
Interpretation questions
1. Look at the following aspects for each of the key characters in Samuel:
    a. What are their leadership qualities?
    b. Who contrasts with them in action, motive or personality?
    c. Are they good parents; why or why not?
    d. Do they keep the covenant and what does this imply about godly character?
    e. Refer to *Creative interpretation* for a deeper study on the main characters in this book.
2. How does the book of Samuel equate success to the keeping God's laws?
3. Consider the people's request for a king.
    a. Why did the people ask for a king?
    b. Why was God not enough for the people?
    c. What was God's view of the request?
    d. How did Samuel respond to it?
    e. What was wrong with them wanting a king?
4. Review the conditions for the king listed in Deuteronomy 17:14-20.
5. Read the following verses, which dictated the role of the kings and predicted what life would be like underneath one: 1 Samuel 8:11-18; 12:13-15; 12:22-25; 16:7.
6. What change did the Holy Spirit bring? See: 1 Samuel 10:6, 9-10; 11:6-11; 16:13-14; 23:1-7; 2 Samuel 23:1-6.
7. Read the following passages and comment on the importance of the Ark. Refer to: 1 Samuel 4:10-11, 22; 5:1-7:1; 2 Samuel 6:1-7, 9-13.
8. The psalms reveal that King David delighted in the Law of the Lord and

meditated on it day and night.

    a. Knowing the above, read 2 Samuel 11:3-4 and then consider his actions in light of Exodus 20:14 and Leviticus 20:10.

    b. Skip to 2 Samuel 11:15 and consider his private command in connection with Exodus 20:13 and Numbers 35:30.

    c. Reflect on David's response to the events in 2 Samuel 13:1-22 taking a look back on God's Law in Deuteronomy 22:28-29.

    d. Reflect on King David's knowledge of the grace of God. He did not live a perfect life and the book of Samuel clearly published his flaws. Nevertheless, in 2 Samuel 22 he repeatedly declared himself to be righteous, clean, and blameless in God's sight.

9. What leadership principles can you take from Samuel? Here are some passages to get you started: 1 Samuel 24:6; 26:9-11, 23; 30:23-26; 2 Samuel 16:11-12; 18:3-4.

10. What can be learnt about how character is built from the book of Samuel? Some starting passages include: 1 Samuel 15:22-23; 16:11; 22; 23:14; 25; 2 Samuel 12:1-14; 22:1.

11. Linking the Old Testament to the New Testament:

    a. Read 1 Samuel 21:4-6 and Matthew 12:2-4; Mark 2:24-26; Luke 6:1-5.

    b. How did Jesus interpret the passage in 1 Samuel?

    c. How did He use it in His teaching?

    d. How might the Pharisees have responded to Him quoting this passage to them?

12. God's covenant with David was recorded in 2 Samuel 7. Notice God's use of the personal pronoun "I".

    a. What did God promise to do?

    b. What did David have to do, if anything?

    c. Read Psalm 89, a Messianic Psalm (a psalm predicting the coming of Christ). Note the "who" in verse 20, the unconditional promises in verses 28-29 and 34-37, and the conditional statement in verses 30-33.

    d. The promise of the eternal kingdom is ultimately fulfilled in Christ. Read Matthew 1:1.

Creative interpretation

1. Character summaries:

The book of Samuel focuses on the character of individuals and some of the main characters have been listed below. The subjects and passages listed underneath each character give guiding passages and attributes that you may wish to focus on, but are in no way exhaustive. Write a summary on each of the following characters:

- God
  - 1 Samuel 2:6-9; 12:22; 14:15; 15:10-11; 15:22-23; 16:7; 2 Samuel 5:9-10; 7:4-16; 7:22-26; 21:1, 14.

- Samuel
  - Early years, and dedication to God as a Nazarite (1 Samuel 1:11, 3:19).
  - Faithfulness to God, and his relationship with God (1 Samuel 3:1-4:1a; 15:10-11; 16:1-4a; 7:15).
  - Interactions with Saul (1 Samuel 10:1; 13:7b-14; 15:13-35).
  - Interactions with the people (1 Samuel 7:3-11; 7:15-17; 8; 12).
- Saul
  - His family (1 Samuel 18:17-30; 19:1-2; 19:11-13, 17; 20:30-31).
  - Relationship with God (1 Samuel 10:10-11; 11:5-13; 15:23).
  - As a warrior and his attitude in battle (1 Samuel 11:6-11; 13:7b-14).
  - Consider Saul's strengths and flaws as a man, a king, and a father.
  - Contemplate on how Saul could have ended his life well.
- Jonathan
  - Loyalty in friendship and faithfulness to his promises (1 Samuel 18:1-4; 19:1-7; 20; 23:15-18; 2 Samuel 1:26).
  - Recognising David as the chosen king (1 Samuel 18:3-4; 23:15-18).
  - Relationship with God (1 Samuel 14:8-10).
- David
  - Distinguished warrior (1 Samuel 17:32-37, 45-47, 50; 23:1-5; 30:1-22; 2 Samuel 5:20-25; 8; 10:17-19; 21:15-17).
  - The lessons he learned as a fugitive (1 Samuel 22:1-2; 23:10-14).
  - His response to dark times; for example, when facing the imminent death of his young son (2 Samuel 12:15-23; 13:21-22).
  - His response to the death of his enemies (2 Samuel 1:11-27; 2:4-8; 3:26-37; 4:8-12; 18:5, 33).
  - Faithfulness/ unfaithfulness (2 Samuel 9; 10:1-2; 16:1-4, 19:24-30; 19:21-23; 21:7).
  - Concern for worship and his relationship with God (1 Samuel 17:26, 22:5; 30:23-25; 2 Samuel 1:15-16; 5:19; 6:5-23; 7; 11:27-12:13; 21:1-5-6, 8-9; 22-23:7; 24:1-17 24:18-24).
  - Do not forget that David was a song writer (Psalms as a fugitive: 59, 56, 142, 52, 54, and 57. Psalm 3 relates to his son, Absalom)!
  - How did David become a person who listened to God, did not retaliate, and trusted in the Lord (1 Samuel 23:10-14; 24; 26:9-12)?
  - David and women (1 Samuel 25:32-35, 39-44; 2 Samuel 1:26; 5:13; 11:1-17, 26-27; 15:16).
  - David and his family (1 Samuel 27:3; 30:5, 18; 2 Samuel 5:13; 12:15-25; 13; 14:21-24; 14:25-27).
- Joab
  - Faithfulness to David (2 Samuel 2:13; 11:14-25; 12:27-28; 14:1-3; 18:11-17; 24:3-9).
  - As an advisor (2 Samuel 3:23-27; 19:1-8; 20:14-25; 24:3).

- Absalom
  - 2 Samuel 14-18.
- David's mighty men
  - What was the character of David's men (1 Samuel 22:1-2; 2 Samuel 21:15-22; 23:8-39)?

2. Character contrasts:

Look at the following characters and comment on how they contrast with one another:

- Eli's sons and Samuel (1 Samuel 2).
- Samuel and the people, when they asked for a king (1 Samuel 8, 12).
- David and Goliath (1 Samuel 17:37-51).
- David and Saul (1 Samuel 18:7-9; 18:12-16; 18:20-27; 22:5, 17-23, 28:4-11; 24; 26:9-12, 21-25).
- Jonathan and Saul (1 Samuel: 19:1-7; 20:30-34).
- Abigail and Nabal (1 Samuel 25).
- Uriah and David. Note that Uriah was a Hittite and yet this non-Jew was shown to be the one doing the godly thing, when the king of Israel was not (2 Samuel 11:1-21; 23:39).
- Absalom and Jonathan (1 Samuel 18:4, 23:17; 2 Samuel 15:1-6, 10, 13-14).
- Saul and Abner being related compared with David and Joab being related (2 Samuel 2:8-32; 3:6-21; 24-27).

Application inspiration

- Play worship music and dance before the Lord with abandon, giving Him praise.
- Is your life a contrast? Do people see you as different in a good way? Do they see that you do not do certain socially-accepted things due to your faith and ask why? The lives of God's people should call others to ask questions, standing in contrast to the unbelieving world.
- Does you life proclaim who you are and what you believe? Do you want to be like the world?
- In what area do you stand out? Do you read Scripture on the bus to work? Do you make an effort at work parties to talk with those who are uncomfortable? Are you the first to introduce yourself to, and befriend, new families moving into your street?
- In what areas are you tempted to fall into the patterns of the world when you know God would have you live otherwise? Do you feel compelled to buy the latest fashion accessories, or electronic goods, to "keep up with the Joneses"? Do you swear when work pressures get to you? Do you struggle with managing anger in a godly way when your child accidentally breaks a good vase?
- The world is not your model, and its ways should not be your passion. Believers are to model righteousness to the world.

[1] 1 Samuel 8:4-9

1 & 2 KINGS

The Reason for the Exile

Still the LORD did not turn from the burning of his great wrath, by which his anger was kindled against Judah, because of all the provocations with which Manasseh had provoked him. And the LORD said, "I will remove Judah also out of my sight, as I have removed Israel, and I will cast off this city that I have chosen, Jerusalem, and the house of which I said, My name shall be there." – 2 Kings 23:26-27

Take time in the study of these books. Remember that 1 & 2 Kings were originally one book and should be studied as such. Set aside time for these books because they lay the foundations for the books of the prophets. It will make the study of the prophets an easier task if you have laid good ground work in the books of 1 & 2 Kings, and also in the books of 1 & 2 Chronicles.

As the assignment for 1 & 2 Chronicles builds on the one for 1 & 2 Kings, it would be beneficial to study them together. Why are these books so similar and yet different? Kings is written from the perspective of the *prophets*, whilst Chronicles gives the perspective of the *priests*.

During your first reading

Themes to track
- Obedience/ disobedience to the covenant
- Character of God
- Character of the prophets
- Leadership principles

During your second reading

Things to notice in the text
- God's character; look at His responses, commands, and actions.
- Whether a king is good or evil. Look for the phrase "did right in the eyes of

the Lord", compared with "did evil in the eyes of the Lord".
- Prophets: their words, actions, and reactions.

Chapter summaries

These are optional as they can be time consuming for the larger books. If you choose to do them, you will receive a much deeper appreciation of the book. By the end of The IBSC, you will have paraphrased the entire Bible! Go through each chapter and try to summarise it in one paragraph, using your own words; force yourself to stay big picture and capture the heart of each chapter.

After your initial readings

Setting of 1 & 2 Kings
Author

The specific author remains unknown, but the work is widely credited to one or more of the prophets.

Recipient

Kings was written to the exiles in Babylon.

Date and place of writing

It was completed during exile in Babylon, placing the date of completion between 586 and 550 BC.

Reason written

The original readers were in exile believing they had been unjustly punished. The prophets wanted to show the people that they were there because of their disobedience to God, having broken the covenant. Kings called them to nationally repent of their sins before God so that He might restore His nation.

Big picture
Historical background

Kings recounts the history of the people of God from 970 to 586 BC. Take note of the change to whom the name "Israel" refers. When the nation divides, Israel no longer defined the nation as a whole, but rather the northern kingdom. Judah became the name of the southern kingdom. The book ends with both the northern and southern kingdoms of Israel having been conquered, and the people sent into exile. The Northern Kingdom was the first to be sent into exile in 722 BC, with the southern kingdom following in 586 BC.

The time of kings falls during the "age of empires"

At the time of Israel's fall, the Assyrians were the dominant world power. The Assyrian Empire was the world power between 900 and 612 BC (just after the time of King Solomon). Assyrians were known for cruelty and the horrors they inflicted on prisoners of war. There were jobs in the Assyrian Empire specifically devoted to thinking up new punishments and ways to induce pain. Examples of the torture they inflicted on captives included:

- Flaying prisoners of war (removing the living victim's skin);
- Impaling victims on stakes through the anus and leaving them to die in excruciating pain over the course of days;
- Putting hooks through the noses of captives and marching them naked across the desert;
- Burying people alive with only their heads above ground, fixing their heads with a nail through the mouth.

By the time of Judah's fall, Babylon had risen to become the prevalent power of the world. The Babylonian Empire was the world power between 612 and 539 BC.

The Persian Empire was the world power between 539 and 330 BC. It was the ruling power when the prophet, Daniel, was alive. It was the Persians who allowed the Judean exiles to return to their land, seventy years after the fall of Jerusalem.

Character portrayal – original readers in exile

"Why did God send us here? Why did He allow Judah to fall? Why are we being punished? It was our fathers who sinned, not us!" Tobias was in a foul mood.

"And now we are here and He has no authority in Babylon. Their gods have the power here," Cephas replied, as one accepting his fate. "The God of our ancestors cannot save us now."

"It isn't fair! Because our fathers disobeyed, we get cursed. We have done nothing wrong and yet our God abandoned us so that the Babylonian gods could punish us as slaves."

"It could have been worse. We could have fallen to the Assyrians as Israel, our brothers, did."

"Small comfort," was the bitter retort.

Book overview

God's mercy is beyond all comprehension. Whilst Kings ends badly for the people of Israel and Judah, one must remember that there were forty-two kings and one queen who ruled before they were taken into exile, amongst whom only a few were faithful. Most of the rulers led God's people astray. Even the kings who "did right in the eyes of the Lord" did not walk in full obedience to His ways. The number of kings before exile shows God's longsuffering.

Neither were the people innocent before God. They did not turn from their ways despite the prophets calling them back to the covenant. God longed for His people to return to Him. He tried over and over again to win them back, but eventually He had to send them into exile in faithfulness to the covenant conditions.

God is faithful and therefore He had to keep the conditions of the covenant, which stipulated blessings for obedience and curses for disobedience – see Deuteronomy 28. The prophets who composed Kings were determined to show the people that they went into exile because they were unfaithful. The exiles could not lay the blame at anyone's door, but their own.

The prophets who penned this book were angry! Historical records do not often reveal the embarrassing or shameful details of a nation's history, and yet the prophets recorded it all. They wanted to show that God does not care about accomplishments, but obedience. The prophets were calling the people to take responsibility for their sins, acknowledge them before God, and repent. Kings was written as a call for the exiles to seek the grace of God.

Interpreting the books of 1 & 2 Kings
Interpretation questions

1. Look back on your character study of David from 1 & 2 Samuel.
   a. What other aspects of his character do you see in 1 Kings 1:1-2:13?
   b. What do you learn of the relationships within his family?
2. David was held up as the standard for the good kings, the kings faithful to God.
   a. Did David deserve the amount of favour God gave him; why or why not?
   b. Was this favour due to understanding on David's part? Was it because of the covenant God had with him? Was it because of his repentant heart? Read 1 Kings 11:38, 2 Kings 8:19, and Romans 4:5-8.
3. How did Solomon start and end his reign as king?
   a. What caused the contrast?
   b. What was his greatest strength and what was his greatest weakness?
   c. Why was wisdom not enough for him?
   d. What does this show you about obedience to God?
4. The evil kings were all compared to Jeroboam.
   a. What made his sins so vile in God's eyes?
   b. Why was he held up as worse than Ahab, who was declared in 1 Kings 16:30 to have done more evil than all who went before him? Was it because he set up the idols or perhaps the change he made to the priestly order? Was it simply because he was first or perhaps because he caused the kingdom to divide?
5. What stirs up God's anger, as shown through Kings?
6. Re-read the information on the Assyrian Empire and the punishment they inflicted on captives, given in *historical background* above. Consider God's judgement upon His people, knowing that He sent Assyria to defeat Israel.
7. Why did God keep sending His prophets to the Northern Kingdom when king after king did not turn from the evil of their fathers before them?
8. Consider the fact that God pursued both Ahab and Jezebel, who were more evil than any who had come before them. God knew they would not repent and yet He continued to pursue them. What does this show about God?

9. One of the sins frequently listed against the evil kings is that they "caused Israel to sin". For example, 1Kings 14:16; 15:26; 16:12-13; 2 Kings 13:2. Read Luke 17:1-2. What implications does this have for those in leadership?

10. The prophets were keepers of the covenant. Contemplate how the people were to keep the covenant when the book of Law was lost (2 Kings 22:8).

11. The prophets were not concerned about military might, but whether the king and the people kept the covenant. They called the people back to God and to repentance. What does this show about the measures God took to offer mercy and grace to His people?

12. Consider the emotions of the prophets:
    a. How do you believe the prophets would have felt looking back on the sins of their nation?
    b. Can you feel their anger as you read through Kings?
    c. Read 1 Kings 19:4 and think about the thankless job that these prophets had been given. Today they are held up in places of honour in the church, but think about what their lives would have been like as they showed a rebellious people their sins against God.

13. Refer back to the covenant promises, and the associated blessings and curses, in Deuteronomy 28:1-7 and 18:58-68.
    a. How do these passages provide evidence against the people? Use these passages to explain why they were ultimately sent into exile.
    b. In light of this, why did it take God so long to send His people into exile?

14. The nation of Israel was at the height of its power in Solomon's day. In today's monetary values, the money coming into Israel during Solomon's reign from other nations alone tallied in the (USD) billions. Yet at the end of his the nation was crumbling because of his unfaithfulness. Consider:
    a. What would have happened if Solomon had listened to God and walked in obedience?
    b. Read 1 Kings 4:20-21.
    c. Would Israel have become the first world empire?

15. Recall that God's intention for His people was for them to be an example to the surrounding nations, drawing others into His people.
    a. What relationship did Israel and Judah have with the surrounding nations, as revealed throughout Kings?
    b. Consider what you saw in Judges of their relationship with the surrounding nations.
    c. How did the people of God, who were meant to bring light to the nations, end up walking in the darkness of idolatry?

16. What does Kings teach about:
    a. The character of God?
    b. Obedience and disobedience?
    c. Godly leadership?

    d. The importance of godly parenting?

Creative interpretation

    1. See *Special study – Kings and Chronicles*

When completing the special study, take note that sometimes the kings co-reigned with their sons for a number of years. Refer to Introduction to the rulership of Israel for the dates of the kings' reigns.

Making the time to compile this information will provide you with a very handy resource which you will refer to regularly when studying the books of the prophets.

Application inspiration

Obedience

- What are some of the worst excuses you have given (in general, or to God)?
- Ask God for wisdom, but also the desire to obey Him and the discipline to walk faithfully in His ways.
- How often do you blame someone or something else for putting off what God has asked you to do? What about the problems and struggles you faced this past week: where did you lay the blame? Do you have a complaining spirit or is it a joy to do God's will?
- Do you try to impress God by accomplishments or obedience?

Personal walk with God

- In addition to what you saw of man's character in Kings, consider Romans 1 and 2. Man needs a Saviour! Left alone mankind goes to lust, greed, power, and other acts of unrighteousness. Nothing changes this – not encounters with God, worship times, nothing. Without Jesus, man remains wretched. Turn to God.
- Kings shows how great men can make horrible decisions when they tune God out of their lives, or even just a part of their life. You are not exempt from this. It is not an issue of forgiveness, for God will forgive, but the consequences can last for a lifetime. Pray to God for a humble heart. Cling to accountability and to the Word of God.

Family

- What parenting principles can you gain from Kings?
- How do you currently mix family with ministry? How can you actively put your children before ministry? What boundaries can you set? Maybe you can move the timing of a church commitment to get to your child's basketball game. Or perhaps you need to de-clutter one day of the week to have as a family day.
- You are not bound to the decisions of your forefathers. Be comforted in the knowledge that a parent's dysfunction does not have to be given to the child. Their children are able to choose to turn back to God and make a conscious decision to walk in His ways.

- The next generation needs to have the lessons you have learnt passed on; ministries need to be handed over to the next generation; future planning within the church should be continual. Do not keep the passion to yourself, but pass it on to others! Share what you know – regardless of how little you feel that may be.

1 & 2 CHRONICLES

Temple; from Building to Burning

The LORD, the God of their fathers, sent persistently to them by his messengers, because he had compassion on his people and on his dwelling place. But they kept mocking the messengers of God, despising his words and scoffing at his prophets, until the wrath of the LORD rose against his people, until there was no remedy. – 2 Chronicles 36:15-16

Remember that 1 & 2 Chronicles were originally one book and should be studied as such. It is advisable to study 1 & 2 Chronicles after you have studied the books of Samuel and Kings, as Chronicles builds upon these books. Invest time into your study of these books, as they lay the foundations for the books of the prophets.

Why are the books of Kings and Chronicles so similar and yet different? Why is it necessary to study both books? Kings is written from the perspective of the *prophets*, whilst Chronicles gives the perspective of the *priests*.

During your first reading

Themes to track
- Treatment of the temple
- Obedience (to the Law) and revival
- God's character
- Divided, but still part of God's people

During your second reading

Things to notice in the text
- Choose a colour for each of the themes. When you see this theme in a passage, draw a coloured line corresponding to that theme in the column beside it.

Chapter summaries

These are optional as they can be time consuming for the larger books. If you choose to do them, you will receive a much deeper appreciation of the book. By the end of The IBSC, you will have paraphrased the entire Bible! Go through each chapter and try to summarise it in one paragraph, using your own words; force yourself to stay big picture and capture the heart of each chapter.

After your initial readings

Setting of 1 & 2 Chronicles
Author
Ezra, a priest and scribe, is traditionally held to be the author of Chronicles due to the correlations between Chronicles and the book of Ezra.

Recipient
Chronicles was written for the Israelites returning from Babylon, following seventy years in exile. Returnees were mainly from the nation of Judah, the southern kingdom, although a few descendants from the northern tribes of Israel also chose to return to the Promised Land.

Date and place of writing
It would have been written after the return from exile in 539 BC as the returnees are mentioned in 1 Chronicles 9. Ezra arrived in Jerusalem in 458 BC and it is reasonable to believe that he compiled the book whilst officially there to compile information for the Persian king. The suggested date range for compilation falls between 440 and 400 BC as Nehemiah returned in 444 BC, bringing important reference material from the library.

Reason written
Chronicles was written to encourage the returning exiles to have hope, worship God, and follow His commandments. They were shown that, regardless of their situation and trials, He is faithful and remains true to His promises. The author wanted to show them how to live after exile whilst warning them not to repeat history and so avoid a return trip to exile.

Big picture
Historical background
Important dates in Israel's history
- 931 BC – Kingdom of Israel divides;
- 733 BC – Israel taken into exile;
- 586 BC – Judah taken into exile;
- 539 BC – Fall of Babylon and the rise of the Persians.

When Persia took over as the world empire, they allowed the Jews to go back to their lands and rebuild the temple. This event is recorded at the very end of Chronicles.

The intended audience of this book were the Jews returning to their land after seventy years as captives, and who faced persecution during the rebuilding of God's temple. They may have had their land back, but they were still under Persian rule and surrounded by enemies. Remember that the Promised Land was repopulated by foreigners during the reign of the Babylonian Empire. These foreigners came to see the land as their own and persecuted the returning Israelites.

As mentioned previously, the book was written from the perspective of the priests. The people had been in a foreign land and were assimilated into the cultures surrounding them. As they returned to rebuild the temple, God also restored His Levitical priesthood. This was one of the reasons why the author invested time into the recording of their genealogy. The priests were calling the people to put aside foreign gods and serve the One True God.

Character portrayal – questions asked by the returning Jews
- Where do I start rebuilding in this land? Will I have what I had in exile or what my father boasted of having previously in the land of Judah?
- Are His promises still in force? Is the covenant still applicable to me and my family?
- What is our relationship to the Israel of old? Are we still part of God's nation?
- Is God still with us? Does He still rule over the land?
- Why did I return? Did we make the right decision?

Book overview

Knowledge of history builds hope for the future. Chronicles shows that God is faithful to His promises, bringing the promised blessings for obedience and the curses for disobedience (see Deuteronomy 28). However He is also merciful. He restores those who repent of their sins, and humble themselves before Him.

Chronicles clearly shows that the covenant is their guideline for what is godly and ungodly character. Success is found in keeping the covenant. Even the king must submit to the covenant and Law. Rulers and leaders are influential over the people and can lead them towards God or away from Him, but man is not the ultimate ruler.

God is sovereign and in control over the dynasties of man. This can be seen in the contrast between David and Saul. Saul did not keep God's commandments and so he was put to death by the Lord, with the kingdom handed over to David. It was the Lord who determined that David should be the shepherd of His people. However David and all the kings of men are only stewards for a moment in time; God is the Eternal King.

God is also the ultimate Victor. It is impressive to read of the feats of David's mighty men, but even in these God is shown to be the One who gave them victories. All glory, power, victory, and majesty belong to the Lord. His ark is holy and He will not abide it being dishonoured. He expects His people to keep His commands. He is an awesome God, worthy of praise and worship; He is worthy to be honoured and revered. Chronicles called the people to remember the Almighty God of Israel.

Interpreting the books of 1 & 2 Chronicles
Interpretation questions
   1. Why were the genealogies included in the first chapters? Break them up:
      a. Firstly, the genealogy of David is traced. Read 2 Samuel 7:11-16; 1 Chronicles 17:10-14; and Matthew 1:1. What is reflected in these verses of God's faithfulness to His people? Remember His covenant with Abraham.
      b. Remember the original readers as you look through the genealogy. How would this have demonstrated to them that they were still the people of God? How did it connect them with their past? Why would this have given them encouragement, as they headed back to Jerusalem from exile?
      c. The sons of Levi received great attention in their genealogy. How would this have helped to re-establish the priesthood?
   2. In Samuel, you looked at the character of David's mighty men (1 Samuel 22:1-2; 2 Samuel 21:15-22; 23:8-39). What further information do you gain about them in 1 Chronicles 11:10-12:22?
   3. Refer back to Deuteronomy 10:8.
      a. Why did Uzzah die in 1 Chronicles 13:9-10?
      b. What does this reveal about God and the Ark of the Covenant?
      c. What lesson did this teach David (1 Chronicles 13:11-14 and 15:2, 12-13)?
      d. What did the Ark of the Covenant represent?
      e. Why was the Ark of the Covenant important to God and His people?
   4. Look back on your character study of David from Samuel and Kings and then answer the following questions.
      a. What other aspects of his character do you see in 1 Chronicles 16:7-36; 17; 21:1-22:1; 28-29:20?
      b. What further is revealed of his family dynamics (1 Chronicles 16:43)?
      c. Who propelled David's heart towards the building of God's temple (1 Chronicles 28:12, 19)?
   5. Look at the temple of Solomon:
      a. What was the significance of God choosing Solomon, rather than David, to build His temple?
      b. Why was David prevented from building it?
      c. David still worked faithfully on the preparations of the temple. Why was this? What was his motivation?
   6. Why was it important to organise the priesthood in preparation for the temple?
   7. David seemed to see the importance of the musicians, gatekeepers, and treasurers. What value did each of these roles have in the service of God?
   8. What do 1 Chronicles 23-27 reveal about the importance of having

organisation within a kingdom, and the diversity of roles within it?

9. Consider King Solomon:
    a. Why did God favour Solomon's request for wisdom?
    b. Why were other nations led to come to him – as vassals, to seek his wisdom or to give gifts?
    c. Why did the author of Chronicles not spend much time on the end of Solomon's reign? Remember the author's reason for writing the book.
    d. What accomplishments of Solomon did the author uphold?
    e. Was Solomon aware of his sin? What was the reason for his actions in 2 Chronicles 8:11?

10. Consider the new temple, rebuilt by the returned exiles:
    a. Consider the events, which occurred as the Judeans were taken into exile, as recorded in 2 Chronicles 36:15-19.
    b. Consider the significance of the temple to the people and priests, as they return from exile.
    c. How would David's passion for the temple in 1 Chronicles have been an encouragement to the returning Jews? See: 1 Chronicles 17; 22:2-19; 28-19:20; Chronicles 2-5; 7:21; 24:4-14; 28:24-25; 29:3,15-17; 33:4-5; 33:7-8; 36:22-23.

11. With the people returning from exile, why was Solomon's intercessory prayer in significant to the original readers (2 Chronicles 6)?

12. What does Chronicles illustrate about the importance of godly advisors?
    a. See: 2 Chronicles 10:6-14; 22:3-6; 24:1-3,17-22; 25:14-15; 26:3-5.
    b. Bring this to personal application. Who do you turn to for advice when you have questions, concerns or decisions to make?

13. What leadership principles do you see in Chronicles? Refer to: 1 Chronicles 10:14; 11:9; 18:14; 2 Chronicles 1:10-12; 20:3-4; 30:6-9; 34:19-21,29-31.

14. Consider the priests who lived during the reign of the kings.
    a. How were the priests portrayed in Chronicles?
    b. What was their relationship with the kings?
    c. What duties did they perform?
    d. Were they faithful to God?
    e. Refer to: 1 Chronicles 15-16; 2 Chronicles 10:19; 11:13-17; 13:8-12; 19:4-11; 22:10-23:21; 26:17-18; 29:4-36; 30:15-17; 31:9-19; 35:1-9; 36:14.

15. Consider what Chronicles records regarding the Law and man's faithfulness.
    a. In what context was the Law shown?
    b. Were the people being faithful to God?
    c. What was the Law's importance in relation to the faithfulness of the people and their worship practices? Look at: 2 Chronicles 17:9-10; 19:4-10; 23:11; 25:3-4; 31:1-4; 34:14-28.
    d. What do you learn of man's obedience/ disobedience and how

God views man's faithfulness? Some verses you may wish to look back on include: 1 Chronicles 10:13-14; 2 Chronicles 11:7; 12:1-4; 15:9-15; 18:6; 20:18; 22:16-17; 24:17-19; 26:16; 27:6; 18:1,5-6; 28:22-23; 29:1-2; 30:1-9; 32:7-8; 33:9,10; 36:15-18.

16. Comment on the significance of man's motives and his heart after reviewing the following: 2 Chronicles 12:14; 20:18; 25:2; 32:24-26; 33:1-17; 34:27-28; 34:31; 36:12-13.

17. Consider: 2 Chronicles 7:1-6; 9:8; 15:8-15; 17:10; 20:18-19; 20:29; 21:13; 24:7-10; 24:18-19; 29.
    a. What was the response of the people when they were called back to the Lord?
    b. What was the response of the surrounding nations?
    c. What was the response of the people when the kings lead them astray?

18. What is revealed of God's character, particularly His faithfulness?
    a. For example, 1 Chronicles 12:5-8 (Teacher); 1 Chronicles 20:5-17 (Defender of His name).
    b. Here are some verses to get you started: 1 Chronicles 17:1-4; 21; Chronicles 6:4-6; 6:10-11; 13:10-20; 14:4-7; 14:11-13; 15:1-2; 17:3-6; 18:30-31; 20:35-37; 21:6-7; 24:20; 26:4-5; 28:9-11; 32:20-22; 33:10; 33:13; 36:16-17; 36:21,23.

19. How would the following verses have encouraged the people to rely on God as their King and Provider? 2 Chronicles 13:18; 14:7; 16:1-3,7-9; 19:1-2; 30:15-20.

Creative interpretation

    1. See *Special study – Kings and Chronicles*
When completing the special study, take note that sometimes the kings co-reigned with their sons for a number of years. Refer to *Introduction to the rulership of Israel* for the dates of the kings' reigns. In addition, remember that Chronicles has some repetition to Kings so in your study only add information that is unique to Chronicles, rather than repeating the information.

Making the time to compile this information will provide you with a very handy resource to reference which you will refer to regularly when studying the books of the prophets.

Application inspiration
- The author links the kings' treatment of the temple to how well they honoured God.
    o How does this impact on how you honour the presence of God, given that your body is the temple of the Holy Spirit?
    o Do you honour God in how you live, worship, and treat others?
    o Do you seek to honour Him above all else?
- Read back over 2 Chronicles 36:22-23. Chronicles ends with hope, whereas

Kings ends with the people entering exile. They could hope in God and His faithfulness.

- o Will you trust Him to bring you out of the exiles of life? Trust Him to establish and restore broken or painful places in your life. Do not lose hope in God.
- o Is there a past hurt that you are too afraid to give into His care or that is too painful to think on? Trust in Him. Give it to Him in prayer and have hope that He will heal the brokenness.
- o Is He the steadfast anchor in your life?
- o How does your hope in God influence how you serve Him?

- • Something to ponder: God can be worshipped in all the spheres of society and one of these is arts and entertainment.
- o For those of you who have seen the movie "300", why does this movie create inspiration in the hearts of men? Is this the type of entertainment people want? And, if so, why are there not movies about the feats of David's mighty men?
- o Surely, there are some worthwhile stories needing to be told from the pages of Scripture! Can you think of some creative ways these could be presented on the world stage?
- o Think of a story captured in the pages of Chronicles that you think worthy of telling. Tell the story to a friend this week.

Responding to God:

- • Worship the Lord for He is faithful.
- • Acknowledge Him as King and give Him dominion over your life.
- • Repent before Him with a humble heart. Everyone needs to become right with the Lord.

SPECIAL STUDY – KINGS AND CHRONICLES

Remember that the book of Kings was written from the *prophets'* perspective, whilst Chronicles was written from the *priests'* perspective. Kings ends with the Israelites entering exile, whereas Chronicles ends with hope, as the Israelites were given permission to return to Jerusalem.

Refer to *Introduction to the rulership of Israel* for the dates of the kings' reigns.

The King of Israel and Judah

Instructions

1. List the name of the king, the years of his reign, and key Scripture references.
2. Work your way through the book of Kings. For each of the kings listed, answer the questions given below.
3. Go through the book of Chronicles and add any additional information that it contains of the king's reign.

An example is given after the application section below. The example uses the life of King Azariah (also known as King Uzziah). If you are working on a computer, you may find it helpful to draw up a prototype form of the questions before you begin so that the layout does not need to be repeated for each king.

Questions

1. What were the major historical events that occurred during his/her reign?
   a. How did the king's response affect the outcome of the event?
   b. Could they have responded better?
2. Observe their relationship with God.
   a. Did they walk in obedience to His Law?
   b. If they "did evil in the sight of the Lord", what was the nature of their sin? For example, "he led the people into idolatry", or "he committed murder".
   c. Did they repent?
   d. What were the consequences of their attitudes and actions

towards God and the covenant?
3. Who were their enemies?
    a. Were they from foreign nations or within Israel/ Judah?
    b. Which nations had significant involvement in the events of Israel/ Judah during their reign?
4. Who were the prophets that spoke?
    a. Did they speak directly to the king?
    b. What did they say?
    c. Did the king respond and, if so, what was his response?
    d. When did their prophecies come about? When were they fulfilled?
5. How did the king treat the temple? (This question is unique to Chronicles)
    a. How did they treat the priests and Levites?
    b. Was judgement or were blessings brought upon them?
6. Give a summary of their reign from the perspective of the author of Kings (the prophets) and of Chronicles (the priests). Things you may wish to observe include:
    a. Was he a good or bad king?
    b. Note any comparisons or contrasts that were made between the king in question and other kings.
    c. What would their reign have meant to the original reader?
    d. Other significant information from his reign.

Application

For at least twenty-five of the kings, bring your observations through to an application for leadership. Aim for a mix of specific and general applications.

For example:

- A general application would be: "The Lord is faithful to those who place their trust in Him. Utter reliance on God will not lead one astray"; whereas
- A specific and personal application would be: "Seek guidance from those who will faithfully seek the heart of the Lord, rather than those who will relay what they think will please me. I am making a decision about changing jobs this week. I will talk it over with Mrs Smith and Mary because I can trust them to give me sound, godly counsel and pray for me as I make the decision."

Example

AZARIAH/ UZZIAH (King of Judah)
767 – 740/39BC (coregent from 791/0); 2 Kings 15:1-7; 2 Chron. 26

2 Kings 15:1-7
Key historical events
God touched him with leprosy until the day of his death

- *Results?* He lived in a separate house and Jotham, his son, was over the king's house, governing the people of the land.

Relationship with God/ Obedience to the covenant

He did what was right according to the ways of his father, but still the high places remained where people worshipped foreign gods.

Summary

The king was compared to his father. He sought to do right by the Lord, but did not remove the high places, which were key contributors to idolatry flourishing within the land.

2 Chronicles 26

Key historical events

God prospered the king as long as Uzziah sought Him.

- *Results?* He had victories against the Philistines, Arabians, and Meunites. The Ammonites paid him tribute and his fame spread to the border of Egypt as he grew strong.
- *King's response?* He built towers in Jerusalem and in the wilderness and fortified them with war engines. He helped the farmers and vine dressers for he loved the soil. He grew proud in his might, which led to his destruction.

Enemies

Philistines, Arabians, and Meunites.

Treatment of the temple, Levites, and covenant

Pride led him to be unfaithful to the Lord. He went to burn incense in the temple, a role sacred to the priests. Azariah the priest with eighty others, who were men of valour, withstood him, declaring it was for the priests alone to burn incense. He became angry. The Lord struck him and leprosy broke out on his forehead in the presence of the priests.

Prophets

Zechariah: the king sought God under the instruction of Zechariah, who taught him to fear the Lord. God prospered him as long as Uzziah sought Him.

Summary

Pride led Uzziah astray. One's might and victory may be given by the Lord, but it does not make you holy in your own right. The author appeared to want the people to understand the holiness of God and the sanctity of His dwelling place. Their fathers desecrated the holy place of God.

Leadership application

- A good king looks after his people and seeks their protection. A good leader values the role and contribution of everyone. _____ *is my quietest student in my grade 3 class. I will make sure to ask questions specifically to her this week that I know she can answer. I pray that she will gain confidence in giving contributions before the class.*

- There is danger in success. It can cause one to become prideful and think oneself above the Law. Leaders need to continuously humble themselves before God and know it is He that sanctifies and makes clean. Leaders need God. *God, I ask that you will keep me in a place of humility. Each day this week I commit to spending ten minutes in prayer with my morning coffee. During this time, I will declare your victories in my life so that I do not become proud.*

INTRODUCTION TO THE PROPHETS

The prophets were ordinary people inspired by the Holy Spirit to proclaim the Word of God. God has sent prophets to the nations throughout history. There are sixteen prophetic books in the Bible, which are classified into the Major Prophets and the Minor Prophets. They are as follows:

- Major Prophets: Isaiah, Jeremiah, Ezekiel, and Daniel.
- Minor Prophets: Hosea, Joel, Amos, Obadiah, Jonah, Micah, Nahum, Habakkuk, Zephaniah, Haggai, Zechariah, and Malachi.

The terms minor and major are not indicative of contrasting importance. Rather, they refer to the length of the books.

God used His prophets to: speak messages of warning, calling the people to repent or face the judgement of God; pledge restoration with the promise of healing, reinstatement in the land after exile, and renewal; give messianic prophecies, relating to Christ who would bring redemption; and to proclaim God's character.

The prophets constantly called the people back to God, reminding them of the covenant and its associated blessings and curses. However, most of the prophets lived under intense persecution and saw little, if any, fruit from their labour. They were faithful to God, but the people were not. Their messages usually fell on deaf ears and hard hearts.

The prophets gave emotional messages to the people of God through the spoken word, the written word, and prophetic enactments (see *enacted symbols* below).

Common tools used by the prophets

Enacted symbols

Sometimes the prophets were called to use physical actions to visually illustrate God's message. For example in Ezekiel 4:1-5:17, which records God's command to Ezekiel to act out different elements of the final siege against Jerusalem.

Visions

God gave the prophets visual images and pictures that represented His message. For example, Ezekiel 1:5-28 depicts Ezekiel's vision of the four living creatures and the wheel within a wheel.

Lament

Laments are passionate displays of grief. The prophets were blessed with God's heart for the people, which was often bitter sweet as the people rebelled and the prophets watched God's judgement fall upon them. The most famous lament is recorded in Lamentations and is attributed to Jeremiah.

Analogies/ allegories

An analogy seeks to make a difficult concept easier to understand by relating it to something familiar, which shares common features with it. Allegories are a type of analogy, as are metaphors and similes. Allegories use story form of something known to symbolically represent a deeper meaning, intangible concept or to depict a message. For example, Hosea's life became an allegory for God's relationship with the people of Israel.

Oracles

The prophecies that the prophets gave to the Israelites and surrounding nations often had predictable elements to them. Three common forms of oracles are found in the prophets, as follows:

1. *Lawsuit oracles* – God is the Judge, who calls the people or nations to come before Him on trial. He lists their sins (the charge and evidence), and then declares judgement upon them (the verdict). For example: Amos 1:3-5.
2. *Woe/ ah oracles* – God prepares the people or nations for distress to come upon them for their iniquities. He announces that it will come, gives the reason why (their sins), and predicts their downfall. For example: Isaiah 10:5-19.
3. *Salvation oracles* – Amidst the judgement declared by the prophets, God also gave His people hope. He refers to a future time, lists the change that will have occurred (usually in the people), and then gives the promise (of restoration, peace, and prosperity). For example: Jeremiah 30:8-10.

Principles of prophecy fulfilment

Bear these principles in mind when interpreting the fulfilment of a prophecy.

Single fulfilment

There is one fulfilment of a prophecy.

Closest fulfilment option

For physical prophecies, choose the nearest possible fulfilment date that adequately fulfils the predicted outcome or event. The physical prophecies listed in the books of the prophets usually fall in the period between 800 and 400 BC.

Types

A type occurs when there was a physical event, action or person at the time of the original readers that would fit with the prophecy, but the ultimate fulfilment points to something fulfilled in Christ; the initial physical thing foreshadowed Christ. For example, the physical temple was a type for the Holy Spirit coming to dwell in believers. The New Testament is the authority on what a type is and what is merely a similarity.

Progressive prophecies

Sometimes a prophet may give a chronological series of predictions, with each predication having different fulfilment dates in history. To the prophet it would have looked like one upcoming event, but looking back on history one is able to define multiple elements to the prediction. This kind of prophecy is often used to build faith. When one part of the prophecy is fulfilled, it gives hope that the remaining parts of the prophecy will also see fulfilment.

Telescopic prophecies

These are similar to progressive prophecies. There are usually two elements to the prophecy. The first element contains a contemporary prediction, which promises something coming in the physical for the original hearers or readers of the prophecy. There then follows an element that looks to the future, such as the first or second coming of Christ.

Cyclic

Parallel passages appear throughout a book, which restate the same coming events. For example, the book of Revelation is cyclical of the final battle.

Non-literal/ spiritual

These are prophecies that are fulfilled in ways the original readers would not have expected. For example, the Jews expected a King who would defeat Rome, but Christ came to defeat sin. Remember to look at New Testament interpretation for these prophecies; look to see if they have been quoted or commented on in the New Testament.

Prophecy fulfilment

Following is a list of common nations prophesied against in the books of the prophets, and main prophecy fulfilments.

God's judgement on the nations:
- Israel (Samaria) – Israel fell to the Assyrians in 722 BC.
- Judah – In 701 BC, Assyria destroyed forty-six of Judah's cities. Judah finally fell to the Babylonians in 586 BC when Jerusalem was taken by siege.
- Edom – Edom came under Babylonian suzerainty in 604 BC. They were reportedly destroyed by Babylon during the sixth century BC, according

to archaeological findings. The land of Edom came under Arab control in the fifth century BC. The inhabitants moved in the fourth century to a land South of Judah due to the Arabs and became known as the Idumeans. In 120 BC, the Maccabeans had a victory over the Idumeans. From 70 AD, with the destruction of the temple of Jerusalem under Titus, the Edomites disappeared from history.

- Assyria – Assur, a capital of Assyria, fell in 614 BC, with the nation following in 612 BC, at the hands of the Babylonians.
- Babylon – Babylon fell to the Medes and Persians in 539 BC.
- Aram (Damascus was the capital of Aram) – In 732 BC, Tiglath-Pileser III of Assyria captured the city and took the Arameans captive.
- Philistia – Gaza, Ashod, Ashkelon, Ekron, and Gath were all main cities of Philistia. Gaza was to be burned, which was fulfilled in 734 BC by Tiglath-Pileser III. The Assyrians conquered many cities of the Philistines during their reign as world power. The nation passed out of all existence during the time of the Maccabeans (169-134 BC).
- Tyre, of Phoenicia – In 332 BC, the city was conquered by Alexander the Great of Macedon.
- Ammon – Ammon was invaded by Tiglath-Pileser III of Assyria in 734 BC. It was finally conquered by Nebuchadnezzer of Babylon around 582 BC.
- Moab – Moab was conquered by Sargon II of Assyria during his campaign in 715 BC. It disappeared completely from historical records during the time of the Persian Empire.
- All nations – At Christ's second coming.

Options for the fulfilment of salvation prophecies:

- Immediate – the restoration of the Israelites to Judah following exile in Babylon;
- First coming of Christ;
- Church age – being the present time;
- Millennial (1, 000 year) kingdom referred to in Revelation; or
- The age to come – the second coming of Christ bringing the fullness of the Kingdom of God.

EZRA

Temple Rebuilt, but was the Lesson Learned?

"For we are slaves. Yet our God has not forsaken us in our slavery, but has extended to us his steadfast love before the kings of Persia, to grant us some reviving to set up the house of our God, to repair its ruins, and to give us protection in Judea and Jerusalem." – Ezra 9:9

During your first reading

Themes to track
- The temple
- The people
- Character of Ezra
- Opposition

During your second reading

Things to notice in the text
- Responses of the returning exiles, Ezra, and the leadership of the returned exiles.
- The actions of the kings of Persia and the Gentiles who were settled in Judah.

Chapter summaries

These are optional as they can be time consuming for the larger books. If you choose to do them, you will receive a much deeper appreciation of the book. By the end of The IBSC, you will have paraphrased the entire Bible! Go through each chapter and try to summarise it in one paragraph, using your own words; force yourself to stay big picture and capture the heart of each chapter.

After your initial readings

Setting of Ezra

Author

The book was written by Ezra, who was a teacher of the Law as well as a trusted scribe of King Artaxerxes of Persia.

Recipient

The book was written for the returned exiles, who had completed the rebuilding of the temple in Jerusalem and were now beginning new lives in the land.

Date and place of writing

To coincide with the completion of the temple, the book must have been written, or at least completed, after 450 BC. A date of 458 BC is likely as this is the year that Ezra was sent to Jerusalem by King Artaxerxes.

Reason written

Ezra wrote this account so that the exiles would not intermarry and merge with the people of the land. This was to protect them from taking on false gods through marriage, as their fathers had done. Ezra's goal was for the people to remain faithful to the Law, walking in obedience to the commandments of God. He emphasised that the people could trust in God because He is faithful to His Word and promises.

Big picture

Historical background

The returning Jews (the original readers)

The Jews who had returned to Judah from exile came in two groups with a third one followed later. The first group returned with Zerubbabel in 539 BC, and the second group returned with Ezra in 458 BC.

The text states that the Jews were returning from an "area near the Chebar River", which suggests that they had been settled on good land when they were sent into exile and were not necessarily doing poorly in Babylon. They were living a normal life, their needs were being met, and they were living in peace. See Psalm 107, written from exile.

Given their situation in exile, it is somewhat unsurprising that the majority of Jews chose to remain in the land of their exile rather than return to Jerusalem. After seventy years in exile, those who had known life in Jerusalem would be well-advanced in years, whilst the younger generations would have had no knowledge of life in the Promised Land.

Approximately 18 to 40 thousand people were taken into Babylon from Judah. An approximated 120 thousand returned to Jerusalem. Whilst this may seem a large number, one must account for population growth during the years of exile, making the number of Jews who chose to return only a fraction of the total population in exile.

The Persians

Unlike the Babylonians, who took Judah into exile, the Persians practiced religious tolerance. They also allowed captured peoples to live in their native regions under Persian governance. The Jews were not the only ones given the opportunity to return home, but God was the only god that was acknowledged as the True God by the Persian kings. In addition, the temple of God was the only foreign temple that the kings of Persia financed.

The temple was rebuilt over a period of eighty two years, during which time God worked in the hearts of the Persian kings. However, not all of the kings during this time cared about the temple or allowed the work to continue on it.

The kings of Persia during the rebuilding of the temple were:

- Cyrus; 559-530 BC.
- Cambyses, the son of Cyrus; 530-523 BC.
  Cambyses killed his brother to avoid contention for the throne, yet the throne was usurped whilst he was away in Egypt. There is nothing about Cambyses in the book of Ezra.
- Smerdis (or a Magus usurper); 522 BC.
  It is recorded by Darius that Smerdis was, in fact, an usurper by the name of Gaumata. Whether this is true is not overly important as Smerdis only lasted about ten months after stealing the throne. Again, he is not mentioned in Ezra.
- Darius; 522-486 BC.
  During his governance, the Jews had peace and prosperity. The prophets Haggai and Zechariah spoke during his reign and the temple rebuilding began.
- Ahauerus (Xerxes); 468-464 BC.
  He was t king during the time of Esther.
- Artaxerxes; 464-423 BC.
  Artaxerxes was king when the book of Ezra was written. He allowed Nehemiah and Ezra to return to the Promised Land.

Character portrayal – to go or not to go?

"The King is giving us the chance to go home! We can go back to the Promised Land!"

"Home? What home? Take a good look around you, my dear, this is our home! This is where we built. This is where we work. It is here that we have raised our families."

Adena was crestfallen. How could Shahar not want to return to the land of promise, the land of their forefathers? It was not their fault that they were exiled. God had made a way for them to go home and she was eager to take it; only, to do so would mean leaving many loved ones behind. This included her beloved elder brother, Shahar. She did not want to leave him in this foreign land, but it was clear his feelings were not the same as her own.

Adena had always noticed a difference between herself and those around her. Few people felt the way she did toward the old land and the old ways. God had placed a string around her heart that pulled her towards Judah. The thought of leaving behind all that she knew was a daunting prospect, as was entering an unknown land. However, it was the land God had given to her people and that sent shivers of excitement through her body.

Home. Her brother may have found it in Babylon, but she had not. For her, home meant the Promised Land. She was willing to face the long, dangerous, and expensive journey from Chebar to Jerusalem, if it meant the opportunity to go *home*.

Book overview

The first half of Ezra is a record of the rebuilding of the temple. There was opposition to the rebuilding from the Gentiles in the land, who had begun to think of the land as their own. They persecuted the returned exiles and this caused the Jews to fear their neighbours. The work on the temple was ceased at one point because the returned exiles gave in to fear of their opposition. The people began to build their own homes and lives, rather than the Lord's temple.

The returned exiles were at a cross-road. They came very close to following the path of their parents: turning from God, taking on the culture of the land, and with time their foreign gods too. So it is amazing that when Ezra came with a rebuke from the Lord, they confessed their sins and returned to Him. The rebuilding that was stopped was taken up with new zeal and the temple was completed. The consecration of the Lord's temple occurred amidst celebration. However, the physical temple was only a shadow of Solomon's, which had been destroyed during the fall of Jerusalem.

The book of Ezra also shows how various kings and influential leaders submitted themselves under God and to His will. Cyrus was obedient to the call of God on his life in regards to the rebuilding of God's temple. He recognized the True God. The king submitted himself under the power of God and called his officials to do likewise, showing that God influences the influential. Furthermore, the book demonstrates God's faithfulness in fulfilling His promises. He was not only having His temple rebuilt, but He was rebuilding the people of His nation. God was calling for a reformed people, whose hearts were for Him and His Law. The people chose to respond and came back to work alongside God.

Interpreting the book of Ezra
Interpretation questions
1. Look back on the physical restoration that was promised in:
    a. Jeremiah 25:11-14,
    b. Jeremiah 29:10,
    c. Isaiah 44:28,
    d. Isaiah 45:13, and
    e. Isaiah 44:26.
2. Consider what you see of God in the book of Ezra.
    a. What do you see of God's sovereignty?
    b. What other aspects of His character were revealed?

   c. What role did God play in His people returning from exile?

   d. What part did God take in the rebuilding of the temple?

   e. How did He provide for the people upon their return to Judah?

3. Why did many of the exiled Jews choose not to return to Judah when given the opportunity?

4. How do you think the original readers felt, who had chosen to go back to Judah? Perhaps: apprehensive, excited, scared, fearful, overwhelmed, feeling that it was going to be better back in Jerusalem . . .? Remember that most of these returning Jews had never been in the Promised Land. They were returning to a place that they had not seen and did not know.

5. When looking at the genealogies, ask:

   a. Why was it important for the original readers to know these lineages? Consider God's laws on land rights and the role of the Levites.

   b. Why distinguish the different groups, and their roles?

   c. Who were the groups being listed?

   d. How would defining these roles have helped in the rebuilding of Jerusalem?

6. What was the importance of laying the foundation of the temple?

   a. Why would this event be worth celebrating?

   b. What did it represent?

   c. Why did the older generation respond differently to the younger generation when the temple foundations were laid (see Ezra 3:10-13)?

7. Consider the dedication of the temple in light of the events that occurred at the dedication to the former temple. Compare Ezra 6:13-18 with 1 Kings 8:10-11.

   a. What was different this time around?

   b. What was the significance of this?

8. Follow the theme of opposition in the book of Ezra.

   a. What was the nature of the opposition and what was motivating it?

   b. What were those opposing the Jews hoping to achieve?

   c. How did the returned exiles respond in each situation?

   d. How did the various Persian Kings respond?

   e. In what way did the past history of the people play a role in Artaxerxes' decision in chapter 4? What are the implications of this?

9. Who was Ezra?

   a. What do you learn of him from the following verses: Ezra 7:1-5; 7:6; 7:14-26; 8:21-23; 9:3-15; 10:1; 10:10-11?

10. In chapter 8, the second group of returning exiles arrive with Ezra.

   a. Do you think there would have been conflict between the two groups; why or why not?

   b. Would the first group who returned have felt they had risked more than their later-returning brethren?

   c. How were they kept together?

   d. What moulded them together, bringing unity?

11. Why did Ezra feel it was important to weigh and record the silver and gold articles provided to him by the king at the start and finish of his journey (Ezra 8:24-36)? What did this achieve?

12. What was the big deal about intermarriage?

   a. Read back over Numbers 25:1-9. What clues does this provide?

   b. What about the commands in Deuteronomy 7:1-5?

   c. What do these extra passages show about God and His purpose for the laws on intermarriage?

   d. How was Ruth different (see Ruth 1:16)? This is not about racial mixed marriages, but about faithfulness to God and not being led astray from Him. In this context, consider 2 Corinthians 6:14-15.

   e. How did Ezra respond to the marriages between the returned Jews and their Gentile neighbours?

   f. As a scribe and one who knew the scriptures, how would the above passages in Numbers and Deuteronomy have fuelled Ezra's response upon hearing of these marriages?

13. What was the significance of the events in Ezra 10 to the faith of the returning exiles?

   a. What changes had occurred to make the people zealous for the Lord and His Law?

   b. What did it show about the new leadership?

   c. What did it show of the outcome of exile?

Creative interpretation

1. Make a comparative observation table for the books of Ezra, Nehemiah, and Haggai to track the events that occurred as the Jews returned from exile. Feel free to add any extra observations that you would like to track!

Observations	Ezra	Nehemiah	Haggai
Key leaders:			
Prophets who spoke:			
Progression of the building — temple, wall, time frames, delays, etc:			
Actions of the people/ key emotions:			

Actions of God:			
What was God communicating?			
Response of the Gentiles in the land – opposition etc:			
Response/ actions of the kings:			
Other significant events which took place:			
Other observations:			

Application inspiration
Facing opposition in the faith

- How do you respond in the face of opposition? Do you give up or do you cling to God's direction and your faith?
- Obedience is on the heart of God. He desires a faithful people dogged in their determination to follow through according to His will. Do you value obedience to God higher than anything else, even in the midst of opposition?
- Do you have a never-give-up spirit to be obedient, despite hard times? Will you press on regardless of how you feel?

A passion for the Law

- What is your passion for the Law/ Word of God?
- Is your communication of the Law something that will ignite a passion for it in others?
- Do you desire to see truth and obedience to the Word put into practice around you and in your own life? Do you lovingly challenge others in their walk with God?
- Are you willing to sacrifice things that are important to you for the sake of following and obeying the Lord?

NEHEMIAH

Rebuilding & Renewal

So the wall was finished on the twenty-fifth day of the month Elul, in fifty-two days. And when all our enemies heard of it, all the nations around us were afraid and fell greatly in their own esteem, for they perceived that this work had been accomplished with the help of our God. – Nehemiah 6:15-16

During your first reading

Themes to track
- Covenant renewal
- Spiritual revival of the nation
- Opposition and persecution
- Character of Nehemiah
- Prayer
- Remembrance
- Leadership

During your second reading

Things to notice in the text
- Responses of Nehemiah, as well as the Levites, Israelites, and Gentiles.
- Rebuilding of the wall
- Rebuilding of the nation
- Highlight: lists, emotions, and the repeated word "Law".

Chapter summaries
These are optional as they can be time consuming for the larger books. If you choose to do them, you will receive a much deeper appreciation of the book. By the

end of The IBSC, you will have paraphrased the entire Bible! Go through each chapter and try to summarise it in one paragraph, using your own words; force yourself to stay big picture and capture the heart of each chapter.

After your initial readings

Setting of Nehemiah
Author
    Authorship is attributed to Nehemiah.

Recipient
    The book was written to the people of God who chose to return to Jerusalem, from their exile in Babylon.

Date and place of writing
    It would be likely that Nehemiah wrote it whilst still in Jerusalem, prior to returning to the king's service in Susa, alternatively known as Shushan. This dates the book around 432 BC.

Reason written
    The book was written to encourage continued strength in the face of opposition, by reminding the returned Jews of God's past faithfulness. It was to motivate the people to continue rebuilding the nation whilst trusting God to protect them.

Big picture
Historical background
    As a cupbearer to the king, Nehemiah drank of the king's wine prior to the monarch so that, if a drink was poisoned, he would be the first to die. The cupbearer was also required to always be cheerful in his lord's presence. Nehemiah journeyed to Judah with the third group of returning exiles in 444 BC in order to accomplish the restoration of the wall.

    By this time, the temple had been rebuilt. The returned exiles had seen God's protection and provision first hand in their native land. Whilst having received many blessings, the people remained in danger as the wall of Jerusalem remained in ruins, offering them no protection from those seeking their harm. The ruined walls would also have caused them shame, acting as a reminder of their previous exile and current slavery to the Persian Empire.

Key dates to remember:
- 722 BC – Assyria is the world power; Israel is taken into exile.
- 612 BC – Babylon conquers Judah.
- 605 BC – First deportation of Judeans into exile.
- 597 BC – Second deportation into exile.
- 586 BC – Third deportation into exile, and the fall of Jerusalem.
- 589 BC – Persia conquers Babylon; Cyrus is emperor.

- 538 BC – Cyrus allows Jews to return to Judah; first group of exiles returns to Jerusalem.
- 516 BC – Rebuilding of the temple in Jerusalem is finished.
- 486-465 BC – Xerxes rules as emperor of Persia.
- 457 BC – Second group of Jews returns to Judah with Ezra.
- 444 BC – Third group of Jews returns to Judah with Nehemiah.

Character portrayal – Nehemiah observes the people

Nehemiah looked out upon the people as they listened attentively to Ezra reading from the Book of Law. His heart swelled. It was right that the people of God should hear of His ways and walk in reverent fear of their Most Holy God. It was because the Law had been discarded by their forefathers that they had been made to suffer the humiliation of exile. Even now, they remained as slaves under the rule of the Persian Empire. Still, the people of God could once again call Jerusalem home. It was a start.

So too was the people's fervour for the Lord. Watching them cry, laugh, and sing with joy as they reflected on what God had done for the patriarchs, hope rose within his breast. Surely, if the people continued in such dedication, they would never again be subjected to the horrors of the past wars or the shame of defeat. If God's chosen people continued to hunger after God's Word, and faithfully keep His commandments, then they had no need to fear from the enemies that surrounded them. And one day, God would send the promised Messiah to set them free; one glorious day, God would send a Saviour to establish His nation over all other nations.

Book overview

Nehemiah returned to Jerusalem with the third group of exiles to coordinate the rebuilding of the wall. The work took place amidst taunts, ridicule, and threats from their foreign neighbours. The Jews were fearful of these people, yet in spite of this, they put their trust in God under Nehemiah's governance. It was significant that they gave acknowledgement to God for the completion of the work.

Having returned to the Promised Land, the people were hungry to hear more about their God. They sought understanding of how to live for Him and how they were to walk in obedience to His Laws. It was because their forefathers failed to obey God's Law that the nation fell, and the people were taken into exile. The returning Jews were eager to avoid repeating history. They responded with worship as they were given understanding and insights into the Law.

The book of Nehemiah records the spiritual revival that took place in the land. A nation was rebuilt as they rebuilt the physical wall of Jerusalem, and their covenant with God was renewed.

Interpreting the book of Nehemiah
Interpretation questions
   1. Look at the character of Nehemiah. Take specific note of his responses,

emotions, and prayers. Ask:

    a. What was important to him?

    b. What made him passionate for God?

    c. What was his relationship like with God, the people, and the king?

    d. How did his knowledge of Scripture impact his actions and his relationship with God?

    e. In what circumstances did he pray? What did he include in his prayers? What events were occurring when he prayed? Is a response from God, Nehemiah or the people recorded that came as a result of the prayer? What do you learn about prayer from the prayer life of Nehemiah?

    f. How did he remain faithful to God in the midst of persecution? How did he respond to hostility from the enemies of the Jews?

    g. What was Nehemiah's desire for the people of God?

    h. Why was Nehemiah favoured by the king?

2. Look at the theme of leadership.

    a. What leadership qualities do you see in the book of Nehemiah? See: Nehemiah 1:6; 1:8; 1:11b; 2:1; 2:5,8; 2:11; 2:12; 2:13; 2:18; 4:3,6; 4:23; 5:7; 5:14-17; 6:3,11; 6:15,16; 13:8,25.

    b. Why did the people stray from God's commands after Nehemiah returned to the king?

    c. What does the book of Nehemiah, and particularly the record in chapter 13, show about the importance of strong and God-fearing leaders?

    d. What makes a strong leader?

3. What opposition did the returned Jews face?

    a. Was it coming from within the nation, or did the antagonism stem from an external source?

    b. Why were their neighbours antagonistic towards them?

4. Why was it shameful for the Jews to see the wall of Jerusalem in ruins?

5. Consider the details that Nehemiah records amidst the rebuilding.

    a. For what reasons would Nehemiah have listed who had been responsible for each section of the rebuild?

    b. Why did he record the list of those who returned from captivity?

    c. Give reasons why it was important to record the names of those who signed the document of covenant renewal.

    d. Was it necessary for Nehemiah to record those who remained in Jerusalem to live, and, if so, why? Likewise, why was it deemed necessary to list the priests and Levites?

6. Consider the theme of remembrance in Nehemiah.

    a. What importance does the book of Nehemiah give to remembrance?

    b. What were the people called to remember?

    c. How was remembrance shown to be linked to obedience and faithfulness?

     d. What had the people learnt from the history of their nation and the sins of their fathers?

     e. What importance did the book attach to knowing the Word of the Law and the commands of God?

     f. Why was the Book of Law read repeatedly?

     g. How would hearing the Law on numerous occasions benefit the people?

     h. What was the response of the people to hearing the Word of God? How was this significant in the rebuilding of their nation?

7. What factors contributed to covenant renewal?

     a. Was it driven by the people, priests or God?

     b. Why did the people make it an oath and sign a sealed document? What was the significance of this act?

8. God's heart for the poor and needy is revealed throughout Scripture. The issue of social justice is once more raised in Nehemiah.

     a. What was said in relation to social justice?

     b. How did Nehemiah lead the way?

     c. Why did Nehemiah have a heart for the poor?

     d. From where did his compassion flow?

     e. What do you remember of social justice in God's Law, from your study of the Pentateuch? Can you find example verses from the books of Moses which state God's will for protection of the poor and needy?

9. Look back on the Law of Moses. Give consideration to the reason why the people fell away from God and went into exile. Now consider why Nehemiah was adamant that foreigners were to be excluded from the people of God.

Creative interpretation

1. Consider the responses of Nehemiah and what they show of his character. Complete the following table as you consider his circumstances, the possible outcomes, and his response. An example has been given, as well as some initial verse references.

Passage reference	Current circumstances and potential outcomes of events	Nehemiah's response	Actual outcome of events
1:1-2:6	Hanani comes from Jerusalem and tells that the people have great trouble and shame and that the wall remains in ruins. Being the king's	He sought information from the captives. Wept and mourned. Fasted and prayed for the Lord to help His people	Nehemiah goes before the king with a sorrowful face, which was not allowed of the king's cupbearer. The king notices his distress and allows

	cupbearer, Nehemiah could have accepted not being able to help them and forgotten about the issue, leaving the exiles to their own troubles.	and keep His covenant promise.	Nehemiah to return to Judah and oversee the rebuilding of the wall of Jerusalem.
2:1-2:8			
2:9-2:16			
2:17-2:20			

2. Make a comparative observation table for the books of Ezra, Nehemiah, and Haggai to track the events that occurred as the Jews returned from exile. Feel free to add extra observations you would like to track!

Observations	Ezra	Nehemiah	Haggai
Key leaders:			
Prophets who spoke:			
Progression of the building — temple, wall, time frames, delays, etc:			
Actions of the people/ key emotions:			
Actions of God:			
What was God communicating?			
Response of the			

Gentiles in the land – opposition etc:			
Response/ actions of the kings:			
Other significant events which took place:			
Other observations:			

Application inspiration

Responding to the Word of God

- Is the Word of God touching your heart? Is it causing change to take place?
- What is your response as you study, as you read, and as you go through your day? Do verses come to mind, or situations in Scripture, that help as you are "out and about" in the world?
- Ask God to prevent the Word become stale in your life. Ask Him to use it to transform your heart and mind.

Responding to persecution

- Are you prepared for opposition to the tasks God has set before you?
- Have you already faced persecution? What did it look like? Was it from those who do not believe, from family or friends, or from within the church? How did you respond?
- How can you be prepared for hostility? Will you give up or press through?

Responding in prayer

- When given a task by God, how much time do you invest in prayer? Do you seek further guidance from God before you begin?
- Are there any elements of your prayer life that need to change in response to what you learnt in Nehemiah?

Responding to social injustice

- Who are the social outcasts in your community?
- How can you care for the vulnerable?
- How can you help to rebuild lives?
- Are you prepared to suffer personally in your support of the poor and needy? What costs are you prepared to pay?

ESTHER

Courage amidst Persecution

Then Queen Esther answered, "If I have found favor in your sight, O king, and if it please the king, let my life be granted me for my wish, and my people for my request. For we have been sold, I and my people, to be destroyed, to be killed, and to be annihilated. If we had been sold merely as slaves, men and women, I would have been silent, for our affliction is not to be compared with the loss to the king." – Esther 7:3-4

During your first reading

Themes to track

- God's sovereignty and protection
- Persecution
- Obedience
- Character of Mordecai and Esther

During your second reading

Things to notice in the text

- God's name is not mentioned once! (Yet His finger prints are all over this story)
- Emotion
- Main characters: King Xerxes, Queen Vashti, Mordecai, Queen Esther, and Haman.

Chapter summaries

These are optional as they can be time consuming for the larger books. If you choose to do them, you will receive a much deeper appreciation of the book. By the end of The IBSC, you will have paraphrased the entire Bible! Go through each chapter and try to summarise it in one paragraph, using your own words; force

yourself to stay big picture and capture the heart of each chapter.

After your initial readings

Setting of Esther

Author

The author remains unknown. It was probably written by a Jew who was a court official through these events. Alternatively, Mordecai or Queen Esther may have ordered a written account of the events.

Recipient

The book was written for a Jewish population. The original readers were the Jews throughout the Persian Empire, including those who had returned to Jerusalem.

Date and place of writing

It was customary not to write about a king until after his death. This would mean that the book was likely written within a twenty year time period following King Xerxes' death in 465 BC. It would have been written from Susa, which was one of the capitals of the Persian Empire.

Reason written

The book of Esther gave the Jews the background of the feast of Purim, showing how they were protected and preserved by the Lord. It also gave them the story behind their strange salvation; one day they heard a decree ordering them to be killed, the next they were given permission to kill their would-be killers. This book gave them the explanation, the behind the scenes version of the tale.

Big picture

Historical background

Key dates to remember:

- 722 BC – Assyria is the world power; Israel is taken into exile.
- 612 BC – Babylon conquers Judah.
- 605 BC – First deportation of Judeans into exile.
- 597 BC – Second deportation into exile.
- 586 BC – Third deportation into exile, and the fall of Jerusalem.
- 589 BC – Persia conquers Babylon; Cyrus is emperor.
- 538 BC – Cyrus allows Jews to return to Judah; first group of exiles returns to Judah.
- 516 BC – Rebuilding of the temple in Jerusalem is finished.
  [This is where the story splits, with many choosing to remain in the land of exile, and a few opting to return to Jerusalem.]
- 486-465 BC – Xerxes rules as Emperor of Persia.
- 483-473 BC – Events of the book of Esther.
- 457 BC – Second group of Jews returns to Judah with Ezra.

- 444 BC – Third group of Jews returns to Judah with Nehemiah.

What's in a name? Names of the king:
- Greek name = Xerxes
- Persian name = Khshayarsha
- Hebrew name = Ahasuerus

King Darius was the father of King Ahasuerus. It was Darius who allowed the captive peoples across his empire to go back to their native lands, including the exiled Jews.

Fast facts about the Persian Empire (the ruling power during the time of Esther)
- At this time, development was occurring throughout the kingdom. Xerxes was known for building infrastructure, including houses and roads. His father was known for developing financial and postal systems.
- It was common for the king to have advisors, but the role of the advisor was to ensure the best interest of the king, not the people.
- Leadership made decisions when drunk, as this was believed to connect them to the spiritual world. It was standard practice to drink whilst making important decisions. At banquets, the guests were required to drink whenever the king drank.
- Military power was important to the Persians. They were pushing out the boundaries of their kingdom. It is believed that the one hundred and eighty day feast referred to in Esther could have been a military gathering as the Persians prepared to attack Greece. The five year gap between chapter 1 and chapter 2 fell during the time the king was away from Susa, fighting. Susa was their winter capital.
- When the Persian Empire conquered foreign groups, they let them live freely amongst their people. This resulted in the captives being assimilated into Persian culture. A captive was free to buy a house and get a job; hence, bringing them into Persian society. It was therefore significant that the Jews maintained their own identity amongst the Persians. However, this would not have concerned the Persians, provided that the Jews did not attempt rebellion.
- Zoroastrianism was the Persian religion. They believed that good and evil coexisted and balanced each other out. They did not see it as good versus evil, but rather that both were needed in order to maintain balance.
- A hierarchy existed within the king's harem. It included all women, even those who worked in the kitchens. Their lives were rigidly controlled, and not by themselves. No person could enter the king's presence unless he called them by name and the only person these women could be alone with was the king.

The Jewish people in Susa

The Jews were still practising their own laws, but had become accustomed to Persian culture and adopted some of their practices. They were Jewish by heritage and religion, but influenced by the Persian culture. The Jews in Persia were self-sufficient, distant from the other people, and distant from their God.

Character portrayal – Esther wrestles with her call

"Why was I chosen for this task?" Esther wondered, anxiety rising up within her.

Mordecai, her dear Mordecai. Surely he knew that she was not up to this task? He had read the scriptures to her since she was a girl. She knew well that courage did not always flow from the expected source. She might not have might, and she certainly did not have power, but it seemed that God had set this task before her, and her alone.

The events of the past few years began to make sense. What had Mordecai conveyed through the guard? *"And who knows whether you have not come to the kingdom for such a time as this?"*[A] Yes, that was it. As Esther sat on her mat in the Harem, she began to see events from a new perspective. When she had arrived at the palace, summoned by the king's edict, she had seemed small and insignificant. God had seen fit to have the king choose her from amongst all the other women; nevertheless, the king rarely called her to him, and that caused her anxiety.

Over the past few years, she had known fear, loneliness, heartache, and the loss of innocence. She had made friends and she had learnt that a title can instil jealousy in the heart of those who do not have one. And now, when she had finally accepted life as one of thousands, she felt God pulling her to step out and mark herself as different. Be marked for death, too, as was more than likely to be the case. No one went uninvited before the king. She would. She would go because the Lord had chosen her. That knowledge would have to be her strength and support.

"God, grant me strength for this task. Let me be as Joshua – strong and courageous," Esther prayed. *"Please, O Mighty God, fight once more for your people. Do not let Haman murder your people for what we have not done. Protect my life before King Ahasuerus and, by doing so, O King of nations, save your people."*

Book overview

God's chosen people were scattered through the nations and were living under Persian rule, but God had not forgotten them or abandoned them to their fate. He is both sovereign and a providential protector. His people were in need and He worked the events of history to enable a saviour to arise in the hour of their need. The saviour was once again somewhat unexpected: a young and beautiful woman, chosen by the king to be his bride. Yet the task set before her would not have been easy for Esther to complete.

Mordecai called her to intervene for the people when they became threatened with annihilation. However, she was locked in the Harem and was subject to the whims of the king. Queen she may have been, but she was understandably scared. To go uninvited before the king was to invite death. Yet she did not go alone before the king – unseen, God was nevertheless with her and His people.

Esther, one small and seemingly insignificant, captive woman, became queen of an empire and the saviour of her people. One person can change the course of history. One person can influence the course of *nations*! The book of Esther illustrates that individuals can make a difference, when they walk with the Lord.

Interpreting the book of Esther
Interpretation questions

1. How do you believe the Jews felt when they received the edict declaring they were to be killed at a set date and time by command of the king, without reason?
2. Consider the actions of Mordecai before Haman.
   a. Why would Mordecai not bow to Haman?
   b. Was he right not to bow?
   c. How do you believe the Jews would have felt about Mordecai not bowing down to Haman?
   d. How was this similar to the actions of Daniel and his three friends in Daniel 1:8, 3:12, and 6:10-13?
3. Consider Esther's situation as well as her emotions and responses within them.
   a. What was the significance of Esther winning favour with the palace staff, as well as the king?
   b. Why do you think she won favour? Was it her physical beauty, her character, her God, her accent, a combination . . .?
   c. Why would Mordecai warn Esther not to reveal her identity when taken to the palace?
   d. How could she have felt being taken into the harem and away from family and friends?
   e. What do you believe she would have felt when she heard the edict of the king?
4. Consider the actions of King Xertes:
   a. What was the significance of King Xertes giving his ring to Haman? What was he effectively doing?
   b. What about when he gave his ring to Mordecai?
   c. What did these actions convey about his leadership?
   d. Contrast this with the historical background that records that the king was responsible for developing his empire's infrastructure.
5. Do you think that the outcomes listed at the end of Esther would have made the Jews remaining in exile more or less likely to join the second and third waves of Jews returning to Jerusalem in 457 BC and 444 BC?
6. What do you see of courage in the face of persecution in this book? What motivated the courage?
7. What lessons do you learn of obedience in the book of Esther?
8. God's name is not mentioned in the book.
   a. Can you see Him in it?
   b. In what ways was He present?

    c. Do you think that the original readers would have acknowledged Him?

    d. Why might His name have been left out of the book?

<u>Creative interpretation</u>

1. Complete a short summary of the personality and traits of each of the main characters (Esther, Mordecai, Xertes, and Haman) in the book of Esther.

    a. What motivated their actions?

    b. Why did each character respond as they did?

Application inspiration

- The book of Esther shows how one person can make a difference – to an entire nation!
  - Are you ever discouraged that your life cannot make a difference? What do you think causes these emotional beliefs? How does the story of Esther and Purim challenge these emotions?
  - How can you make a difference in your community? What event or program could you become involved in? For example, if you are an athlete, maybe there is a community sport's team that needs a coach for the young ones.
  - Who could you help this week? Could you cook a meal for someone? Perhaps there is a family at church you know who is struggling that you could slip a $50 note into their Bible.
- Sometimes obedience involves taking risks. Are you prepared to step out of your comfort zone for the Gospel?

[1] Esther 4:14

JOB

Do the Righteous Suffer?

Then Job answered the LORD and said: "I know that you can do all things, and that no purpose of yours can be thwarted. 'Who is this that hides counsel without knowledge?' Therefore I have uttered what I did not understand, things too wonderful for me, which I did not know. 'Hear, and I will speak; I will question you, and you make it known to me.' I had heard of you by the hearing of the ear, but now my eye sees you; therefore I despise myself, and repent in dust and ashes." – Job 42:1-6

During your first reading

Themes to track
- God's character and sovereignty
- Suffering, loss, and illness
- Comforting friends during suffering

During your second reading

Things to notice in the text
- Who is speaking
- Conditional statements: "if x, then y"
- Views on wisdom
- Discussion of suffering and sin

Chapter summaries
These are optional for Job due to the titling of conversations in *creative interpretation* for this book.

After your initial readings

Setting of Job
<u>Author</u>
The author remains unknown.

<u>Recipient</u>
The intended readers remain unknown.

<u>Date and place of writing</u>
It is believed that Job lived during the time of the patriarchs; however, it is not known exactly when the events occurred, or when they were transferred from oral tradition to written form. Job is mentioned in Ezekiel, which means that the story was recorded prior to 593 BC. The book was likely written from within Israel. Refer to the *historical background* given below for information about the land of Uz, where Job lived.

<u>Reason written</u>
Job was written in defence of a just and holy God, amidst a world of suffering. For thousands of years people have been wrestling with the questions: "Why do the righteous suffer?" and "How can an Almighty and Holy God allow such suffering?" The author declared that it is through knowledge of God that suffering is brought into perspective.

Big picture
<u>Historical background</u>
Job lived in the land of Uz, amongst the people of the East. Where is this eastern land? The Israelites reading Job's story would relate "east" to east of the River Jordan. The land of Uz is mentioned twice more in Scripture: Lamentations 4:21, in association with Edom, and Jeremiah 25:20-21, separate to Edom. In Genesis 10:23, Uz is recorded as a son of Aram (son of Shem, son of Noah). Some scholars suggest that the land of Uz could have been named after this Uz, the son of Aram. Furthermore, they suggest that Uz could have bordered Edom (modern day northern Arabia).

Middle near-eastern culture believed in retribution theology, which held that evildoers had evil befall them and do-gooders could expect blessings to come upon them. They believed sinful men caused suffering, and they attributed illness to personal sin.

<u>Character portrayal – Elihu listens to Job and his friends</u>
Elihu stood in the shadow of his elders, listening as they discussed Job's plight. He found it hard to look at Job, whose skin sat loose over his bones and bore red, blistering boils, yet he found it harder still to listen as Job spoke.

Elihu's jaw clenched as Job justified himself, rather than God. How could Job declare that God denies him justice? Elihu thought in anger. The Almighty could not pervert justice and yet Job was implying that there was no profit in living a godly life! And why did Job declare that God should answer him? Who was he that the Creator of All Things should come at the bidding of a mere man? Elihu was scornful and outraged. God was greater than man and had no need to justify Himself to His creation!

Elihu could not believe the conceit of his four elders. He had remained silent out of respect due to his elders, but silent he could remain no longer! He must speak!

"I am young in years, and you are old,"[1] he began.

Book overview

The book of Job is classed as speculative wisdom literature, which asks the question "why?" In the book of Job, the author is asking: "Why does God allow the righteous to suffer?"

The book must be read as a whole in order to follow the author's train of thought. The discussions of the characters do not always proclaim truth. The author included discussions containing truths, half-truths, misapplied truths, wrong assumptions, and totally incorrect beliefs. The dialogues between Job and his three friends contain assumptions. Remember that assumptions are ideas that have not been tested; they are at the lowest level of knowledge.

In wisdom literature, such as Job and Proverbs, principles can be discovered by which to live, but it must be remembered that these principles cannot always be taken as promises. A promise is something that God has said will, or will not, happen; a principle is formed by man, based on what they have seen of God's character and ways. Take the wisdom in Job as principles, not promises.

True wisdom is revealed at the end of Job. It is seen that God is God and there is no questioning of His actions. He does not need to answer: "Why?" and He is not under obligation to explain His ways to man.

The book of Job also shows that not all suffering is the direct consequence of personal sin. This is seen at the beginning of the book during God's discussion with Satan, and at the end when God declared that Job's friends were wrong in their assumptions about Job's suffering.

Interpreting the book of Job
Interpretation questions

    1. Consider Job's responses.
        a. To whom, or what, did Job attribute his suffering?
        b. What concept of God did he hold?
        c. Did these change through the course of events?
    2. Consider the responses of Job's wife.
        a. To whom, or what, did she attribute his suffering?
        b. What was her concept of God, His judgement, and His mercy?
        c. What image did she hold of Him?
    3. Consider the responses of Job's three friends.
        a. To whom, or what, did Job's three friends attribute his suffering?
        b. What was their concept of God, His judgement, and His mercy?

    c. What image did they hold of Him?

    d. Did their views change through the course of events?

    e. What was their understanding of wisdom?

4. What advice did the friends give?

    a. Was it sound advice?

    b. Why did God reprove them?

    c. What do other scriptures outside of the book of Job say in support or dispute of their views?

5. Consider the responses of Elihu.

    a. To whom, or what, did Elihu attribute Job's suffering?

    b. What was his concept of God, His judgement, and His mercy?

    c. What image did he hold of Him?

    d. What was his understanding of wisdom?

6. Consider Job's response to his suffering.

    a. Particularly, why did Job take his complaint to God, rather than remain silent?

    b. Compare Job's response to suffering to that of King David's (for example, Psalms 43 and 69).

    c. What was Job's hope? Did he hold to it?

    d. Did Job's response change through the course of events?

    e. Was God pleased with Job's response or aspects of it? How did you come to this conclusion?

7. What was revealed about man's character and of man's response to suffering?

8. Look at the comfort offered by Job's friends.

    a. Did Job's friends believe they were comforting him? Was that the intention of their words?

    b. Why was Job dissatisfied with his friends, and the comfort they offered him?

    c. How should they have responded?

    d. Consider the implications of the book's message in regards to comforting friends when they are suffering.

9. What implications can be drawn from Job's story in relation to suffering and hardships?

    a. How should such times be viewed?

    b. What should man's response be during them?

    c. Consider John 9 in relation to sin and illness. See also Acts 9:11-16 and James 5:10-11.

10. What do you learn of God through the book of Job?

    a. What did the book teach of God's character?

    b. Did God inflict Job with suffering?

    c. What was revealed of God's judgement and justice?

    d. What was shown of His sovereignty?

11. Consider what was said of wisdom.

    a. What was said of wisdom by each of the main characters? Were

they correct; if so, in which parts?
  b. What did God imply is wisdom?
  c. What other scriptural references discuss wisdom?
12. What was said of the fate of the righteous and the wicked?
  a. What assertions were correct based on God's answer and in the context of the rest of Scripture?
  b. Look at what Christ said on suffering.
  c. Look at what the New Testament says about suffering.
13. Consider God's rebuttal in the final chapters.
  a. How did God put Job back in his place?
  b. What did God reveal of His character, His ways, and His deeds?
  c. What was Job's response to God's correction?

Creative interpretation
  1. Track the characters: Job, his wife, his friends, and Elihu. For each main character, list their point of view on suffering, God, and wisdom.
  2. Give each of the following passages an appropriate title, which includes the speaker's name, and then summarise the content of each passage in one or two paragraphs:
    o 1:1-1:22
    o 2:1- 13
    o 3:1-26
    o 4:1-5:27
    o 6:1-30
    o 7:1-21
    o 8:1-22
    o 9:1-10:22
    o 11:1-20
    o 12:1-14:32
    o 15:1-35
    o 16:1-17:16
    o 18:1-21
    o 19:1-29
    o 20:1-29
    o 21:1- 34
    o 22:1-30
    o 23:1-24:25
    o 25:1-6
    o 26:1- 14
    o 27:1-23
    o 28:1-28
    o 29:1- 31:40
    o 32:1-22
    o 33:1-34:37
    o 35:1-16
    o 36:1-37:24
    o 38:1-38
    o 38:39-41:34
    o 42:1-6
    o 42:7-17

Application inspiration
Reflection on suffering
  • How do you respond to suffering?
  • How has the book of Job challenged your belief regarding the cause of suffering?
  • How will increased knowledge of God help bring perspective during times of suffering?
  • Describe the most severe time of testing that you have encountered as a

Christian. It need not be suffering because of your faith; suffering may also be emotional, financial, health-related etc.

- o During your time of testing, what was your attitude towards God? What did you learn about God's character during that time? What did you learn about your own character?
- o Briefly describe the advice or counsel that you received during your time of testing and say why it was either biblical or non-biblical advice. If it was biblical, was it also helpful and appropriate for you?
- o What advice or counsel would you give to someone who is going through a difficult situation? Would it be different from the counsel you received? Explain why or why not.

Wrestling with hard questions

- Are you at ease with the fact that God does not have to explain His actions or purposes to you?
- Are you content to walk in faithful obedience without always understanding His reasons?
- If one you love is terminally ill, or has a chronic injury, are you able to continue trusting God and declaring Him good, whilst observing their suffering?
- It is okay to wrestle with God and question God. Consider how you can do this with humility, as Job did, rather than in pride, like his friends.

[1] Job 32:6

PSALMS

The Lord, worthy of praise!

Blessed is the man who walks not in the counsel of the wicked, nor stands in the way of sinners, nor sits in the seat of scoffers; but his delight is in the law of the LORD, and on his law he meditates day and night. – Psalm 1:1-2

Studying the psalms

The book of Psalms needs to be studied differently from other books in the Bible as it is a collection of songs, rather than a book or letter written with a particular audience in mind. The study questions and information included below reflect this need for a different study approach.

Treat the psalms as a series of devotionals; for example, study one psalm a week, in addition to your usual Bible study. Meditate upon the chosen psalm over the course of the week.

During your first reading

Themes to track
- Character of God
- Character of man
- Worship
- Trust in the Lord – God is greater than man's problems
- The righteous and the wicked

During your second reading

Things to notice in the text
- Figures of speech; such as similes, metaphors, hyperbole, and personification.
- Emotion

- Historical events and landmarks (some of the psalms were written about specific events, such as battles, in the author's life or Israel's history).
- Author (if declared) and other information provided in the prefix to the psalm.

After your initial readings

Setting of Psalms
Author

The book of Psalms has numerous authors, including: Moses, King David, King Solomon, Asaph, the Sons of Korah, Heman the Ezrahite (a Son of Korah), and Ethan the Ezrahite. The main author associated with Psalms is King David, to whom are attributed over half of the psalms. The authorship of some psalms remains unknown.

Recipient

Some psalms were written for personal devotion, whilst others were penned for communal worship. The psalms were written during many generations of Israelites, so the audience depended on the author.

Date and place of writing

The Psalms are estimated to span a period of one thousand years. Psalm 90 is the oldest, having been written by Moses. Psalm 137 is the youngest, having been written during the time of exile in Babylon. The majority of the psalms were written in Jerusalem.

Reason written

The psalms were written for a number of reasons, including: as an individual's communication with God, to call the people to remembrance of a historical event, and to lead the people in worship.

Big picture
Historical background

As King David wrote more than half of the psalms, consider the *historical background* given for 1 & 2 Samuel. You may also wish to study the book of Samuel before starting study of Psalms.

Some psalms are written about specific historical events; for example, Psalm 52 informs its readers in the prefix that it was written *"when Doeg, the Edomite, came and told Saul, "David has come to the house of Ahimelech."* Why do you boast of evil, O mighty man? The steadfast love of God endures all the day." Such information enables you to explore further historical background. In the case of Psalm 52, further information can be gained from reading 1 Samuel 21 and 22.

Styles of the psalms

The psalms were written in different styles and with different focuses, including:

- Offering praise to God;
- Grieving an event before God;
- As a prayer;
- Confession of sin;
- Recording Israel's history;
- Writing of Jerusalem and the temple;
- Telling of battles that were lost;
- Crying out to God for justice against the wicked (imprecatory psalms);
- Messianic, proclaiming the Christ; or
- Offering wisdom from the author.

It is believed that the psalms were placed in their current order during the time of Ezra and Nehemiah, after the exiles returned to Judah. It became the hymn book of the Jews after exile.

Book overview

The psalms carry truths about God's character that are not seen elsewhere in the Bible. Like journal entries, they are intensely personal, revealing the emotions of their author. The authors related honestly to God, allowing the reader to catch a glimpse of their relationship with God.

Remember that they are a collection of poetry, which use many figurative illustrations to portray their message. They are dramatic and extreme, making use of hyperboles. The psalms communicate doctrine in a unique way through illustrations and emotion.

The psalms also reveal the sovereignty of the Lord and His accessibility to man. They demonstrate that God's ways are above man's understanding, whilst also offering hope, as they tell of how He acts on the behalf of the righteous.

Interpreting the book of Psalms
General interpretation questions

Take one psalm at a time and consider the following questions:

1. Does the psalm refer to an event in the author's life, or in Israel's history? Can you gain background information on this event from elsewhere in Scripture?
2. Look at the psalmists' emotions.
   a. What did the psalm mean to the author?
   b. With what emotion did the author commence the psalm?
   c. In what tone does he conclude the psalm?
   d. If there is a change in emotion during the course of the psalm, consider what may have caused it?
3. What does the psalm reveal about the character of God?
4. Is the psalm quoted in the New Testament? If so, how did the New Testament author interpret the psalm, or use it in his argument?
5. Did a theme stand out to you as you read the psalm (see the list of common

themes given below)? If so:
    a. What did the psalm convey about the theme?
    b. What other scriptures come to mind as you consider this theme?
    c. Look up the verse or passage and note it down. How does it relate to the psalm?
6. Summarise the overall message of the psalm.

Common themes to explore include:
- Worship
- Character of God
- God's nearness to man
- Relationship with God
- Trusting in the Lord
- Hope for the righteous
- Righteousness
- The righteous/ saints
- Oppressed, poor, and needy
- End of the wicked
- Character of David
- Israel

Historical psalms

Some of the psalms record or reflect on events in Israel's history. For these psalms, consider:
1. What event was being described?
2. Was the event mentioned elsewhere in Scripture? If so, where?
3. How does the psalm add to the telling of the event?
4. What would it have meant to the reader?
5. Why was it recorded? For example, the author might be calling the people of God to remember His deeds, which were performed on their behalf.

The Messianic Psalms

The following psalms contain predictions about Christ: Psalm 2, 8, 16, 22, 34, 40, 41, 45, 68, 69, 72, 89, 102, 109, 110, and 118. When studying these psalms, consider:
1. How did Christ fulfil what was written?
2. What does the psalm show of Christ's character?
3. What does prophecy convey about the intentionality of God's redemption plan for mankind?

Creative interpretation

1. Write a poem in the same style as the psalm, such as penitential, praise or remembrance.
2. Illustrate the psalm, depicting the overall theme, event, emotion or key

verses.

3. Characterise the author and their relationship with God based on the content in the psalm.

4. Ask the author a list of questions and answer in the voice of the author, such as:
   a. Where was he when he wrote the psalm?
   b. What trials was he facing?
   c. How did he feel towards God?

Application inspiration

- Psalms can teach you how to relate honestly with God.
  - What did the psalm mean to you?
  - What emotions do you need to bring before the Lord?
  - Pray through the psalm.
  - Meditate through the psalm.
- Write a letter to an unbeliever based on the principles of the psalm or reflecting what you learnt of God through the psalm. Make sure to write in love; do not preach. You do not have to send the letter – this exercise will help you attain a better understanding of the psalm's message.
- Model a journal entry on the psalm. For example, using Psalm 20:
  - Start with a prayer for the faith of a close friend;
  - Pronounce what you are trusting Christ to do for your friend, and the joy this will bring to you;
  - Praise God that He answers prayers and acts from heaven for His anointed ones;
  - Declare your faith and trust in the Lord.
- Give glory back to God for what He has done for you, in your church, and in the lives of those around you.

PROVERBS

Wisdom = Walking in the Fear of the Lord

The fear of the LORD is the beginning of wisdom, and the knowledge of the Holy One is insight. –
Proverbs 9:10

Studying Proverbs

The book of Proverbs needs to be studied differently from other books in the Bible. It is a collection of works, rather than a book or letter, written with a particular audience in mind. The study questions and information included below reflect this need for a different approach to study.

Chapters 1 through 9 introduce the book, as Solomon gives the purpose of the proverbs. The proverbs are contained in the remaining chapters (10-31). Do not take them as promises, but principles to live by for a godly life. They need to be read within their broader scriptural context.

During your first reading

Themes to track
Overlying theme:
- Wisdom = Fear of the Lord

Repeated themes in the Proverbs:
- Wise and foolish
- Righteousness and wickedness
- Money, loans, and debt
- Greed
- Laziness/ aimlessness
- Discipline

- Social injustice
- Violence
- Poor/ needy
- Righteous women
- Family
- Adultery
- Humility and pride
- The tongue/ speaking
- Drunkenness
- Leadership and rulers
- Life and death, health

During your second reading

Things to notice in the text
- Figures of speech, such as similes, metaphors, hyperbole, and personification.

The proverbs (chapters 10 through 31) do not follow a natural progression of thought. To make it easier to trace the themes, choose a different symbol or colour for each of the above themes and place a mark in the side column each time a proverb relates to a particular theme.

After your initial readings

Setting of Proverbs
Author
The book of Proverbs is structured around its authors. The following verses highlight the various authors:

1:1, 10:1, 25:1 – Solomon, who wrote most of them;
22:17, 24:23 – The Wise;
30:1 – Agur; and
31:1 – King Lemuel, who recorded the proverbs that his mother had taught to him.

Recipient
The text tells us that Solomon wrote his proverbs down for his son. Another possible audience may have been the Israelites living during the reign of King Hezekiah, as Hezekiah had his scribes copy the proverbs of Solomon.

Date and place of writing
King Solomon reigned from 971 to 930 BC, out of Jerusalem. King Hezekiah, who had his men copy the proverbs of Solomon, ruled between 715 and 687 BC.

Reason written

The purpose of the proverbs was to establish fear of the Lord in the hearts of the readers so that they might walk in righteousness, keeping their feet from sin.

Big picture

Historical background

The identities of The Wise, Agur, and King Lemuel remain unknown. Scholars believe that King Lemuel was not an Israelite. Events in the life of King Solomon can be read in 1 Kings 1-11 and 2 Chronicles 1-9. Key events in the reign of King Hezekiah are recorded in 2 Kings 16-21 and 2 Chronicles 29-32.

King Solomon

Solomon commenced his reign in love with the Lord, walking in obedience to God's commands (1 Kings 3:3). He understood that his father, King David, was blessed by God because he had walked before the Lord in faithfulness (1 Kings 3:6). In light of this, Solomon was humble before the Lord, proclaiming that he did not know how to be a good king. His request for wisdom came from his motivation to govern well (1 Kings 3:7-9), and God granted his request.

So was wisdom enough for Solomon? During his reign, the kingdom of Israel reached its peak in strength and riches. Their land spanned from Egypt to the Euphrates, in line with God's promise to Abraham. In 1 Kings 9, God appeared to Solomon a second time to give a warning, but it went unheeded. Two chapters later, in 1 Kings 11, God became angry with Solomon, whose heart had turned away from the Lord.

Solomon knew the laws of the Lord and yet he failed to live them out. His biggest weakness was for foreign women who led him into greater sin as he adopted their ways and their gods. The kingdom of Israel divided after his death, and never again experienced the wealth and prosperity it had known during his reign.

King Hezekiah

King Hezekiah did right according to the Lord as David had done. He removed the high places, pillars, and Asherim, which were places of worship to idols and false gods. He broke the bronze serpent of Moses, which had become an idol, and trusted in the Lord, holding to Him and His ways. As a result, the Lord prospered Him and went with him.

Sadly, even a king with the heart of David ended his days foolish and callous. At the end of his reign, Hezekiah became proud of all that God had given him and foolishly showed it off to envoys from Babylon. He became heartless. He did not care that his action sentenced the nation of Judah, and his own sons, to exile so long as there was peace and riches in his days, for him to enjoy.

Book overview

The proverbs address real questions of everyday life and give principles for achieving success. The proverbs are NOT LAW.

To transgress a proverb is not a sin, but they do strive to give principles that will prevent sin. For example: rather than commanding: *"Do not commit adultery"* (Exodus 20:14), the proverbs say: *"Let your fountain be blessed, and rejoice in the wife of your youth, a lovely deer, a graceful doe. Let her breasts fill you at all times with delight; be intoxicated always in her love. Why should you be intoxicated, my son, with a forbidden woman and embrace the bosom of an adulteress?"* (Proverbs 5:18-20).

The proverbs are a tool to prevent ungodliness by giving the consequences of righteous living compared with wickedness. For example, Proverbs 7:25-26: *"Let not your heart turn aside to her ways; do not stray into her paths, for many a victim has she laid low, and all her slain are a mighty throng."* The proverbs call people to walk in fear of the Lord and give principles for righteous living.

Interpreting the book of Proverbs
Guidelines to follow

1. Do not be deductive. Do not take a verse in isolation; consider it in the context of the book and the whole of Scripture.
2. Take them as principles, not promises. A promise is something that God has said will, or will not, happen. A principle is formed by man, based on what they have seen of God's character and ways.
3. Do not take the proverbs too literally. Seek to understand what the author is using the imagery to convey. For example, Proverbs 26:13 says: *"The sluggard says, "There is a lion in the road! There is a lion in the streets!""* Here, the author's intended message is that lazy people will make excuses to avoid work.
4. Remember culture. Consider the ways and customs in the time of King Solomon. This will help you to correctly interpret the meaning of the figures of speech.

Interpreting by theme

Since you marked the themes as you read the text, it should be easy to pick out which verses relate to an individual theme. For each theme, choose at least six verses or passages in Proverbs that relate to the theme, and a further two from scriptures outside of the Proverbs.

Considering the scriptures you have found:

1. What is the message given from each of the proverbs?
   a. What does it teach?
   b. Do any proverbs seem to contradict one another?
2. If imagery is used:
   a. What did it mean in the setting of its culture at the time of King Solomon?
   b. How does the imagery show the author's point?
3. What additional information do the scriptures from outside of Proverbs shed on the theme?
4. Give an overall theme summary.
5. Consider what truths can be taken from the passages that will remain true throughout all time. Application of these truths is looked at in *Application*

inspiration below.

An example

Theme chosen: adultery

Verses from Proverbs: 2:9-19; 5:3-6; 5:18-20; 6:23-35; 7:4-5; 22:14; 23:27; 30:20.

Scripture outside of Proverbs: Exodus 20:14; Matthew 5:27-28; Mark 7:20-23; John 8:3-11.

Figures of speech utilized:

- *House sinks down to death, none who go to her . . . regain the paths of life* (Proverbs 2:9-19):
    - Adultery leads one away from God. It is just the beginning. Once you step off the path of righteousness, you will sink down further and the end of sin is death.
    - Once abandoned to sin, one becomes numb to the call of the Holy Spirit.
- *Mouth drips with honey; end is bitter as wormwood* (Proverbs 5:3-6):
    - Wormwood is a species of plant of the genus Artemisia. The herbs and shrubs are usually bitter to taste and have strong aromas.
    - The imagery means that whilst her words might be temptingly sweet, one should be careful not fall for them. They are deceptive words. The first moments of adultery might seem sweet, but only pain and disillusionment await the guilty parties.
- *Can a man carry fire next to his chest and his clothes not be burned?* (Proverbs 6:23-35):
    - The end of adultery is sure. You cannot escape the cost of adultery.
- *She eats and wipes her mouth and says, "I have done no wrong."* (Proverbs 30:20):
    - Those lured into adultery will make excuses for their wrong doing. They will make excuses for you to follow their ways. Do not listen to words or emotions, but rely on the Word of God to lead you in righteousness.

Messages:

- *Proverbs 2:9-19:*
    - Adultery breaks the covenant of marriage, which is made as a covenant before God.
    - People who are lured into adultery are no less guilty than those who go willingly. Allowing yourself to be flattered and flirted with is the starting point of the spiral towards an affair.
- *Proverbs 5:18-20:*
    - Focus on your life partner.
    - It is a choice to be satisfied with your husband/ wife. Choose to

"remain in love". Choose to be intoxicated by them. Find their strengths and praise them.

- o No one satisfied in their marriage will commit adultery. If you have eyes only for your spouse, you will not stray.
- *Proverbs 6:23-35:*
  - o To get caught in the web of adultery is a sign of a lack of sense for it is known to end in ruin. Adultery is a sin, which will be punished.
- *Proverbs 30:20:*
  - o Do not rely on the words of man, for man does not recognise his own sin, saying: "I'm not so very bad", but rather dwell in the Law of the Lord.

Connections:

- Adultery is linked to walking counter to wisdom (Proverbs 2:9-19; 7:4-5).
- Those who seek after wisdom have it as a shield to protect them from the trap of adultery (Proverbs 7:4-5).
- Marriage is made as a covenant before God (Proverbs 2:9-19).
- Straying from the Lord is to walk towards sin. Turning away from God separates you from His Holy Spirit, leaving you vulnerable to traps, such as that of adultery (Proverbs 22:14; 23:27).

Additional scriptures:

- Do not commit adultery – it is against the Law (Exodus 20:14)!
- Adultery starts in the heart. A man does not just walk into an affair; it starts well before the act (Matthew 5:27-28; Mark 7:20-23).
- Christ forgave the woman caught in adultery. Those who turn to Christ with a repentant heart will be forgiven. He is the One able to forgive sins. He is the hope of sinners (John 8:3-11).

Theme Summary:

Adultery is a sin. It breaks the holy covenant of marriage; a covenant made with God. It begins in the heart, with a lustful look or a flattering word. Once one begins to step away from the Lord, their heart hardens to His discipline and turns from the wisdom of Scripture. Abandoning oneself to adultery is a sure way to fall away from God, which can only lead to death. The only way back is through the blood of Christ, who died for all sins. Protection against adultery and lust is found in the Word of God. Those who delight in His ways, soak in His Presence, and dwell on His Word will be kept safe from temptation.

Reading as devotionals

Many people enjoy reading a proverb a day in their quiet time with God.

1. First read through Proverbs 1-9 to gain the heart of the proverbs.
2. For each proverb, carefully consider the words. Think about their meaning.

Consider it in the light of the rest of Scripture; do not take an individual verse out of its wider context.

<u>Creative interpretation</u>

Many of the proverbs utilise figures of speech.

1. Consider the meaning in the context of the original readers' culture.
2. How was the author using the figure of speech to portray the message? – reflect on this.
3. Lastly, think of a figure of speech that would make sense in today's society, which parallels the author's intended message.

Application inspiration

- Wisdom is useless if it is applied. Consider your theme summary. What needs to change in your life in light of these truths?
- Are you walking in fear of the Lord? Ponder what it means to walk in fear of Him.
- After studying a theme in Proverbs:
    o What truths can be taken from the proverbs that are applicable today, tomorrow and always? Look back on the author's message and your theme summary.
    o What are the likely results of walking in this truth? How would you be affected if you did not walk in light of the biblical truth?
    o How would walking in the biblical truth make a difference to your life or bring transformation to the church? Consider your work environment, the government, your child's education, family life, and the church.

ECCLESIASTES

The Search for Life's Meaning

The end of the matter; all has been heard. Fear God and keep his commandments, for this is the whole duty of man. For God will bring every deed into judgment, with every secret thing, whether good or evil. – Ecclesiastes 12:13-14

During your first reading

Themes to track

- Vanity/ meaningless
- Living under God compared with not living under Him
- Wisdom and folly
- Labour/ toil

During your second reading

Things to notice in the text

- Repeated phrase: "Under the sun"
- Repeated word: "Meaningless"/ "vanity"
- Time elements
- Contrasts; for example, wisdom compared with folly
- Lists

Chapter summaries

These are optional as they can be time consuming for the larger books. If you choose to do them, you will receive a much deeper appreciation of the book. By the end of The IBSC, you will have paraphrased the entire Bible! Go through each chapter and try to summarise it in one paragraph, using your own words; force yourself to stay big picture and capture the heart of each chapter.

After your initial readings

Setting of Ecclesiastes
<u>Author</u>

Solomon is believed to have written Ecclesiastes 1:2-12:8, with an editor thought to have added Ecclesiastes 1:1 and 12:9-14 at a later date. This division has Solomon's writings starting and finishing on the words "vanity of vanities".

<u>Recipient</u>

Solomon wrote Ecclesiastes for himself, in order to reflect on life. However, the writings were probably released to the people of Israel after his reign ended, with the additions of the editor.

<u>Date and place of writing</u>

Solomon would have written his reflections towards the end of his life (around 930/1 BC) from within Jerusalem. The writings would have been released within a couple of hundred years of his death.

<u>Reason written</u>

Solomon was reflecting back over his life as it drew to its end, seeking to find meaning within it. He pondered the value of what he had pursued and where he had found pleasure, seeking to discover whether any of it had been of worth.

Big picture
<u>Historical background</u>

What does Kings shows us about Solomon's reign? (See 1 Kings 1-11 for further details)

1 Kings 5:1-9

Solomon made a marriage alliance with Pharaoh, king of Egypt, which was against the Law. He began his reign in love with the Lord and walking according to the statutes of his father, David. However, the people of Israel were already copying the religious practices of surrounding nations.

1 Kings 3:10-4:34, 6:14-7:51, 10:11-28

God granted Solomon both riches and honour. His reign as king was unparalleled in any of the surrounding nations. Israel dwelt in safety during his reign. Solomon built the house of the Lord, the temple. His income in one year alone was six hundred and sixty-six talents, which is estimated to fall within USD 2-4 hundred million; this excludes the further income he received from explorers, the business of merchants, kings of the west, and governors of the land.

1 Kings 12:25-14:20

Solomon's reign did not end well. He loved many foreign women and his heart did not remain true to the Lord. He turned to foreign gods and made sacrifices to them. Following his death, the kingdom of Israel divided, never to reunite.

Who were the original readers of Ecclesiastes?

Israel reached its political peak during the reign of Solomon. The people knew security, wealth, and prosperity. They knew that Solomon "had it all". After Solomon's reign, they lost everything. Their kingdom split into two, they went away from God, neighbouring nations began to take territory from their borders, and they went from receiving tithes from surrounding nations to giving tithes to greater world powers. They lost all they had under Solomon's reign. The Israelites would have been reflecting upon Israel's fall from the glory and power of Solomon's reign and wondering how this had happened.

Character portrayal – a disenchanted original reader
(Remember that the original readers lived in the few hundred years following Solomon's life).

King Solomon had it all! Uzzi reflected. Our fathers had it all under his reign! They knew peace, they knew what it was to have wealth, and they prospered. What do we have? War, trouble, a broken kingdom . . . and brother turns against brother. What was the point of it? King Solomon had everything and yet he declared it meaningless. If one such as he could not find meaning then what chance do I have of finding it? What is the point of living? What is the point of this life?

"Fear God and keep his commandments, for this is the whole duty of man . . ."[1] the words echoed through his mind.

Fear God. King Solomon had all wisdom, granted to him from God, and yet . . . and yet, did he fear the Lord? What a treacherous thought – to doubt the king – and still, it seemed to be a fair question. Perhaps that was the whole matter: fear God and obey His commands. Did the man who had it all get it all wrong? It seemed God counted obedience of more value than man's wisdom. Interesting! He needed to think on this further . . .

Book overview

In this book, remember that Solomon's perspective came from a man who did not believe in eternity and thus he saw all as vain because, by his reasoning, nothing he had done in his life had lasting value.

The type of writing in Ecclesiastes is known as pessimistic wisdom literature and most of what was written is wrong. Solomon had tried everything that the world saw as meaningful and declared that none of it mattered because none of it lasts. This was the core of his argument. He tried to find pleasure in earthly pursuits and materialism, but none of it satisfied his soul.

Solomon also saw life as vanity because he believed that the same fate fell upon the righteous as the wicked. He felt that this was unjust and thought that there was no point in living a godly life if there was no gain to be had in following God's laws. He was looking for material gain. He wanted to know that his work had meaning, but he did not see value in it because he believed all people would die and their works come to nothing.

True wisdom is given at the end of Ecclesiastes, from the editor: *"The end of the matter; all has been heard. Fear God and keep his commandments, for this is the whole duty of man. For God will bring every deed into judgement, with every secret thing, whether good or evil"*[2].

True wisdom is not found in knowledge. Rather, wisdom is found in fearing God and seeking knowledge of Him. The foundation of a meaningful life is found in God. The editor called his readers to live focused on God, walking in obedience to His commands.

Interpreting the book of Ecclesiastes

Remember that wisdom literature is an author's reflections; it contained principles to live by, not promises. When considering a principle offered by the author, be sure to compare it against the rest of Scripture to confirm the truth of it.

<u>Interpretation questions</u>

1. List what the author denoted as being meaningless. Go to the gospels and explore what Christ says has meaning.
    a. What is the significance of your two lists?
    b. What has meaning?
    c. What did Ecclesiastes depict as meaningful for man? Is this confirmed by what you see in the Gospels?
    d. What other references can you think of from Scripture that discuss man's purpose?
2. What was said of God?
    a. How did the author perceive Him?
    b. How does the author's view stand against the truth of Scripture?
    c. Did the author have an accurate or distorted view of God? Where was he correct and where was he at fault?
3. For each of the following topics, consider what was said by the author of Ecclesiastes, and by the rest of Scripture, and then form a list of true principles based on your findings:
    a. Meaningless/ purpose of life;
    b. Man's lot in life;
    c. Work and toil;
    d. Wisdom and folly;
    e. Living contrasted with the dead;
    f. Wealth and poverty;
    g. Judgement, justice, and oppression;
    h. Fairness and equality;
    i. Vows;
    j. Speech, words, and tongue;
    k. Wickedness versus righteousness;
    l. Joy and sorrow;
    m. Friendship.
4. Consider the commands for living and the worldly advice the author offered to his audience.
    a. What would be the outcome of following each command?
    b. Should one follow such advice?
    c. What scriptures support or dispute his counsel?

      d. Which of his commands were sound?

5. List the evils given to exist "under the sun".

      a. Consider them firstly from a worldly (temporal) perspective, and secondly from a kingdom (eternal) perspective.

      b. Was the author correct in his statements; why or why not?

6. Consider the conclusion of Ecclesiastes.

      a. What was the end of the argument?

      b. Look at two conclusions: Ecclesiastes 12:1-8, which is the proposed original ending, and Ecclesiastes 12:9-14, believed to have been added as a postscript.

      c. What advice was given to youth?

      d. Do you believe that the author would have lived differently in light of his observations; why or why not?

      e. For what reason do you believe the editor added his own thoughts to the ending?

Creative interpretation

1. Contrast key figures:

      a. First, consider Solomon's life perspective recorded in Ecclesiastes. Write a summary about what he sought pleasure in, where he found meaning, and what became his outlook on life. Here are some passages to get you started: Ecclesiastes 2:1; 2:24-26; 5:18-20; 8:15; 9:9.

      b. Secondly, look at the following passages relating to Paul's life perspective and complete a similar summary: 2 Timothy 4:6-8,18; Philippians 1:21; 2 Corinthians 5:6-10; 2 Corinthians 11:16-33; Romans 8:16-19; Romans 12:1-3; 1 Corinthians 2:6-10; Galatians 5:19-26.

      c. Most importantly, consider the attitude of Christ: Luke 2:49; John 3:4; John 5:30; John 6:35-40; John 12:27-28; Matthew 8:19-21; Luke 4:1-13.

      d. Contrast Paul and Solomon, and how they aligned with Christ.

          i. Who had it right?

         ii. What do you learn from the contrast?

        iii. What are the implications for living in the fear of God compared to the pleasures offered by the world?

        iv. Consider the implications for witnessing to non-believers.

2. Consider the commands of Christ, compared with the advice given in Ecclesiastes. Review the following passages as starting references for Christ's commands: Matthew 16:23-27; Mark 10:21; John 12:24-26; Matthew 5:3-7:27.

Application inspiration

Challenging questions to explore

- If you gained one billion dollars what would you do with it? Would life get

better?
- Why do bad things happen to good people? Why must godly men and women suffer through atrocities?
- How could a good God allow the suffering, which exists in the world?

Reflecting on the meaning of life
- Do you believe that life has meaning?
- Where does your society say that one finds meaning?
- Where does Scripture say that you should find meaning?
- From what are you currently seeking meaning?
- Does it matters how you live?
- Are you walking in the fear of the Lord and in obedience to His commandments?
- How can you walk out Christ's greatest commands: to love the Lord and to love your neighbour as yourself?
- How can you keep an eternal perspective?
- Reflect on Paul's words in 2 Timothy 4:6-8,18.

[1] Ecclesiastes 12:13
[2] Ecclesiastes 12:13

SONG OF SONGS

Love between Man and Woman

I am my beloved's and my beloved is mine; he grazes among the lilies. – Song of Songs 6:3

During your first reading

Themes to track
- Faithfulness
- Physical beauty
- Awakening the heart

During your second reading

Things to notice in the text
- Pronouns: him, they, your, I, my, he, mine, we, who, you.
- Figures of speech: comparisons (more than, better than), similes (like, as), metaphors/ analogies (comparisons that do not use "like" or "as").
- Emotion
- Contrast between the Beloved's relationship and Solomon's marriages.

Chapter summaries

These are optional as they can be time consuming for the larger books. If you choose to do them, you will receive a much deeper appreciation of the book. By the end of The IBSC, you will have paraphrased the entire Bible! Go through each chapter and try to summarise it in one paragraph, using your own words; force yourself to stay big picture and capture the heart of each chapter.

After your initial readings

Setting of Song of Songs

Author

The author is unknown, but the comparisons made with Solomon indicate an author from amongst his subjects.

Recipient

The book was written to the people of God, during the reign of Solomon.

Date and place of writing

Song of Songs was written during the reign of Solomon, when he had sixty wives, dating it between 970 and 931 BC. It was most likely written from within Jerusalem.

Reason written

Song of Songs is a collection of poetry between a real man and a real woman, extolling their love for one another. It shows that love, as God designed it to be, is worth seeking and protecting. It is worth waiting for this love. It also condemned the model set by Solomon, saying what he had was not love and did not bring satisfaction.

Big picture

Historical background

Some historians argue that Song of Songs is an allegory between man and God. However, this does not fit with the culture of the time. The original readers never would have understood such an allegory between themselves and God.

The Old Testament laws must also be taken into consideration, where anything to do with sexual acts was to be well away from the temple. These laws were given because sexual religious practices were common amongst the surrounding nations. Temple prostitution was common practice amongst Israel's neighbours; the belief was that the temple prostitute momentarily took on the persona of the god during sexual intercourse and was therefore able to manipulate the actions of that god. God would have none of this from His holy people. God wanted it clearly communicated that: "sex is good, but it belongs in marriage, not in relationship with Me".

Literature type – love poems

Good love poetry uses in-depth descriptions. It uses emotional language, rather than plain descriptions of reality, so do not take all the illustrations literally; they are imagery and need to be looked at as such. Remember not to interpret the metaphors and similes according to today's understanding. Make sense of it according to their culture. In their society, these images were indicative of beauty.

Character portrayal – the Beloved; a modern paraphrase of her thoughts

I am not a classic beauty, but I have allure to my Beloved. My skin is not flawless, I am frumpy and my hair lacks shine. I did not attend a finishing school and I had no sisters to teach me the crafts of make-up. Wonderfully, these things are of little value to my Beloved. He calls to me and I am drawn to him. He delights in my looks and my body, and I delight in his. He is the one that my soul loves.

I waited patiently for him in my youth and now my reward is the sweetness of our love. It is made still more verdant by the purity which we shared as we waited. In the fullness of God's timing, He has given me the gift of a loving husband in whom my body, soul, and mind delight. My husband is my lover, he is my best friend, and he is the one I long to run home to each evening. I dream about him; my body longs for him when he is away; his image is ever before my eyes. Oh, how sweet the love is between my Beloved and me!

Book overview

Faithfulness is a must in marriage and is depicted in Song of Songs. When a nightmare took hold of the Beloved that she cannot find her Lover, she went seeking for him and, upon finding him, clung to him. She sealed her love of him with marriage. She compares her relationship to that of Solomon's, who had seven hundred wives and three hundred concubines. She declared that it was better to be the delight of one man than to have thousands of men, but only know of lust. Being faithful brings the blessing of love.

Faithfulness starts before marriage, by protecting oneself against stirring up love before it awakens. As a wall, or as a door, Song of Songs conveys the need for singles to protect themselves in the season in which God has them. It is a choice, and something that needs to be continuously protected and worked on, even during marriage. True love is affirming, focuses on the positives, and is passionate.

Song of Songs looks back at Genesis 1 and 2 and shows how it should have been between man and woman; it shows how it still can be. God does not place a divide between secular and sacred. This was seen in the laws in Leviticus and is shown again in Song of Songs. God cares about all areas of life.

So often, the church can become focused on the bad news. Youth groups often drill home the message of purity before marriage without conveying the benefits of remaining pure. What Song of Songs shows is the beautiful awakening of passion that comes in the marriage that God desires for man and woman. God wants to give His people something good, and the book shows that following His heart for relationships results in something that is beautiful. His way of giving the message to remain pure is so different from what is often given in the church.

Interpreting the book of Song of Songs
Interpretation questions
1. What do you learn about the following areas of marriage through Song of Songs:
   a. Marriage should be a safe place;
   b. Exclusivity in marriage (Three starting places include: Song of Songs 2:16; referring to the repeated words "my beloved" and "mine", and considering 1 Corinthians 7:3-4);
   c. The place for physicality;
   d. Passion, adoration, and love;
   e. Friendship;
   f. Affirming your spouse / language you use with your spouse;

g. Protecting your marriage/ relationship with your spouse;

h. Mutuality and giving in marriage.

2. What does Song of Songs teach about the following:
    a. Supporting others in their relationships;
    b. Offering wisdom to others from a godly marriage;
    c. Including others in your relationship/ sharing love with others;
    d. Seeking advice;
    e. Waiting for marriage;
    f. Raising children in purity.

3. Compare what you know of Solomon from Kings and Chronicles with what is said of him in Song of Songs.
    a. What comparison was the author bringing?
    b. Why was the author critical of Solomon?
    c. Why did she claim that what she had was better than what he had?

4. How does what you see and read in Song of Songs compare with that of 1 Corinthians 7?
    a. How do these passages build upon one another?
    b. How do they support each other?

Creative interpretation

1. What does Song of Songs teach about faithfulness? What practical strategies does it give to support faithfulness in marriage?

2. Describe how Song of Songs gives young men and women encouragement to wait for sex and physicality until they are within the blessing of marriage.

Application inspiration

To the married

- How can you affirm your spouse in words and in action today? Write a list for the next week, with one item per day that you can do to affirm and love your spouse.

- Have you seen the movie "Fireproof"? Perhaps you may wish to watch it on your own and think through some of the strategies it offers. Perhaps you can watch it as a couple and reaffirm your love for one another at the end of it.

To the single

- Song of Songs gives a beautiful image of the gift of love in marriage. Wait for the best. You can work towards a marriage that is affirming and selfless.

- One way of learning selflessness now is with how you relate to others. Wait for your spouse to come to you and in the meantime practice selfless love in your friendships.

In friendship and discipleship

- A common world view is that individuals are responsible for their own purity, but in Song of Songs 8:9 a different picture is drawn. The Others were asking how they could help their young sister remain pure. How can you help your friends, brothers, and sisters remain pure, both in relationships and before relationships?

ISAIAH

Salvation through the Suffering Servant

You will say in that day: "I will give thanks to you, O LORD, for though you were angry with me, your anger turned away, that you might comfort me. "Behold, God is my salvation; I will trust, and will not be afraid; for the LORD GOD is my strength and my song, and he has become my salvation." – Isaiah 12:1-2

During your first reading

Themes to track
- Salvation
- Trust versus unbelief
- Pride and humility
- Sin/ judgement/ restoration
- Social injustice
- Messianic visions, foretelling the Christ

During your second reading

Things to notice in the text
- Track the themes
- Repeated phrase: "In that day"
- Selfless Servant (Jesus) revealed
- God's heart for the nations
- Character and words of God
- Isaiah's character

Mark re-occurring ideas and images (motifs)
- Righteousness

- Salvation
- The Holy One
- Zion
- Remnant (stump, holy seed, branch, shoot)
- Vineyard
- Wounds and healing
- Highways
- Hand stretched out
- Trees
- Banners
- Deserts
- Gardens
- Fertile fields
- Children

Chapter summaries

These are optional as they can be time consuming for the larger books. If you choose to do them, you will receive a much deeper appreciation of the book. By the end of The IBSC, you will have paraphrased the entire Bible! Go through each chapter and try to summarise it in one paragraph, using your own words; force yourself to stay big picture and capture the heart of each chapter.

After your initial readings

Setting of Isaiah
Author

Some commentators believe that this book was written by multiple authors; however, the text proclaims Isaiah as the author and the New Testament supports this claim. Furthermore, the theme of idolatry in chapters 40-66 would not be as applicable after Isaiah's time, as the returned Jews did not struggle with idolatry after the exile.

Date prophecies were spoken

Isaiah prophesied from 740 BC until at least 701 BC, a forty year period.

Recipient – hearers

The prophecies were spoken to the nation of Judah.

Recipient – readers

There were two groups of intended readers. Chapters 1-39 were written to those in Judah before 701 BC, as a call to repentance. From chapter 40-66, Isaiah was writing to give those in exile a hope to cling to, calling them to trust in God's promised salvation.

Date and place of writing

The prophecies were recorded during a period from 740 BC until 689 BC from within the nation of Judah. Jewish tradition holds that Isaiah died during the reign of Manasseh, which spanned the years from 687/6 to 642/1 BC.

Reason spoken

The people of Judah were walking in idolatry and God was showing them that He is the One True God. Isaiah was calling the people back to God and showing them that His coming judgement upon them was just.

Reason written

Chapters 1-39 were written to show the people that the judgement coming upon them was a result of their disobedience, in a hope that they would repent. From chapter 40-66, Isaiah was writing to give those later to be in exile a hope to cling to, calling them to trust in God's promised salvation, and to those who later returned from exile and would need strength during the rebuilding of their nation.

Big picture
Historical background

The book spans three significant periods of history. The first of these covers chapters 1-39 of the text and falls during Isaiah's lifetime, from 739 BC to 701 BC. The second and third periods were long after Isaiah's death. The second period was that of Judah's exile, from 605 BC to 539 BC, covered in chapters 40 to 55, and the third period was that of the return from exile, covered in chapters 56 to 66. The return from exile occurred from 539 to 400 BC, but Isaiah only covers events falling between 539 and 500 BC.

Isaiah lived through at least four monarchs as listed in Isaiah 1:1 *". . . in the days of Uzziah, Jotham, Ahaz, and Hezekiah, kings of Judah"*. Jewish mythology holds that Isaiah met his end by being sawn in half by Manasseh and that Hebrews 11:37 gives reference to this event. Although admired by believers today, Isaiah was not appreciated by the people of God during his lifetime. The prophet Micah was a contemporary of Isaiah.

Judah during the first period; Isaiah's lifetime

Overall, Uzziah was depicted as a faithful king and, as such, during his reign Judah was less affected by apostasy. Apart from Uzziah's one attempt to act as high priest (2 Chronicles 26:16-21), for which he was punished by leprosy for the rest of his life, he was faithful to God.

Judah enjoyed a period of recovery under the reigns of Uzziah (792-740 BC) and Jotham (740/39-732/1 BC), who were roughly contemporary with the reign of Jeroboam II in the northern kingdom. This restoration that Judah experienced was primarily a flow-on effect of the renewal of their northern brethren, during the reign of Jeroboam II.

The nation's revival came to an end after Tiglath-Pileser III rose to power in Assyria. This occurred in 745 BC. In 722 BC, Judah watched as Israel fell to Assyria and their northern brethren were dispersed throughout the Assyrian Empire.

During this time frame, the Judeans also had to compete with Damascus, a less powerful opponent than the Assyrians, but closer geographically. This nation, at the hands of King Rezin, fell to Assyria just before Israel in 732 BC.

Judah during the second period; Judah's exile

Refer to the *historical background* given for the books of Jeremiah, Ezekiel, and Daniel.

Judah during the third period; return from exile

Refer to the *historical background* given for the books of Daniel, Haggai, Zechariah, Malachi, Nehemiah, and Ezra.

Character portrayal – original hearers in exile

Unwinding the newly recovered scroll, Chaim stood up in the public square and began to read from the word of Isaiah:

"Ah, Ariel, Ariel, the city where David encamped! Add year to year; let the feasts run their round. Yet I will distress Ariel, and there shall be moaning and lamentation, and she shall be to me like an Ariel. And I will encamp against you all around, and will besiege you with towers and I will raise siegeworks against you. And you will be brought low; from the earth you shall speak, and from the dust your speech will be bowed down; your voice shall come from the ground like the voice of a ghost, and from the dust your speech shall whisper." [1]

As he progressed, a crowd began to gather around him.

"But the multitude of your foreign foes shall be like small dust, and the multitude of the ruthless like passing chaff. And in an instant, suddenly, you will be visited by the LORD of hosts with thunder and with earthquake and great noise, with whirlwind and tempest, and the flame of a devouring fire . . ." [2]

A chill ran through the people who stood listening. These words! The people marvelled at them. They described all that had happened to them and to the surrounding nations. God had been faithful. They were in exile because of their disobedience, not because God was not strong enough to defeat the Babylonian gods.

Heaviness seeped into their hearts as they weighed their guilt and sins. They were slaves in Babylon because they deserved to be. There was no hope left for them. Why would the reader not cease? The crowd was held still as if under an enchantment. Why did he continue to pour out his words of conviction against them? The implications were ripening in their minds.

The public speaker of the scroll also desired to end the stream of words. His own heart was repulsed by the actions they, as a people, had committed against God. He was weighed down by their unfaithfulness. And yet, he was compelled to go on. He could not stop. They were in exile, but he needed to know more about this awesome and fierce God of their fathers. Who was He? Why had they strayed from His Law?

And then the mood shifted with the words, which now seemed sweet, promising refreshment. They were more delightful than honey, more satisfying than a drink from a cool stream. The words of promise flowed into their hearts brining hope for restoration.

"*. . . But now thus says the LORD, he who created you, O Jacob, he who formed you, O Israel: "Fear not, for I have redeemed you; I have called you by name, you are mine.*

'When you pass through the waters, I will be with you; and through the rivers, they shall not overwhelm you; when you walk through fire you shall not be burned, and the flame shall not consume you. For I am the LORD your God, the Holy One of Israel, your Savior. I give Egypt as your ransom, Cush and Seba in exchange for you. Because you are precious in my eyes, and honored, and I love you, I give men in return for you, peoples in exchange for your life.

'Fear not, for I am with you; I will bring your offspring from the east, and from the west I will gather you. I will say to the north, Give up, and to the south, Do not withhold; bring my sons from afar and my daughters from the end of the earth, everyone who is called by my name, whom I created for my glory, whom I formed and made . . ." [3]

They were not deserving of such great love and mercy. They deserved His wrath. Despite this, here He was promising them a future and a hope. Oh, what a God they served!

Book overview

The book of Isaiah has a distinct transition from judgement to restoration, which occurs at the end of chapter 39.

Isaiah commenced by bringing the original readers through chapter after chapter of God's anger. God's wrath was shown to be fierce, all consuming, terrifying, and ferocious. The author intended to weigh his audience down by the judgement coming upon them. Perhaps, if he sobered them enough, they would repent and God would stay His hand from these tragedies.

In these chapters, God likened Himself to a vineyard owner. He tends to man the way a vine dresser tends to his crops. He protected His people from pestilence (illness, famine, and pain) and from the outside animals (influence of the world). He gave them water and nutrients (His Word, priests, and prophets) to enable growth. From this He expected fruit and the original hearers, those in Judah, were not producing fruit. They were evil and had left the ways of God to worship dead idols. Isaiah proclaimed that God's wrath was coming upon Judah and the nations because of man's pride, idolatry, and social injustice.

The people were warned that if, at the end of these "seven years" (the average time it takes for a new vineyard to begin producing), no crop had been produced (they had not accepted Him as their God and King), then He would judge them unworthy, unrighteous, and clear the land with death and destruction. His wrath is mighty and ferocious. It is a thing of terror beyond description. Those who do not chose God will be thrown into the wine press of His wrath. And He is not afraid of getting dirty in the press – blood will splatter!

Do not lose hope. Good news remains. The book did not end proclaiming His anger and wrath. The good news was saved for last. In contrast to the image of a vengeful, just, wrathful, and almighty God, who conquers and destroys His enemies, was given the picture of God's compassion, love, nurturing heart, desire to heal, and tenderness. He is a God who abundantly blesses those who receive His salvation. He promises redemption for those who accept Him. The book gives a picture of the

Suffering Servant, the Christ, who came to be mankind's Saviour and Redeemer.

This is the Christ, prophesied: *"The Spirit of the Lord GOD is upon me, because the LORD has anointed me to bring good news to the poor; he has sent me to bind up the brokenhearted, to proclaim liberty to the captives, and the opening of the prison to those who are bound; to proclaim the year of the LORD's favor, and the day of vengeance of our God; to comfort all who mourn; to grant to those who mourn in Zion-- to give them a beautiful headdress instead of ashes, the oil of gladness instead of mourning, the garment of praise instead of a faint spirit; that they may be called oaks of righteousness, the planting of the LORD, that he may be glorified."* [4]

The book shows God's character and that He is different from man. He is the only God. He is the True God. He is active in the world and will save those who cry out to Him. Man expected a warrior king coming in the physical realm to establish a kingdom on earth. In Isaiah, God revealed His plan to send a suffering servant, His Son, who was persecuted, abused, falsely accused, and died for the sins of man. Jesus was mocked for carrying man's transgressions. What other god, idol or man would so humble himself?

His kingdom is also revealed, which will reflect His attributes. It shall be a kingdom of righteousness, peace, prosperity, joy, safety and comfort. There shall be no wars, no evil, and no fear. He will bring the end of grief, mourning, and pain. He will restore all things. He is the Giver of Life.

Interpreting the book of Isaiah
Interpretation questions
1. Look into God's character. Seek, pursue, and hold on to God as you study this book!
    a. How is God unique? How is He separate from idols and false gods?
    b. What do you see of His character and authority? What aspects of His nature are revealed?
    c. Look at why He was angry with the people. How does He describe their sin? What feelings did He display towards their sins?
    d. Why did Isaiah use so many names to describe God?
    e. Look at "I am . . ." proclamations of God. Look at the repeated idea of "for my sake". What was God's intention in giving these pronouncements? What was He trying to convey to His audience?
2. The people of Judah struggled with idolatry. Consider:
    a. Why was idolatry condemned?
    b. Why is it an abomination to God?
    c. What did Isaiah show of the worthlessness of idols?
3. Chapters 13-24 denote the judgement coming upon the nations – both individual nations and the world. Note why each nation was being judged.
    a. What were they doing?
    b. Why was He judging them?
    c. How were they to be judged?
4. Look at the use of imagery in Isaiah. Look at the motifs that you marked as you read. For each, consider:

    a. What did the image represent?

    b. What was its meaning?

    c. Did the image progress?

    d. How was it developed? How was it built upon throughout the book?

5. You marked the repeated phrase: "In that day", which represented promise (salvation) oracles. Looking at these, answer:

    a. How did His restoration come?

    b. What comfort would these promises have offered to the readers who were in exile?

6. Consider the implications of the following connections between the Old Testament and New Testament. Consider when and how the prophecies were fulfilled. Wrestle with any questions they might raise in your heart.

    a. Isaiah 53:9 - Matthew 27:57-60;

    b. Isaiah 19:16-25 – Ephesians 2:13-14, 19;

    c. Isaiah 28:14-29 – Romans 9:32-33;

    d. Isaiah 32:9-20 – Galatians 5:22-23;

    e. Isaiah 34:15-17 – Revelation 20:12, Luke 1:32-33;

    f. Isaiah 35:8-10 – Revelation 21:27;

    g. Isaiah 62 – Revelation 21:3;

    h. Isaiah 63:10-64:7 – Matthew 12:32;

    i. Isaiah 65:1-16 – Revelation 3:5, Revelation 20:15.

7. Look at the following passages, and where they were quoted in the New Testament. You will notice that the majority fall in the second half of Isaiah. Ask why they were quoted in the New Testament? What was the prophecy's fulfilment?

    a. Isaiah 6:8-13 – Matthew 13:13-14;

    b. Isaiah 7:10-17 – Matthew 1:23;

    c. Isaiah 8:11-15 – 1 Peter 2:4-8;

    d. Isaiah 29:15-24 – Matthew 5:1-11;

    e. Isaiah 40:3 – Matthew 3:3, Mark 1:3, Luke 3:4-6, John 1:2;

    f. Isaiah 40:3-5 – 1 Peter 1:24-25, James 1:1;

    g. Isaiah 40:13 – Romans 11:34;

    h. Isaiah 52:15 – Romans 15:21;

    i. Isaiah 53:1 – John 12:38; Romans 10:16;

    j. Isaiah 53:4 – Matthew 8:17;

    k. Isaiah 54:1 – Galatians 4:27;

    l. Isaiah 54:13 – John 6:45;

    m. Isaiah 55:3 – Acts 13:34;

    n. Isaiah 52:53:7-8 – 1 Peter 2:23, Acts 8:32;

    o. Isaiah 53:9 – 1 Peter 2:22;

    p. Isaiah 53:11-12 – Romans 5:18-19;

    q. Isaiah 45:23 – Romans 14:11;

    r. Isaiah 52:11-12 – Romans 2:24;

    s. Isaiah 52:11-12 – 2 Corinthians 6:17;

     t.   Isaiah 56:1-8 – Matthew 21:13, Mark 11:17, Luke 19:46;
     u.   Isaiah 54:13 – Romans 3:15-17;
     v.   Isaiah 59:20-21 – Romans 11:26;
     w.   Isaiah 61:1-4 – Luke 4:18-19.

8. Imagine the readers in exile in Babylon. How would the following passages have given them hope and encouragement? Isaiah 40:1-2; 40:11; 40:28-30; 41:9-10; 43:1-4; 46:3-4; 49:13; 51:11.

9. In chapters 40-48, compare the greatness of God to the vanity of idols.

10. In chapters 49-57, focus on what is said of God's salvation through the Suffering Servant.

11. What do chapters 58-66 reveal of the glory of God and the future Kingdom of God?

Creative interpretation

1. Look at the image God gave displaying Himself as the Vine Dresser and Israel as the vineyard.
    a.   What were His hopes and desires for the vineyard?
    b.   How did He act as the Vine Dresser?
    c.   How were His people displayed in this image?

2. Focus on the division in this book.
    a.   Hear God's pain, frustration, and judgement throughout chapters 1-39. Experience the wrath of God being directed at His people and the sheer lack of hope. Consider how this would have impacted on their hearts and the emotions of those who were reading this book in exile, after the prophecies had been fulfilled.
    b.   Then turn to chapters 40-66 and hear the good news of salvation! How would this have affected the people in exile?

Ongoing prophets' project

Start a separate document from your Isaiah notes that you can add to as you study the books of the prophets. Note down what you learn about the "day of the Lord" versus the "great day of the Lord" from Isaiah. Keep adding to this document as you work through the prophets.

Application inspiration

This book should stir a deep desire to worship God and know Him more. You may have felt depressed through the first thirty-nine chapters, but even these reveal the power of the Almighty God, His justice, and His wrath. It shows His passion for justice and the protection of the weak. It shows how highly His name is to be valued and that He is deserving of all the glory!

- Allow this book to stir emotional responses in you as you read.
- Did you feel overwhelmed at the greatness of God?
- Where do you go when things get difficult?
  - Do you truly put your trust in God before anything else? Or are

you known to run to movies, friends, yourself, books, logic, food or money?

- o In what order do you turn to God compared to these other comforters?
- o Isaiah reveals that you can put your trust in God, and that in Him alone should you place it. Ask Him to help you trust Him.

- Accept His grace, peace, love, salvation, restoration, redemption, saving grace, and tender mercies.
- Let application come from your spirit: gratitude, awe, fear, delight, hope, joy, peace, comfort, delight in God, pursuit of Him, hope in Him, delight in Him, adore Him, and/or desire Him.
- Isaiah uses so many names to try and describe God and label His attributes. Listen to the "That's My King" sermon by the late Dr. S.M. Lockeridge. Multiple audio copies can be found on the internet, such as on YouTube. Ponder the names of God that are used in an attempt to comprehend and describe Him.

[1] Isaiah 29:1-4
[2] Isaiah 29:5-6
[3] Isaiah 43:1-7
[4] Isaiah 61:1-4

JEREMIAH

Judgement falls on Judah

"Then fear not, O Jacob my servant, declares the LORD, nor be dismayed, O Israel; for behold, I will save you from far away, and your offspring from the land of their captivity. Jacob shall return and have quiet and ease, and none shall make him afraid. For I am with you to save you, declares the LORD; I will make a full end of all the nations among whom I scattered you, but of you I will not make a full end. I will discipline you in just measure, and I will by no means leave you unpunished." – Jeremiah 30:10-11

During your first reading

Themes to track
- Sovereign Lord/ King of the nations
- Unfaithfulness of the people
- (Broken) covenant/ hearts
- Jeremiah and his ministry
- Opposition in ministry

During your second reading

Things to notice in the text
- The book of Jeremiah is <u>not</u> chronological!
- Highlight the repeated words "adultery", "faithless", "prostitute", "whore".
- Highlight the repeated words "idolatrous", "idol", "idolatry".
- Mark themes in the column beside the text as you read. For example: a yellow line to mark the names of God and His actions, a purple line to mark passages revealing Jeremiah's character, a red line to highlight opposition in ministry, and an orange line to signal text relating to the covenant.

Chapter summaries

These are optional as they can be time consuming for the larger books. If you choose to do them, you will receive a much deeper appreciation of the book. By the end of The IBSC, you will have paraphrased the entire Bible! Go through each chapter and try to summarise it in one paragraph, using your own words; force yourself to stay big picture and capture the heart of each chapter.

After your initial readings

Setting of Jeremiah
Author

Authorship is credited to Jeremiah although his scribe, Baruch, probably did most of the writing.

Date prophecies were spoken

The prophecies were spoken over a sixty year period commencing in the thirteenth year of Josiah's reign and continuing until Jehoiachin's release from prison; from 627 BC until 561 BC.

Recipient – hearers

The prophecies were spoken to the people of Judah over three time periods: before, during, and after the exile.

Recipient – readers

The original readers also spanned over three time periods: the people of Judah before, during, and after the exile.

Date and place of writing

Jeremiah penned his account over a sixty year period, which commenced in the thirteenth year of Josiah's reign and continued until Jehoiachin's release from prison; from 627 BC until 561 BC. The book of Jeremiah was mostly written in Judah; although, some sections may have been written in Egypt.

Reason spoken

God was telling His people very clearly that they were going into exile for choosing foolish and worthless idols rather than the true God, their Creator. He left no doubt in their minds that they were sent into exile because they "played the whore" against Him with idols.

Reason written

The book was written so that they would know why they were sent into exile, yet also to give hope to those who returned to Him. God saw His people as rebellious whores, and they were being judged for their sins against Him. His heart was for them, He loved them, but they were to be judged and sent into exile for their unfaithfulness. The book shows that it was the people that broke their covenant with God, and He was just in His judgement of them.

Big picture
Historical background

Jeremiah was called to be a prophet in the thirteenth year of King Josiah's reign (614 BC). He prophesied during the reigns of King Josiah (627-609 BC), King Jehoahaz/ Shallum (609 BC), King Jehoiakim (608-597 BC), King Jehoiachin/ Jeconiah/ Coniah (597 BC), and King Zedekiah (597-586 BC). This totals sixty-six years of public ministry, faithfully serving God, which commenced when he was about twenty years old!

Jeremiah saw little fruit from his ministry, and lived through the fall of Jerusalem at the hands of the Babylonians. The people believed that God would not let His temple be destroyed. The tabernacle was the symbol of God's Presence with His people, so when Jeremiah said that *everything* would be destroyed, they did not listen to him.

The Babylonians did not scatter captives throughout their empire (to break up national identities), as the Assyrians had done before them. As a result, the exiles of Judah were settled in one, concentrated area. The Babylonians tried to make the Judeans part of their nation, being willing to educate them and assimilate them into their culture.

Take note of the history recorded in the book of Jeremiah, particularly the events of the fall of Jerusalem.

Character portrayal – Jeremiah asking God: "why?"

"Why do these people not listen? God, you have given them warning after warning. You have given them a Law to guide them, and a covenant promising blessings for obedience, and yet they turn away from you.

"Wickedness surrounds me, and yet you do nothing. Why, God? How long must I watch the righteous suffer? You promise destruction of the wicked, and yet they prosper. They mock me for my words. They imprison me for speaking your message. But what has changed, O Lord? Change their hearts, change their ways, or bring destruction upon them. Only do not, O Lord, remain silent and unmoving."

Book overview

God took the breaking of His covenant very seriously. He does not abide disobedience. In Jeremiah, He showed that it is a choice to obey His commands. The people of Judah chose not to obey and so were being judged for their disobedience. God listed examples of their sins, particularly breaking the covenant, but also failing to show hospitality, murdering, and living in the ways of violence. His wrath came upon them as a result of their sin.

His judgement came, leaving their city in ruins and the people being carried into exile. His curses came because they walked in disobedience (Deuteronomy 28). His people continued not to obey His voice over and over again and as a result the remnant who ran to Egypt were also judged. God requires faithfulness and obedience from His people.

God showed clearly that he is the King of nations; He is the world power; He is sovereign.

Interpreting the book of Jeremiah
Interpretation questions

1. Refer back to your colour-coded themes in the columns of your Bible. Consider the character of God.
    a. What do you see of the sovereignty of God?
    b. How did He depict Himself?
    c. How did He show Himself to be the King of kings?
2. Again referring back to your colour-coded themes in the columns of your Bible, consider the character of Jeremiah.
    a. What do you learn of Jeremiah?
    b. How did he relate to God and the people?
    c. How had he hoped the people of Judah would respond?
    d. How would he have felt as he watched the unfolding of the events he had prophesied would come?
    e. Look at Jeremiah's confessions in the following passages: 11:18-23; 12:1-6; 15:10-11,15-21; 17:14-18; 18:18-23; 20:7-18.
3. Consider the opposition Jeremiah faced, using your colour-coded themes in the columns of your Bible.
    a. How did Jeremiah respond during times of opposition in ministry?
    b. Who was opposing him and what were their reasons?
    c. How did God encourage him to continue?
    d. Notice the repeat in Jeremiah 15:19-21 of God's promise to him in chapter 1. Why might Jeremiah have needed to hear this again? What does this show of God? How would this have been a support and comfort to Jeremiah in his ministry?
    e. What do you learn of how God defines success in ministry?
4. Using the colour-coded themes in the columns of your Bible, consider the covenant:
    a. What do you see of how God upholds the covenant?
    b. How do the passages on a broken covenant display the people's guilt?
    c. What promises did God give regarding the covenant (blessings, curses, promises of a new covenant)?
5. You marked the repeated words "adultery", "faithless", "prostitute", and "whore".
    a. Who were these words describing?
    b. Why was God using such graphic language?
    c. How did this relate to the Ten Commandments?
6. The repeated words "idolatrous", "idol", and "idolatry" are also seen throughout the book of Jeremiah.

      a. Why was this close to God's heart?

      b. What turned the people to idolatry?

      c. Why did they continue in it? Why was it a worthless practice?

7. Jeremiah is a book of emotion!

      a. Consider the author's emotion.

      b. How would the original readers have been feeling as they read this book? Remember that there are three groups of readers: before, during, and after exile.

8. What was the attitude of the people of Judah?

      a. See Jeremiah 2; 5:12; 5:23-28; 6:10-11; 7:9-11; 8:5-12.

      b. What charges were brought against the people by God? Look closely at chapter 2.

9. What was said of the priests/ leaders of Judah? See Jeremiah 2:8; 5:4-5; 5:30-31; 6:13-15; 8:10-12; 14:13-18; 20:1-6; 23:1-2; 23:9-40; 28; 29:24-32; 36.

10. Look at Jeremiah 7:21-26; 11:6-8; 16:10-13; 44:1-14.

      a. Why was history brought to the fore?

      b. What did the people forget?

      c. Why was it so important for the people to remember?

11. Look at Jeremiah 10:46; 51:15-19.

      a. How does God compare to idols in the book of Jeremiah?

      b. Consider the idolatry of the people; for example, in Jeremiah 44:15-28?

12. God warned His people that judgement was coming.

      a. See His purposes behind His actions in Jeremiah 6:16-18; 22:21; 25:3.

      b. What did He require of them as expressed in Jeremiah 7:1-15?

13. God gave Jeremiah the command not to intercede on behalf of the people three times: Jeremiah 7:16, 11:14 and 14:11. What was God conveying through this command?

14. In the passages Jeremiah 17:5-11; 21:8-10; 26:1-6:

      a. Look at the conditional statements, choices given, and comparisons that were made.

      b. What does this demonstrate about an individual's responsibility in their faith?

15. What was revealed about God in the book of Jeremiah?

      a. What do the following passages reveal about God's heart: Jeremiah 3:11-13; 3:19; 4:1-4; 4:18-19; 9:23-24; 22:1-5; 35:1-19; 36:1-3?

      b. Look at the names used to describe Him.

      c. Look at the following passages: Jeremiah 10:6-10; 18:1-10; 22:13-17; 23:23-24,29; 48:31-32,36-37; 49:11; 50:33-34.

      d. How was He shown to be the World Power in 18:6-10; 27:5-11; 51:20-24?

16. How does Jeremiah 9:23-24 link to 1 Corinthians 1:17-2:16 and 2

Corinthians 10:12-18?

17. Look at the temple in Jeremiah: 7:1-15; 11:15; 12:7; 23:11; 27:16-22; 28:1-9; 32:31-35; 50:28, 51:11; 51:49-53. Look at Exodus 40:34-35.

    a. Why was it significant to the people that the temple was destroyed?

    b. Why did they not believe that God would allow the temple to be destroyed?

    c. How would these beliefs have impacted on the degree of credit they gave to Jeremiah's prophecies?

    d. What impact would this have had on their worship?

18. What is said about the "day of the Lord" in Jeremiah 4:9; 7:30-8:3; 6:9; 39; 52?

19. What do you see of Babylon and the coming army? Refer to Jeremiah 6:1; 6:22-30; 15:12-14; 25:8-14; 27; 32.

20. What is said about the "great day of the Lord" in Jeremiah 9:25; 25:15-38?

21. What is conveyed about the nations and/ or the Kingdom of God in Jeremiah 12:14-17; 16:19-21; 23:7-8; 24:1-7; 30-31; 46:27; 48:47; 49:5; 49:39?

22. In chapters 46-51, God listed His coming judgement upon the nations. Notice the starting words "concerning_____*(nation)*___".

    a. What were the sins listed against each nation?

    b. Was there significance in the imagery used to describe the coming wrath on the different nations in relation to what actions and practices they were famous for as a nation?

    c. What role did God play in their judgement?

    d. Who would God use to fulfil His purposes?

23. Consider the letter that Jeremiah sent from Jerusalem to the surviving elders, priests, prophets, and people, whom Nebuchadnezzar took into exile (Jeremiah 29:1-23).

    a. What does the Lord convey through the letter?

    b. How was this against Hananiah's prophecy in chapter 28?

24. Look at the following Messianic passage, foretelling Christ: Jeremiah 23:1-8.

25. God's promise of restoration pops up every now and then throughout the book. Look at the following passages: Jeremiah 5:18-19; 16:14-15; 23:1-8; 27:22; 30-33; 46:27-28; 50:19-20.

    a. What would these verses have meant to the original hearers (those listening to the words of Jeremiah)?

    b. What would they have meant to Jeremiah?

    c. How about the original readers before, during, and after exile?

26. In chapter 32, look at what is said about the people in verses 30-35 and then the promise that is given in verses 36-41. Look at the contrasting promises God makes in Jeremiah 33:1-5 and then 33:6-9. What does this show about God?

Creative interpretation

1. Complete a character study on Jeremiah. Consider:
    a. What helped him to remain obedient to God?
    b. What did he bring to God in prayer?
    c. How did he respond to times of trial? Did this affect his attitude towards the people?
    d. What fruit did he see in his ministry? Did this affect his relationship with God?
    e. How did he view God?
    f. From where did he draw strength?
    g. How did Jeremiah define success in ministry?
    h. Did he show fear? Was he disobedient or unfaithful?
    i. What caused him to become angry?
    j. How did Jeremiah view himself? Was he critical of himself or the people?
2. Idolatry is a recurring theme in the books of the prophets. What does the book of Jeremiah reveal about God's heart on this issue?

Ongoing prophets' project

Take out the separate document that you started during your Isaiah study. Add to it what you learn about the "day of the Lord" versus the "great day of the Lord" from Jeremiah. Keep adding to this document as you work through the prophets.

Application inspiration

- Do not give up for lack of visible fruit in your ministry. Let God change your view of how success should be defined. Push in. Do not be deterred by obstacles.
- Will you do the jobs and ministries "without glory"? Will you serve in the kitchen, on grounds maintenance, with the Sunday school or in the finance department at your church?
- God desires a people faithful and obedient to Him.
    o   Do you desire to walk in faithfulness to God?
    o   Are you listening to His voice, determined to walk in obedience to His call?

LAMENTATIONS

Jeremiah weeps for Judah

The LORD gave full vent to his wrath; he poured out his hot anger, and he kindled a fire in Zion that consumed its foundations. The kings of the earth did not believe, nor any of the inhabitants of the world, that foe or enemy could enter the gates of Jerusalem. This was for the sins of her prophets and the iniquities of her priests, who shed in the midst of her the blood of the righteous. –
Lamentations 4:11-13

During your first reading

Themes to track
- Grief and sorrow
- Questioning God
- Jeremiah's character

During your second reading

Things to notice in the text
- Emotion
- Questions

Chapter summaries

These are optional as they can be time consuming for the larger books. If you choose to do them, you will receive a much deeper appreciation of the book. By the end of The IBSC, you will have paraphrased the entire Bible! Go through each chapter and try to summarise it in one paragraph, using your own words; force yourself to stay big picture and capture the heart of each chapter.

After your initial readings

Setting of Lamentations

Author

Lamentations is assumed to have been written by the prophet Jeremiah, but his authorship is not certain.

Recipient

Lamentations may have been written for the people of Judah, or alternatively, in response to the author's personal grief.

Date and place of writing

The book was written as a remnant of God's people fled to Egypt after the fall of Jerusalem, in 586 BC. It was likely written in Egypt or Judah.

Reason written

The book of Lamentations was written to remember the tragic fall of God's nation and to express grief for His people.

Big picture
Historical background

Jeremiah was called to be a prophet in the thirteenth year of King Josiah (614 BC). He prophesied during the reigns of King Josiah (627-609 BC), King Jehoahaz/ Shallum (609 BC), King Jehoiakim (608-597 BC), King Jehoaichin/ Jeconiah/ Coniah (597 BC), and King Zedekiah (597-586 BC). This totals sixty-six years of public ministry, faithfully serving God, which commenced when he was about twenty years old! He saw little fruit from his ministry and lived through the fall of Jerusalem.

The tabernacle was the symbol of God's presence with His people. When Jeremiah said that everything would be destroyed, the people did not listen. This was because they believed that God would not let His temple be destroyed. Following exile, Lamentations was read every year by the Jews as a funeral poem to remember the loss of the city.

Take note of the history recorded in the book of Jeremiah, particularly the events of the fall. The fall of Jerusalem is covered in Jeremiah 39-44. Look at the detailed and graphic images that the writer of Lamentations depicted, surrounding the events of the fall of Jerusalem.

Character portrayal – Lamentations 2:20, 4:4-5, 9-10

"Look at us, God. Think it over. Have you ever treated anyone like this? Should women eat their own babies, the very children they raised? Should priests and prophets be murdered in the Master's own Sanctuary? [1]

"Babies have nothing to drink. Their tongues stick to the roofs of their mouths. Little children ask for bread but no one gives them so much as a crust. People used to the finest cuisine forage for food in the streets. People used to the latest in fashions pick through the trash for something to wear. [2]

"Better to have been killed in battle than killed by starvation. Better to have died of battle wounds than to slowly starve to death. Nice and kindly women boiled their own children for supper.

This was the only food in town when my dear people were broken." [3]

Book overview

Lamentations recognises that it was God who brought the destruction down upon Jerusalem and that knowledge was painful to the author, who was clearly overwhelmed by the destruction of the city.

The grief and sorrow expressed in Lamentations was personal, as the writer struggled to see the greatness of God and His holiness. He was struggling to move past the sight of destruction, chaos, pain, and anguish. The author wrestled with what he had seen and observed. He knew that God is sovereign, as demonstrated through the wrathful destruction of His people and His Temple, but was asking: Can the goodness of God still be found? Can hope be found in the midst of the pain, my questions, and grief?

Interpreting the book of Lamentations

Interpretation questions

    1. How did the author convey the fall of Jerusalem?
       a. What did it look like?
       b. How would the original readers have felt as they relived these moments through his words?
       c. Why did Jeremiah choose to be graphic in the details he recorded?
       d. How would instilling fear of God into the remnant of Judah help them to remain obedient to God during exile in a foreign land?
    2. At whose door did Jeremiah lay the blame for the defeat of Judah?
    3. In each chapter, consider how God is portrayed.
       a. Did the author's portrait of God change?
       b. In chapter 2, look at the list recording what "He has" done.
    4. How did the view of God in Lamentations contrast with the view of Him given in Jeremiah?
    5. Is there a difference between how Jeremiah looked on the people of Judah in Lamentations compared with Jeremiah?
    6. Note the contrast in chapter 3. In Lamentations 3:1-20, the author listed his injuries and wounds, but then in verse 21 there is a significant shift where he transitioned to recalling what he knew of God.
       a. Why did this offer him hope even in the midst of his suffering?
       b. What comfort would this have given to the original readers?
    7. What personal insults and injuries did the author report?
       a. Did his suffering show strength or weakness in his faith?
       b. Was there a break in the author's relationship with God?
    8. What do you see of God the Almighty? What do you learn of His character?
    9. Read 1 Peter 2:21-25 in conjunction with Lamentations 5. How do the two passages relate to one another?

<u>Creative interpretation</u>

1. Read Lamentations out loud in a dramatic reading. Try to express the emotions of the author, think on the imagery he used, and relate to the people of Judah who lived through these times of horror and destruction. Take yourself back to the time of the fall of Jerusalem as they were conquered by Babylon.

Application inspiration

- Sharing your grief or the consequences of sin you have experienced can keep future generations safe from the same transgressions.
  - o Are you open to sharing your pain and hurt with others when called to, if it will make a difference to their faith?
  - o Are you willing to be vulnerable in order to enable the growth of others? This needs to be done with wisdom and in a place of safety, but there are times where God desires to use personal testimonies of grief and sorrow to encourage others in their faith. Are you willing to be used in this way?
- It is okay to be real with God. It is okay to grieve. Comforting those in grief is often telling them that it is okay to mourn their losses. Sometimes the best thing you can do for people is to tell them that it is okay to bring their grief before God.

[1] Lamentations 2:20 (The Message)
[2] Lamentations 4:4-5 (The Message)
[3] Lamentations 4:9-10 (The Message)

EZEKIEL

So they will know that I am the Lord

"And I will vindicate the holiness of my great name, which has been profaned among the nations, and which you have profaned among them. And the nations will know that I am the LORD, declares the Lord GOD, when through you I vindicate my holiness before their eyes." – Ezekiel 36:23

During your first reading

Themes to track

- God's judgement
- "For the sake of My name"
- Spirit of God
- Restoration for the people of God
- Ezekiel and his character

During your second reading

Things to notice in the text

- Highlight the repeated phrase "know that I am the Lord".
- Highlight the repeated words "prostitute", "whore", "harlot", "promiscuity", "lewd", and "lust".
- The dates that the visions came to Ezekiel (with the first vision in Ezekiel 1:1 coming in 593 BC; however, please note that there is some conjecture on exact dates).

Chapter summaries

These are optional as they can be time consuming for the larger books. If you choose to do them, you will receive a much deeper appreciation of the book. By the

end of The IBSC, you will have paraphrased the entire Bible! Go through each chapter and try to summarise it in one paragraph, using your own words; force yourself to stay big picture and capture the heart of each chapter.

After your initial readings

Setting of Ezekiel
<u>Author</u>
The book was written by the prophet, Ezekiel.

<u>Date prophecies were spoken</u>
Ezekiel's prophecies fell between the dates of 593 BC and 571 BC.

<u>Recipient – hearers</u>
Ezekiel predominantly spoke his prophecies to the people of Judah who were amongst the first group taken into exile to Babylon. In one short space of the book, Ezekiel was speaking to those remaining in Jerusalem during the siege.

<u>Recipient – readers</u>
The book was predominantly written for the people of Judah in exile in Babylon, but also to those who led the way home from exile in 528 BC, when King Cyrus of Persia issued a decree permitting them to return to Judea and rebuild the temple.

<u>Date and place of writing</u>
It can be assumed that the prophecies were written over the same period they were spoken (between 593 BC and 571 BC). Ezekiel was in exile in Babylon when he composed the book.

<u>Reason spoken</u>
God wanted the nations and His people to know that He is the Lord and He is mighty in action. The prophecies declared God's judgement upon Judah, whilst also giving individuals a chance to repent, turn from their wickedness, and live. Ezekiel declared that each individual would be judged for their own actions.

<u>Reason written</u>
Ezekiel recorded these prophecies to show the nations and God's people that God is the Lord and faithfully fulfils His word. It gave individuals the chance to choose the way of righteousness, promising that they will be judged for their own actions. The final chapters gave instructions for when they returned from exile.

Big picture
<u>Historical background</u>
The people of Judah were taken into exile in three stages. In 605 BC, the treasures of the temple as well as the best and brightest young men, including Daniel, were taken to Babylon. The second stage occurred in 597 BC, when Ezekiel and 10

thousand captives were carried off into exile. Finally, in 586 BC, the city of Jerusalem fell and the third and final group went into exile.

The original readers were the Judeans in exile. They felt like God had abandoned them. They were without hope. They did not believe that God could reach them anymore, as they thought gods were territorial, meaning that the God of Israel could not act in Babylon. Conversely, they also appeared to think exile would only be for a short time.

Whilst Ezekiel received little positive fruit during the years of his ministry, the following decades witnessed more than 120 thousand people returning from exile, totally weaned off idolatry and eager to rebuild God's temple and the city of Jerusalem. Ezekiel was a contemporary prophet of Jeremiah, Nahum, Habbakuk, and Obadiah.

Character portrayal – the life of a puppet; Ezekiel

"I cannot walk unless my Master lifts me up. I have strings through my hands and strings through my feet. I even have one that comes out through the top of my head. To be able to stand, my Master must lift me up. I can only speak the words of my Master.

"People pass me by and laugh at my act, but they fail to hear the message that I proclaim. No one values my words or takes heed of the warning contained within them. To the people, I am simply entertainment – a silly puppet, speaking silly things, to keep them amused. Yet, through me, my Master is speaking words of life and death. He is giving the people a choice, and they are choosing the way of folly.

"They think I am foolish, but they are the ones that do not see. I may walk in complete obedience to the will and whim of my Master, but if they had one glimpse of the One they defied, they would fall prostrate to the ground. No, they would die from gazing on His Holy Presence.

"I pray for them and cling to hope that the people of God will turn back to Him. I don't know how many acts He has planned for them through me, His puppet, and I fear what is coming after the closing act . . ."

Book overview

God is concerned with His name and how it is portrayed, not just within the land of Israel and His people, but to all the nations on the earth. The phrase "that you may know that I am the Lord" is repeated about forty times throughout Ezekiel. It is clear God wants to make His name known throughout the earth. His anger is aroused when His name is profaned.

God's judgement is shown to come when people mock Him, speak ill of Him or belittle His power. Through His judgement, He also makes His holiness known to the lands of the earth. For the sake of His name, He restrained Himself many times from unleashing His wrath against His people for their sins, but no longer. They continued to practice abominations and so His wrath came. However, He also warned that woe would come upon those who accused Him of not being mighty enough to save His people. Those who laughed at, or rejoiced over, His people's demise would learn the hard way that He is God, and is mighty in action.

However, hope remained for God's people. He promised to be with them, even in exile, and a remnant would have a chance at restoration. He is shown to be sovereign over the dominions of men and world powers. He can restore and bring to life what is dead. Once the nations have been judged, God will gather the righteous remnant into an eternal kingdom and establish an everlasting covenant of peace.

<u>Assistance with symbolism</u>
The four living creatures and the wheels – chapters 1 & 10

- They are connected with the Spirit of God, going wherever the Spirit goes. Whenever these four creatures appear, the presence of God is also "in the house".
- Look at Revelation 4:7-8. It seems that the living creatures are also related to worship of the One True God.
- What are they? They could be representative of all creation worshipping before the Lord, showing that even the mightiest of creation bows before Him. This is suggested because of the Rabbinical saying at the time, which held that *"the mightiest among birds is the eagle, the mightiest amongst domesticated animals is the ox, the mightiest amongst beasts is the lion, and the mightiest of all is man"*.
- The wheels within a wheel represent a mobile throne. It is also associated with the presence of God. The coal from the wheels is symbolic of the presence of God.
- Why are they important? They reveal the glory of the Lord and the coming of His presence. The Spirit is not physically visible so they might clearly represent His presence to man.
- The wheels can move in any direction. It would have been an encouragement to the people in exile to hear that God was on the move and could follow them. God is not limited to the physical territory of Judah. This imagery was showing the people that God is not found in a temple; He is not confined to one space or nation.
- Consider the significance of Ezekiel being unable to describe what they looked like.

Gog and Magog – chapters 38 & 39

- There are mixed views as to what the prophecy against Gog and Magog represented; however, it is clear that these prophecies painted a picture of deliverance for the people of God. A lot of similarities can be seen between this passage and Revelation. Refer to Revelation 19:17-20:10.
- The names and places:
  - Gog – Who or what Gog was remains unknown. Gog is called a person in Ezekiel 38:2, but in Revelation it is a place.
  - Magog – 1 Chronicles 1:5 and Genesis 10:1 indicate that Magog was a physical place, which existed in space and time.
  - Meshech and Tubal – see Ezekiel 32:26, 27:12-13, Psalm 120:5-7,

and Genesis 10:2, which indicate that Ezekiel was familiar with these places.

- o Meshech – Meshech is identified with a place in Turkey.
- o Tubal – Tubal is identified with a place near Cilicia. See the list of people in Genesis 10:2 and the place being judged in Isaiah 66:19.
- o Rosh – Rosh means "chief prince of. . .", so Rosh could mean "Gog of Rosh", or "Gog, the chief prince".

- Possible interpretations for this passage include:
  - a. A historical battle.
  - b. Armageddon; a future, physical battle.
  - c. The final battle of history; a spiritual battle.
  - d. Perhaps a reverse telescope; it starts by depicting a spiritual battle, but then, in verse 25, it comes back to the physical restoration of the nation of Judah.

- What to focus on:
  - o These chapters would have given hope to the original readers because of the restoration they promised to Judah.
  - o God's people can trust Him to protect them and give them peace.
  - o Look at the character of God. He is going to defeat a LARGE, ungodly army that will assemble against His people. God is a mighty protector. He will justify His name and judge justly.
  - o It looked like evil would win, but in the end, God triumphs.

Interpreting the book of Ezekiel
Interpretation questions

1. Think about what God was trying to communicate as He gave these prophecies to the people.
2. What do you learn of the character of God through the book of Ezekiel?
3. What do you learn of the Holy Spirit? How was the Holy Spirit revealed through the book of Ezekiel?
4. Consider the life that Ezekiel lived and what he faithfully walked through at the command of the Lord. Look particularly at chapters 2-4 (his call), chapter 24:14-27 (personal suffering), chapter 32:1-20 (the watchman) and chapter 33 (amusement of the people). Do not forget that God made him mute for the majority of his ministry, only allowing Ezekiel to speak the words of God.
5. God gave His people visual illustrations to communicate His truths in an attention grabbing way. For each of the enacted symbols that Ezekiel carried out, consider what the original viewers would have thought, what the symbol represented, how Ezekiel would have felt as he carried them out, what it revealed of God, and what God desired to convey to His people. Remember that Ezekiel was mute as he carries out these symbols. The commanded symbols:
  - a. Siege with bricks (Ezekiel 4:1-3);

b. Lie on your side (Ezekiel 4:4-8);

c. Cook food over dung (Ezekiel 4:9-17);

d. Cut your hair with a sword (Ezekiel 5:1-4);

e. Two sticks joined to form one (Ezekiel 37:15-23).

6. Consider the information given above in *Assistance with symbolism* for help interpreting the Four Living Creatures and the Wheels.

   a. What was the significance of this imagery?

   b. What does it reveal about God?

   c. How would it have given hope to the exiles?

7. In Ezekiel 2:9-3:3, Ezekiel was given a scroll to eat. Compare Ezekiel's experience with that of John in Revelation 10.

   a. What are the differences?

   b. What are the similarities?

   c. Consider the difference in taste as it could relate to judgement; final judgement compared with the physical judgement of Judah.

   d. By eating the scroll, how could this be seen as Ezekiel making the message his own?

8. Ezekiel 4-7 declares judgement upon Judah and Jerusalem.

   a. For what are they being judged?

   b. What did it reveal of the religious state of Judah?

   c. What did He think of the religious state of Judah?

   d. What was the attitude of the people?

   e. How would they be judged?

   f. How would this have made the original hearers feel, who were already in exile without hope and blaming God?

9. Ezekiel 8-10 depicts the abominations occurring in God's temple. Remember that the people did not think that God would allow His temple to be destroyed.

   a. What was happening in God's temple?

   b. What did it reveal of the religious state of Judah?

   c. How would the original readers have responded to hearing that God had removed His presence from the temple (chapter 10-11)?

   d. How does this compare with what is seen when God's presence falls on a place? See Exodus 19:16-22; 34:4-7; 40:38; 1 Kings 8:1-13?

10. What hope would the final words of the book have given to the original readers (Ezekiel 48:35)? How would they have gained hope from the promise in Ezekiel 11:16-21?

11. See Ezekiel 11:1-14; 13:1-16; 19:1-9; 34:1-10.

   a. What was spoken against the leaders of Israel?

   b. What judgement was coming upon them for their sins?

   c. Why did God hold the leaders to a higher standard than the people?

   d. What effect did the action of the leaders have on the people of Judah?

e. How does this contrast with the passages in Ezekiel 18 and 33:1-20 when God proclaimed that each person would be judged for his/ her individual ways?

12. How does the Good Shepherd contrast with the leadership that the people had experienced at the hands of the priest, princes, kings, and prophets of the land (Ezekiel 34)?

13. When were the prophecies against Judah fulfilled? Use the book of Jeremiah as an aid when considering the fulfilments. For example, look at Jeremiah 39:1-7 alongside Ezekiel 12:1-16.

14. What would Ezekiel have felt as he spoke these words to the exiles? Remember that his audience was already in exile (the first of those deported from Judah) and yet mocked his words.

15. What do you learn of the Judeans through Ezekiel?
    a. Consider Ezekiel 12:21-25; 22:29; 33:30-33.
    b. How would the mindset of the original readers (living after the fall of Jerusalem, and fulfilment of the prophecies) be different from that of the original hearers (living before Jerusalem had fallen?

16. Further to what insights you gained in chapters 8-10:
    a. What does Ezekiel convey of the religious state of the nation in Ezekiel 13:1-14:11; 16; 22; 23?
    b. What do you see of God's heart and desire for His people in Ezekiel 16?

17. The original readers were in exile and Jerusalem had fallen.
    a. What encouragement would they receive as they read Ezekiel's prophecies against the nations (Ezekiel 21:28-32; 25-32; 35)?
    b. Would this change how they felt towards God?
    c. Would it give them hope?
    d. Why was each of these nations being judged?
    e. Why were some condemned to complete destruction, whilst others were only to suffer for a period of time?
    f. How would God judge them?
    g. When were these prophecies fulfilled?

18. Throughout Israel's history when judgement was coming, God turned aside His wrath at the pleas of a few righteous people.
    a. What is the significance of Ezekiel 14:12-23?
    b. How does this relate to Jeremiah 7:16, 11:14, and 14:11?
    c. What did God want to convey to the people?
    d. What reasons did God give for having stayed His hand in the past (Ezekiel 20:1-29)?

19. Consider the figures of speech God gave Ezekiel. See Ezekiel 15:1-5; 17; 19; 21:6-17; 23; 24:1-14; 37:1-10.
    a. Bring the image into your mind and think of what was being conveyed.
    b. What significance did these images have to the people of God?

20. Ezekiel proclaimed the judgement of God coming upon the nation of

Judah.
   a. What about the individual?
   b. What was the significance of the passages in Ezekiel that proclaim life for those who chose the way of righteousness?
   c. If they were all going into exile, what life was being offered to the righteous (Ezekiel 18 and 33:1-20)?
21. Look at the promises of restoration in Ezekiel.
   a. Consider whether they relate to the physical return from exile or to the coming Kingdom of God.
   b. What would these promises have meant to those in exile? See Ezekiel 11:16-21; 20:39-44; 34:11-31; 36:8-15, 24-38; 37?
   c. What is learnt of Christ in these passages?
   d. Are they prophecies that concern Christ's first or second coming?
   e. What was said of the Spirit?
22. Ezekiel 40-48 depicts the building of a new temple in Jerusalem. Remember that, to the original readers, the temple was central to faith and worship. This was an important vision for them to hear.
   a. Why would this have given the people hope?
   b. What was God communicating to the exiles?
   c. For further context to the new temple, compare the details listed in Ezekiel to that of Revelation 21.
23. When looking at Ezekiel 40-48, remember that the temple took centre stage, but also consider what was said of the prince, and the high priest, especially their allotted roles.
24. Ezekiel 12:2 is quoted by Matthew in the New Testament (Matthew 13:13). Christ, Himself, spoke these words.
   a. What was Christ conveying through them?
   b. Why did Matthew record them?

Creative interpretation
      1. The temple and the prince; Ezekiel 40-48
There is discussion amongst theologians as to whether this is speaking of a physical restoration for God's people or a spiritual restoration – whether it foretold the end of the exile in Babylon or was a representation of the coming Kingdom of God. There is also debate surrounding who the prince is – was he an ordinary man who will rule a physical nation or was he the Christ?

Temple options:
   1. Literal, physical temple:
      a. Ezra's temple, which was built when the exiles returned to Jerusalem.
      b. Herod's millennial temple, being the temple at the time of Christ.
      c. A temple that will exist during the millennial period, the one thousand years told of in Revelation.
   2. Spiritual temple

a. Giving a concept of heaven. It is not about physical materials, but a state of being, and a way of life.

Prince options:
1. Person, if a physical prince;
2. Jesus, if a spiritual prince.

For this passage (Ezekiel 40-48):
- Complete a two- to three- paragraph summary on what is said about the temple, and what you believe it represents. Consider first what it would represent to the original readers, and then consider what it represents now that we can look back through history. Take a guess and say whether, and why, you think the temple predicted was to be physical or spiritual.
- Consider: who is the prince?
- Consider what this vision meant to the original readers in exile.

Ongoing prophets' project

Take out the separate document that you started during your Isaiah study. Add to it what you learn about the "day of the Lord" versus the "great day of the Lord" from Ezekiel. Keep adding to this document as you work through the prophets.

Application inspiration
- Ezekiel seemed crazy to his peers because he did what God asked him to do. He listened to the Holy Spirit, and acted.
  o Would you? Do you?
  o How often do you seek to hear what the Spirit is asking of you?
- Allow God to challenge you. Seek and ask for a prophetic enactment this week from God that symbolises something that He is doing in your life or what He is teaching you. Be challenged to step outside of your comfort zone. Be open to God giving you a physical act to perform, which will denote a change that is happening within your heart or to your mindset.
- God condemned the leadership of Israel for leading His sheep astray. The king, princes, priests, and prophets were all judged for the sins they caused the people to commit. Think of two good and two bad leaders who have had influence or authority over you.
  o What made them good or bad examples?
  o What were the characteristics they displayed?
- Consider the promises of restoration given to the people of God.
  o What hope can you draw from them?
  o What about the gift of the Holy Spirit that has been given to you?
  o What is said concerning this joyful gift?
  o How does this promise impact on your life?

DANIEL

Whatever comes, God is Bigger. Full stop.

"And in the days of those kings the God of heaven will set up a kingdom that shall never be destroyed, nor shall the kingdom be left to another people. It shall break in pieces all these kingdoms and bring them to an end, and it shall stand forever." – Daniel 2:44

During your first reading

Themes to track
- Sovereignty of God
- Kingdom of God
- Character of Daniel
- Character of the kings
- Character of Shadrach, Meshach, and Abednego
- Pride and humility

During your second reading

Things to notice in the text
- Who – people and their responses
- Prayer
- Imagery
- Visions

Chapter summaries

These are optional as they can be time consuming for the larger books. If you choose to do them, you will receive a much deeper appreciation of the book. By the end of The IBSC, you will have paraphrased the entire Bible! Go through each chapter and try to summarise it in one paragraph, using your own words; force

yourself to stay big picture and capture the heart of each chapter.

After your initial readings

Setting of Daniel
Author

Daniel was the author as supported by the personal pronouns he uses in the book.

Date prophecies were spoken

The events of the book occurred over a period of about seventy years, spanning from 605 BC to 536 BC.

Recipient – hearers

The prophecies were given to the Babylonian kings, who had received visions from God, as well as to the Jews in exile.

Recipient – readers

The book seems to have been written for a mixed audience of Jews and Gentiles. Daniel wrote part of the text in Hebrew, to his Jewish audience, and some of it in Aramaic, suggesting a wider target-audience.

Date and place of writing

These events were recorded from Babylon during or shortly after the time they took place; from 605 BC (when Daniel was amongst the first Judeans taken into exile), until about 536 BC.

Reason spoken

The lives of Daniel, Shadrach, Meshach, and Abednego showed their fellow exiles how to live for God in an anti-God society. The visions that came to the kings and to Daniel declared that the Most High God is living, active, and ruler over all kingdoms of men.

Reason written

The writings of Daniel showed the people how to live in expectation of the coming Kingdom of God. They would have offered encouragement and enabled the Jews to wait for God's kingdom, even knowing that they would experience martyrdom and persecution. This is the first book in the Bible that speaks of persecution of the people of God for their faith, not as judgement resulting from covenant unfaithfulness.

Big picture
Historical background

Kings of the exile and the years of their reign:

- Nabopolassar (625-605 BC);

- Nebuchadnezzar II (605-562 BC);
- Amel-Marduk (562-560 BC);
- Nergal-sharezer/ Neriglissar (560-556 BC);
- Labashi-Marduk   (556 BC);
- Nabonidus (556-539 BC);
- Belshazzar (co-regent 553-539 BC);
- Cyrus II of Persia (559-530 BC, Cyrus defeated the Babylonians in 539);
- Cambyses (530-523 BC);
- Smerdis, or a Magus usurper, (522 BC);
- Darius I (522-486 BC).

*Note that there is contention over whether or not Cyrus II and Darius are the same, or different, rulers.

The five kingdoms to come (as depicted in Daniel 2):
- Head of gold = Babylon, 625-539 BC.
- Chest and arms of silver = Media-Persia, 539-331 BC.
- Waist and thigh of bronze = Greece, Alexander conquers known world.
- Legs of iron, with feet and toes of iron and clay = Rome.
- Stones not cut with human hands = Kingdom of God.

Important battles that took place:
- 609 BC – First battle of Carchemish, and the death of King Josiah.
- 605 BC – Second battle of Carchemish, a decided victory to the Babylonians against the Egyptians and remnant of the Assyrians. The first deportation of Jews into exile in Babylon, including Daniel, Shadrach, Meshach, and Abednego.
- 597 BC – Second deportation of Jews into exile, including Ezekiel.
- 539 BC – Babylon falls to the Persians.

Prophets speaking at the time:
- Jeremiah prophesied to those still left in Jerusalem; 626 BC until the fall of Jerusalem, in 586 BC.
- Ezekiel prophesied to the exiles in Babylon from 593-570 BC.
- Daniel prophesied to the nobility in Babylon from 605-535 BC.

Character portrayal – into the flames

A speaking look passed between the three countrymen, certifying that they would all give the same answer. Their choice was to bow down and worship the golden image that King Nebuchadnezzar had set up, or keep the commands of the One True God. To bow down would be to appease the human king and avoid the flames, but sin in the eyes of the Almighty God and bring His judgement. To refuse the king would be to accept the inevitable punishment of being thrown into the fire. Some may have considered it a tough decision, but it was no decision at all to Shadrach, Meshach, and Abednego.

The three answered of one accord: *"O Nebuchadnezzar, we have no need to answer you in this matter. If this be so, our God whom we serve is able to deliver us from the burning fiery furnace, and he will deliver us out of your hand, O king. But if not, be it known to you, O king, that we will not serve your gods or worship the golden image that you have set up."* [1]

The certainty in the voices of Shadrach, Meshach, and Abednego raised Nebuchadnezzar's ire. Who were these foreign youth to be refusing him, the great and mighty king over nations? Nebuchadnezzar raged internally. Who was it who had plucked them from their diminutive country and set them up in his court? He fed them the finest foods, clothed them in splendid garments, and educated them. And now they turned their backs on him? And who was their God who still held their unshakable faith even though He was unable to save them?

In his wrath, King Nebuchadnezzar did not pause to consider the faithful way in which these three had diligently served *him*. He did not consider that their only crime against *him* was not bowing to a statue. The only command they had placed above his was that of their God. Yet that was enough to send black and red spots dancing before the king's eyes. He would not be denied. They must die! And with no more thought, King Nebuchadnezzar commanded the three to be thrown into the fire.

All of a sudden there were four within the flames. The guards that carried out the king's command perished, becoming ashes. The king shuddered as his eyes lingered on the fourth figure in the flames. His eyes went wide as he realised the ramifications of what he was seeing: God had placed His protection over His three faithful servants . . .

Book overview

The book of Daniel declares over, and over, and over again, in many different ways, that God is sovereign over the kingdoms of men. God is the Almighty. God is the Most High Ruler. God is sovereign over rulers and their kingdoms. He sets them up and brings them down according to His timing. God allowed Babylon to conquer His people, but He also extended a hand of protection and favour upon Daniel and his companions.

The lives of Daniel, Shadrach, Meshach, and Abednego show how to live godly lives in the midst of a secular world. They provide encouragement to take the challenging option to stand in faithful obedience to God in the midst of persecution. The book of Daniel also teaches about the effectiveness of prayer. It shows the value and power of individual prayer and intercession.

In the later part of the book, Daniel recorded the visions he was given of the things that were to come in the kingdoms of men. God gave details of what would come and their fulfilment can be seen by looking back through the history books. God knows the future and believers can be comforted in the knowledge that He is in control of it.

The prophecies show that times of tribulation will come on the people of God, but comfort is also offered in the final chapters of the book. He declares that there will be an end to the persecution and suffering, and that those who continue in faith will receive eternal life. The prize is worth the fight. Furthermore, it shows that persecution no longer comes as God's judgement upon sin, but falls on the righteous because of their faith. God was revealing the new covenant, which came with Christ. Those in Christ will suffer persecution for their faith, but those who overcome until the end will receive eternal comfort.

Assistance with the visions (chapters 7-12)

It is easy to focus on the end times when studying these chapters, so remember to look at the big picture of the book and why Daniel was recording these prophecies. Also remember to ask what it would have meant to the original readers. It is okay to ask questions about these visions – Daniel did – but do not allow yourself to miss the big picture as a result of narrowing in on the details.

Beasts and horns – chapter 7
- Lion (king of beasts) = The Babylonian Empire, which fell with the end of Nebuchadnezzar's reign. As seen in chapter 4, God made Nebuchadnezzar go mad until the king humbled himself before the Lord.
- Bear (might) = The alliance between Medes and Persia. The Persians rose up higher than the Medes.
- Leopard (speed) = Greece. Alexander the Great, the first king of Greece, conquered the known world in a short period of time, only to die at thirty-three years of age. The four heads splitting represented Alexander's four generals who divided the kingdom upon his death.
- Fourth Beast = Rome. Why Rome? It is the next kingdom and the original reader would expect it to be the next kingdom of man.
- Ten Horns = This may represent the fact that Rome was an enduring kingdom; it was in power for an extended time frame and saw the rise and fall of many Caesars.
- Little Horn = There are three main views of what this represented:
    a. Titus/ Vespation, who destroyed the (second) temple of Jerusalem in 70 AD.
    b. A symbolic representation of anti-Christian governments and leaders throughout the church age. The church age is this period we are in now that stretches between Christ's first coming and His return.
    c. The antichrist has also been suggested – the man of lawlessness, who is spoken of elsewhere in Scripture and who will rise up at the end of days.

The ram and the goat – chapter 8
- Ram = Media and Persia
    o North, south, and west represent Media (the bigger horn on the ram);
    o Persia is in the east (the shorter horn on the ram).

- Goat = Alexander the Great
    - He defeated King Darius, the last Persian Emperor.
    - Again, the four kings who arose were his four generals who divided the kingdom:
        - Cassander (ruled Macedonia);
        - Seleucus (ruled Syria);
        - Lychimachus (ruled Thracia and Bethynia);
        - Ptolemy (ruled Egypt).
- The other horn = King Antiochus Epiphanes
    - Antiochus Epiphanes became king over the Syrian part of the kingdom in the 137th year of Greece, 175 BC.
    - In verse 13, "the transgression of desolation" refers to how Antiochus Epiphanies mercilessly persecuted Jews during the period of 176-164 BC. He came against Jerusalem and pillaged the temple to the horror of the Israelites. In 168 BC, Antiochus ordered that the temple be dedicated to the worship of Zeus, sacrificing a pig (an unclean animal) upon the altar.
    - In verse 25, Daniel writes that he will "even rise up against the Prince of princes". This refers to Antiochus making a coin for himself that declared: "Theos Epiphanes" or "God manifest". He set himself up as god.
    - Continuing in verse 25, that "he shall be broken—but by no human hand" foretells the cause of Antiochus's death. He was killed by a flesh eating disease that ate him from the inside out.

Seventy sevens – chapter 9

- Remember the context; Daniel was praying and interceding that his people be restored to Jerusalem and this chapter is God's response to the prayer. It can be assumed to be linked with the restoration of Jerusalem.
- The three sets of seven:
    a. First set of seven, the seventy weeks, and the call to rebuild until the coming of the Anointed One.
        - Option 1: Nehemiah goes to rebuild the temple with the first group of Jews returning from exile. The majority of theologians support this option.
        - Option 2: Referring to the time between the first and second comings of Christ.
    b. Second set of sevens, the sixty two weeks, when the rebuilding shall be in troubled times.
        - Option 1: Time from Ezra and Nehemiah until Jesus. It did not get easier for the Jews after the rebuilding of Jerusalem.
        - Option 2: The church age (current age).
    c. Third set of seven, the one week, where the Anointed One shall

be cut off. The city and temple are destroyed by prince's people. The prince makes a strong covenant with many for one seven, and for half of this week, the offerings cease and there is a desolating abomination. The interpretation of this final seven, which depicts the final end, is where the greatest contention exists between scholars.

- Option 1: Crucifixion of Jesus and then the fall of Jerusalem in 70 AD, to Rome/ Titus.
- Option 2: Coming of the Antichrist and tribulation for the church.

- Do not forget the purpose of the vision and how it ends! The Anointed One will come and all of this tribulation and trouble will be done away with. The sacrificial system shall be done away with. God is saying that what Daniel was praying for (the restoration of the temple and sacrifices) would not be needed any more!

Chapter 10

- Why was this vision given? Refer to Revelation 1 for context. In both Daniel and Revelation, the man in white linen came to bring comfort and give encouragement to the people of God who were suffering. God was bringing the message that He is in control.
- The princes of Persia and Greece, and an angel, were strengthening the prince of Medes, Darius, the King. This passage was still dealing with physical kings; therefore, there is very little evidence that this is about demons and spirits. In context, it seems to point to a physical king.

Chapter 11

- Chapter 11 mentions a series of kings that were to come [2], which are generally held to be as follows:
  - Persia:
    - The "three more kings" in verse 2 are taken as Cyrus, Cambyses, and Darius, and the "fourth king" as Xerxes.
  - Greece:
    - The "mighty king" in verse 3 is held to have been Alexander the Great.
  - Kings of North and South (Ptolemy and Seleucid):
    - The "king of the south" in verse 5 is Ptolemy I.
    - The "king of the south" in verse 6 is Ptolemy II.
    - Ptolemy III is referred to in verses 7 and 9.
    - The "king of the north" in verse 8 is Seleucus II, who is also referred to in verses 9 and 10.
    - In verse 10, "his sons" were Seleucus III and Antiochus III. Antiochus is the "king of the north" in verses 10-19
    - In verse 10-15, the "king of the south" is Ptolemy IV.

o Antiochus Epiphanes:
- Antiochus Epiphanes is the "contemptible person" in verse 21 and is referred to until verse 39, with some holding he is also referred to in verse 40-45.
- Ptolemy VI is referred to in verses 22-27 as the main antagonist to Epiphanes.

o The interpretation for verses 40-45 remains uncertain.

Chapter 12
- Time, times, and half a time = symbolic of an indefinite, incomplete or undefined period of time.

Interpreting the book of Daniel
<u>Interpretation questions</u>

1. Take note of the two types of literature in the book of Daniel:
   a. Narrative: mainly chapters 1-6
   b. Prophetic: mainly chapters 7-12
2. It can be easy to fall into looking only at the end times when studying Daniel, but to do so is to lose track of the main reason it was written. When studying Daniel, be sure to focus on the original readers who were in exile. Focus on:
   a. How would this book have impacted the original readers?
   b. How did the exiles respond to these revelations?
   c. How did they wait for the kingdom knowing that they were to be martyred and persecuted?
3. Consider the faith and responses of Daniel, Shadrach, Meshach, and Abednego:
   a. How might these four have felt as youth when they were carried into exile? Would this have changed when they were set in high positions to be taught in the king's court for the purpose of entering his service?
   b. What enabled Daniel to be steadfast in his beliefs despite the temptations of rank and position within a foreign country? How did he respond when placed in a position of compromise?
   c. Look at Shadrach, Meshach, and Abednego's response to the king when threatened with death for choosing not to worship an idol. In a time in their history when God's Law was often neglected or rejected, what does show of these men that they knew the Law?
   d. How did these four men balance serving a foreign king with living as servants of the One True God? How does this relate to Jesus' command: *"Render to Caesar the things that are Caesar's, and to God the things that are God's"* [3]?
   e. Look back at Exodus 20:3-6. Which situations were Daniel, Shadrach, Meshach, and/ or Abednego placed in that could have caused them to break these commands?

    f.   What do you learn of Daniel's character through his actions? What is said of his daily life that the jealous satraps could find no means by which to condemn him, not even the smallest of indiscretions (Daniel 6:1-5)?

4. Consider the image of the statue that God gave to Nebuchadnezzar.
    a.   Why did God give this vision to the king?
    b.   What did God want to convey?
    c.   Consider the four kingdoms. What were they?
    d.   What was revealed of God's coming kingdom?

5. Consider God's pursuit of Nebuchadnezzar.
    a.   Why did God continue to pursue Nebuchadnezzar?
    b.   Why did He give the vision of the tree?
    c.   How does this vision's fulfilment change Nebuchadnezzar?
    d.   Consider his responses to God and his later actions after considering the parable of the soil, which Jesus gave (Mark 4:1-20).

6. Consider the character of King Nebuchadnezzar.
    a.   What do you learn of his motives, his religious beliefs, how he ruled, and his personality from the book of Daniel?
    b.   What do his actions in Daniel 3:1-7 convey of the understanding of God he displayed in Daniel 2:46-47?
    c.   How did his quick temper get him into trouble?
    d.   What do you see of his decision making processes?
    e.   How would his temper have affected the people under his rule?
    f.   What is the significance of the declaration he made to all the people, humbling himself before them, and heralding God as the Most High God?
    g.   Did King Nebuchadnezzar end his reign well?

7. Furthermore, what is implied in the book about hasty decisions?
    a.   Look at Daniel 2:12; 3:12-15; 6:6-9.
    b.   How could the kings have been wiser in their actions, commands, and decrees?
    c.   What difference would this have made?

8. God also gave warnings to Nebuchadnezzar's son, Belshazzar.
    a.   Why did Belshazzar reward Daniel for interpreting the dream and yet not take action to humble himself before God?
    b.   What excuses may he have made to harden his heart?
    c.   Could this relate to the New Testament passage: Luke 12:16-21?
    d.   What does it signify about the need for immediacy in response to God's commands?

9. What is revealed in Daniel about the sovereignty of God over kings and nations?
    a.   How did God reveal His desire to be acknowledged and praised?
    b.   What is once again revealed about His propensity to protect His name and to act "for the sake of His name"?

    c. What else do you see revealed about the character of God?

10. What do you see of God through the visions that He gave to Daniel (chapters 7 and 8)?
    a. How did Daniel receive them?
    b. What would these have meant to the original readers?
    c. What do you learn of the Kingdom of God?
    d. What was the importance of Daniel 7:36-28 to the original readers?

11. For Daniel, these prophecies were overwhelming and wrenched at his heart. Remember he was not looking back in history, but had lived through atrocities and then, as he looked towards the end of exile for his people, he was told that more bad times are on the way. How may he have been feeling?

12. What does chapter 9 reveal about Daniel's understanding of the Law, his study of Deuteronomy 28, and how it shows that he had likely read Jeremiah's writing?

13. What encouragement would God's words have given to Daniel that He heard his prayers? What about to the original readers in exile?

14. What was the purpose of the seventy sevens, as listed in Daniel 9:24? Keep this as the focus when you read on. God is not concerned with the physical land of the Jews, but with the sins of the world.

15. What was revealed of God in the final three chapters?
    a. How do they show God to be sovereign over the nations?
    b. What do you see of Daniel and his character?
    c. How did Daniel receive these visions?
    d. How would the events in chapter 10 have brought Daniel and the exiles comfort, even knowing that more suffering was on the way?

16. How does Revelation 1:13-15 relate to Daniel's experience? Contrast this passage in Revelation with Daniel 10:5-6. What further information do you learn of whom this image represented? What differences, if any, are there?

17. Consider the historical background in *Assistance with visions* when interpreting chapter 11. You may wish to explore the historical events of the kings listed, for further assistance interpreting the visions.

18. What promises of resurrection were given in Daniel 12?
    a. Would the original readers have understood this?
    b. Should they have understood; why or why not?

19. What was told of God's coming judgement?
    a. Who will be judged?
    b. What will be the result of judgement?
    c. Consider Daniel 12 in the added context of Revelation 20:12-15 and Revelation 21. What will be removed and what will remain when Christ returns?

20. Consider Matthew 24 for additional context to Daniel 12. When considering time elements, consider Christ's words in Matthew 24:36.

    a. If the focus was not on the time, then what do you believe Daniel's focus would have been on?

    b. What was the big picture of these prophecies?

Creative interpretation

1. Make a study on the lives of Daniel, Shadrach, Meshach, and Abednego. Write a two to three paragraph summary on how they remained faithful to God in an ungodly environment, amidst temptation and persecution. Make sure to consider what enabled them to remain steadfast in their beliefs.

Ongoing prophets' project

Take out the separate document that you started during your Isaiah study. Add to it what you learn about the "day of the Lord" versus the "great day of the Lord" from Daniel. Keep adding to this document as you work through the prophets.

Application inspiration

- The application of the book of Daniel – hope – remains the same today as it was for Daniel, when he heard of the evil coming upon his people; for the readers in the time of the Maccabees, as they faced persecution under Antiochus Epiphanes; and for the early church, which was under persecution when John wrote his Revelation from Christ. Hope enables believers to endure persecutions, trials, and uncertainties. It gives God's people confidence, knowing that they will partake in Christ's inheritance and enter into the eternal Kingdom of God with the rest of His saints. Look up 2 Timothy 2:8-13 and reflect on the words.
- How can you live in the world, but not of the world, as Daniel and his three friends?
  - See John 17:11,16.
  - Are you living as light and salt to those around you?
- The book of Daniel shows that the choice of obedience is a daily decision.
  - Are you walking in obedience every day?
  - Are you obedient in the small, seemingly trivial things?
  - How can you live faithfully in the small, daily choices you must make?
- Is it enough for you that God knows the time of Christ's return? Does it frustrate you that you do not have more details or do you find it easy to release this to God?
- When you are faced with a situation you do not understand, are you able to take comfort in the knowledge that God understands it?

---

[1] Daniel 3:16-18
[2] Smith, R. (2004).

[3] Matthew 12:14-17

HOSEA

Israel plays the Whore

And the LORD said to me, "Go again, love a woman who is loved by another man and is an adulteress, even as the LORD loves the children of Israel, though they turn to other gods and love cakes of raisins." – Hosea 3:1

Notes

This is a graphic book in which God revealed His passionate and jealous heart for His people. The title of this chapter is appropriate. Whilst reading Hosea may make some uncomfortable, one must remember that it should be an unpleasant read! Its intention was to reveal God's heart to His people and show them how He viewed their idolatry. It is not mere religion to God; the sins of His people broke His heart, like man's hearts would break if their partner committed adultery.

The books of Amos and Hosea were set at the same time, but view God's judgement on Israel from different angles. Amos was written from the viewpoint of an outsider, whilst Hosea was written from a local's perspective. It is beneficial to study the books together.

During your first reading

Suggestion: Read through the book once, highlighting only the words "unfaithful", "adultery" and "whoredom". Take a break after this first read, and then read through it a second time. What emotions did the two readings elicit from you?

Themes to track
- God's judgement
- Faithlessness/ adulterous nation
- God's heart for His people
- What true love does

- God's character (faithfulness/ love)

During your second reading

Things to notice in the text
- Highlight the repeated words "un/faithful", "adultery", and "whore".
- Mark the passages containing judgement; for example, use a red "J".
- Mark the sins listed – the reason for judgement; for example, put a red "X" next to passages containing a list of the people's sin.
- Mark the passages promising restoration or giving hope; for example, with a green line.

Chapter summaries
These are optional as they can be time consuming for the larger books. If you choose to do them, you will receive a much deeper appreciation of the book. By the end of The IBSC, you will have paraphrased the entire Bible! Go through each chapter and try to summarise it in one paragraph, using your own words; force yourself to stay big picture and capture the heart of each chapter.

After your initial readings

Setting of Hosea
Author
The book was penned by the prophet, Hosea.

Date prophecies were spoken
Hosea spoke the prophecies during the reign of Jeroboam II (782-753 BC) of Israel and during the reigns of Uzziah (767-740/39 BC), Jotham (740/39-732/1 BC), Ahaz (732/1-716/5 BC), and Hezekiah (716/5- 687/6 BC) of Judah.

Recipient – hearers
The prophecies were spoken to the Northern Kingdom of Israel.

Recipient – readers
The prophecies were recorded for the southern kingdom of Judah, as a warning.

Date and place of writing
The book was written sometime between Israel's defeat by the Assyrians in 722 BC, and when Judah fell to the Babylonians in 687 BC. Hosea most likely fled to Judah when Israel fell, making it the place where the book was composed.

Reason spoken
Hosea brought God's sentence against Israel, who had continually spurned God's love and rejected His grace and mercy. Their punishment was just, but God still loved them despite their sins and was trying to call them back to Him. The message proclaimed God's redeeming love. It was a message of hope for the nation.

Reason written

The book of Hosea was written as a warning to the people of Judah. God had called Israel to judgement and Judah needed to steer clear of the sins of their northern brethren if they were to avoid the same end. It called the people of Judah to repentance so that God might heal them.

Big picture

Historical background

Words used to refer to Israel

- Ephraim: one of the biggest tribes of the northern kingdom; a source of pride for them.
- Israel: the name of the nation.
- Samaria: a captive city of Israel.

Israel under Jeroboam II

Israel experienced a period of prosperity during the reign of Jeroboam II, before entering a period of spiralling corruption and decay in their last years, leading to their defeat in 722 BC. The four kings that followed Jeroboam II were all assassinated, during a period of turmoil within Israel.

Surrounding nations

Assyria was the world power at the time these prophecies came to the northern kingdom. Israel had sought aid from both Egypt and Assyria at various times, for protection against enemies.

Character portrayal – Hosea's prayer to the Lord

"Holy God, how do you cope with the heartache that you feel for these people? Gomer's betrayal tore my heart. It has been shattered into irreparable shards. Yet still, you call me to love her. How am I to overcome the grief, anger, and pain that I feel, in order to once again bring her under the protection of my name?

"She is beautiful, yes, but is she worth it? What makes this nation worth it for you? Why do you love this faithless people? Let your wrath come against them and have done with it! If you show them mercy, they will only sin against you once again.

"Who is like you, God? Help my heart to love Gomer as you call me to love her. Help me to bring her home in accordance with your command. I do not understand it, but I will walk in obedience."

Book overview

This is a story of the redeeming love of God. It shows that His love and commitment to the unfaithful people of Israel is unchanging. God's love was a redeeming love, which fought to bring His people back to Him. His love is true, pure, and selfless.

Hosea proclaimed God's purpose and desire for His people: *"Come, let us return to the LORD; for he has torn us, that he may heal us; he has struck us down, and he will bind us up.*" [1]

God desired to heal and restore His people. His love went beyond the love one returns to one who shows kindness. God showed that true love continues to pursue, even in the face of rejection. God's love always chooses the option to forgive, and then restore, broken relationship. However, God being just will bring punishment on those who continue to reject Him for other gods. He is jealous of His people and demands all of their worship and praise.

Hosea's life was lived to reflect God's relationship with the people of Israel. Hosea was to represent God's passionate devotion to His people by lovingly and persistently pursuing his wife. Gomer's unfaithfulness, in stark contrast to her husband's love, represented the people of Israel in the story. Sadly, no matter what God did, His people kept running away from Him, back into prostitution with false gods and idols.

God's heart is always to restore people to Him. He does not desire to bring judgement, yet His holiness demands it against sin. He is always willing to put aside His wrath for those who return to Him in true repentance of heart. Even His judgement shows His mercy; it reveals to mankind their sin and thus their need of a Saviour. God is the only Savour. God is the one with the power to restore man to relationship with Him.

Interpreting the book of Hosea
<u>Interpretation questions</u>

1. It was suggested that in your first reading, you highlight only the words "unfaithful", "adultery", and "whoredom", and that after that reading you take a break, and then read through the book for a second time.
    a. How did you feel at the end of the first reading? What about at the end of the second reading?
    b. How would the Israelites have felt and what would their response have been?
    c. Would the Israelites have accepted this message?
    d. What about Judah, reading these words as they watched the Assyrians invade their northern brethren?

2. As you study Hosea, make a table of who was being sentenced by God. For each nation or people group called out for judgement, list the following:
    a. What were the sins listed against them? Can you put them into a category, such as: social oppression, idolatry, pride or rebellion?
    b. What punishment was coming against them?
    c. When did the prophecy take place? What was its fulfilment date, and what did the fulfilment of the prophecy look like? Refer to *Introduction to the prophets.*
    d. Compare your findings to the ones you made when studying Amos.

3. Consider the emotional cost of Hosea's call.
    a. How would he have felt about marrying a prostitute?

    b.   What emotions would have arisen when naming his children as per God's commands, and raising them in a household where their mother came and went?

4. Why would God want a real-life illustration of His heart for the people? Why was a story not enough?

5. What was God communicating to Israel about their relationship with Him through:

    a.   Hosea's marriage in Hosea 1:2-3?

    b.   His first son, Jezreel, in Hosea 1:3-5?

    c.   His daughter, Lo-Ruhamah, in Hosea 1:6-7?

    d.   His second son, Lo-Ammi, in Hosea 1:8-9?

    e.   Bringing his wife back in Hosea 3:1-5?

6. What message of hope was given in Hosea 5:15-6:3?

    a.   Did this passage give hope, in light of the text on either side of it?

    b.   What response did Hosea want from the people?

7. The following verses display God's desire to heal His people: Hosea 6:5-7:11; 9:10; 11:1-7; 13:4-6; 14:1-3. Take note of the contrasting responses from the Israelites.

8. The judgement on Israel can be seen as a lawsuit against them. Identify the following elements in Hosea 4, 5, 8 and 11:12-12:14:

    a.   God calls them (in a lawsuit, this would be the summons to appear); then

    b.   God lists their sin (charge and evidence); and finally

    c.   God proclaimed their judgement (the verdict).

    d.   What was the likely fulfilment for the judgements given? Refer to *Introduction to the prophets*.

9. Look at the "woe oracle" in Hosea 7:13. Give:

    a.   The reason for distress (sins of the people; the words "woe", "alas", or "ah" are usually hints);

    b.   The prediction of doom (their coming judgement); and

    c.   When it was likely fulfilled.

10. Can you pair verses from Hosea, and the judgement God foretold, with those He warned the people would come for disobedience in Leviticus and Deuteronomy?

11. The judgement coming upon Israel should not have been a surprise for the people, if they had known the Law. For example: Hosea 2:2 and Deuteronomy 28:39 both promise that God will lay waste to their vineyards as a curse for disobedience. Re-read through Deuteronomy 28 and take note of the curses promised for disobedience.

12. Consider the following passages: Hosea 1:10-2:1; 3:14-23; 11:8-11; 14:4-9.

    a.   What was portrayed through God's promise of restoration?

    b.   Which of these passages relate to the "great day of the Lord" and are promises for all the people of God who call upon Christ as their Saviour?

    c.   When were, or will, these restoration promises be fulfilled. Refer to *Introduction to the prophets*.

13. What does this book show of God's heart for His people?
    a. What does Hosea show of His jealousy over His people, His desire for them, and His unending love towards them?
    b. What do you see of His wrath?
    c. What do you learn of His grace and mercy?
14. Read Romans 9:22-28.
    a. What hope is given through these words to the people of God?
    b. What is their significance?
    c. What are the implications for Christians and non-Christians?

Creative interpretation

1. The book of Hosea used the illustration of a faithless bride to reflect upon the sins Israel had committed against God. Looking at the illustration of unfaithfulness:
    a. Why did God show His heart to Hosea in this way?
    b. What emotions do the images bring up?
    c. What aspect of God's heart was revealed? What new insights did you see of God's heart, love, and desire for relationship with man?
    d. Was Israel to pursue God or did God pursue Israel? Was it a mutual pursuit?
    e. Is God's discipline really loving; why or why not?
    f. How was Israel unfaithful?
    g. What response to these warnings did God want from the people?
    h. How does this imagery redefine your view of true love? What actions does this love take? What does it reveal about loves' ability to heal and restore?

Ongoing prophets' project

Take out the separate document that you started during your Isaiah study. Add to it what you learn about the "day of the Lord" versus the "great day of the Lord" from Hosea. Keep adding to this document as you work through the prophets.

Application inspiration

Of the heart

- Study the Word to seek God's heart, rather than for knowledge alone. He wants to be your focus.
- It is seen in Hosea that it can be costly and painful to be given God's heart for a person, country or issue. Yet it also brings a new level of intimacy with God. Do you believe it is worth the cost? Pray for more of God's heart wisely, and remember that its rewards are worth any heartache that comes with it. It can be a painful thing to share God's love – to experience His heart for another person, a nation or an area of society – but what a privilege and blessing too.

- Think over your life. What part of His heart has He shared especially with you? Is it for children, some of your workmates, societal "lepers", a specific nation, the church . . . ? How are you going to give out His love to these people?

[1] Hosea 6:1

JOEL

Coming day of the Lord

"Yet even now," declares the LORD, "return to me with all your heart, with fasting, with weeping, and with mourning; and rend your hearts and not your garments." Return to the LORD your God, for he is gracious and merciful, slow to anger, and abounding in steadfast love; and he relents over disaster. – Joel 2:12-13

During your first reading

Themes to track
- Day of the Lord
- Great day of the Lord – final judgement, the end of days.
- Judgement
- Repentance

During your second reading

Things to notice in the text
- God's character and promises
- God's actions
- Coming judgement
- The call to respond (to the message)
- Use of language; for example: "like lions", "like a virgin grieving", "like dawn".

Chapter summaries

These are optional as they can be time consuming for the larger books. If you choose to do them, you will receive a much deeper appreciation of the book. By the end of The IBSC, you will have paraphrased the entire Bible! Go through each chapter and try to summarise it in one paragraph, using your own words; force yourself to stay big picture and capture the heart of each chapter.

After your initial readings

Setting of Joel
Author
The book was written by Joel, the son of Pethuel.

Date prophecies were spoken
There is contention over the time frame of these prophecies. Three main time periods are suggested by scholars as follows:

- Pre-exile: During King Joash's youth, whilst the nation was under stewardship. This would account for why a monarch was not mentioned. During this time the temple still stood, as supported by the text. King Joash took the throne at seven years of age, reigning from 835 BC to 796 BC.
- Early post-exile: After the rebuilding of the temple and the wall of Jerusalem, as the book uses past-tense language that the people had been scattered. This also fits the text not mentioning a king or the nations of Assyria and Babylon. The suggested date range for this option is 444-400 BC.
- Late post-exile: This date range has gained support due to the heavy use of quotations within Joel from other books, such as Isaiah and Ezekiel. The suggested date range for this option is 400-180 BC.

Recipient – hearers
The prophecies were spoken to the nation of Judah.

Recipient – readers
The prophecies were written for the nation of Judah.

Date and place of writing
The prophecies were written at the same time that they were spoken. Again, three options exist: pre-exile (835-796 BC), early post-exile (444-400 BC) or late post-exile (400-180 BC). Although the internal evidence does not make the place of writing clear, the references to Zion, Judah, and Jerusalem make it reasonable to assume that it was written from within Judah, and probably from the city of Jerusalem.

Reason spoken
The message is clear: the people needed to repent for the day of the Lord was coming. Disaster had come upon them for their sins and they needed to repent as more judgement was on the way. God was showing the people that there was a solution to their misery – they needed to rend their hearts and not their clothes. God was calling them to return to Him with all their hearts.

Reason written

Similar to the reason spoken, the book was a call to repent for the day of the Lord was coming. It called the people to acknowledge their guilt before the Lord and call upon His mercy. They were to rend their heart in grief and acknowledge their sin before God.

Big picture

Historical background

Pre-exile

During the reign of Joash, the priests were in a position of authority, the temple was still standing, and sacrifices were considered important (836-796 BC). If Joel lived during the reign of Joash, then the original readers lived in the desperate financial years of Judah. Queen Athaliah's reign had just ended and the Lord had begun to cut off parts of the territory of the Northern Kingdom of Israel.

During this time, Assyria was under the rule of Shalmaneser II and Syria was under the rule of Hazel. In 790 BC, the Syrians came up against Joash and executed judgement upon Judah.

Note that the language of the text surrounding the "day of the Lord" is similar to that of the prophet Zephaniah who prophesied during the reign of Josiah, king of Judah (640-609 BC).

Post-exile

During this time, the priests were in a position of authority, the temple had been rebuilt, and sacrifices were considered important (500-400 BC). The Jews were under the rule of the Persians and had no king of their own.

The locusts

Locust plagues have three stages:
1. The initial cloud, or swarm, comes through. They consume the greenery and lay eggs. Each female can lay about one hundred eggs.
2. The eggs hatch. The juveniles cannot fly, but rather hop around and consume any greenery close to them.
3. The second generation grow wings and take off to wipe out anything eatable that was left by the first generation.

Some suggest that the locust plague referred to in Joel was a metaphor to describe the total destruction that would occur in the land, leaving nothing behind. The description in the book gives an impression of three stages, which matches the cycle that occurs in literal locust plagues, so it could also have been predicting that a real plague would come upon the land. A third interpretation is that the prophesied locusts were fulfilled both metaphorically and literally against Judah.

Character portrayal – discussion of the prophecies

"Maybe the words of Joel are true," Benjamin said with a slight tremor in his voice.

"The other prophets do not agree with him," Erez replied, holding to common opinion.

"Yes, but the locusts last year . . ."

"Wouldn't you insert that into a false prophecy? I say that Joel is the odd one out amongst the prophets, and that suggests he is the one making things up."

"Events in the land have improved a little since Joash became king and people began to worship the God of David again." Benjamin referred to the restoration Joel promised would come upon Judah if they turned back to their God.

"Benjamin is right," Hadar voiced his opinion. He was not hasty to speak, but his wisdom, when given, was well-respected in their town. "Our lot has improved since the king called us to repent before the Lord."

"The God of our fathers is with us once more," Benjamin replied with rising spirits.

"Perhaps." Erez remained sceptical. "Let us hope that the Almighty will do as He promises through your prophet Joel and crush our enemies. The Syrians are growing in strength . . ."

Book overview

The book of Joel looks at both the day of the Lord and the great day of the Lord.

The "day of the Lord" referred to the judgement that would befall the nation of Judah if they did not repent before the Lord. It was a physical judgement that was coming upon the nation for its sins. No one would be able to endure it, but if they repented, He would turn His wrath aside from them. God was using judgement to draw His people back to Him.

The "great day of the Lord" refers to the final judgement of God, at which time He will judge all nations and all people. There will no longer be a chance to repent. Those who are in Christ will be safe, but all others will be utterly destroyed. God will gather the nations for judgement, but His people will receive salvation. His judgement will come upon the nations in retribution for the wrongs they have done His people. Those who call on God shall be saved from His wrath and will see His wonders on the great day of the Lord.

Help with difficult passages

Cut off offerings; Joel 1:9,13

Judah could not face a greater calamity than the suspension of the daily sacrifice. The Law and covenant was what made them distinct from other nations. If they could no longer sacrifice offerings, they would lose the one thing that defined them as a nation. It was a physical sign that God had rejected His people. With the fields in ruin, they could not bring the sacrificial offerings, even if they had wanted to, as there was nothing left for them to bring.

Between the vestibule and altar; Joel 2:17

This was as close to the curtain of the temple as they were allowed to come under the old covenant and sacrificial system. God was saying: "Get closer, get closer to me".

Valley of Jehoshaphat; Joel 3:1-8

Jehoshaphat means "judgement". This was not physical language, referring to a physical valley; it was referring to bringing the people into a place of judgement.

Language usage – the "day of the Lord"

Note that there is a difference between the "day of the Lord" and the "great day of the Lord". Every mention of the day of the Lord in Joel was followed with the opportunity for repentance. When the great day comes, there will be no opportunity to repent.

Interpreting the book of Joel

<u>Interpretation questions</u>

1. Who was being judged?
   a. Upon whom was God calling out judgement?
   b. Why was judgement falling?
2. What curses for covenant disobedience are seen (refer to Deuteronomy 28)?
3. Consider the description of the locust plague that had come upon the people. Consider the devastation this would have caused to an agricultural nation. How would the people have felt as they saw the locusts coming upon their crops?
4. Why would God first let only one curse fall on them, and then tell of the ones still to come if they remained unrepentant?
   a. What did He want them to do?
   b. How was He trying to get them to change?
   c. What response was He seeking from the people?
5. Consider the devastation that sin causes, as seen in Joel 1:1-11.
6. Look back at 2 Kings 12 and 2 Chronicles 24, which record the reign of Joash.
   a. If the locust plague occurred during his reign, what significance may it have had on the events of which you read?
   b. How was the author of Joel linking the destruction they were seeing with the sins of his readers?
7. Read over chapter 1:1-2:11 and pause.
   a. How would the original hearers have felt at this point?
   b. Read on until the end of the book. Would their emotions have changed?
8. What do you learn of the day of the Lord?
9. What was said about the great day of the Lord?
10. What should the people's response have been to the coming judgement?
11. List the promises that God gave to His people. How would these promises have strengthened the hearts of the Judeans when they saw God's judgement fall upon them?
12. Who was the great army mentioned in the prophecies?

13. Notice the change in who was being judged. At the start, God was judging His people, but in chapter 3 He began judging the nations.
14. Look at the New Testament fulfilment of the prophecies in Joel 2:28-32.
    a. Read Joel 2:28-29 and Acts 2:17-18. What was the significance of Pentecost?
    b. Read Joel 2:30-32 and Romans 10:12-13. What are the implications of these passages?

Creative interpretation

1. Consider the illustrations that the author gave to the people and their implications. For example, in Joel 1 he called the drunkards to weep, for there would be an end to the wine. A drunkard is one who has become dependent on alcohol to drown out their sorrows or is physically reliant upon alcohol, as a coping mechanism. They would suffer withdraw systems that may even lead to mental illness.

Ongoing prophets' project

Take out the separate document that you started during your Isaiah study. Add to it what you learn about the "day of the Lord" versus the "great day of the Lord" from Joel. Keep adding to this document as you work through the prophets.

Application inspiration

Living in the light of eternity

- Are you mindful of eternity?
- Would you give up your comfort now, to bring another into the eternal Kingdom of God? Do you value other people's eternity?
- The day of judgement coming on the great day of the Lord is not something to rejoice over. Be motivated by other people's eternity. Intercede through prayer for those in your life who do not know Christ or have turned from Him.
- Praise God for His mercy, compassion, and love that have turned His anger aside from you. Be thankful for what the Lord has done and come before Him with your heart and life as an offering.

AMOS

Judged for Injustice

But let justice roll down like waters, and righteousness like an ever-flowing stream. – Amos 5:24

Notes: The books of Amos and Hosea were set at the same time, but view God's judgement on Israel from different angles. Amos was written from the viewpoint of an outsider, whilst Hosea was written from a local's perspective. It is beneficial to study the books together.

During your first reading

Themes to track
- Social injustice
- Oppression of the poor
- Pride
- Laziness
- Idolatry

During your second reading

Things to notice in the text
- Highlight repeated words (these will help you find patterns in the text):
    - "For three sins . . . , even for four"
    - "Not returned to me"
    - "Though they . . ., from there . . ."
    - "Woe"/ "ah"
    - "I saw"
- Mark the passages containing judgement; for example, use a red "J".
- Mark the sins listed – the reason for judgement; for example, put a red "X" next to passages containing a list of the people's sin.

- Mark the passages promising restoration or giving hope; for example, with a green line.

Chapter summaries

These are optional as they can be time consuming for the larger books. If you choose to do them, you will receive a much deeper appreciation of the book. By the end of The IBSC, you will have paraphrased the entire Bible! Go through each chapter and try to summarise it in one paragraph, using your own words; force yourself to stay big picture and capture the heart of each chapter.

After your initial readings

Setting of Amos
Author

The prophet Amos was the author of this book. Amos was from Judah, but was sent to prophesy against his northern brethren in Israel.

Date prophecies were spoken

Amos spoke during the days of King Uzziah of Judah (767-740/39 BC), and of King Jeroboam II of Israel (782/81-753 BC).

Recipient – hearers

The prophecies were spoken to the nation of Israel (the northern kingdom).

Recipient – readers

The prophecies were recorded for the nation of Judah (the southern kingdom).

Date and place of writing

Amos spoke during the days of King Uzziah of Judah (767-740/39 BC), and of King Jeroboam II of Israel (782/81-753 BC). He would have penned his record during this time whilst in Israel or after returning to his native land of Judah.

Reason spoken

Amos brought his message urging the people of Israel to repent during a time of national prosperity, under the reign of King Jeroboam II. God was calling the people to repent from their lives of social injustice, idolatry, and pride.

Reason written

The book of Amos was written to Judah, as a warning to them against committing the sins of their brothers in Israel.

Big picture
Historical background
Israel

Israel was at the height of their wealth and territorial possession under the rule of

King Jeroboam II. He restored the borders of Israel from the entrance of Hamath as far as the Sea of the Arabah [1]. He also restored Israelite control over much of the Transjordan [2].

Amos was not sent to a land feeling a desperate need for the Lord. The Israelites, to whom this prophecy was brought, were enjoying their wealth and living in luxury. This can be seen in the text as you read of their summer and winter houses and the wine that they were drinking [3]. Their response to wealth was corruption (both religious and political), oppression of the poor, injustice in business, and violence. Israel's place of religious worship was also a place of idolatry [4].

The world power

Assyria was the world power during this time of history. They were particularly feared for their cruelty and brutality. For example, captives of war were strung together in lines by a rope that went through rings inserted into their noses. The prisoners were then forced to walk like this for days as they were marched to Assyria.

Fulfilment

These prophecies came to fulfilment in 722 BC when Israel was defeated by Assyria and exiled to Damascus.

Character portrayal – Amos speaks of his unlikely call

"I was but a lowly shepherd. I have no education and no knowledge of governing, kingship or the priesthood. Despite this, God called me and so I obeyed. He sent me to Israel where I was not welcome and my words brought nothing aside from isolation and loneliness in the world. Despite the consequences, I could not cease my words. His people were sinning against Him. They had forgotten their Maker and were oppressing the poor amongst them. Injustice was rife in that land and I could not stand by knowing it was occurring.

"The life of a shepherd is a simple and beautiful one, yet I was called away from it to go to an unfaithful nation, whose sins were bringing judgement upon the land. They did not listen to me. They did not want to hear my message. Yet I was faithful and that is all that the Lord God Almighty required of me. A simple shepherd, I became a prophet by His grace."

Book overview

God has a heart for social justice. This is reflected in His Law, His Word, and His judgements. The nations surrounding Israel were judged for the wrongs they had done to their neighbours during war. His people were not exempt from the consequences of sin, with God promising that His judgement would come upon them too.

In Israel, sin abounded. There was affliction of the needy and the righteous. The wealthy were turning aside from those who lacked basic life needs, whilst taking bribes to further enrich their own lives. There was also slavery, the buying of the poor. People were deceitful in their business practices. The rich stretched themselves out in gluttony and laziness, whilst they kept the gleanings for themselves, selling even the chaff, rather than letting the poor collect this pittance for food. Israel had become greedy and without compassion for the poor. They sought the way of violence, having rejected righteousness and justice. For all of this, they were to be judged.

The prophets show that His judgement and mercy fit together. His punishment was given with the desire to restore and bring the people back into His grace, just like a parent who disciplines their child in reproof in order to teach the child without causing them harm. He did not delight in having to inflict judgement upon them. He longed to bring them back to Him.

Help with the use of language
Wormwood = poison, bitter

Wormwood is a species of plant of the genus Artemisia. The herbs and shrubs are usually bitter to taste and have strong aromas.

Plumb line = measuring instrument

A plumb line is an instrument used in construction to make sure a building is straight. Symbolically, it was representative of God's perfect standard, the Law.

Interpreting the book of Amos
Interpretation questions

Remember that the original hearers of these prophecies were the people of Israel, whilst the original readers were the people in Judah.

1. As you study Amos, make a table of who was being sentenced by God. For each nation or people group called out for judgement, list the following:
    a. What were the sins listed against them? Can you put them into a category, such as: social oppression, idolatry, pride or rebellion?
    b. What punishment was coming against them?
    c. When did the prophecy take place? What was its fulfilment date, and what did the fulfilment of the prophecy look like? Refer to Introduction to the prophets.
    d. Compare your findings to the ones you made when studying Hosea.
2. Many of the sins listed in this book are listed in the books of Leviticus and Deuteronomy. As you read of the sins listed against Israel and the nations, refer back to the Law that God gave to His people.
3. Response to the message:
    a. What would the original hearers have been thinking as they listened to the words recorded in Amos 1:1-2:3 and heard of the coming judgement upon their enemies?
    b. What would the original readers have been thinking as they listened to the words recorded in Amos 1:1-2:3?
    c. Read James 4:1-12 and comment on how they should have responded to the predicted downfall of their enemies.
4. The judgements on the nations were listed much like a lawsuit might be

conducted. List the following elements for the judgement of each of the six nations and Judah (Amos 1:3-2:5):

    a. God first called them (in a lawsuit, this would be the summons to appear), then.

    b. He lists their sin (charge and evidence), and finally.

    c. He pronounced the judgement (the verdict).

    d. What was the likely fulfilment of these prophecies for each of the nations listed? Refer to *Introduction to the prophets.*

5. Three "words" were given against Israel in Amos 3:1-5:17.

    a. At whom within Israel were these aimed?

    b. What were their sins, and how were they to be judged?

    c. Was there any hope for restoration?

6. Read Amos 4:4-5 and 5:14.

    a. What do these verses imply about how the Israelites viewed their relationship with God?

    b. Having responded with pride to the proclamations in Amos 1:1-2:3, how would they react as they listened to the words of Amos recorded in Amos 2:4 onwards?

7. What point was God trying to get across with the imagery in chapter 3:1-7? How would this imagery have drawn the original readers in by grabbing their attention?

8. You marked the repeated words "not returned (to me)" in chapter 4:6-12.

    a. What was God trying to achieve amongst His people?

    b. What was His desire and hope?

    c. What does this reveal about His character?

    d. Why was the author listing these?

    e. What response was Amos seeking from the Judeans?

9. What was Amos' aim in chapter 5:14-15?

    a. What was he calling the original hearers to do?

    b. What does this reveal about God's continued desire for His people even in the face of His wrath against injustice?

10. Three "woes" are listed in Amos 5:18-6:14 (some translations do not list the third woe in Amos 6:4). For each woe, give:

    a. The reason for distress (sins of the people). The words "woe", "alas", or "ah" are usually hints.

    b. The prediction of doom (coming judgement), and

    c. When the judgement was likely fulfilled.

11. What do you learn about the day of the Lord from Amos 5:18-27?

12. Amos lists five visions that the Lord gave to him (Amos 7:1-9:10). From these visions:

    a. What do you learn about Amos? What actions did he take?

    b. Was Amos able to make a difference to the fate of the people?

    c. List the sins of the people that are specified.

    d. What did God show of Himself? What was revealed of His character?

e. Give a list of the judgements that fell or are to fall.

f. How did the imagery of the visions add weight to their message?

13. What point is God trying to get across about the coming judgement in Amos 9:2-4?

14. How would the original hearers (Israel) have felt by the time they heard chapter 9:11-15?

a. Would they get hope from this message?

b. What did it convey about what the future holds for them?

c. Would the response of the original readers (nation of Judah) have been different to that of Israel?

15. What image of Himself did God portray through the words of Amos? Read Amos 2:9-11; 4:13; 5:14-16; 9.

16. Look back on the special study that you completed for Kings and Chronicles.

a. What was the situation in Israel during the reign of Jeroboam II, son of Jehoash (2 Kings 14:23-29)?

b. Were the people well off, facing natural disasters or plagued by war?

c. How may this have impacted on how the people responded to the prophecy of Amos (Amos 7:10-13)?

17. What do you learn of Amos and his character from the following verses: Amos 1:1-2; 7:2; 7:5; 7:10-16; 8:3?

18. Read 1 Corinthians 1:26-31. How does this relate to God's call on Amos' life?

19. Israel's place of worship in Bethel held two gold calves that were worshipped as idols. And yet Amos spends little time on their idolatry compared to social injustice. What is the significance of this?

Creative interpretation

1. Oppression and social injustice are recurring themes in the books of the prophets. Take note of some of the situations of social injustice listed through Amos, then answer the following:

a. Was there a social divide?

b. Who were listed as the poor?

c. Who were the oppressed?

d. What or who was causing the oppression?

e. What should the rich have been doing for their brothers in need? Refer back to God's commands given in Leviticus.

f. How did the Law call them to live?

Ongoing prophets' project

Take out the separate document that you started during your Isaiah study. Add to it what you learn about the "day of the Lord" versus the "great day of the Lord" from Amos. Keep adding to this document as you work through the prophets.

Application inspiration

A heart for social justice

- Ultimately, nations can be changed when they practise social justice. Every individual is valuable.
    - How will you model this to your children and to others around you?
    - Individuals can make a change for social justice. Can you think of a way you can aid the oppressed, poor or neglected in your community?
    - Does your church have a social justice group in which you could become involved?
    - Is this a topic that you could bring up in Bible Study?
    - What issues are in the media that you could pray into, focusing on God's heart for social justice?
- Consider the life of William Wilberforce: He strove for years to have the slave trade aborted. How long did he get to celebrate this achievement? He died only three days after hearing that the Slavery Abolition Act had been passed. Yet his one life made a difference, not only in England, but world-wide and across generations.

[1] 2 Kings 14:25
[2] Amos 6:13; 1 Chronicles 5:17
[3] Amos 3:15-4:1
[4] 1 Kings 12:28-29

OBADIAH

Sins against a Brother

"Because of the violence done to your brother Jacob, shame shall cover you, and you shall be cut off forever. On the day that you stood aloof, on the day that strangers carried off his wealth and foreigners entered his gates and cast lots for Jerusalem, you were like one of them." – Obadiah 1:10-11

During your first reading

Themes to track
- Pride
- God's judgement upon pride
- Unbrotherly actions
- Day of the Lord
- Kingdom of God

During your second reading

Things to notice in the text
- Edom's wrongs against Judah
- God's judgement
- Restoration of God's people

Chapter summaries

These are optional as they can be time consuming for the larger books. If you choose to do them, you will receive a much deeper appreciation of the book. By the end of The IBSC, you will have paraphrased the entire Bible! Go through each chapter and try to summarise it in one paragraph, using your own words; force yourself to stay big picture and capture the heart of each chapter.

After your initial readings

Setting of Obadiah

Author

The prophet Obadiah is credited with writing this book. There are fourteen others named Obadiah that are referenced in the Bible, but none can clearly be established as being the same person as the author of this book.

Date prophecies were spoken

Two time frames are proposed for when these prophecies were spoken:
1. Early date: 845 BC; pre-exilic.
    Edom revolted against Judah (2 Chronicles 21:8-10,16-17); however, they did not physically take arms against Judah at this time whereas the book of Obadiah implies that Edom physically came against Judah.
2. Late date: 586 BC; during exile.
    The words Jeremiah recorded in Jeremiah 49:7-13 parallel those recorded in Obadiah 1:10-15, which suggests that Edom was being judged because they watched the fall of Jerusalem with glee. Psalm 137:7 also links the date of Obadiah's prophecy to after the fall of Jerusalem to the Babylonians in 586 BC.

Recipient – hearers

The book of Obadiah does not mention that the prophet went to Edom. If these prophecies were spoken, as opposed to just written, it would likely have been within the nation of Judah; although word of his proclamations may have reached the Edomites.

Recipient – readers

The book of Obadiah was written for the people of Judah.

Date and place of writing

The prophecies were recorded at the same time they were spoken. Again, two main dates have been proposed: an early date of 845 BC or a later date of 586 BC. If the early date is taken, the book would have been written in Judah, but a later date of writing would imply that Obadiah wrote from exile in Babylon. The book is written in past tense implying that Edom had already committed these wrongs against their brothers.

Reason spoken

The prophecies were spoken to show that God had seen Edom's sins against their brother Judah and that judgement would fall upon them for their deeds.

Reason written

The book was written to encourage the surviving Judeans with the message that God had not abandoned them and justice would be served upon Edom.

Big picture
Historical background
Early date – 845 BC

The early date would fall during the reign of King Joram (also named Jehoram), making Obadiah a contemporary of the prophet Elijah. During his reign, Edom revolted against the rule of Judah and set up a king from their own people. Key enemies at this time were the Philistines and Arabians, who invaded the camp of Judah. They took away the king's possessions, his sons, and wives. The only son left to him was his youngest, Jehoahaz (also named Ahaziah). See 2 Kings 8:16-24 and 2 Chronicles 21 for further background information.

Late date – 586 BC

Zedekiah was king over Judah from 597-587 BC. Jerusalem finally fell to Nebuchadnezzar, king of Babylon, in 586 BC. Edom did not come to Judah's aid when they were conquered. This date would make Obadiah a contemporary of Jeremiah, as indicated by Jeremiah 49. See 2 Kings 24:18-25:30 for further background information.

Geographical borders of Edom
- Northern = Wadi Zered (Zered River).
- Southern = The Gulf of Aqabah; Elath and Ezion-Geber.
- Eastern = Desert; its inhabitants were the Kedemites .
- Western = There was probably no fixed western boundary, being contested with Judah.

History between Judah and Edom
- 1900s BC – Jacob and Esau.
- Around 1400 BC – Edom denied Israel passage through its territory.
- 1040 BC – King Saul fought against Edom.
- Around 1000 BC – Abishai killed 18 thousand Edomites in the Valley of Salt. The Edomites became David's servants.
- 860s BC – Edom was ruled by Jehoshaphat.
- 840s BC – Edom revolted against Jehoram.
- 780s BC – Amaziah defeated 20 thousand Edomites in the Valley of Salt.
- 586 BC – Edom participated in the fall of Jerusalem.

Prophecy fulfilments (Edom judged)
The fall of Edom was progressive:
- 860-850 BC – Ammonites and Moabites attacked Mt. Seir (2 Chronicles 20).
- 8thC BC – Edom came under pressure from Arabian tribes.
- 732 BC – Edom became tribute-payers of Assyria.
- 604 BC – Edom fell under the suzerainty of Babylon.

- 6thC BC – Nomadic tribes forced Edom into the Negeb, which became known as Idumea.
- 312 BC – Edom was dislodged from Petra by the Nabateans.
- 165/4 BC – The Idumeans (formerly Edomites) were driven from the Negeb by Judas Macabaeus.
- 126 BC – Judaism, including circumcision, was forced upon the Idumeans by John Hyrcanus, during the time of the Maccabees.
- 70 AD – After 70 AD, Edom (Idumea) disappears from history. This is the same time that Jerusalem fell to Rome at the hands of Emperor Titus.

Character portrayal – leaders of Edom; a chorus of voices

"Nebuchadnezzar is preparing to march on Judah," Anat spoke vindictively.

"Shall we side with him?" Barauch asked. He was unsure how their nation should respond.

"They are our brothers. We cannot fight against them!" Koppel opposed.

"They are no brothers of mine!" Anat said, with stubborn hatred.

"Or mine. If they are God's chosen, let Him save them," said one who had recently joined the group.

"It does not look to me as if they are His chosen anymore," Anat sniggered. "Perhaps this is a sign that God has come to our side. We will reap the benefits of Judah's fall."

"So we sit and wait?" Barauch asked.

"We sit and wait. Let us see whose side God is on!"

Book overview

In Obadiah, the nation of Edom was being judged for the hatred it had towards its brother nation, Judah. They could not forgive their brothers, and so God declared their sentence to be one of destruction. They were being judged because they had chosen to stand by and watch their brothers be overthrown by the Babylonians. The start of this brotherly feud is recorded right back in Genesis, between the brothers Esau and Jacob. Generations later, the wounds still festered between families that had grown into two separate nations – Edom and Judah.

Edom had boasted in the fall of their brother-nation, Judah. They chose to side against their brother, rather than to stand side by side with them in the day of Judah's distress. God was judging Edom because they harboured bitterness and judgement against their brothers, God's chosen people, for generations. They allowed past issues to fester until it caused them to act against their brothers. Neither side should have allowed the issues to remain unresolved or leave the wounds uncleaned and unhealed.

Edom showed pride rather than mercy. They chose revenge over love, and they opted for passive delight in their brothers' downfall instead of joining their brothers' fight. God made it clear that Edom was being judged for their vengeful hearts and for standing passively to the side, watching Judah's fall with glee. Judah may have revolted against Him, but He promised to redeem them and see their enemies punished. At the end, the book looks back on the people of Judah. God wanted them to know that He is the Defender of His people.

Interpreting the book of Obadiah
<u>Interpretation questions</u>
1. Consider the following passages, which look at the brotherly feud: Genesis 25; 27:18-45; 32:1-21; 33; 36; Exodus 15:15; Numbers 20:14-21; Deuteronomy 2:1-18; 23:7-8; 1 Samuel 22 (Psalm 52); 2 Samuel 8:13-14; 2 Chronicles 21:8-10,16-17; Psalm 83.
    a. What caused the bitterness between the two nations?
    b. What does this show about the heart and nature of man?
2. Look at the actions of Edom.
    a. How did Edom wrong their brothers?
    b. How did this cause self-harm?
    c. How could Edom have sought reconciliation with their brothers (at the time of the prophecy, but also through the history of the two nations)?
    d. What should Edom have done when Judah fell?
3. Why was God judging Edom?
    a. What further information does Numbers 20:14-21, Ezekiel 25:12-14, and 1 Samuel 22:17-18 provide about why Edom fell to God's judgement?
    b. What does the prophecy reveal about God's view of pride?
4. Consider the judgement to befall Edom:
    a. Edom judged elsewhere: Jeremiah 49:7-22 (nearly identical to Malachi's message); Malachi 1:2-4; Isaiah 34:5-6; Ezekiel 25:12-14, 35:1-13; Joel 3:19; Amos 1:11-12.
    b. How were they to be judged?
    c. When was this fulfilled?
    d. Would the original readers have seen Edom's fall during the years of their exile?
5. Consider the original readers:
    a. What thoughts may the Judeans have had towards Edom as they lived in exile?
    b. How might they have felt as Edom stood free and they were in captivity?
    c. Would this have affected their view of God?
    d. How would the reading of this prophecy encourage the Jews in exile?
    e. How would the righteous of Judah have felt when they heard of God's coming judgement upon Edom?
6. What is seen of God's character in this book? What is revealed about God's sovereignty over the nations of the earth?
7. Why is bitterness damaging?
    a. What does Obadiah show about the danger of holding grudges?

  b. Why is reconciliation vital?

  c. Why is the topic close to God's heart?

 8. Consider the following verses, which resonate with the message of Obadiah: Proverbs 24:17-18; 1 Corinthians 6:1-8; 1 Corinthians 13:13-14.

Creative interpretation

  1. Family history

Copy out and complete the following table, which looks at the relationship between Judah and Edom through the generations:

Scripture reference:	What event occurred?	What was Esau's/ Edom's response?	How did Jacob/ Judah respond?	How did it affect their relationship?
Genesis 25				
Genesis 27:18-45				
Genesis 32:1-21				
Genesis 33				
Genesis 36				
Numbers 20:14-21				

Deuteronomy 2:1-8a				
Deuteronomy 23:7-8				
1 Samuel 22/ Psalm 52				
2 Samuel 8:13-14				
1 Kings 11:9-16				
2 Kings 8:20-22/ 2 Chronicles 21:8-10, 16-17				
2 Kings 14:7-10 2 Chronicles 25:11-13				

Ongoing prophets' project

Take out the separate document that you started during your Isaiah study. Add to it what you learn about the "day of the Lord" versus the "great day of the Lord" from Obadiah. Keep adding to this document as you work through the prophets.

Application inspiration
Reconciliation

- God would have His children seek reconciliation with those who have wronged them or whom they have hurt. Is there a wound that you have allowed to sit and fester, unforgiven? Does anyone, anything or any situation come to mind? Pray, listen to God, and act if He asks you to do so.

- Is there someone who you need to forgive? Even if you do not "feel" able to forgive, you can still pray it out to God that you choose to forgive them, asking God to release you from bitterness.

- The people of God are to be witnesses to the world by how they act towards each other. God is not happy when believers let their wounds fester. Read 1 Corinthians 6:1-8.

- Pray for the nations of the world and also for healing between individuals, people groups, and countries.

Walking in brotherly love

- God requires His children to stand beside their brothers and sisters in Christ. How can you do this? This could be standing beside each other in prayer, in ministry or in practical ways, such as helping a congregational member move house or cooking meals for a family facing hard times, illness or stress.
- Remember that the body of Christ is called to walk in love towards one another. Even in the face of hurt, the aim is always to walk in love. Whom can you build up this week in brotherly love? Take time to notice people. Focus on their strengths. Encourage them in the giftings you see in them, and help them to develop these gifts further.

JONAH

Grace available to all people

When God saw what they did, how they turned from their evil way, God relented of the disaster that he had said he would do to them, and he did not do it. – Jonah 3:10

Note: Jonah shows the nation of Assyria choosing repentance. You may wish to study the book of Nahum after Jonah. The book of Nahum is not the next book of the prophets chronologically, but it also relates to the nation of Assyria.

During your first reading

Themes to track
- God's heart for nations
- God's sovereignty over creation
- Presence of God
- Prayer
- Love thy enemy
- Jonah's character

During your second reading

Things to notice in the text
- Responses of:
    - The fisherman
    - Jonah
    - The king of Assyria
    - The people of Nineveh
- God's character

Chapter summaries

These are optional as they can be time consuming for the larger books. If you choose to do them, you will receive a much deeper appreciation of the book. By the end of The IBSC, you will have paraphrased the entire Bible! Go through each chapter and try to summarise it in one paragraph, using your own words; force yourself to stay big picture and capture the heart of each chapter.

After your initial readings

Setting of Jonah

Author

Authorship is credited to the prophet, Jonah.

Date prophecies were spoken

Jonah prophesied during the reign of Jeroboam II of Israel (782-753 BC).

Recipient – hearers

Jonah spoke to the citizens of the city of Nineveh, within the nation of Assyria.

Recipient – readers

The original readers of Jonah's account were the people of Israel, the northern kingdom.

Date and place of writing

The prophecies were recorded between 782 BC and 753 BC, during the reign of Jeroboam II, from within Israel.

Reason spoken

The prophecy was given to warn the Assyrians of the wrath of God that was about to come upon them for their sins, whilst providing them with an opportunity for repentance.

Reason written

God has mercy on everyone who turns to him in repentance. Israel's enemies accepted this mercy and Jonah was using the event in the hope that Israel would also heed the call to repentance, humble themselves, and return to the Lord.

Big picture

Historical background

Who was Jonah?

Jonah is seen in 2 Kings 14:25 to have been a prophet to the Northern Kingdom of Israel.

Nation of Assyria (to whom the prophecies were spoken)

Assyria was the world power and a feared nation when Jonah was sent to prophecy against them. Nineveh was the capital city of the Assyrian Empire.

Renowned for cruelty in warfare, Assyria was more brutal than any other nation. Examples of their cruelty included skinning people alive (including babies), impaling captives on poles, and cutting off the hands, feet, and noses of captives. Piles of dead were left in front of captured cities to cower other nations into submission. Captives from each nation were scattered across the Assyrian Empire to strip them of their national identity.

Asshur was the nation's chief god, whom they used to justify their cruelty in warfare. The Assyrians believed that every object of nature was possessed by a spirit and hence their gods were represented by things of nature.

The reigning kings of Assyria through this period were:

- Shalmaneser IV; 783-773 BC
- Asherdan III; 773-755 BC
- Asher-nirari V; 755-745 BC

Religious and political climate of Israel (to whom the book was written)

Jeroboam II was said to have walked in the ways of Jeroboam I, ushering the nation into idolatry. At this time in Israel's history, national pride was high. Having seen their affliction, God had restored land territory to them, increasing their borders. The Israelites interpreted God's mercy as a sign of favour, stemming from righteous living.

The people of Israel did not turn to God in times of need, but rather to man; for example, when they turned to the Assyrians for help (Ezekiel 16:28; Hosea 8:9). Politically, the nation was without a threat until the reign of Tiglath-pilesar, also known as Pul, of Assyria. The Assyrians overthrew the Northern Kingdom in 722 BC, following a three year siege.

See 2 Kings 14:23-29 for further background information regarding Israel during the reign of Jeroboam II.

Character portrayal – Jonah grumbles at God's mercy [1]

Jonah was relieved when God caused the plant to grow up over him. The sun had been scorching down upon him, adding thirst and light-headedness to his burning anger. He sat under its shade as evening fell upon the land of Assyria. A land that should have been destroyed by now, he thought bitterly. Why had God shown them mercy? The Assyrians deserved death for their cruel and vicious ways!

Heat and emotional exhaustion finally lulled him into slumber. He awoke with a dry throat, blistering skin, and the sun's harsh light once more beating down upon him. He saw that the tree had withered overnight and knew instinctively that only the Lord could have turned its fortune so quickly. Leaning over and dry retching, Jonah wished he could die. He was angry at the Lord for saving Nineveh. He also believed that God was harsh to kill the tree, which had been his only comfort, and the heat of the day was making him ill.

God's voice broke in on his bitter reflections: "Is it right for you to be angry for the plant?"

Jonah replied: "Yes, I am right to be angry. I am angry enough to die!"

The Lord returned: "You pity the plant, for which you did not labour or cause to grow, which received life in a single night and likewise perished in a night. If you feel this way for a mere plant, then should I not pity Nineveh, that great city, in which there are more than 120 thousand people who do not know My Laws or their right hand from their left?"

Book overview

God's sovereignty is revealed through Jonah's personal journey to the nation of Assyria. He is shown to have control over the wind, sea, land, and animals. God is the Creator who is at work in the world. The will of man cannot prevail over that of God for He is sovereign over all things.

Jonah's life should have ended when he was swallowed by the sea creature, yet God was able to protect Him. This is significant during a time where people believed in territorial gods – the belief that a god of any given nation or people only has power in that region. It is also important given that Jonah was making his way into a land that worshipped gods representing all living things, including a sea god and gods of animals.

The book of Jonah tells how the feared nation of Assyria came to acknowledge that their fate was in the hands of the Lord. A nation that was cruel and arrogant, filled with pride, and worshipped false gods, humbled themselves before the power of the One True God. They worshipped spirits of nature, but here they are seen to bow before the True and Living God, who holds salvation in His hands. God alone stands as Judge over the nations.

Through Jonah's journey, God teaches Jonah of His grace, which He extends even to the enemy of His people. He loves all nations and people.

Interpreting the book of Jonah

Interpretation questions

    1. Reflect on the following contrasts:
        a. Jonah and the sailors;
        b. The disobedience of Jonah opposed to the obedience of the fish;
        c. Jonah's hateful heart versus God's compassionate heart for the nations.
    2. Why did Jonah run from God's command?
    3. Why would he run to Tarshish (consider 1 Kings 10:22; 2 Chronicles 9:21)?
    4. What do you learn of Jonah through his prayer to God? What does this show about Jonah's awareness of God's character?
    5. What do verses 2:8-9 reveal about Jonah's change of thinking?
        a. What had Jonah learnt through his ordeal on the ship, and inside the fish?
        b. What does this declare about God's character and salvation?
        c. Consider the following New Testament verses: Acts 4:11-12 and Revelation 7:9-10.
    6. What would Jonah desire the people of Israel to gain from hearing of

Assyria's repentance?

7. How might the original readers have responded to the message? Consider the situation of their nation at this time.

8. Read through the book of Nahum and see the atrocities for which Assyria was renowned.

    a. How does this impact on your understanding of how far God's grace will extend?

    b. How does this influence your view of Jonah's reactions throughout the book?

9. Consider the significance of Jonah 3:6-10, remembering that Assyria did not know much about the God of Israel, and mocked the gods of other nations. What does this show about God's mercy and power to save?

10. It took humility for Jonah to record the humbling events of chapter 4.

    a. Why did he feel that it was important to pass this message on to the Israelites?

    b. What did he hope for them to gain?

11. What does chapter 4 reveal about God's character, His grace, and His love for man? Is there significance in how God chose to explain His heart for Assyria to Jonah in a way Jonah would understand?

12. Consider Jonah 4:5-10 in the light of John 3:16.

13. What do you learn of God's sovereignty over creation?

14. In what ways was God's grace revealed through the events recorded in the book of Jonah? Consider His grace in the lives of Jonah, the fisherman, and the people of Assyria.

15. There is contention surrounding whether the story of Jonah really occurred or was given as an allegory. An allegory is a fictional story told to make a point or conceptualise an idea.

    a. Read Matthew 12:39-41, Matthew 16:4, and Luke 11:29-32.

    b. Comment on whether or not you believe the story to be telling of actual events that had occurred or whether it was written as an allegory.

Creative interpretation

1. Write your own children's version of the story of Jonah. Example perspectives from which you may wish to write:

    a. Jonah's perspective, as he ran from God (Jonah 1), to God (Jonah 2), alongside God (Jonah 3), and ahead of God (Jonah 4).

    b. Assyrians' perspective: showing their nature as a cruel nation, and how a world power came to humble themselves before the Lord.

    c. A geographical perspective: Jonah in the ship (Jonah 1), in the belly (Jonah 2), in Ninevah (Jonah 3), and under the shade of the tree (Jonah 4).

Application inspiration

- The book of Jonah is a call against a bitter and unforgiving spirit. Look into your own heart. Is there any bitterness or unforgiven hurts that you need to release?

- Allow the book of Jonah to prompt you to obediently follow God's call, regardless of your feelings.
  - o Is there something God asked you to do that you still have not obeyed?
  - o What are you running away from in your relationship with God?
- Take confidence in the fact that you can make a difference through ministry because it is God who changes hearts; it is not up to you to bring the change in another person.
- Are there people who you believe are "beyond God's grace" to save? Or are there people who you would rather not see saved because of insults, pain or injury that they have caused to you, or atrocities they have committed? Pray for these people, knowing that no one is beyond God's saving grace.

[1] Interpretation and paraphrase of Jonah 4:1-11

MICAH

Lord of Justice

He has told you, O man, what is good; and what does the LORD require of you but to do justice, and to love kindness, and to walk humbly with your God? – Micah 6:8

During your first reading

Themes to track
- God's heart for nations
- Social injustice
- Judgement and justice
- Sins of Judah
- Messianic visions

During your second reading

Things to notice in the text
- Connectives; look for "because", "for", and "therefore".
- Repeated phrases: "In that day" and "In the last day"/ "in the latter days".
- Figures of speech: personification, metaphors, similes, etc.
- Mark passages speaking of judgement.
- Mark passages promising restoration and hope.
- Prophets of the land being called to account.

Chapter summaries
These are optional as they can be time consuming for the larger books. If you choose to do them, you will receive a much deeper appreciation of the book. By the end of The IBSC, you will have paraphrased the entire Bible! Go through each chapter and try to summarise it in one paragraph, using your own words; force

254

yourself to stay big picture and capture the heart of each chapter.

After your initial readings

Setting of Micah
<u>Author</u>
The book was written by the prophet Micah, of Moresheth.

<u>Date prophecies were spoken</u>
Micah spoke these prophecies during the reigns of Jotham, Ahaz, and Hezekiah of Judah, placing Micah's ministry between 740 BC and 687 BC.

<u>Recipient – hearers</u>
The prophecies were primarily spoken to the nation of Judah, except for chapter 1, which was spoken to Israel.

<u>Recipient – readers</u>
The prophecies were written for the people of Judah.

<u>Date and place of writing</u>
Micah recorded his prophecies during the years of his ministry, 740-687 BC, from within Judah. It was either penned from Micah's home town or, more likely, from Jerusalem, where he ministered.

<u>Reason spoken</u>
The prophecies were a call to repentance before the judgement of the Lord came against Judah for their sins of social injustice. Micah also proclaimed the coming of Christ.

<u>Reason written</u>
Micah hoped the book would instil fear of the Lord into the people, and bring them to a place of repentance, in order to save them. In the midst of a troubling time, full of anxiety and uncertainty, the faithful in Judah would have received hope from the promise of peace given in the book of Micah.

Big picture
<u>Historical background</u>
Judah
Micah prophesied during the reign of Jotham (750-732 BC), Ahaz (735-715 BC), and Hezekiah (715-686 BC), when many political and national crises were occurring within Judah.
Overall, King Jotham "did right by the Lord". Decay of justice followed his reign when Ahaz came to power. King Ahaz had a blatant disregard for the Lord's temple, plundering it and closing it off so that the people could not worship God. After meeting the king of Assyria, he determined to build a replica altar to the Assyrian

god in Judah. He was a callous man who burnt one of his sons to death as an offering to a foreign god. Following Ahaz was another of his sons, Hezekiah.

King Hezekiah was Judah's shining star. He tore down the altars, restored treasures to the temple, and commanded that the Passover be kept for the first time in generations. However, war and tension continued to plague Judah. Hezekiah refused to pay tribute to Assyria and for retribution the Assyrians destroyed forty-six of the nation's cities in 701 BC. When the Assyrian army came before Jerusalem, Hezekiah humbled himself before God in sackcloth and fervent prayer. God heard his prayer and delivered Jerusalem from the Assyrians.

Refer to the *special study* that you completed for Kings and Chronicles for further insight into the events that occurred during the reigns of Jotham, Ahaz, and Hezekiah.

Assyria

The Assyrian Empire began to dominate the Ancient Near East around the year 740 BC and both Judah and Israel became tribute-paying vassals to the Assyrians. The cities of Judah listed in Micah 1:10-16 are all believed to have been on the war path of Sennacherib, King of Assyria, who destroyed forty-six cities and towns en route to Jerusalem. At this time, Sennacherib sent the first group of Judeans into exile.

Character portrayal – Hezekiah before the Lord [1]

King Hezekiah heard the words that the chief of the Assyrian army had declared before the gates of Jerusalem. How was he to withstand this cruel and mighty nation that struck fear into the hearts of men? He could not. He could do nothing against them. He could do nothing to defend his people.

In grief and helplessness, he tore his clothes and covered himself with sackcloth before going to the one place where help could yet be found. Hezekiah entered into the House of the Lord.

Kneeling down and touching his forehead to the ground in utter abasement of spirit, King Hezekiah prayed before the Lord: "O Lord, we have watched and waited as the kings of Assyria laid waste to the nations, and cast their gods into the fire. The gods of the nations were not gods; only the work of men's hands, wood and stone, and now they are destroyed. But you, O Lord, are mighty to save. I beg you, Mighty God, to save us from the hand of Sennacherib and his army. By such an act will all the kingdoms of the earth know that you, alone, are God."

The Lord responded to the earnest cry of the king. He gave His answer through His servant, Isaiah, who said: *'This is what the Lord says, concerning the king of Assyria: 'He shall not come into this city, or shoot an arrow there, or come before it with a shield, or cast up a siege mound against it. By the way that he came, by the same he shall return, and he shall not come into this city,' declares the Lord. 'For I will defend this city to save it, for My own sake and for the sake of My servant David.'"* [2]

And that night the angel of the Lord went out and struck down 185,000 in the camp of the Assyrians. When the people within the city of Jerusalem arose early in the morning, behold, the army that had come against them were dead to a man.

<u>Book overview</u>

God desires His people to seek justice and kindness and be humble in heart. However, the people of Judah were not living according to this requirement. False prophets in the land, and the nation's leaders, were causing the people to stray. Micah went amidst his false peers as a true prophet to offer God's warning to the people of Judah, foretelling the judgements that would come upon them if they did not repent and return to God.

In 2 Kings 18:1-20:21 and 2 Chronicles 29-32, King Hezekiah is seen to have turned to God in repentance. What would have been the result if Hezekiah had not humbled himself before God? A proud and arrogant leader could have seen Jerusalem destroyed in 701 BC. Micah was one of the few prophets rewarded with fruit during the years of his ministry; he saw King Hezekiah turn to God in repentance, and God stay His hand of judgement over Judah.

The physical kingdom of Judah was not the only one discussed in Micah's prophecies. Micah was given words regarding the eternal Kingdom of God to come. God promised that He shall be King again over His people and lead them into rest, safety and peace. Christ is foretold; the True Saviour who is the only way to redemption, mercy and entrance into God's eternal kingdom.

Interpreting the book of Micah

<u>Interpretation questions</u>

    1. What are the sins listed against Israel in chapter 1?

    2. Look at the "woe oracle" against Judah in Micah 2:1-5.

        a. Give the reason for distress (sins of the people), the prediction of doom (coming judgement), and when the prediction was likely fulfilled.

        b. What further evidence can be gathered against the people by looking at the Law in Exodus 20:15, 17 and Numbers 36:7?

    3. What sins were listed against the false prophets and the leaders of Judah?

        a. Look at Micah 2:6-11 and 3:1-12.

        b. Why was God's wrath aimed specifically at the leaders?

        c. How should these leaders have acted and lived?

        d. How does this relate to the New Testament verses: Matthew 18:6, Mark 9:42, and Luke 17:1-2?

    4. What was Micah's response to the prophecies? How did he respond to the coming judgement upon Israel and Judah?

    5. Consider what Micah reveals about God:

        a. What was revealed about God's passion for social justice?

        b. What did God say about the oppression and injustice that was occurring in the land (see chapters 2, 6 and 7)?

        c. What was God's desire for His nation?

        d. What does Micah 2:12-13 reveal about God? See also 1 Samuel 12:12, 1 Timothy 1:17 and Revelation 15:3.

        e. What does Micah 6:1-8 reveal about God? See also: James 1:27

and 2:17.

6. What is said of the people of God and His eternal kingdom in the following passages:
    a.   Micah 2:12-13;
    b.   Micah 4:1-8; and
    c.   Micah 7:8-20?

7. Look at the Messianic visions in Micah 4 and 5.
    a.   What do you see of Christ and His reign?
    b.   Compare this passage with Matthew 2:6.
    c.   How did Jesus contrast with the false prophets? You may wish to find New Testament references to support your answer.
    d.   How did Christ embody the concepts of justice, kindness, and walking in humility?
    e.   How does Micah 5:7-15 provide a contrast between the people of God and those who reject Christ? Look at the following New Testament references: 1 Corinthians 1:18 and 2 Corinthians 2:15-16.

8. In chapter 6, look at the sins of the nation and God's coming judgement. The judgement on Israel can be seen in the light of lawsuits, brought against them by God. Can you identify the following elements:
    a.   God first calls them (like a summons to appear in court); then
    b.   He lists their sin (charge and evidence); and finally
    c.   He pronounces His judgement (the verdict).

9. How does Deuteronomy 16:19-20 add weight to the evidence against Judah given in Micah 7?

10. Consider the response of Micah's original readers.
    a.   How would those in Judah have felt when they arrived at the final verses in Micah 7?
    b.   What hope would these final verses have given to them?

Creative interpretation

1. Discuss the glorious picture of Christ that the book of Micah gives to its reader.
    a.   What is revealed of His nature and character?
    b.   Discuss the picture that is given of the kingdom that Christ will establish.

2. Oppression and social injustice are a recurring theme in the books of the prophets. How did God speak out against social injustice through His prophet, Micah?

Ongoing prophets' project

Take out the separate document that you started during your Isaiah study. Add to it what you learn about the "day of the Lord" versus the "great day of the Lord" from Micah. You can also compare the pictures given from the phrase "in that day" versus "in the last day"/ "in the latter days". Keep adding to this document as you work through the prophets.

Application inspiration

- Accept His peace and live in hope for the coming King!
- God ALWAYS desires to heal and restore. He is always ready to bestow grace upon you. Your disobedience is forgotten when you cry out to Him with a truly repentant heart, desiring to renew the intimacy of your relationship with Him. Even now you can accept His grace and receive restoration from sins. He is a place of safety for you. Turn to Him. Allow Him to restore your peace.
- What trials or persecution (minor and major) are you facing at the moment? Take these to God in prayer. Cling to Him in hard times and in trials, knowing that He will bring freedom from the pain you endure in this world. Place your hope in Christ during times of suffering.

[1] Based on 2 Kings 18-20
[2] 2 Kings 19:32-34

NAHUM

Assyria Judged

Behold, I am against you, declares the LORD of hosts, and I will burn your chariots in smoke, and the sword shall devour your young lions. I will cut off your prey from the earth, and the voice of your messengers shall no longer be heard. – Nahum 2:13

During your first reading

Themes to track
- God's heart for nations
- Character of God
- Wrath of God

During your second reading

Things to notice in the text
- Figures of speech/ illustrations
- Emotion
- The Lord Almighty
- Sin and judgement

Chapter summaries

These are optional as they can be time consuming for the larger books. If you choose to do them, you will receive a much deeper appreciation of the book. By the end of The IBSC, you will have paraphrased the entire Bible! Go through each chapter and try to summarise it in one paragraph, using your own words; force yourself to stay big picture and capture the heart of each chapter.

After your initial readings

Setting of Nahum
<u>Author</u>
The book was written by the prophet, Nahum.

<u>Date prophecies were spoken</u>
From events recorded and predicted in the book, it can be determined that Nahum spoke these prophecies between the years of 633 and 628 BC.

<u>Recipient – hearers</u>
It is likely that the nation of Judah was the original hearer of these prophecies, even though they were spoken concerning the Assyrians.

<u>Recipient – readers</u>
Nahum recorded his prophecies for the nation of Judah.

<u>Date and place of writing</u>
Nahum was written before Assyria's fall, but not necessarily before the Scythians attacked Assyria. This puts the dating of the book between 633 and 612 BC. It was most likely composed from within Judah.

<u>Reason spoken</u>
Judah had seen their northern brothers fall to God's judgement, for which the Assyrians were His chosen tool. However, this did not excuse the Assyrians for the brutality, greed, and pride they showed in their victories. God was declaring Himself personally against the Assyrians at a time when no nation would have believed that Assyria could be defeated.

<u>Reason written</u>
These prophecies were recorded as evidence to show that God comes in vengeance against disobedient nations. It was a promise to the nation of Judah that He would break the Assyrian bond that was over them and restore their nation. He was giving hope to His people.

Big picture
<u>Historical background</u>
Assyria
The national symbol of Assyria was the lion and this imagery is used in Nahum 2:11-12. They were the world power when the nation of Israel was taken into exile in 722 BC. Known for their cruelty in war and the horrors they bestowed upon their captives, Assyria was a much-feared nation at the height of its power. Refer to the *historical background* given for Jonah for more information.

In 628 BC, Assyria was attacked by the Scythians and left considerably weakened before its fall in 612 BC. At its fall, the nation split into a confederacy of three nations: the Scythians, Medes, and Babylonians. Assyria's fall was three-fold, which is hinted at in Nahum's figures of speech. The fall of Assyria occurred as follows:

1. By war: Cyaxares, the Mede, and Nabopolassar of Babylon, combined forces. Sinsariskun, king of Assyria, went to the Scythians for help, but they betrayed him and sealed the downfall of Assyria.
2. By water: The three nations (the Medes, Scythians, and Babylonians) dammed the Khoser River and directed its flow into Nineveh. The flood of water destroyed the walls of the great city.
3. By fire: Seeing that the city was captured, the King of Assyria heaped up his treasure, concubines, and eunuchs, and set light to the palace to avoid capture, burning them all to death.

Character portrayal – pride in their heyday

Assyria was used as the instrument of God's judgement, and yet they did not acknowledge the Lord. They believed that from their own might and power they had become a great nation. They humbled themselves once before the Lord (when Jonah was sent to prophesy against them), but they did not continue to seek God or His ways. They thought they were ruling the world by their own capacity and force. Added to their sins were cruel and unjust practices.

The Assyrians proclaimed: *"By the strength of my hand I have done it, and by my wisdom, for I have understanding; I remove the boundaries of peoples, and plunder their treasures; like a bull I bring down those who sit on thrones. My hand has found like a nest the wealth of the peoples; and as one gathers eggs that have been forsaken, so I have gathered all the earth; and there was none that moved a wing or opened the mouth or chirped."* [1]

Book overview

The book of Nahum shows the wrathful side of God's character against evil and the wickedness of man. His adversaries are those who do not bow before Him. God is jealous and avenging. He will repay the evil of His enemies with all-consuming might. Yet the book also shows God's love, mercy, and grace. He is shown to be a place of safety and love for those whose faith rests in Him. He is a God of wrath and vengeance, mercy and grace.

God's wrath is shown to be worthy of the fear of His enemies. It is mighty and destructive, and it was coming against an evil nation. Assyria was judged for its pride and greed. He will not tolerate the sins of the nations forever. He is All Powerful and no nation can withstand His fierce judgement. Assyria did not – no one, and no nation, can – endure His wrath.

Interpreting the book of Nahum
Interpretation questions

1. What is revealed about the character of God?
   a. How did He choose to define Himself in this book?
   b. Which of His attributes did He display?
2. What sins were listed against the nation of Assyria?
   a. Why were they being judged?

3. Look at the "woe oracle" in Nahum 3:1. Give:
    a. The reason for distress (sins of the people).
    b. The prediction of doom (coming judgement).
    c. When the prediction was fulfilled. The *historical background* given above will help you to determine the fulfilment of the prophecies.
4. Look at how Assyria fell according to history. Comment on how this supports the fulfilment of Nahum's prophecies.
    a. By water/ flood – Nahum 1:8; 2:6; 2:8; 3:14.
    b. By military power/ war – Nahum 1:12; 1:14-15; 2:1,15a; 2:3-5; 2:13; 3:2-3:12.
    c. By fire – Nahum 1:6; 1:10; 2:4; 2:12; 3:13; 3:15.
5. What additional or supporting information can be gleamed about the fall of Assyria from Isaiah 10?
6. Look at the figures of speech (illustrations) listed in Nahum.
    a. What do they denote?
    b. What were they predicting?
    c. What emotion do they add to the prophecy?
    d. What imagery do they create in the mind of the reader?
    e. What were they proclaiming?
7. How would these prophecies give hope to the original hearers and original readers? How would they be feeling as they listened to God's coming wrath on Assyria?
8. Look at the "promise oracles" in Nahum 1:15 and 2:2.
    a. What was the promise given?
    b. When was its fulfilment?
9. Paul quotes Nahum 1:15 in Romans 10:15.
    a. What was its intended meaning in its New Testament context?
    b. What was the fulfilment of Nahum's prophecy?

Creative interpretation

1. After looking at the books of Jonah and Nahum, as well as reading the historical background related to Assyria, comment on how the Assyrians went from a cruel nation, to a repentant one (recorded in the book of Jonah), and finally back to their sinful ways.
    a. What does this show of man's character?
    b. What does this teach about the choices that nations make?
    c. How could Assyria have continued in humility before God?
    d. What further action did they need to have taken to draw near to God and learn of His ways?
    e. How could they have walked humbly and yet retained their political power, keeping their empire stable?

Application inspiration
Reflecting on God's wrath and judgement
- Today's society often lacks a perspective of God's wrath.

- o Do you have a revelation of God's wrath, and His hatred of sin?
- o How do you feel about the wrathful God depicted in Nahum?
- o What emotions did you experience reading about God's judgement on the nation of Assyria?
- o The Lord displays Himself as the Almighty God in the book of Nahum. Are you able to see Him in this light?
- His judgement falls on the nations because of disobedience, idolatry, lies, cruelty, leading others into sin, and pride.
    - o Do you consider some of these things as "not that bad"? Take the notion of a white lie for an example – does that cause your spirit unease; why or why not? What sins do you think are worthy of God's wrath, and which ones do you find it hard to believe deserving of it?
    - o Do you believe that God's wrath on Assyria was deserved?
    - o Read Romans 1:18-3:20. Do you truly believe that every man and woman is deserving of the wrath of God?
    - o Ask God to grant you understanding of the horror of sin. Pray that He will give you His heart for issues of injustice and cruelty in the world.
    - o Read Romans 3:21-25. Take hope in the gift of God, Jesus Christ.

[1] Isaiah 10:13-14

HABAKKUK

Questioning God amidst Unrighteousness

"Behold, his soul is puffed up; it is not upright within him, but the righteous shall live by his faith." – Habakkuk 2:4

During your first reading

Themes to track
- Questioning God; asking "Why, God? Why?"
- Answers
- Social justice/ social conscience
- Faith

During your second reading

Things to notice in the text
- Habakkuk's character
- Habakkuk's questions
- God's answers
- Majesty and character of God

Chapter summaries

These are optional as they can be time consuming for the larger books. If you choose to do them, you will receive a much deeper appreciation of the book. By the end of The IBSC, you will have paraphrased the entire Bible! Go through each chapter and try to summarise it in one paragraph, using your own words; force yourself to stay big picture and capture the heart of each chapter.

After your initial readings

Setting of Habakkuk
Author

The book was penned by Habakkuk, a prophet of God.

Date prophecies were spoken

Habakkuk spoke during the reign of Jehoiakim, king of Judah between 609 and 606 BC.

Recipient – hearers

The prophecies were spoken to the people of Judah during the reign of Jehoiakim.

Recipient – readers

The prophecies were recorded for the people of Judah.

Date and place of writing

Habakkuk wrote the book before the exile, between 609 and 606 BC, from within Judah.

Reason spoken

Habakkuk was wrestling with God as he looked upon the justice and violence occurring in the world. He was asking God when it would cease, and whether God planned to do anything to stop the perversion of justice. The purpose of the prophecies was to let the people of Judah know that judgement was coming, but that they could trust in God if they walked in faith, even when it seemed that the unrighteous would triumph.

Reason written

The prophecies were written to encourage the people of Judah during the coming hardship and distress. Judgement was coming, but they could trust in God as they walked through it.

Big picture
Historical background

Habakkuk 3:19 suggests that Habakkuk had a tie to the priesthood. It is believed that he was a contemporary of the prophet Jeremiah. His name in Hebrew was Chabaqquwa, which meant "to embrace" (Strong, J., 1989)[1] or "to wrestle". Both of these meanings are appropriate for Habakkuk as he both wrestled with God, and embraced Him.

Habakkuk spoke during the reign of Jehoiakim (609-606 BC). At this point in history, the power shifted from the nation of Assyria to that of Babylon. The fall of the Assyrian Empire occurred in 612 BC. King Jehoiakim was a vassal of Egypt, meaning that Judah was paying tribute to the Egyptians; however, the Egyptian

Empire also fell to Babylon, being defeated in 605 BC. The Babylonians were rising up as the dominant world power and the people of Judah would have been growing in fear of them.

For more information about what was occurring in Judah at this time, refer to: 2 Kings 23:34-24:7 and 2 Chronicles 36:4-8.

What is a dragnet (Habakkuk 1:15-26)?

A dragnet is a large fishing net. One side of the net has floats, keeping it at the top of the sea, and the bottom side has weights, to drag it downwards. The net is dragged along between two boats to scoop up everything. It collects what is wanted and what is not wanted; nothing escapes!

Character portrayal –Habakkuk's choice to praise God

Habakkuk listened to God's reply with a sinking heart; Judah was to fall to the Babylonians. He could not understand why God would chose to deal justice on the sins of His nation by bringing a still more sinful nation against them. It sounded as if it would be a painful downfall too. Their nation was built on agriculture and yet it seemed as if their livelihoods were to be stripped away from them before their final fall.

Habakkuk continued to wrestle in anguish, brought upon him by God's answers. He recalled what he knew of his great God. God was God. There was no one like Him. God was merciful and loving. However, God was also just. God must have His reasons for choosing Babylon as His tool of judgement, to fall upon Judah. Habakkuk took a deep breath and made his declaration:

"Though the cherry trees don't blossom and the strawberries don't ripen, Though the apples are worm-eaten and the wheat fields stunted, Though the sheep pens are sheepless and the cattle barns empty, I'm singing joyful praise to God. I'm turning cartwheels of joy to my Savior God. Counting on God's Rule to prevail, I take heart and gain strength. I run like a deer. I feel like I'm king of the mountain!" [2]

He would trust in God, come what may. He would forever praise the name of the Lord.

Book overview

The book of Habakkuk records a conversation between God and man. It depicts a man bringing the questions that were on his heart before God. It is the record of how a man wrestled with the violence he saw, and the answers he received from God.

Habakkuk could not understand how a righteous God could sit idle and watch the sins of His people. God answered that He was not idle; He was about to send the nation of Babylon to judge His evil nation. God's reply only served to throw Habakkuk into further confusion. How could God be sending a godless nation against His own people?

Yet despite the heaviness of his questions, Habakkuk did not doubt God's character. He struggled to understand how such a judgement could be in line with the character of God, but eventually came to a place of peace and acceptance. Even if he could not understand the plans of God, he chose to trust Him.

The book of Habakkuk shows that joy in God is not limited to times of plenty, security or ease. Just like a deer, believers can walk sure-footed through trying times if they place their trust in God. He enables His people to endure trials and hardships.

Interpreting the book of Habakkuk
<u>Interpretation questions</u>

1. Look at Habakkuk's character through your study. Consider what the text reveals about his faith and his relationship with God.
2. What was Habakkuk's first question?
   a. What was his complaint?
   b. What does it convey about the events occurring within Judah at that time?
   c. What does it show about the religious state of Judah?
3. What was God's response to Habakkuk questioning Him and His justice? How does God's promise in Matthew 7:8 relate to His actions in Habakkuk?
4. Consider Babylon, God's judgement rod:
   a. What image of Babylon was painted in the book?
   b. How would this have instilled fear in the hearts of the Judeans?
   c. How did Habakkuk want his people to respond to the image?
   d. Why would the people of Judah not believe that God would bring the Babylonians against them?
   e. Why would they not understand God using a foreign nation as His judgement rod?
   f. What is revealed of God's character that He chose to use Babylon as His instrument of judgement on Judah?
5. God proclaimed that His works cannot be understood by man.
   a. Why would knowing this have reassured the original readers?
   b. How would this have given them hope in the face of God's coming wrath?
   c. Would it have brought them comfort or distress?
   d. Read 1 Corinthians 13:12-13.
6. Habakkuk 1:5 is quoted in Acts 13:40-41. Read Paul's sermon from Acts 13:13-13:43.
   a. What was the author of Acts using the quote to convey?
   b. Of what was Paul warning his audience through the quote?
   c. Did they pay attention to the warning?
7. What was Habakkuk's second complaint?
   a. What does it reveal about Habakkuk's understanding of God?
   b. What does it show of Habakkuk's world view?
   c. What does it show about the religious state of Judah?
8. How did God's second reply confirm His first? How would this cement the certainty of His intent?
9. Habakkuk 2:4 is quoted three separate times in the New Testament:

Romans 1:17, Galatians 3:11, and Hebrews 20:37-38.
   a. Read these quotes in a few different Bible translations.
   b. Try to get an understanding of how the New Testament authors were using the quote.
   c. Seek understanding as to why it was significant enough to be used three times.

10. Look at each of the "woes" listed against Babylon.
   a. List the reason for distress (why is God against them), give the prediction of doom (how they will be judged), and when the prophecy was fulfilled.
   b. What hope would the original readers have drawn from these woes?
   c. What does it reveal about God's character?
   d. Are there implications for the nations of the world, today?

11. Habakkuk 3:1-15 chronicles the events in the history of the nation, and what God had done for them.
   a. Why was Habakkuk calling the readers to remember these events?
   b. Why was he reminding himself of them?
   c. How would this history lesson have instilled trust in God?

12. How does Habakkuk's ending prayer reveal how he had come to a deeper understanding of God's character?
   a. What had he learnt?
   b. How did this affect his faith and trust in God?
   c. What does it show of God?

Creative interpretation

1. Habakkuk was struggling with some BIG questions. What does he ask and discover about:
   a. God's justice?
   b. God's decisions?
   c. Why God was waiting to act against injustice?

2. Look at Habakkuk's relationship with God. He was real and open with God. What enabled him to trust God in this way?

3. Considering what you have read in Habakkuk (and the other books of the prophets), consider: Is God a God of justice? Support your answer with what you have seen in Scripture. Turn your answer into a poem declaring what you have learnt of His character.

Application inspiration
Wrestling through your questions with God

   • When God does not seem to be answering your questions, which path will you choose: the road of trust and faith, which leads to God, or the path of cynicism and bitterness, which will take you away from Him?

   • Do not let circumstances determine your trust in God. Turn back to His

Word and focus on what you know of His character. Wrestle through your questions with God. It is okay to have questions about injustice and difficult circumstances, yet make sure to take them to God and seek His answers.

- Let this book give you comfort in difficult circumstances. This book was written by a real person who was asking hard questions. Take comfort from knowing God listens to your questions.
- Read through Hebrews 11. What additional insights does this passage give to living by faith and having hope in God?
- It is a choice to wrestle with God, rather than against Him. It does not mean a fake and happy smile when you have questions, face trials or experience moments of doubt. It does mean going to God in these times and seeking to journey with Him through them, clinging to the goodness of His character.
- Take time and write down questions that you have in your heart. Seek God's response and write down the answers you feel He is giving to you.

[1] Strong, James, S.T.D., LL.D., (1989). *Strong's Hebrew and Greek Dictionaries, e-Sword,* Ver. 9.7.2, Dictionary, H2265.
[2] Habakkuk 3:17-19 (The Message).

ZEPHANIAH

The choice is yours!

Seek the LORD, all you humble of the land, who do his just commands; seek righteousness; seek humility; perhaps you may be hidden on the day of the anger of the LORD. – Zephaniah 2:3

During your first reading

Themes to track
- God's heart for nations
- Day of the Lord
- Judgement
- Cleansing/ purification
- Messianic predictions

During your second reading

Things to notice in the text
- Underline "I will" and "I shall" statements
- Character and nature of God

Chapter summaries

These are optional as they can be time consuming for the larger books. If you choose to do them, you will receive a much deeper appreciation of the book. By the end of The IBSC, you will have paraphrased the entire Bible! Go through each chapter and try to summarise it in one paragraph, using your own words; force yourself to stay big picture and capture the heart of each chapter.

After your initial readings

Setting of Zephaniah
Author

Authorship is credited to the prophet Zephaniah, who is believed to have been a member of royalty, as indicated by his genealogy.

Date prophecies were spoken

The prophecies were spoken during the reign of Josiah, king of Judah between 640 and 609 BC.

Recipient – hearers

The prophecies were spoken to the people of Judah who lived during the reign of Josiah.

Recipient – readers

The prophecies were written for the people of Judah who lived during the reign of Josiah.

Date and place of writing

The book of Zephaniah was written during the reign of Josiah, between 640 and 609 BC. As Zephaniah was of the royal family, he most likely lived in Jerusalem, and so it can be assumed that he penned this record from there.

Reason spoken

The prophecies proclaimed judgement against Judah and the nations. They were given as an attempt to urge the people of Judah to humble themselves before God. The people were being called to turn and seek the Lord, in the hope of avoiding His wrath. God was giving the people a choice: chose faith or chose judgement.

Reason written

The prophecies proclaimed judgement against Judah and the nations. They gave the reasons why the people were about to go into exile. The people were responsible for their sin; they could not blame the king or their nation's leadership. The book of Zephaniah shows that it is an individual's choice to pursue or reject God.

Big picture
Historical background

Zephaniah prophesied during the time that Josiah was King over Judah, as did the prophet Jeremiah. Both Zephaniah and King Josiah trace their lineage back to King Hezekiah, inferring that Zephaniah was part of the royal family. This is important to remember as it changes the dynamics of the book by impacting on the author's concerns. Zephaniah was speaking judgement upon his family. He also may have had the king's ear, and been a member of Josiah's court. It is also possible that it was his family relations that influenced the reforms Josiah instigated throughout the land of Judah during his reign.

Josiah was a king who walked in obedience to the Lord and brought religious reform to both Judah and Israel. Unfortunately, the love he had for the Lord was not mimicked in the hearts of the people. Josiah made the people live in obedience to the Law and reinstated their covenant with God, but it was not a choice that the people made with their hearts. It was Josiah who initiated all the work and it was by his command that the people returned to God.

During his reign, Josiah removed idols from the land and purged it of the priests who were serving false gods. He began restorative work on the temple and, when the Book of the Law was discovered during this undertaking, his response was heartfelt repentance for the nation's sins. He reinstated the commands of the Law in the lives of the people. Under his rulership, the nation of Judah kept the Passover for the first time since the days of the judges.

Review 2 Kings 22-23 and 2 Chronicles 34 for further background information.

Character portrayal – possible response of the unrighteous in Judah

"Josiah has us keeping all the laws of God, so what more can God want from us? Why is Zephaniah stirring up trouble by proclaiming these words against us? We are serving God as best we can. We are doing as we are told! What more is there that we can do?" Maayan proclaimed, rebelliously.

"Yeah!" his friend, Noach, agreed. "I'm not cut out to roll around in the dirt and rip my clothes just because we lost some book for a few years. That wasn't our fault; our fathers lost it!"

"I think Zephaniah has it wrong," Maayan persisted. "We are doing what is in the Law. We kept the Passover this year. That will keep God happy with us. But I'm glad that He is going to finally do something about the Moabites and Ammonites! It really is about time they were punished!"

Book overview

In the book of Zephaniah, two separate fulfilments are given to the day of the Lord. One refers to the coming judgement on Judah, as a physical nation, and the other refers to the great day of the Lord, when Christ will return to judge all nations.

God promised that His judgement on Judah would cause wailing and see the destruction of their homes and livelihood. God's wrath and judgement was also promised upon the physical nations surrounding Judah. God gave His people a choice to choose repentance or judgement. Despite godly leadership during the reign of Josiah, the people made the wrong choice. Zephaniah shows the importance of personal choice, and personal responsibility, over one's salvation.

The day of the Lord that marked the fall of Judah was nothing when compared to the agony and complete destruction that will be seen on the great day of the Lord. The great day will see all mankind bowing before the Lord in His consuming jealousy. Mankind will be judged for their sins. Coming with the great day of the Lord will be restoration for God's people, who will be saved from amidst the destruction; the Lord will save His people on that fearful day. This restoration is worthy of praise and should cause the heart to exalt in God's goodness.

Interpreting the book of Zephaniah

<u>Interpretation questions</u>

1. Chapter 1 focuses on the nation of Judah.
   a. What sins had they committed?
   b. How did the Judeans view themselves, God, and their relationship with Him?
   c. What does chapter 1 reveal about the state of Judah's heart and its religious practices?
   d. How does this compare with 2 Kings 22-23 and 2 Chronicles 34?
2. What judgement was declared upon Judah?
   a. What was spoken about their day of judgement?
   b. What was represented by the imagery Zephaniah used?
   c. How complete was the judgement depicted?
   d. When were these prophecies fulfilled?
3. What do you learn of the great day of the Lord, the final judgement of the world, in Zephaniah's prophecies?
   a. What will the final judgement look like?
   b. What response should this have inspired in the original hearers?
   c. When will these prophecies be fulfilled?
4. Chapter 2 looks at God's judgement upon the nations.
   a. Who was He judging, and why?
   b. What did God reveal about His character in this chapter?
5. Zephaniah 3:1-8 returns the focus to the people of Judah. Look at the "woe oracle".
   a. What were the sins it lists against the people?
   b. How would they be judged?
   c. What do you learn of God and the purpose behind His judgement in Zephaniah 3:5-7?
6. Zephaniah 3:9-20 depicts a time of restoration for the humble remnant.
   a. Who is the "remnant" that God was speaking of – the Jews that returned to Judah after exile in Babylon or the spiritual people of God?
   b. What do these verses reveal about the coming eternal Kingdom of God?
7. What further insight do you gain of God's character in Zephaniah 3:15-20?

<u>Creative interpretation</u>

1. Gain a big picture of the book by asking:
   a. What did the righteous in Judah have to look forward to, as promised in these prophecies?
   b. How would these prophecies have called them to place their hope in God?
   c. What picture does the book paint for those listeners not walking

in the way of God, but rebelling against Him?

2. Sketch some of the imagery used in Zephaniah about the coming judgement to help you visualise what God had promised to bring against His people.

Ongoing prophets' project

Take out the separate document that you started during your Isaiah study. Add to it what you learn about the "day of the Lord" versus the "great day of the Lord" from Zephaniah. Keep adding to this document as you work through the prophets.

Application inspiration

- Do not distance yourself from the people of Judah. You have the same choices to make between faith or cynicism, and trust or bitterness. Desire to develop trust with God so that, when you are faced with a crossroad, you will choose the road of faith.
- God's wrath and anger is fierce and very real. It is coming on mankind. This should cause believers to spread the Gospel, the Good News. Even more so, the beauty of the blessings God will bestow on His people should cause the Gospel to spread. Have you been keeping such beautiful promises to yourself?
- Do not forget the significance of the Word of the Lord. When God says something will happen – it happens!
- God has spoken.
  - o He said He will come back. Does this affect your thinking?
  - o He says you will have eternity with Him. Does this change your focus?
  - o Do you look to the eternal kingdom or remain focused on the physical world around you?
- The people of Judah had become accustomed to the ways of the nations around them and had adopted those ways. They no longer saw what God describes as "abominations" as wrong.
  - o What does this say about the ability of culture to blind us to God's Word, and His ways?
  - o What things in your culture have become so normal that you accept them, when in God's eyes they are horrific?

HAGGAI

"Build My House!"

"Go up to the hills and bring wood and build the house, that I may take pleasure in it and that I may be glorified, says the LORD. You looked for much, and behold, it came to little. And when you brought it home, I blew it away. Why? declares the LORD of hosts. Because of my house that lies in ruins, while each of you busies himself with his own house." – Haggai 1:8-9

During your first reading

Themes to track
- The temple
- The people

During your second reading

Things to notice in the text
- The responses of Haggai, the returning exiles, and the leadership of the returned exiles.
- God's actions and commands

Chapter summaries

These are optional as they can be time consuming for the larger books. If you choose to do them, you will receive a much deeper appreciation of the book. By the end of The IBSC, you will have paraphrased the entire Bible! Go through each chapter and try to summarise it in one paragraph, using your own words; force yourself to stay big picture and capture the heart of each chapter.

After your initial readings

Setting of Haggai
Author
The book was written by Haggai, the prophet.

Date prophecies were spoken
Haggai spoke these prophecies in 520 BC.

Recipient – hearers
The prophecies were spoken to the returned exiles.

Recipient – readers
The prophecies were written for the returned exiles.

Date and place of writing
Haggai recorded the prophecies in the same year that they were spoken, in 520 BC, from within Judah.

Reason spoken
God's message, given through Haggai, was to reprimand the people for neglecting His house in preference for material concerns. He had given them warnings through economic trials, but they did not listen. Haggai's message was another outpouring of God's grace upon His people, to prevent them from having a second turn in exile. Through this message, He reminded them of who they served and gave them motivation to resume the building of His temple.

Reason written
The book was written to remind the people that they were still under covenant with God; there remained blessings for obedience and curses for disobedience. The book encouraged the people to be strong in the Lord and to trust Him for provision and protection. It should also have renewed their hope in God, through the promise that His glory would return to the temple.

Big picture
Historical background
By decree of Cyrus, king of Persia, the Jews were given the opportunity to return to Jerusalem and rebuild the temple. The first group of exiles returned to Jerusalem in 538 BC, from exile in Babylon. They commenced work on the temple before ceasing the work due to fear of their hostile neighbours. Instead of completing the work on God's house, the people turned their energy towards building their own homes and lives.

Work on the temple stopped between the years of 535 and 520 BC. Haggai's prophecies urged the people to recommence their work on the temple. Darius became king of Persia in 522 BC and he allowed work on the temple to recommence. The work was finally completed in 516 BC. Refer to the historical background given for the book of Zechariah for more information surrounding the temple rebuild. Haggai was a contemporary of the prophet Zechariah.

Signet rings

The signet ring, also known as a "seal", comes from the Hebrew word "hotam" and the Greek word "sphragis", and was used universally throughout the ancient world. It was a ring with a seal imprinted on it that was used like a signature – a legal stamp used to sign letters and documents. Think of the kings of England sealing documents by putting dobs of melted wax on a parchment and then stamping their ring into it. The signet ring was also a symbol of authority and power.

Character portrayal – forgotten conditions of the covenant

"I work, and work, and yet I receive no gain. It is the same with all of us! We are a pioneering community, rebuilding our homes in the Promised Land. God promised Moses that is would be 'a land flowing with milk and honey', but I would settle for it simply flowing with rain at the moment! The earth is bare; the soil, hard and dry.

"My wife and I have a beautiful house, I cut the timber myself from the finest wood in the region, but what good is a beautified house when we do not have enough food for the table or clothes for warmth? When we were in Babylon we may not have lived on our own land, but we had all that we needed. There is some muttering that perhaps we, who chose to return, made the wrong decision; I suppose time will tell . . ."

Book overview

Haggai is a book that shows God's desire for obedience over sacrifice. God was addressing the group of returned exiles, after they had returned to Jerusalem and commenced rebuilding the temple.

After laying the foundations, work on the temple was set aside in order to build and beautify their own homes. The book shows how the people became consumed with their own possessions and lives, to the neglect of the Lord's house. Haggai called the people to walk in obedience. His message declared that it was not right to be concerned with material things and neglect the Lord; God was to come first in their lives.

The returned exiles were still making offerings to the Lord, but God declared that these were unclean and unworthy before His eyes. He was not concerned with their sacrifices, since they did not come from the heart. The book of Haggai shows that the reason they were not prospering in the land was because they had broken covenant with God, and were therefore living under the covenant curses listed in Deuteronomy 28. The people responded to this reprimand by returning to the task God had set them. The building of God's house recommenced, with the people acting under righteous fear of the Lord.

As they worked, they realised that the new temple would not be a rival of the former one that Solomon had built (see 1 Kings 6). God drew their attention to this fact, but also called them to be strong and trust in Him. He promised that His temple would be restored to its former glory and He would gather the treasures of all the nations to Himself for His glory. Looking back in history, it can be seen that God's promise was not one of physical glory for the temple, as it never returned to the glory of Solomon's day; God was promising glory for His spiritual temple.

What is the spiritual temple? The body of Christ, as seen in 2 Corinthians 6:16. God declared that He will shake the nations of the earth and bring the glory in for Himself. The fulfilment of this will occur at the time of Christ's second coming. At His return, Christ will judge the nations and rule over all the heavens and earth. When this occurs, the people of God will receive their inheritance because they have been sealed by Christ. Jesus is the sealing "signet ring" that declares believers belong to the Father.

Interpreting the book of Haggai
Interpretation questions

1. How did the actions of the returned exiles in Haggai 1:1-4 compare with that of King David in 2 Samuel 7:1-13? How did God want His people to respond?
2. God called the people to look around them as he lists what they did and did not have in Haggai 1:5-6.
   a. What does this imply?
   b. Should the people have known that the size of the harvest or their lack of gain was due to their disobedience; why or why not?
   c. Give scriptures from the Law (first five books of the Bible) in support of your answer.
3. Why was it important for the people to rebuild the temple upon their return to the land?
4. The people were rebuilding their homes before they rebuilt the temple.
   a. Why was God angry that His people were building their homes?
   b. Could they be justified in wanting to provide shelter for their family?
   c. Why were their actions sinful?
5. Haggai 1:12 records a significant turning point for the nation.
   a. Why was the response of the leadership and people important?
   b. What was the significance of their response?
   c. How did it differ from the response of their fathers to the prophets, pre-exile?
6. Notice God's response in Haggai 1:13-15, which He gave immediately after the people's response.
   a. How would this have been an encouragement, point of strength, and motivator for the people?
   b. What had they feared and what did they now have to fear?
7. How did God encourage their continued obedience in Haggai 2:10-19?
   a. What was He calling them to remember?
   b. Would the people have considered this a re-establishment of the

covenant; why or why not?

    c. Look back on the covenant promises – listing blessings for obedience and of curses for disobedience (Deuteronomy 28).

8. Read Ezra 3:11-13. How did God respond to their sorrow, as recorded in Haggai 2:1-9?

9. The presence of the Spirit appears to be related to God's command not to fear.

    a. Are there New Testament passages that also support the Spirit's presence dispersing fear?

    b. What would this have meant to the original readers?

    c. How would it have strengthened them as they lived amongst their neighbours (who did not want the Jews back in the land, having come to see it as their own)?

    d. How does knowledge of the Spirit's presence enable all believers to live without fear of temporal circumstances?

10. The book of Hebrews was also written to a group of believers facing persecution for their faith. Look at the author's use of God's promise in Haggai 2:6-9,20-23, and in Hebrews 12:26. Read Hebrews 12 in its entirety.

    a. How does this reading of Hebrews impact on your interpretation of Haggai 2:6-9,20-23?

    b. What was the promise that God was giving to the returned exiles?

    c. Would the original readers have interpreted this promise in the same way as the author of Hebrews? If not, what would it have meant to the original readers?

11. What was the significance of the temple in the New Testament?

    a. What did Christ say of it in John 2:19-22?

    b. Also consider Paul's words in 1 Corinthians 3:16 and 2 Corinthians 6:16-18 in your answer.

12. In Haggai 2:20-23, Zerabbabel was called the Lord's signet ring. Consider:

    a. What is the promise that was given with the ring?

    b. What encouragement would the promise have brought to the original readers? What would it have meant to the returning exiles?

    c. Note the mention of time – "on that day". What else is occurring on the day God will take Zerabbabel, His servant?

    d. He was also to "shake the heavens and the earth", which, from Hebrews, seems to imply Christ's second coming. Given this, to whom was this promise prophetically relating? Remember that Zerubbabel was a direct descendant of David, of the royal line; this was probably why he was chosen to be governor of Judah. See Matthew 1:12-23, Luke 3:27, and Luke 30:33.

13. Consider the character of God, as revealed in the book of Haggai.

    a. What do you learn of the jealousy of God?

    b. What do you learn of His provision?

    c. What is the greatest provision that He has given?

Creative interpretation

    1. Make a comparative observation table for the books of Ezra, Nehemiah, and Haggai to track the events that occurred as the Jews returned from exile. Feel free to add extra observations you would like to track!

Observations	Ezra	Nehemiah	Haggai
Key leaders:			
Prophets who spoke:			
Progression of the building – temple, the wall, time frames, delays, etc:			
Actions of the people/ key emotions:			
Actions of God:			
What was God communicating?			
Response of the Gentiles in the land – opposition etc:			
Response/ actions of the kings:			
Other significant events which took place:			
Other observations:			

Application inspiration

- Read Matthew 6:33 and Luke 16:13.
  - o Are you focused on material possessions or on building God's kingdom?

- o How can you remain focused on being obedient to the Lord over the call of money?
- 1 Corinthians 3 gives a call for believers to be active in building His church. What does this look like in your life?
    - o How could you serve at church or in the local community?
    - o How can you build the Kingdom of God in your workplace?
    - o Do you live in a godly way towards your colleagues?
    - o Do you serve willingly and joyfully?
    - o Consider how you will build. What stones will you lay in the temple?
    - o How do you reflect the glory of the Most High?
- Let fear of God, and knowledge of who He is, call you to walk in obedience to His will.

ZECHARIAH

Coming King, coming Kingdom

And say to him, 'Thus says the LORD of hosts, "Behold, the man whose name is the Branch: for he shall branch out from his place, and he shall build the temple of the LORD. It is he who shall build the temple of the LORD and shall bear royal honor, and shall sit and rule on his throne. And there shall be a priest on his throne, and the counsel of peace shall be between them both."' –
Zechariah 6:12-13

During your first reading

Themes to track
- Cleansing/ restoration
- Foretelling of Christ/ messianic predictions
- God's character

During your second reading

Things to notice in the text
- Visions
- Repeated phrase: "In that day"
- Questions and answers
- Judgement on the nations
- Salvation for the people of God

Chapter summaries
These are optional as they can be time consuming for the larger books. If you choose to do them, you will receive a much deeper appreciation of the book. By the end of The IBSC, you will have paraphrased the entire Bible! Go through each chapter and try to summarise it in one paragraph, using your own words; force

yourself to stay big picture and capture the heart of each chapter.

After your initial readings

Setting of Zechariah
<u>Author</u>
The book was written by the prophet, Zechariah.

<u>Date prophecies were spoken</u>
Zechariah spoke these prophecies between 520 and 518 BC.

<u>Recipient – hearers</u>
The prophecies were spoken to the returned exiles during the time that the work on the temple rebuilding had ceased.

<u>Recipient – readers</u>
Zechariah wrote down his prophecies for the returned exiles, who had completed building the new temple and were now seeking to rebuild their lives and city.

<u>Date and place of writing</u>
The book was written shortly after 518 BC, close to the completion of the temple rebuilding in 512 BC, from within Jerusalem.

<u>Reason spoken</u>
The prophecies were spoken to give the people hope in God, and encouragement during the rebuilding. They promised that His blessings would come if the people walked in obedience to God's Law.

<u>Reason written</u>
The book was written to keep the people from turning from God and, as a result, being sent back for a second time in exile. The prophecies also reset the people's expectations for what their new life in Jerusalem would be like, and in what form God's blessings would come upon them.

Big picture
<u>Historical background</u>
Key dates for Zechariah:
- 538 BC – First group of exiles returned to Jerusalem.
    - The Persian Empire took over as the world power and reversed the policy followed by Assyria and Babylon, who had forced captives to leave their lands in order to strip defeated nations of their national identities. In contrast, Cyrus allowed captive people groups to return to their home lands as a means of gaining their loyalty, and ensuring their faithfulness to the Persian Empire.
- 536 BC – Temple foundation was laid.

- o Why the two year gap between when they returned to Jerusalem and when they commenced work on the temple? They built the altar immediately, but feared the people of the land who were standing in opposition to their rebuilding. It is unknown what reasons other than fear may have existed for the delay.
- 535-520 BC – Temple rebuilding was stopped.
  - o Fear, mixed with unmet expectations, led the people to lose faith. They start to think that God's promises were broken, and as a result, they believed they must fend for themselves as best they could.
  - o Ezra 4 reveals that their neighbours were persecuting the returned Jews.
  - o In Ezra 5, a tag-team of God's prophets gets the people back to construction. For fifteen to sixteen years, the people had done nothing towards rebuilding the temple. It was because of the prophecies of Haggai and Zechariah that they recommenced the work.
  - o Haggai 2: the returned Jews stopped work again to build their own homes. They were living in beautiful houses whilst the city lay in ruin and God's temple sat neglected.
- 516 BC – Temple was completed (Ezra 6:15-18).
  - o Key background information can be found in Ezra 1-6.
  - o Ezra 5:1 and 6:14 again shows the tag-team prophets.

The night visions

Zechariah records eight night visions, which were given to him by God. These visions were given to deal with the unmet expectations of the returning exiles. The returned exiles were asking many questions, including:

- "Why do we need a temple when we did not have one in exile?"
- "Why should we invest time and effort to rebuild the temple amidst persecution?"
- "Will judgement come upon our enemies, upon those persecuting us?"
- "When will God do something about the persecution we are suffering?"

Character portrayal – Zechariah seeks understanding

"The Lord gave me eight visions to share with the people, and to record for His glory. Even now I do not really know what they mean.

"I sought understanding from the angel who was with me. What compelled me to ask, I do not know – perhaps it was the Spirit of the Lord. Nevertheless, I did ask. I sought understanding for the visions. And not once did the angel refuse to answer me; not once was my asking in vain. I still do not clearly see what they foretell, but I trust that God will bring them all to fruition.

"These visions . . . they were confusing and seemed fractured: images of baskets, flying scrolls, and horses – what could they mean? Some caused sorrow in my breast, whilst others caused pain. I knew fear, and I knew joy. Yet the greatest seed the visions planted was hope – hope for God's people and hope for mankind. God is going to bring salvation to His people! I will cling to that hope! We can trust in the Lord our God and sing His praises. We can trust in Him as we live in this land, our land, and as we rebuild His temple!"

Book overview

God's heart is for the spiritual restoration of all men. The original readers were impatient in their desire to see the complete physical restoration of their nation, and to once more be considered a dominant world power. They wished to have the temporal prosperity their nation had enjoyed in the days of King Solomon. Yet God said that the surrounding nations were not His main concern. He was concerned with ending sin and cleansing the nations of unrighteousness.

Through the One Pierced, God promised to remove all sin and impurity from the land. The removal of the filthy garments from Joshua, the High Priest, was symbolic of the purification Christ brings upon His people. They shall be clothed with pure vestments. God promised to cleanse the iniquity of the land in a single day, foretelling the cross and Christ conquering over death.

The book foretold spiritual salvation through the Branch, who would make the people of God holy before Him. Christ is the author of salvation. Believers will be set free because of the blood covenant Christ establishes with them. God promised restoration for Jerusalem. He promised that He would once again make His dwelling place in Zion, amidst His people. He will be their protection. Fasts and feasting will be as God desires them. In the meantime, God's people are to be a light to the nations, bringing others into His kingdom.

Zechariah prophesied of a final battle where God and His holy ones will fight against the nations, and God will stand victorious. The land will be left desolate as He destroys His enemies and, afterwards, water will flow from Jerusalem. At this time, all within Jerusalem will be holy, just as the holy items in His temple are holy. God will bring complete sanctification to Jerusalem, bringing about a kingdom of saints. He will be able to dwell in the midst of man because all people will be holy. He has conquered sin, and at Christ's return, believers will welcome in a kingdom of righteousness.

Help interpreting Zechariah

Stay big picture when studying the night visions. Following is a brief summary of what God was conveying to the original readers through each vision:

- Vision 1 – A man among the myrtle trees.
  - o God would bless the returned exiles and help them to rebuild the temple.
  - o They were not to worry about what was happening in the nations for God would be their security.
- Vision 2 – Four horns, four craftsmen.
  - o The text does not tell who these four nations are, but four is

symbolic for totality; therefore, it could be referring to all nations – the whole world.

- o Nations will be judged, but in God's timing.
- o God would protect Judah and repay their enemies.

- Vision 3 – A measuring line.
  - o A measured area was a sign of protection and blessing. They would not need physical walls because God will be their protection.
  - o Babylon was known as a place of greed, materialism, and wealth. God was calling the exiles to flee spiritual Babylon, to let go of Babylon's culture and lifestyle.

- Visions 4 – Joshua, the high priest.
  - o The vision gives a beautiful picture of the cross and Christ's sacrifice.
  - o The priest represents the people. Mankind is guilty of sin, unable to strictly adhere to the Law. The garments represent mankind's current state of sin and uncleanness before the Lord. The vestments symbolise purification, being cleansed and made holy.

- Vision 5 – The gold lamp stand and two olive trees.
  - o The eyes of the Lord symbolise God's sight over the entire world. He will be the Judge over all nations and all people.
  - o The lamp stand is of the type that would have been found in the tabernacle. It was not just for vision, but was symbolic of God's witness to the surrounding nations.
  - o The olive trees are two anointed ones. Looking at Deuteronomy 19:15 and Numbers 35:30, two witnesses can be trusted to speak the truth.
  - o God was bringing them back to the land, and the temple would be a witness to the people around them. This foreshadowed Christ, and the building of the spiritual temple.

- Vision 6 and 7 – The flying scroll and the basket.
  - o The true enemy is seen through these visions to be sin.
  - o The scroll represented the Law and the covenant curses that came for disobedience. A time of judgement is coming upon all who break the Law of God. This will be a final judgement, bringing an end to disobedience and sin.
  - o The basket vision should bring hope. It was a promise that God is going to remove the iniquities of His people far away from them.

- Vision 8 – Four chariots and two bronze mountains.
  - o Chariots indicate that these horsemen are going to war, bringing judgement upon the nations.
  - o The original readers would have recognised the north as being symbolic of the enemies of God because the enemies of Judah came from the north.

- o The enemies of God will be punished.
- o The vision was about the spiritual temple built by Christ, not the rebuilding of a physical temple.

Interpreting the book of Zechariah
<u>Interpretation questions</u>

1. Try not to get caught up in the little details or the controversial passages. Rather, ask:
   a. What was God trying to communicate?
   b. What was happening at the time the prophecies were given to Zechariah?
   c. Why was this important for the original readers to hear?
2. Consider the original hearers.
   a. What did the Jews expect when they returned from exile to the Promised Land?
   b. Look for insight to their mindset as they returned to the land.
   c. How were their expectations different from what actually happened?
3. The very first words of God, recorded by Zechariah, were a call to remembrance.
   a. How might Zechariah have wanted the original readers to respond to his message?
   b. What was he calling them to do?
4. Zechariah records eight night visions, given to him by God. When studying each night vision be sure to consider:
   a. How might it have addressed the questions of the original readers, as noted in the historical background given above?
   b. Did the vision address the surrounding nations, Judah or the spiritual people of God? What did it say about them?
   c. What do you learn of their true enemy (sin), and how God would deal with it?
   d. What did it reveal about God's bigger plans?
   e. Who was God going to send as Saviour? What was revealed about the Messiah/ Branch?
   f. What was revealed about the spiritual temple?
   g. How would Zechariah have felt as he saw these visions?
   h. What was significant about Zechariah asking questions about the visions? What was the importance of his seeking an explanation? Why would he have done this?
5. The laying of the temple's foundation:
   i. Why was the laying of the temple's foundation recorded in the midst of the visions (Zechariah 4:8-10)?
   j. Was it a spiritual promise of things to come or a physical promise?
   k. What encouragement would it have given to the original readers?
6. Through Zechariah 9-14, be sure to consider the following:

a. New Testament quotes – these indicate the fulfilment of the prophecies.
b. What was said of the Branch:
   i. Who is the Branch?
   ii. What would happen when the Branch came?
   iii. Was the promise for physical or spiritual salvation?
   iv. Should the original readers have known that it was talking about spiritual events?
   v. What would the people do to Him?
   vi. What would He achieve?
   vii. How did wrong expectations of the coming Messiah impact on their actions?
c. How would these promises have given hope to the depressed original readers? Remember that, whilst they had returned to the Promised Land, it was no longer their land; they remained under the governance of Persia. Also remember that they were being persecuted by their neighbours.
d. Look at the contrasting pictures of war and salvation.
   i. What is foretold of Christ's second coming?
   ii. What is said of judgement?
   iii. Who will be saved?
   iv. What is told of the Kingdom of God?
e. What warnings were given against sin? Are there sins, such as idolatry, that were specifically mentioned? Why do you think this is? What does it say about God? Why were these warnings important to the original readers, given the idolatrous history of their ancestors?

Creative interpretation

1. Look at the passages that relate to the Branch, the coming Messiah. Also look at New Testament passages that quote the text of Zechariah and consider the meaning of these quotations in their New Testament setting. Write a short summary on the coming Messiah, including:
a. Who is He?
b. What was He to accomplish? What did Christ accomplish?
c. How would the people receive Him? How did the people receive Jesus?

Ongoing prophets' project

Take out the separate document that you started during your Isaiah study. Add to it what you learn about the "day of the Lord" versus the "great day of the Lord" from Zechariah. Keep adding to this document as you work through the prophets.

Application inspiration
Implications for ministry and faith

- What does Zechariah show about the danger of expectations?
  - Things can take longer than we expect, but when this happens will you allow this to kill your hopes or diminish your faith?
  - Are you willing to lay down your expectations for Him or will you allow disappointments to stop you from serving the Lord, and His Gospel?
- The greatest fear of Christians should not be failure, but fear of succeeding at things that do not matter, having no lasting value.
  - What are godly expectations?
  - How can you cultivate godly expectations?
  - How can you have an eternal and spiritual focus?
- What are you more concerned about: doing what you feel is your call or with the spread of the Gospel?
- Is there a ministry right in front of you that you could be serving in, and yet have ignored because you long to be somewhere else?
- When God gives you a vision that you do not understand, do you pursue an answer from Him? Do you seek His clarification when what you see or hear does not make sense?

Truths from the book of Zechariah

Think on these truths from Zechariah, and let them bring you hope and comfort. Find New Testament verses that give further support to them. Here are a number of truths that may comfort you, found in the book of Zechariah:

- God has conquered sin, bringing salvation and spiritual cleansing to His people.
- Everyone was deserving of God's wrath, but likewise everyone can receive life in Christ.
- As a child of God, you are called to focus on what is of lasting value.
- Christ silenced the Accuser; you are now clean and righteous.
- Those of God's kingdom seem weak in the eyes of the world, yet God will make them strong.
- In the Kingdom of God, all will be holy, God will be worshipped, and He will provide for His people.

MALACHI

Here comes the great day!

"Behold, I send my messenger, and he will prepare the way before me. And the Lord whom you seek will suddenly come to his temple; and the messenger of the covenant in whom you delight, behold, he is coming, says the LORD of hosts. But who can endure the day of his coming, and who can stand when he appears? For he is like a refiner's fire and like fullers' soap." – Malachi 3:1-2

During your first reading

Themes to track
- Day of the Lord
- "My name"
- Character of God
- Right sacrifices
- Covenant

During your second reading

Things to notice in the text
- Mark the questions of the returned exiles and God's answers.
- Circle connectives; look for "because", "for", and "so that".
- Highlight the repeated words "covenant" and "My name".
- Promises of God
- Messianic passages
- Emotions/ state of the heart

Chapter summaries
These are optional as they can be time consuming for the larger books. If you choose to do them, you will receive a much deeper appreciation of the book. By the

end of The IBSC, you will have paraphrased the entire Bible! Go through each chapter and try to summarise it in one paragraph, using your own words; force yourself to stay big picture and capture the heart of each chapter.

After your initial readings

Setting of Malachi
Author

Written by the prophet, Malachi, whose name means "messenger", or "messenger of the Lord".

Date prophecies were spoken

The events recorded in the book of Malachi coincide with those occurring at the time of Nehemiah's second visit to Jerusalem. It can therefore be concluded that the prophecies were spoken at this time; 430-432 BC.

Recipient – hearers

The prophecies were spoken to the returned exiles, after the completion of the new temple.

Recipient – readers

The prophecies were written for the returned exiles living in Judah, having completed the new temple.

Date and place of writing

The prophecies were recorded at the time they were spoken; 430-432 BC, from within Judah.

Reason spoken

Malachi rebuked the Israelites for their unfaithfulness to the covenant and for not fearing God. The message clearly conveyed to the people that it was because of their disobedience that their land and works were not being blessed, not because of any unfaithfulness from God.

Reason written

The book was written as a challenge and a warning. It called the people to return to God's ways because if they did not, more curses would come upon them for continued disobedience.

Big picture
Historical background
Mindset of the returned exiles (the original hearers of the message)

The people had lost commitment in their service to God. They had been excited to rebuild their lives and city, but work was slow and tiring, often intertwined with opposition, and involved primitive living conditions.

The people were drifting away from God and His Laws, and had allowed doubt to enter into their hearts. They had begun to question the character of God, His love, and His justice. They had expected to see the Messiah of whom Zechariah had spoken. They had also been looking forward to receiving the blessings He had promised through the prophets. When God did not fulfil their expectations, they chose the path of disobedience. They struggled with the land's poor yield; however, they did not see this as a consequence of their own actions, by their failure to bring a tithe to the Lord or their offering of unacceptable lame animals. The fear of the Lord no longer dictated their actions.

Fall of Edom

The fall of Edom was progressive:

- 860-850 BC – Ammonites and Moabites attacked Mt. Seir (2 Chronicles 20).
- 8thC BC – Edom came under pressure from Arabian tribes.
- 732 BC – Edom became tribute-payers of Assyria.
- 604 BC – Edom fell under the suzerainty of Babylon.
- 6thC BC – Nomadic tribes forced Edom into the Negeb, which became known as Idumea.
- 312 BC – Edom was dislodged from Petra by the Nabateans.
- 165/4 BC – The Idumeans (formerly the Edomites) were driven from the Negeb by Judas Macabaeus.
- 126 BC – Judaism, including circumcision, was forced upon them by John Hyrcanus, during the time of the Maccabees.
- 70 AD – After 70 AD, Edom (Idumea) disappears from history. This is the same time that Jerusalem fell to Rome at the hands of Emperor Titus.

Character portrayal – Malachi's anger at a hard-hearted people

"God chose you!" Malachi nearly spat the words out in his frustration. "What did we, as a people, do to deserve God's favour? How are you better than your brothers in Edom? We were no better! We were sinners before a Mighty and Awesome God, and yet He chose to deliver us. It was our father's disobedience that caused God to send them into exile. But He was faithful to bring us back from Babylon! And what need you do, but tempt Him to exile us once more!"

The people did not understand Malachi's frustration. They looked at him like confused deer. A riot of questions ran through their minds. Questions such as: How has God loved us? How have we disgraced His name? Why are our offerings not sufficient for this God? Where is the justice that God harps on about? and What have we taken from Him?

"Oh, if only the people could see the folly of their ways!" Malachi bewailed on his mat, shaking his head as he thought of the people. He prayed morning and night for them with held breath. Surely they would come back to the Lord now that God had answered their questions. He would present God's case before them and they would listen; they would return to the Law of the Lord and renew their covenant with Him. They had to listen and attend! For Malachi, it seemed the only logical response to the Creator God.

Time would tell if the Jewish people would respond in the same manner as Malachi, God's prophet, or as their ancestors, who were sent into exile for their disobedience . . .

Book overview

God was calling the returned exiles back to the covenant. They were full of questions, which reflected their doubt of God's justice and faithfulness. They did not see the point of following in God's ways, proclaiming that following the Law had brought them no gain. The returned exiles were questioning God's love for them because they did not think they were better off than the nations around them.

God answered their questioning of His character and condemned their sacrifices. He proclaimed that they were cursed because they were breaking the covenant by offering abhorrent sacrifices to Him. Blessings and curses were still conditional upon their faithfulness to His Laws. The Jews, to whom Malachi was prophesying, were being faithless to God's laws, especially those relating to intermarriage and worship of the One True God. They were also being faithless in their marriages. The priests were not leading the people in the truth, but causing them to stray. They were not being faithful in their tithing, but were oppressing the needy. The people had once again turned from God's Law.

God was pursuing His people and calling them to return to covenant obedience. He challenged them to test whether obedience did not bring them blessings, as they were proclaiming. He promised that His blessings would pour down from heaven upon those who acted faithfully to the covenant.

Yet, however bad their situation may have been, God went on to show that there were greater consequences at stake than physical blessings and curses. Those that walk in obedience to the Lord's Law and seek righteousness will be safe on the great day of the Lord, but those who break His Law are doomed to perish in His fierce wrath. Malachi prophesied that the fear of God would enable them to stand on the day of judgement.

Interpreting the book of Malachi

Interpretation questions

1. The book is written in the format of questions and answers. The people were asking questions of God, seeking proof of what He had done for them. How does God answer each of the following questions, asked by the returned exiles:
   a. How have you loved us? (Malachi 1:2);
   b. How have we despised your name? (Malachi 1:6);
   c. Why do you not accept our offerings? (Malachi 2:14);
   d. How have we wearied you? (Malachi 2:17);
   e. Where is the God of justice? (Malachi 2:17);
   f. How shall we return to God? (Malachi 3:7);
   g. How have we robbed you? (Malachi 3:8);

    h.   How have we spoken against you? (Malachi 3:13).

2. Remember that the original readers had rebuilt the wall of Jerusalem and the temple.

    a.   How might the original readers have felt?

    b.   Were these emotions justified?

    c.   How could they have clung to faith in God despite their temporal circumstances?

3. What do you learn of God's character in Malachi?

    a.   What names did He use for Himself?

    b.   What was He communicating to the returned exiles, living under Persian rule, by the names He used for Himself?

    c.   How did He show concern for His name? Why was this important?

4. Look back on the book of Obadiah.

    a.   Why did God judge the nation of Edom?

    b.   What does Malachi 1:2-5 show of how God protected His people, compared to what happened to those who persecuted His chosen people?

    c.   Why would this have been a reprimand to the returned exiles? What had the Jews forgotten?

5. What did God have to say about the priests? In addition to Malachi, refer to Exodus 32:28-29 and Deuteronomy 10:7-9.

    a.   How had they been leading the people?

    b.   Were they shepherding His flock in the way they should have done?

    c.   What was God's covenant with the house of Levi? A covenant with Levi is not specifically mentioned in Scripture until Jeremiah 33. Some scriptures you may wish to consider include: Exodus 32:24-29, Numbers 3:12-13, Deuteronomy 33:8-11, and Jeremiah 33:14-26.

    d.   How was this held as a reprimand against the priests in the book of Malachi?

6. What sins were listed against the returned exiles?

    a.   How had they strayed from His Laws?

    b.   In what ways had they been disobedient?

    c.   Why was God angry with them?

    d.   What was the state of their worship and religion?

    e.   What was happening with their sacrifices? Why were their sacrifices unworthy before the Holy God? Return to Leviticus 1-7.

    f.   What did God say about the covenant? In what ways had the people broken their covenant with the Lord? Can you find scriptural references to support your answer?

7. What curses were upon them?

    a.   How does God show the blessings and curses to be conditional?

    b.   Where in Scripture are these blessings and curses listed; can you

find some references from elsewhere in the Bible?
8. Look at Malachi 3:1, quoted in Matthew 11:10, Mark 1:2, and Luke 7:27.
   a. Who was the fulfilment of the prophecies?
   b. Who was the messenger?
   c. Who was the Lord? What was He to do?
   d. How would the returned exiles have interpreted these prophecies, given that they did not have the privilege of looking back in history at the Christ?
   e. What would these prophecies have meant to the original readers in their circumstances?
9. What is said of tithing in the book of Malachi?
   a. How were the people robbing the Lord?
   b. What did God desire from His people?
   c. What does this show of God's heart?
   d. How was tithing to be an act of worship?
   e. What is said of tithing in the New Testament? Look at Matthew 23:23, Matthew 22:37-39, Luke 12:15, Luke 18:22, 2 Corinthians 8-9, and Galatians 2:10.
   f. Why is tithing no longer specifically commanded in the New Testament?
   g. What is shown of God's heart for the poor and needy?
10. What is said of the day of the Lord's coming?
   a. How will man be judged?
   b. What two groups will be defined on judgement day?
   c. Who shall be saved?
   d. When will this be fulfilled?
   e. What does it show of the Lord?
   f. What response was God seeking from the returned exiles?
   g. What do you learn of the Kingdom of God? How does this compare to the parable Christ told as recorded in Matthew 13:24-30,37-43?
11. Who was the prophet Elijah?
   a. Look at Luke 1:16-17 and Matthew 17:12-13.
   b. What was he to do?
   c. What was his call?

Creative interpretation
   1. Considering the following questions, write a summary about God's covenant with man as seen in Malachi.
      a. What does Malachi show about the covenant?
      b. What covenants are mentioned?
      c. What was God communicating to the original hearers by referencing His covenant?
      d. Why was the covenant so important to God?
      e. What does it show of His character?

f. Find other verses in the Old Testament to add depth to God's message in Malachi.

g. Can you find New Testament references relating to God's covenant with man?

Ongoing prophets' project

Take out the separate document that you started during your Isaiah study and have been adding to throughout the prophets. Finish this study by adding to it what you learn about the "day of the Lord" versus the "great day of the Lord" from Malachi. Well done completing this project!

Application inspiration

- Do you demand proof of God's love when circumstances are not going the way you would chose for them to go? Can you cling to Christ as the greatest illustration of His love in your life, even when you are waiting for Him to fulfil another promise?

- Are you living out what you are learning in His Word? Do you act as He requires or as is expected of you from your community?

Giving and sacrifice

- What should giving look like today? Is a tithe still to be given? Be sure to consider both New Testament and Old Testament passages.

- Do you give God the best of yourself?
  - What does giving look like in your life?
  - What sacrifice has God called you to lay before Him?

- Do you trust Him to provide? Is this something with which you struggle?

- In what ways has He previously shown His faithfulness to you? Write some of these down in a book or your journal to look back on when you doubt His faithfulness.

INTRODUCTION TO THE NEW TESTAMENT

Between the Old and New Testaments

Four hundred years separate the last events of the Old Testament and the first events of the New Testament. These years are known as the "four hundred years of silence". During these years, Alexander the Great conquered the known world and began the process of hellenisation, compelling captive people adopt Greek culture, language, and religion.

Alexander the Great died at the age of thirty-three and four of his generals took over rulership, dividing the Macedonian Empire. Antiochus Epiphanes became ruler of the section into which Judea fell in 175 BC and was determined to have the Jews adopt Greek culture. In 168 BC, he desecrated the temple by sacrificing a pig (an unclean animal) upon the altar. He also demanded that the Jews cease keeping the Sabbath, circumcision of infant boys, religious ceremonies and festivals, and the reading of the Law (Torah). After returning from exile, the Jews became fanatical about keeping the Law, not wanting God to send them back into exile, and so they refused to heed Antiochus Epiphanes' orders. A successful revolt issued, led by a prominent Jewish family known as the Maccabbees.

By the time of the New Testament, Rome had become the world power, but Greek thinking and culture still predominated in society. Under the Roman Empire, the Jews experienced a period of relative independence and were granted some rights of self-governance.

Judaism in the time of the New Testament

The revolt during the time of the Maccabbees epitomised the people's willingness to die for the Law. Following their return from exile, fervour for the Law had overtaken the Jewish people. This fervour led to man-made traditions, becoming the oral law, which acted as a "fence" around the Law of Moses.

Think of the oral law as being a hundred meter perimeter outside the "red flags" of the Law, for the purpose of avoiding accidentally walking too close to the red flags. The Jews became so afraid of breaking the Law that they put safe-guards around each one. It was the role of the Pharisees to ensure that the laws were kept.

Illustration: oral law as a fence around Law of Moses

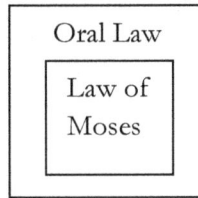

```
┌─────────────────────┐
│  Oral Law           │
│   ┌──────────────┐  │
│   │  Law of      │  │
│   │  Moses       │  │
│   └──────────────┘  │
└─────────────────────┘
```

The temple was the centre of Jewish religion and society. It was where heaven and earth met; it was the house of God's glory, and His dwelling place with man. God's glory entered into the temple of Solomon at its consecration [1], but not upon the temple of Zerubbabel [2], which was built by the returning exiles and later improved upon by Herod the Great. To the Jewish mindset, the glory of God had to come back to the temple to make their deliverance from exile complete, even though this never happened. Similarly, they saw the Promised Land as theirs by right, and Israel as defiled because of the Roman rule.

Sects within Judaism

Sanhedrin

This was the ruling body of the Jews that advised the Chief Priest. The Romans gave some self-governing rights to the Jewish people, which were managed by the Sanhedrin, made up of both Pharisees and Sadducees. The Chief Priest no longer had to be a descendant of Aaron, as the Law demanded, but was appointed by Herod.

Pharisees

The Pharisees were the dominant sect of Judaism. They were responsible for the creation of the oral law and their role was to teach the laws to the people and ensure they were kept. They set themselves apart for the keeping of the Law, promising to keep every single law, both of Moses and the oral traditions. Teaching and worship mainly occurred within synagogues, rather than the temple.

Scribes

The Scribes worked out the oral law and determined the interpretation of Old Testament law; for example, the law that no burden should be carried on the Sabbath, gave rise to an oral law not allowing the lifting of any food weighing more than that of a dried fig.

Sadducees

In opposition to the Pharisees, they held only the Pentateuch to contain God-inspired laws. They also rejected the afterlife and did not believe in angels or demons. Where the Pharisees looked to the religious practices of the people, the Sadducees focused on politics and obtaining power.

Zealots

The Zealots were Jewish extremists, determined to have no foreign ruler over the Jewish people. They openly rebelled against Roman governance; for example, by refusing to pay taxes to Caesar. It was the Zealots that stirred the people up to revolt during the war against Rome, from 66 to 70 AD, which ultimately led to the fall of Jerusalem and the destruction of the temple.

Hellenists

These were the Jews who had adopted Greek culture. They mostly lived outside of Judea. The Old Testament was translated into Greek, and this translation was known as the Septuagint.

Examples of rabbinic teachings and traditions (oral laws)

The Rabbis taught that the oral law was also given to Moses, but in spoken form. It became more fervently abided by and revered than the Law of Moses. These traditions taught legalism, rather than heart-felt worship and a life lived seeking to glorify God.

The following are some examples of the rabbinic teachings and traditions at the time of Christ:

- Rabbis claimed that they had the power to bind or loose, meaning they were able to declare one guilty or innocent.
- Righteousness was equated with the performance of good works, such as the giving of alms to the poor.
- Illness was held to be the result of an individual's sin, not as the result of the fall of man or a consequence of living in a fallen world.
- Lepers were ostracised from all human contact. Not only could they receive no physical touch, but they had to shout out "unclean" to alert people of their presence and had to stay six feet away from others when walking.
- Tax collectors were considered the greatest of sinners as they worked for Rome. They were looked upon as traitors who stole from their own people.
- Children were seen as worthless; they had no rights and were to be despised.
- A man could divorce his wife for a string of reasons, including if he caught her talking to other men, she went into public without a head covering, she spoiled his dinner, or he tired of her in preference for another.
- Forgiveness was only to be extended three times.
- Hands had to be washed to the wrist before and after they ate to avoid defilement.

The relationship between Gentiles and Jews

Gentile views on Jews

The Gentiles made fun of the Jews for their strict adherence to food laws, the keeping of religious festivals, and the practice of circumcision. The Gentiles could not conceptualise a religion in which only One God was served, and so they labelled the Jews as being atheists. They hated the Jews for their temple tax exception, business success and military exception.

Jewish views on Gentiles

The Jews saw themselves as righteous because of their laws and religion. They believed that they had automatic entry into the eternal Kingdom of God purely based on their lineage, tracing back to Abraham. They viewed Gentiles as unclean and "in darkness", because of Gentile ignorance of the Law.

Women in New Testament times

Women held a very low place in Jewish, Greek and Roman society, alike. Understanding the cultural views held upon women will help you to understand how the teachings of Christ, and the apostles (including Paul) were counter-cultural, bringing women value and greater privileges.

Jewish views on women

The Old Testament shows women in that time to be well-respected; however, this had changed by the time of the New Testament. Jewish women were considered only slightly better than Gentiles. There were three courts in the temple and only Jewish men were allowed into the innermost courtyard; the women had to remain in the middle courtyard, cutting them off from God's presence. The women went to the temple and synagogues to hear the Law; only the men could "learn".

The role of women was restricted to servitude within the home. They were to work, remain silent and be kept out of the public way for their seducing ways. They were considered lazy, vain, and full of lust. Women were seen as inferior to men in every way, and blamed for the fall of man.

Greek views on women

The Greek's viewed women with loathing. Legend held that man stole fire from the gods and women were created as man's punishment. Men were said to be made of the gods; women, from one of ten sources: the long-haired sow, the evil fox, the dog, the dust of the earth, the sea, the stubborn donkey, the weasel, a mare, the monkey, or a bee. Only the bee was considered "good" as it was hard-working; hence, only one in ten women could be good. Like the Jews, the Greeks viewed men as superior, the "rulers", and women as inferior, the "subjects".

Roman views on women

The Roman view of women took after that of the Greek's. Female infanticide was common (the practice of killing infant girls, with parents valuing boy children). Husbands would kill their wives for things such as adultery, or drunkenness.

[1] 2 Chronicles 7:1
[2] Ezra 6

INTRODUCTION TO THE GOSPELS

The Gospels were written to testify to the good news of Jesus Christ. Each Gospel was written with a different audience in mind and to meet different needs within the church. The Gospel of Luke was written to an individual, Theophilus, so that he might believe, whilst the remaining Gospels were written to congregations of believers.

The Gospels provide a written account of the life and ministry of Jesus from eye witnesses. They explain how Christ is the fulfilment of the prophecies, the promised Messiah. They also introduce the covenant of grace He brought in, and the eternal Kingdom of God.

Jewish expectations for the Messiah

In order to understand their expectations, one must first understand what made the Jews consider themselves distinct from their neighbours. There were four main reasons why the Jews held themselves aloft from others. These were:

1. The temple and sacrificial system

    The temple was God's dwelling place with man, and the sacrificial system was to have made them a holy nation after the likeness of their holy God.

2. The Law

    The Law was detailed, absolutely holy, and covered every area of life. There was the Law of Moses (written law), and the oral traditions (oral law).

3. The land

    God had given them the land as their inheritance; it was the Promised Land, first promised to their beloved patriarch, Abraham. They had been exiled from it once, and since the return from exile, they had clung to the Law in order to avoid a second time in exile.

4. Their ethnicity

    Their very identity came from their lineage, tracing back to Abraham. They were the chosen people of God, set apart from the nations. They believed that the Jews were the only people who had responded to God's call, and thought they were automatically entitled to inheritance in the eternal Kingdom of God because of their lineage. Physical circumcision set them apart as the people of God.

The Jews were waiting for a physical saviour to return their nation to the former glory days of King David and King Solomon. The temple rebuilt after the return from exile was a mere shadow of Solomon's majestic temple; more importantly, God's presence never returned to rest in the new temple. The saviour was to restore the temple to its former glory and, from its top, he was to declare himself king. They anticipated a mighty warrior king, who would take Israel back from Rome, before he went on to conquer the nations. They also believed that He would enter Jerusalem riding on a cloud.

It is important to remember that not all of these expectations were founded on Scripture or even their interpretation of the prophecies relating to the Messiah. Ultimately, their wrong expectations as well as their unwillingness to compare their traditional beliefs to Scripture, and the person of Christ, hindered many Jews from coming to salvation in Christ.

What expectations did He meet?

There were some expectations of the Jews that Jesus met, whether the Jews recognised this or not. Here are a few of them:

- Christ was the Son of God, and the Messiah they expected was to be ascribed divinity;
- He would work miracles;
- A star would announce His birth;
- The Saviour would subdue Satan, casting him into hell;
- He was to bring freedom from sin; and
- He was to hold power over nature.

Jesus broke the rules

Jesus rattled the mindset of the people and their expectations for the Messiah. He was completely different from the beliefs, which they had held for hundreds of years, about the coming Messiah. He did not come in pomp and ceremony, and was not the son of earthly nobles or kings. He was born in a lowly stable, amidst the animals, and his birth was surrounded by stigma and gossip about his parentage.

Neither did Jesus conform to Jewish traditions. He challenged the Jews to leave their self-righteous ways and move back to the heart of the Law, and heart-felt worship of God. Some of the ways in which He went against the cultural norm and Jewish expectations included:

- The Jews placed huge influence on cleanliness; Jesus ate with sinners, women, and tax collectors.
- The Jews practiced self-righteous acts; Jesus looked at the state of one's heart.
- Jews thought that their entry into God's kingdom was based on ethnicity and sex; Jesus commended Gentiles for their faith, and spoke highly of

women.

- Jews had rigid worship practices and laws; Jesus cleansed the outer court of the temple, which had become a market place, but was meant to have been the place where the Gentiles could worship God.
- The Jews thought the Christ would be a conquering, military king who would save them from the Romans; Jesus told them to give Rome its taxes, whilst He came as the Suffering Servant.
- The Messiah was to rebuild the temple; Jesus predicted the destruction of the physical temple, which occurred in 70 AD. He declared Himself to be the temple and predicted His death and resurrection.
- They did not expect the Lamb of God and they did not expect a Messiah who would suffer; Christ bore insult from His own people, was condemned as a common criminal, died upon a cross, and was crucified for the sins of all mankind, before rising on the third day.
- They thought their Saviour would enter Jerusalem riding on a cloud; He came on a donkey's colt.
- The Jews expected a physical kingdom, a land cleansed from foreign armies and defiled people; Jesus preached a coming eternal kingdom and spiritual deliverance from sin.

Many of the Jews, and particularly the religious leaders of the time, failed to see Jesus through the foggy glasses of their mindset. They thought "He cannot be the Messiah; He is breaking the rules!"

The new covenant of grace

Jesus was not who the Jews were expecting and He brought in a kingdom that was far greater than their greatest hopes. They expected physical deliverance; Christ brought deliverance from sin.

Jesus came as the fulfilment of the Law. No one born of man could perfectly keep God's Law. The old covenant required animal sacrifice for each sin committed; Christ gave His blood as the ultimate sacrifice, once, for all. Under the new covenant, grace, love, and mercy conquer over sin. The old covenant had requirements from man; to uphold the Law through works, which no one could do. The old covenant showed that something better was needed. Jesus brought in a new covenant. Christ's death and resurrection paid the cost of sin, buying freedom for all who believe in Christ for salvation.

Jesus' ministry

Jesus taught the people that God looked to the heart of a person, and that it was what was inside that determined whether one was clean and pure or defiled. He opposed the self-righteous Pharisees and welcomed all who desired to hear the message of God. His life and ministry looked unremarkable to those who wanted a warrior king, but to those who had been ostracised by society, His ministry brought new hope.

Christ was a friend to the lowest in society – to tax collectors, children, women, sinners, and Gentiles. Crowds were drawn to Him for His love and compassion. He walked in perfect accordance with the will of God. He taught that the greatest commandment was to love God, followed by loving one's neighbours. His public ministry lasted only three years. His death and resurrection brought salvation from sin and eternal life to all who placed their faith in Him.

Christ preached to the masses, and to the few; to leaders, and to sinners. He reserved specific teaching times for His close friends and disciples. His teachings focused on salvation, the forgiveness of sins, and the Kingdom of God. The Kingdom of God was brought in by Christ, and yet will not come in its pure form until His return. Christ promised to send the Holy Spirit when He ascended to the Father in heaven. The Holy Spirit is to serve as Witness and Teacher, until Christ's second coming.

The parables of Jesus

Parables were the common way that Jesus challenged the world view of His listeners. Teaching by parables was common in the days of Christ and would have been a method that the people understood. They were designed to draw a response from His listeners. They were not meant to be full of hidden secrets, and they were not given as allegories for only the wise in His audience to be able to interpret. They were given for all. It is evident from the reactions of the people, recorded in the Gospels, that Christ's parables were understood to those wanting to hear and understand.

About the parables

1. Parables generally had only one main point. Not every detail was meant to hold significance.
2. Parables took a concept that was intangible and put it into story form to enable people to grasp the foreign concept.
3. They caught the listener by surprise. Christ talked about a situation that would have culturally made sense and then added a twist that was meant to challenge the way people thought.
4. Christ used the parables to teach or convey something about the Kingdom of God – a principle, Christ's return, who are God's people etc.
5. Christ's parables brought either a message of good news (to those that received the message and responded to God) or bad news (to those that hardened their hearts). The Pharisees fell into the later group; hence, their desire to kill Jesus.

To understand why these parables were received negatively by those hardened of heart, remember that they threatened, attacked, and undermined the fundamental beliefs and cultural practices of the Jews. Jesus was challenging their very lives, as their faith affected every aspect of how they lived.

Interpreting the parables

When interpreting a parable, take note of who Jesus was teaching. Was He addressing the Pharisees and Scribes, a crowd of people, individuals or His disciples? Ask the following questions when interpreting the parables:

1. How would His audience have identified with the story, and the characters in the story?
2. What was Christ's message to his original audience? Look for the main point. Do not look for spiritual meaning in every detail of the parable.
3. What was the twist in the story? What was the unexpected turn?
4. What response did the parable call forth from the original hearers? How was the audience challenged?

GOSPEL OF MATTHEW

Jesus; the Prophesied Redeemer

Now Jesus stood before the governor, and the governor asked him, "Are you the King of the Jews?" Jesus said, "You have said so." – Matthew 27:11

During your first reading

Themes to track

- Fulfilment of prophecies
- The end of the story/ salvation revealed
- Jesus the Christ: Messiah and Holy One of God
- Kingdom of God

During your second reading

Things to notice in the text

- Highlight the repeated words "fulfil" and "sign".
- Mark Old Testament quotes.
- Draw a coloured line down the side panel beside passages related to the Kingdom of God.
- When you come across a parable, mark the audience to whom Jesus was preaching – were the Pharisees present, was He alone with the disciples, or was He in front of a large crowd?

Chapter summaries

These are optional as they can be time consuming for the larger books. If you choose to do them, you will receive a much deeper appreciation of the book. By the end of The IBSC, you will have paraphrased the entire Bible! Go through each chapter and try to summarise it in one paragraph, using your own words; force

yourself to stay big picture and capture the heart of each chapter.

After your initial readings

Setting of Matthew
<u>Author</u>

Whilst the author remains anonymous in the text, tradition supports that Matthew wrote this Gospel. The detailed description of Matthew within the text adds a personal note. It is the only Gospel where he is first named as Matthew, and not Levi, hinting that he may have been the author.

<u>Recipient</u>

Matthew wrote to a Jewish Christian congregation, possibly his own.

<u>Date and place of writing</u>

Speculation surrounds which of the synoptic Gospels – Matthew, Mark or Luke – was written first. There is also conjecture surrounding whether they were written before or after the fall of Jerusalem in 70 AD. The Gospel of John is agreed to be the last Gospel written and as it does not include mention of the fall of Jerusalem, most assume that the others must have also been written before this time. Most scholars place the writing of Matthew between 50 and 65 AD, although some suggest a date as late as 90 AD.

The original readers of Matthew's gospel lived in proximity to both unbelieving Jews and believing Gentiles, which suggests a possible location of Antioch, in Syria.

<u>Reason written</u>

Matthew sought to confirm that Jesus was the Messiah by using fulfilment of Scripture. By strengthening the faith and spiritual life of his congregation, Matthew was also providing them with defence against the unbelievers amongst them who were disrupting the congregation's faith. Furthermore, the Gospel provided an account of Jesus as the promised Messiah, which the Jewish believers could then proclaim to both unbelieving Jews and Gentile Christians.

Big picture
<u>Historical background</u>
Culture at the time of Christ

The Jews built traditions around the Law to keep them from breaking it. Their religion had become about keeping rules, which gave them a sense of security in God and their salvation. Their religion encompassed every aspect of life, leading them to believe that God was perfectly pleased with them, His chosen people. They were waiting in anticipation of the coming Kingdom of God and the prophesied Messiah. However, the picture they had in mind was significantly different to the reality that Christ brought.

The coming Kingdom of God

According to the Jews, the coming Kingdom of God was to be a physical kingdom. The Jews believed that they would once again become a mighty nation on the earth. The Messiah would cleanse the land from foreign armies and defiled peoples. He was meant to rebuild the temple to the splendour of the original temple built by King Solomon. With this restoration, they believed God would once again make the temple His dwelling place with man.

The Jews believed that redemption would be for Israel only; no Gentiles would be part of God's kingdom. They were convinced that they would automatically be welcomed into the Kingdom of God because their genealogy could be traced back to Abraham, to whom God gave His promises.

The Messiah the Jews desired

The Jews thought the Messiah would be a conquering, military king who would save them from Roman governance and rule; He would rule the house of Israel in the new kingdom. They also held that a king should be rich and physically attractive. A star would announce His birth. Furthermore, the Messiah would be ascribed divinity, work miracles, and hold power over nature. The Saviour would subdue Satan and cast him into hell, freeing them from sin. He would enter Jerusalem on a cloud and stand atop the temple proclaiming that he was King.

Insight into the Jewish mindset

The Jews placed a huge emphasis on cleanliness; this lead to social stigma with classes of people viewed as unclean and untouchable (think of India's cast system). Ethnicity was viewed as the way to salvation; as decedents of Abraham, they were the chosen people of God and thus believed they were guaranteed salvation. The Gentiles would not be welcome in God's kingdom.

Refer to the *Introduction to the Gospels* for more information about Jewish culture at the time of Christ.

Events at the time Matthew wrote the Gospel

Remember that the Jews had the above mindset. Christ radically contradicted many of the expectations they held for the Messiah and the Kingdom of God. The Jews would have been trying to determine whether Christ matched the Messianic prophecies. Even more than altered expectations, these Jewish believers were being called to sacrifice their way of life. They had spent their lives working for their salvation by adhering to strict rules that covered every aspect of daily life. Now they were wrestling with the truth that their self-righteous acts were not sufficient for salvation.

In addition to wrestling with their life-long beliefs, all Jewish converts to Christianity had to suffer the loss of their family connections. When Jews turned to Christ, their families held a funeral for them; they were completely cut off. Their decision to convert was well-weighed, as it meant sacrificing all they knew and all whom they loved. They needed to be fully convinced that Christ was the promised Messiah.

Character portrayal – Jewish Christian in prayer

"Most Holy God, please reveal the truth to me. Christ said that we are your children and that you are our Father. I need a Father right now. I miss my family, my earthly family. You said "those who leave their families for your sake . . . will receive a hundredfold" [1] *I pray for strength to endure the loss.*

"The pull to go back to my family and the old Jewish ways is so strong upon me. This life is much harder than I thought it would be. It sounded easier not having to follow the old ways, but now I realise how much they meant to me. I feel like my life has been turned upside down; like my house has been ripped from underneath me and I have no platform to build upon.

"Christ was nothing like we expected. Reading Matthew's letter, I see that Jesus did fulfil the prophecies – just not as we had anticipated. If this truly is the truth, as I feel it is, then I pray for you to give me faith to believe it and peace in my heart. Help me to live as you would have me live. Teach me, I pray. Unravel the truth of the parables Jesus told to us. Let them change the way I live . . ."

Book overview

Jesus is the fulfilment of the Law and the Prophets, and is the end of God's redemption story. Jesus is the Messiah prophesied in Scripture and He completed God's salvation plan, begun in Genesis 3, straight after the fall of man.

Jesus threatened the very existence of the Jewish nation that was built on rules, regulations, and traditions. He broke the rules they held dear and was persecuted for it. He changed the expectations of the people. Jesus did not come to abolish the Law (as He was accused of trying to do), but rather to reveal God's true intention for the Law.

Christ came to save His people and to reveal the Kingdom of God. He taught His followers how to walk in the ways of the Father. He showed how to live according to the will of the Father. Jesus looked to the heart and condemned wrongly-motivated acts of self-righteousness. He will come again to bring the eternal Kingdom of God. In the meantime, believers are to spread the Good News of salvation.

Interpreting the Gospel of Matthew
Interpretation questions
   1. The Jews had fixed beliefs regarding the prophesied Messiah.
      a. What were some of the met and unmet expectations of the Jews? Look back at the *historical background* given above as well as the *Introduction to the Gospels* to review their principal expectations.
      b. Note a number of ways Jesus went against the norm. For example, the Jews placed a huge emphasis on cleanliness and yet Jesus ate with sinners, women, and tax collectors, who were socially stigmatised as unclean.
   2. Christ brought in a new covenant (Matthew 5).
      a. Consider the response of the crowd to whom Christ was preaching.
      b. Consider the response of the congregation to whom Matthew was

writing.

   c. How would they have had to change their thinking or lives as a result of His teachings?

3. For each parable recorded in chapter 13, consider at least four of the following questions:

   a. To what was the Kingdom of God likened in the illustration that was used?

   b. List any significant commands, people, events or time frames mentioned.

   c. What does the parable mean? What was Jesus trying to teach them?

   d. What was revealed about God or man?

   e. What was taught about salvation?

   f. What is learnt about Christ's return?

   g. What is learnt about the kingdom of heaven?

   h. What are the implications of the parable?

   i. What is an unchanging truth about His kingdom that can be taken from the parable?

   j. Comment on what the crowd's response/s may have been to the parable.

   k. How would the original readers of this Gospel have responded to the parable? Consider the possible mix of emotions, thoughts, and actions.

   l. Feel free to look up additional scriptures that may be relevant to the teaching.

4. In addition to the parables in chapter 13, what else was taught of the kingdom of heaven in Matthew? Summarise your findings on the Kingdom of God.

5. What made it so hard for the Jews to accept Jesus as the prophesied Saviour?

6. Look at the journey that the disciples walked with Jesus.

   a. How did they grow in their faith?

   b. How were they taught by Christ?

   c. What was the significance of the commands, teachings, and instructions that Jesus gave to them?

7. Consider the Old Testament quotes that Matthew included in his Gospel.

   a. How were the quotes significant to his argument?

   b. How were they used to support Christ as the Messiah?

   c. Where were the quotes taken from – can you find them in the Old Testament? What was their meaning in their original context?

8. What do you learn about Jesus in the Gospel of Matthew? Consider His:

   a. Ministry;

   b. Power;

   c. Compassion;

   d. Obedience; and

    e. Passion.

<u>Creative interpretation</u>
    1. Write a sermon or teaching discussing how Matthew proved that Jesus is
       the Messiah. For a starting point, look at:
        a. Old Testament Scriptures included by Matthew.
        b. The lineage that was given.
        c. What events of His birth were recorded?
        d. The words "fulfil" and "fulfilled" that you highlighted during your
            reading of Matthew.

Application inspiration

  - Go back to your interpretation of the new covenant in Matthew 5 and the
    parables in Matthew 13. What change do these truths call you to make in
    your own life?

  - Do you truly see Christ as the greatest treasure you can obtain? Do you see
    the Kingdom of God as worth the cost of any suffering that might come
    your way in this world?

  - The cost of choosing Christ was great to the original Jewish converts. What
    cost are you being called to pay in order to put God first?

[1] Matthew 19:29-30

GOSPEL OF MARK

Christ; the Suffering Servant

"For even the Son of Man came not to be served but to serve, and to give his life as a ransom for many." – Mark 10:45

During your first reading

Themes to track

- Suffering
- Christ the Suffering Servant
- Persecution
- Endurance
- Faithfulness of Jesus (to the will/ plan of God)

During your second reading

Things to notice in the text

- Highlight the repeated phrase "Kingdom of God".
- Mark a line down the side column of passages where you see one of the above themes. Preferably, use a different colour to represent each theme.

Chapter summaries

These are optional as they can be time consuming for the larger books. If you choose to do them, you will receive a much deeper appreciation of the book. By the end of The IBSC, you will have paraphrased the entire Bible! Go through each chapter and try to summarise it in one paragraph, using your own words; force yourself to stay big picture and capture the heart of each chapter.

After your initial readings

Setting of Mark
Author

The book is attributed to Mark, a disciple of Peter, who also knew Paul (Acts 12 and 15). It is proposed that he did not sign his name to the Gospel because of the heavy persecution of believers occurring at this time.

Recipient

Mark wrote to the persecuted church in Rome, which consisted primarily of Gentile believers at the time of writing.

Date and place of writing

Speculation surrounds which of the synoptic Gospels – Matthew, Mark or Luke – was written first. There is also conjecture surrounding whether they were written before or after the fall of Jerusalem in 70 AD. The Gospel of John is agreed to be the last Gospel written and as it does not include mention of the fall of Jerusalem, most assume that the others must have also been written before this time. Most scholars place the writing of Mark between 64 and 69 AD.

It has been suggested that Mark penned this account in Rome to preserve Apostle Peter's firsthand account of Christ's ministry, in the lead up to Peter's martyrdom.

Reason written

The Gospel was written to encourage the persecuted church in Rome, during a time of unthinkable suffering. Mark showed that their Saviour had come as a Suffering Servant for all. Mark's readers needed to know what Christ had done for them and that no earthly treasure was worth denying Him.

Big picture
Historical background

Culture at time of Christ

The Pharisees had become incredibly strict and passionate about keeping the Law because they did not want to see the people of Israel return to exile, as the result of disobedience to God's commands. This passion was witnessed during the reign of Antiochus Epiphanes, ruler of the Seleucid Empire from 175 BC until his death in 163 BC. During his reign, he attempted to prevent the Jewish populace from keeping the Law; for example, by banning circumcision. A successful revolt by the Jewish people against Antioch's edicts was led by the Maccabean family.

The Jews were ashamed that they had never returned to being a powerful nation following their exile at the hands of the Babylonians. God had foretold this exile through the prophets, including Jeremiah and Isaiah, but He also gave promises of future restoration for the nation of Israel. The promises of restoration had the Jews expecting a warrior-king, who would come and defeat the Roman Empire and establish Israel as the world's ruling power. They anticipated a return to the former glory days of King David and King Solomon.

Refer to the *historical background* given for the Gospel of Matthew as well as the *Introduction to the Gospels* for more information about the Jewish culture at the time of Christ.

Events at the time Mark penned his Gospel

The Roman Empire was under the control of Emperor Nero. For the first five years of Nero's reign, he governed well and was liked by the populace. Unfortunately for the people of Rome, one of his mistresses encouraged his excesses and he plunged deeper into immorality and crime. To worsen the situation, he got rid of his best advisers. Nero exhausted the riches of the treasury to pay for his personal excesses and began stealing from the nobles.

When a great fire broke out in the city of Rome on July 18, 64 AD, Emperor Nero averted suspicion from himself by turning the blame upon the Christians. Seven of the city's fourteen regions were completely destroyed, and four partially destroyed, in the blaze.

The acts that Nero saw committed against his Christian populace were horrific. Nero showed a disregard for human life, and the Christians in the city suffered the worst of it. For example, the emperor had Christians wrapped up as torches and used them as human lights at his banquets. Further persecution included crucifixion of Christians and wrapping them in animal skins to be fed to dogs for entertainment. Imagine the fear that would have spread through the population – both Christians and non-Christians alike. Picture the noblemen he had stolen from coming to his banquets and having their noses assaulted with the smell of burning human flesh. It was not a good time to live in Rome.

Character portrayal – a picture of Mark in Rome

Mark was tense as he walked through the streets of Rome back to his small lodging, always watchful and alert to danger. He could see the fear in the eyes of the faithful believers. He watched as more and more families withdrew from the church, and heard of friends denying Christ in order to save their families.

Mark's heart ached for his brethren. Each day they were faced with the choice of life or Christ. They needed to be given renewed hope in their Saviour, their Servant King. They needed their faith bolstered that Jesus was the Son of God, who endured all things to the point of death on the cross for their sake. It was time to pen his account, drawing on the testimony of Apostle Peter. His heart quickened as he hastened his pace across the city. Certainty filled his mind. It was taking a huge risk to write such an account, and he would be unable to sign it with his name, but he would do it for his brethren so that their faith might be strengthened.

Mark had often pondered on the suffering that Christ had been willing to endure and he did so again as he sat at his desk, wondering how to begin. He had seen the Lord in the flesh, unlike many of the believers in Rome. Mark felt the weight lifting from his chest as his mind drew him back into the remembered days of following Christ and the twelve. He remembered the night when the Lord was betrayed. He had been there, and he had fled with the others. A rueful smile crept into his eyes as he recalled how his linen garment had flown free that fateful night in the garden of

Gethsemane and how he had fled naked from that place as the Lord was taken into custody.

"Lord, strengthen our hearts," he prayed. *"Let us not flee from you again when persecution overtakes us and when we are faced with the choice of Christ or life. I did not stand with you in the Garden —none of us did. We had expected the prophesied Son of David to come as a Conquering King to free us from Roman governance. Instead, you came as a Suffering Servant, as a Lamb led to the slaughter. You have promised that those who endure to the end, remaining firm in the faith, will receive eternal life. Let us count this life as nothing compared with the surmounting joy of salvation.*

"Strengthen the hearts of those of us in Rome. May our faith only be increased as we live through the torture the emperor is inflicting upon your children. Give us renewed hope and encouragement. May we follow in Christ's example and endure through this time of trial. I ask this in the name of your Son, who died that I might live."

Book overview

Christ knew suffering; He knew persecution. He was delivered over for death because of the envy of the Pharisees. He endured scourging, suffering thirty-nine lashes with a whip made with stones and glass in its tails – forty strikes of this whip was considered a death beating. His skin would have been ripped from His back. He was humiliated, beaten, and mocked. Christ can relate to the pain believers experience.

Christ came as a servant and calls His followers to do likewise, laying down their rights for the sake of the Gospel. The Good News is that, whilst believers are promised persecution in this life, they can cling to the hope of eternal life and glory with Christ. Jesus has the ultimate authority and no ruler on earth is higher than Him. No matter what they suffer, believers can be comforted by the knowledge that God has endured worse for their sake. By His suffering, He won them eternal glory. The kingdom is worth enduring temporary suffering.

The Romans glorified actions over intellect and thus Mark portrayed Jesus as a man of action. For this reason, his account included fewer Old Testament quotes and omitted the genealogies that are found in Matthew's Gospel. These elements were also of lesser important to his predominantly Gentile audience.

Interpreting the Gospel of Mark
Interpretation questions
1. Explore the hearts and motives of the Pharisees and religious leaders.
2. Jesus used parables to provoke and challenge people's way of thinking. He chose to use parables to expose their hearts and force them to a decision. Choose five parables in the book of Mark and focus on Christ's audience who were being addressed – the crowd, disciples or religious leaders.
    a. What was He challenging within their society?
    b. How was He challenging the mindset or actions of His audience?
    c. Would His words have offended them?
    d. How would they have reacted?
3. For chapters 14-16, focus on the emotions Jesus may have experienced as the different events unfolded. Remember that He was not only fully God,

but also fully man. He felt, and as seen through the Gospel, He felt deeply.

4. How was Christ faithful to His call, to God's plan for salvation, and to God's will?

5. Make a list of the sufferings that Christ endured during His time on earth.

6. As you read and study the book, consider what each account of His deeds would have meant to the original readers who were suffering in Rome.

    a. What passages would have given the Christians in Rome hope during the time of Nero?

    b. To what aspects of this Gospel do you think they would have clung?

    c. List some of the emotions they may have felt.

7. It is believed that Mark was a disciple of Peter and would have heard many of these stories during the ministry of Peter. What do you learn of Peter through his stories?

Creative interpretation

1. Write a short story (two to three pages) depicting the emotions of the church in Rome as fear grew under Emperor Nero. Alternatively, write a short story (two to three pages) of how the Roman church may have responded, following receipt of Mark's Gospel. Explore how they would have drawn hope from the Gospel message.

2. Write a summary on how Christ came as the Suffering Servant.

Application inspiration

Suffering for the Gospel

- The people Mark was writing to were literally choosing life or Jesus; sibling or Jesus; mother and father or Jesus; husband or Jesus; children or Jesus. Is there anything in your life that you would choose above Jesus?

- Would anything tempt you to deny Him?

- To be able to stand firm if you are ever faced with intensive persecution:
  - How can you prepare today to be able to make the right choice and face the persecution, clinging to Christ?
  - What needs to change in your heart?
  - What is lacking in your perspective?

- What currently causes you pain or suffering? Perhaps you are ill, facing loss of a family member or friend, depressed, mocked at work, jobless or having difficulty in your relationships at home. Take these to God in prayer. Talk to God about your trials.

GOSPEL OF LUKE

Jesus; Saviour of All

"I have not come to call the righteous but sinners to repentance." – Luke 5:32

During your first reading

Themes to track
- The Kingdom of God
- Prayer
- The Holy Spirit
- The least
- Compassion of the Christ

During your second reading

Things to notice in the text
- Highlight the repeated phrase "Kingdom of God"
- Individuals
- Christ's compassion/ emotion

Chapter summaries
These are optional as they can be time consuming for the larger books. If you choose to do them, you will receive a much deeper appreciation of the book. By the end of The IBSC, you will have paraphrased the entire Bible! Go through each chapter and try to summarise it in one paragraph, using your own words; force yourself to stay big picture and capture the heart of each chapter.

After your initial readings

Setting of Luke

Author

The Gospel is attributed to Luke, a doctor, who also wrote the book of Acts. Luke is unique in that he is the only Gentile writer in the Bible.

Recipient

The Gospel of Luke and the book of Acts were written to an individual named Theophilus, who is assumed to have been a Roman official.

Date and place of writing

Speculation surrounds which of the synoptic Gospels – Matthew, Mark or Luke – was written first. There is also conjecture surrounding whether they were written before or after the fall of Jerusalem in 70 AD. The Gospel of John is agreed to be the last Gospel written and as it does not include mention of the fall of Jerusalem, most assume that the others must have also been written before this time. Most scholars place the writing of Luke between 60 and 62 AD, corresponding to Paul's arrival in Rome and his subsequent Roman imprisonment; although some date the book as late as 85 AD. The dating of the Gospel indicates that it was written from the city of Rome.

Reason written

Luke wrote his Gospel to share the story of Christ with Theophilus – a Gentile writing to a Gentile to share the Good News that salvation is for all mankind, not limited to the Jews. Luke desired to give an orderly account of the Good News of Christ from the perspective of the people most intimately involved.

Big picture

Historical background

Culture at the time of Christ

The culture of Christ's day had distinct social values, boundaries, hierarchies, and status distinctions. Violating these would have been considered dishonourable, shame-worthy, and an attempt to upset cultural stability. People socialised with those who were of the same social, economic, and religious class. Socialising involved returning the favours given; for example, if one invited you to dinner, then you would be expected to host them for a meal at a later date.

The Pharisees believed themselves to be the highest in this ranking system. The Pharisees and Sadducees were the leaders of the Jewish people. A prayer of the Pharisees at this time was:

> *"Blessed be He who did not make me a gentile,*
> *Blessed be He who did not make me a woman,*
> *Blessed be He who did not make me an uneducated man or a slave."* [1]

At the other end of the social ranks were lepers. Lepers had to shout "unclean" as they walked, and were forced to live outside the city. There were also laws regarding the distance one must keep from those with leprosy. Lepers would not have received any form of physical touch from others. Shepherds were also looked down upon in Jewish society. Whilst they were not seen as the least, they were still excluded from some meetings, being labelled as unclean.

Whilst the Pharisees were the leaders of the Jews, the Jewish people fell under Roman governance, much to their displeasure. However, in Jerusalem the Jews maintained some power of self-governance. It was also the only place where they could sentence someone to death. This is why Jesus did not go to Jerusalem until the end of His ministry.

Events at the time Luke wrote his Gospel

In his account, Luke emphasised the humanity of Jesus. During His time on earth, Christ remained fully God, but He was also fully man. Gnostic deviations were occurring within the church, pulling people away from the truth of the Gospel. People believed that flesh was evil, and because of this they were coming to think that Christ could not have been fully man. Luke highlighted the virgin's conception, the suffering of Christ, and the physical resurrection of Jesus to counter these deviations from the truth, which were occurring within the church.

Paul was in prison in Rome at the time the Gospel was written. It is likely that trouble was also beginning to increase in the city of Jerusalem for its Christian populace. Luke emphasised the significance of Jerusalem and the role the city played in Christ's crucifixion.

Character portrayal – Luke

Luke paced his small home, offering him a physical outlet for his distracted mind. He had just returned from the prison where he had spent the day, in between running errands for Paul.

Luke's heart was anxious for Paul, but not as much as it was for Theophilus. He had been talking to the intelligent Roman Official for weeks now and, whilst Theophilus continued to show interest, he had not yet been convinced. Luke longed to see Theophilus come to know the Lord. Luke slowed his pace as his eyes fell on his writing desk. He had always been better with the written word.

Pulling out the humble, old chair, Luke sat down and bowed his head in prayer:

"Dear Father, you are to be worshipped above all others. Your mercy saves and your love heals. I have found joy in Christ and my heart yearns to see others receive this same joy. I see Theophilus as a man whose heart longs for more. He is not satisfied with the routine of this life. I do not know what good this letter may do Paul's case in the courts, but if I can persuade just one more man to come to you, then it will be worth the telling. I pray for your Spirit to guide my account. I pray that I will capture the heart of your Son as I tell the Good News of salvation.

"Speak through my words to Theophilus. May his heart be convinced and his spirit cry out to you. May he receive Christ into his life and may he come to know the healing love of your Spirit . . ."

Pulling his chair in a little closer to the desk, Luke pulled the copy of Matthew's Gospel close to him to use as a reference if he needed it. Then, dipping his quill into the ink, he began to write his labour of love: the account of Christ, written to Theophilus, which became known as the Gospel of Luke.

Book overview

Luke's Gospel shows that Christ chose to associate with the ordinary and lowly people of the world. Jesus went to Gentiles, women, uneducated people, and slaves. Christ was not content to leave societal rankings in place. He did not uphold them. He came to bring in a new kingdom. Christ was different; He was radical; He loved the least, and reached out to the outcast. He came to save sinners, not the righteous.

Luke focused his account of Christ's ministry to those who were seen as the least in society. Luke's attention was on Christ's compassion towards those that society looked down upon: the widows, poor, sick, foreigners, and tax collectors. In the words of Christ: *"Those who are well have no need of a physician, but those who are sick. I have not come to call the righteous but sinners to repentance."* [2]

Luke also recorded how Christ revealed the hearts of men; he showed that Christ cared about the motives behind one's actions. Christ came to bring in an upside-down kingdom; the Kingdom of God that Christ preached went against the Jewish mindset. Luke also revealed the difference between the present time and the kingdom to come.

Interpreting the Gospel of Luke

Interpretation questions

1. Look at the role of the Holy Spirit through the first four chapters of the Gospel. Summarise what you learn of the Spirit.
2. Write two paragraphs regarding what Luke revealed about each of the following:
   a. The Kingdom of God. Look at the parables Christ told about the kingdom and compare this to what the Jews expected.
   b. Prayer.
   c. The least. Who were the least? How were they treated by the disciples, the crowd, the Pharisees, and Jesus?
3. Choose at least two parables in the Gospel to look at in greater detail. Answer the following questions:
   a. Who was present as Christ told the parable?
   b. With what part of the parable would the audience have connected? How did Christ draw them into the story?
   c. What was the twist? What would have shocked His audience?
   d. What was revealed about the Kingdom of God?
   e. What was revealed about the heart or lives of the audience?
   f. To what response did it call the audience? What choices of response did He offer them?
4. What does the Gospel reveal about Jesus? Consider:
   a. The events surrounding Jesus' birth;
   b. His compassion and love for the people;
   c. How He revealed Himself as the Son of God;
   d. The value He placed on individuals.

<u>Creative interpretation</u>

1. Who stood out to you as you read the book of Luke? Which individual drew your attention? Choose one individual that Christ interacted with that is recorded in this Gospel. Re-read the relevant paragraphs of Scripture and then, in character, rewrite their encounter with Christ from the perspective of your chosen individual (at least two paragraphs).

Application inspiration

- Who is considered to be amongst the least in society today? Are there places where you have noticed a division of people? If so, what was used as the ranking system; for example, money, social connection or place of employment?

- Look at how Jesus lived and seek to do likewise. God interacts with sinners. He does not wait for them to "get their lives right" before He went to them and welcomed them in, or before He healed them and showed them the kingdom.
    o Do you have friends that are non-Christians?
    o Are you pursuing relationships with only Christians or seeking out sinners too?
    o God rejoices over just one sinner that comes to Him! Just one! Do you have this joy in salvation or do you take salvation for granted?

Take time to reflect on these questions about the heart

- Are you willing to be different to those around you, and from societal norms?
- Are you willing to live of the kingdom and not of the world?
- Are you comfortable in your world?
- Are you willing to say: "I want to live differently to my culture"?
- Are you willing to count the cost? What is God calling you to give up to Him – family, money, self?

Take time to reflect on your actions

- Do you love those whom Jesus loves?
- Do you show compassion to the outcast? How can you reach out to the outcasts?
- How do you respond to those with illness? Do you back away from those with disease?
- How can you act upon the compassion in your heart? What excuses do you use to continue to neglect the people He had placed on your heart?
- Jesus went from place to place proclaiming the kingdom, but He also healed the sick and fed the people. He met the needs of the people. God desires to work miracles, but He also wants us to meet their needs as we are able. The feeding of the five thousand started with the offering of

physical fish and bread, and then God did the miracle. What can you do today?

[1] Tractate Berachot, chapter 6, Tosefta 26
[2] Luke 5:31-32

GOSPEL OF JOHN

Life in Christ

Now Jesus did many other signs in the presence of the disciples, which are not written in this book; but these are written so that you may believe that Jesus is the Christ, the Son of God, and that by believing you may have life in his name. – John 20:30-31

During your first reading

Themes to track
- Eternal life
- Jesus' divinity
- Miraculous signs
- Discipleship
- Faith/ belief/ evangelism

During your second reading

Things to notice in the text
- The miracles of Jesus
- The "I am" statements of Jesus
- Highlight repeated words "(eternal) life", "light", "abide", and "in Him"
- Circle the word "world"
- Circle key leaders: Pharisees, Sadducees, and Sanhedrin

Chapter summaries

These are optional as they can be time consuming for the larger books. If you choose to do them, you will receive a much deeper appreciation of the book. By the end of The IBSC, you will have paraphrased the entire Bible! Go through each chapter and try to summarise it in one paragraph, using your own words; force

yourself to stay big picture and capture the heart of each chapter.

After your initial readings

Setting of John
Author
The Gospel was written by Apostle John.

Recipient
John wrote to a broad audience of second-generation Christians, consisting of both Jewish and Gentile believers.

Date and place of writing
It is widely accepted that John wrote his account between 90 and 100 AD, although some suggest a date as early as 80 AD. It is traditionally accepted that John wrote his Gospel from Ephesus.

Reason written
John was getting old and penned his account to ensure that the church remained stable after his death. He realised that another generation of believers had arisen who were not eye witnesses to the Christ, and desired to record his testimony to enable the readers to believe in Christ and enter into His salvation.

Big picture
Historical background
Jewish leadership at the time of Christ
The high priest had become a secular, political position, with the high priest being appointed by Rome. The title no longer belonged solely to the descendants of Levi, as commanded by God. The Sanhedrin was the ruling body of the Jewish people. It consisted of Pharisees and Sadducees who liaised with the governing body of Rome. Pharisees were the religious leaders, concerned with faith; Sadducees were concerned with political power and economics.

Recording the events following Christ's death, John 18:15-15 tells us that: *"Simon Peter followed Jesus, and so did another disciple. Since that disciple was known to the high priest, he entered with Jesus into the courtyard of the high priest, but Peter stood outside at the door. So the other disciple, who was known to the high priest, went out and spoke to the servant girl who kept watch at the door, and brought Peter in."* It can be surmised by this account that, not only did John know the high priest, but the guards knew that John knew the high priest. The Jewish society was hierarchical and it is therefore evident that John was a known figure, whose family was of high social standing.

About John's writing
John's Gospel contains the greatest detail of Jewish customs. He makes reference to Jewish feasts, the status of women, Jewish purification rights, Sabbath regulations, the time taken to build the temple, and the Jewish attitude towards Samaritans. John

shows how Jesus is superior to the Jewish heroes of the faith, and how Christ included Gentiles into the community of faith.

Structure of the book

The first twelve chapters record the public ministry of Jesus. John included seven specific signs to give testimony to Jesus as the Messiah. The final nine chapters (13-21) contain details of the private ministry of Jesus.

Character portrayal – a glimpse the Father, through the Son

"You ask who the Father is? I say, "If you had known me, you would have known my Father also. From now on you do know him and have seen him . . . Whoever has seen me has seen the Father." [1]

Who am I?

- *"I am the bread of life; whoever comes to me shall not hunger, and whoever believes in me shall never thirst."* [2]

- *"I am the light of the world. Whoever follows me will not walk in darkness, but will have the light of life."* [3]

- *"Before Abraham was, I am."* [4]

- *"I am the door of the sheep . . . If anyone enters by me, he will be saved and will go in and out and find pasture . . . I came that they may have life and have it abundantly.* [5]

- *I am the good shepherd. The good shepherd lays down his life for the sheep . . . I know my own and my own know me . . ."* [6]

- *"I am the resurrection and the life. Whoever believes in me, though he die, yet shall he live."* [7]

- *"You call me Teacher and Lord, and you are right, for so I am."* [8]

- *"I am the way, and the truth, and the life. No one comes to the Father except through me."* [9]

- *"I am the true vine, and my Father is the vinedresser . . . I am the vine; you are the branches. Whoever abides in me and I in him, he it is that bears much fruit, for apart from me you can do nothing."* [10]

Book overview

John defined eternal life as knowing the only true God and Jesus Christ, His Son. John showed that the Father, Son, and Spirit all have a role in giving life. The Father draws people to Jesus. The Father sent Jesus not to condemn, but to save, because He loved the world. Scripture bears witness that Jesus was the Holy One of God, the promised Messiah. The Son of Man was lifted up to bring eternal life to those who believe. Believers must be born again of water and Spirit to receive eternal life. It is God's will that no one is lost, desiring all to be raised on the last day. The Father's commandment to the Son brought life for all who believe.

For John, eternal life was seen as only a part of the reward that came from knowing Jesus. His Gospel shows that Christ also came to give life in abundance during the present age. The Holy Spirit, Living Water, is given now to those who believe in Christ. The Spirit was given to believers following Christ's glorification.

Believers are born of God; not by flesh, or the will of man, or by the Law.

Interpreting the Gospel of John

Interpretation questions

1. What was the role of John the Baptist?
2. Who was the Christ?
   a. What did Christ reveal of Himself?
   b. What was revealed by His actions?
   c. Who testified to the Christ?
   d. Why did He come?
3. Consider the miracles that Jesus performed.
   a. What did they show of His nature?
   b. Why did John feel these stories were important to pass on, remembering John 21:25?
   c. Were they what the people expected? Consider why Israel rejected Jesus, despite the intentional signs that He gave to them.
4. What do you learn of the Father?
   a. How did Christ reveal the Father?
   b. How do the Father and Son give glory to one another?
   c. What is said of the will of God?
5. What do you learn of the Holy Spirit?
   a. What did Christ tell us of the Spirit's role?
   b. How does the Spirit reveal Himself?
   c. What relationship does the Holy Spirit have with believers?
   d. How do you see the Holy Spirit manifest Himself?
   e. Other scriptures to consider include: Romans 8:1-18; Romans 8:26-27; 1 Corinthians 2:11-14; 1 Corinthians 12; 2 Corinthians 3:4-8; Galatians 4:6; Galatians 5:16-18, 22-25; and Ephesians 4:30.
6. Adventure deeper into your understanding of God's character and the different roles of the Father, Son, and Spirit. Seek out how they interact, their role in the Holy Trinity, and how they are revealed through the Gospel of John.
7. What can you learn about Apostle John from the text, assuming that he is the "one whom the Lord loved"?
8. How does John answer the following questions:
   a. If Jesus was the Messiah, why did Israel fail to recognise Him?
   b. How was Christ shown to be the Son of God?
9. What commands did Jesus give to His disciples?
   a. What was the significance or purpose of the command?
   b. How did the disciples respond?
   c. What response did Christ desire from them?
10. Look at the teachings of Jesus.
   a. When considering His words, make sure you take note of whom He was speaking to – was He teaching the crowd, rebuking the Pharisees, commanding His disciples or conversing with an

        individual?

b. What commands were given?

c. How would His teachings have changed the way the Jews interpreted the Old Testament?

d. How did His audience respond to the teaching?

11. What promises did Jesus make?

12. How did John contrast the old covenant of the Law with the new covenant of grace and truth in the Spirit? Support what you learn in John with the epistles of Paul.

13. Consider the salvation imagery that John used and what he hoped to convey to the original readers. Examples of the imagery he used include:

a. Born again/ life from the Spirit;

b. Children of God;

c. Taken from slavery to freedom;

d. Quenching spiritual thirst;

e. Experiencing this life in abundance;

f. Light/ see.

14. Consider at least two of the following questions as you read about the life of Jesus:

a. What is taught of love and peace?

b. What is seen of unity, serving, and stature?

c. What is said of guilt, sin, forgiveness, and freedom?

d. What cultural barriers were being broken?

Creative interpretation

1. Look at Christ's interaction and relationship with key individuals: Nicodemus; the Samaritan woman; the official with the sick son; the lame man; His mother, Mary; the boy who supplied the bread and fish; the woman caught in adultery; the blind man; and Mary, Martha and Lazarus. Answer the following questions:

a. How did Jesus interact with them?

b. What questions did Jesus use to draw these people out of themselves, their culture or their circumstances?

c. What emotions did Christ display?

d. What did He reveal of Himself to them by His speech or though His actions?

2. Take one of the themes of the book and write a debate using the recordings of John. For example, use the Gospel of John to argue that Christ brings eternal life or that the miraculous signs of Christ declared His divinity.

3. Write an article for a Christian magazine that shows that Jesus gives abundant life for believers today, as well as eternal life. Alternatively, write an article explaining what you see of the intimate and mutually submissive relationships within the Holy Trinity – Father, Son, and Holy Spirit – as revealed in John.

Application inspiration

- Christ came to bring eternal life, but He also came to bring joy, hope, and peace to believers.
  - o How does your mindset need to change in light of this truth?
  - o Do you share testimonies of God acting in your daily life or only of your initial salvation?
  - o What works has God done in your life?
  - o How have you seen Him act this week, month or year?
- Do you seek the Holy Spirit's input in your life?
- Where do you find it easiest to pray – do you prefer to be in nature, at a busy bus stop or writing the prayer out in your room? Retreat to a place where you find it easiest to connect to God and reach out to the Holy Spirit in prayer.
- To whom do you find it hard to show compassion? Whom should you look at differently, seeing them with the eyes of Christ rather than ones of condemnation?
- How is God calling you to walk in love? Whom can you serve today? To whom can you show practical love and support this week?

[1] John 14:7-9
[2] John 6:35
[3] John8:12
[4] John 8:58
[5] John 10:7-10
[6] John 10:11-15
[7] John 11:25-26
[8] John 13:13
[9] John14:6
[10] John 15:1-5

ACTS OF THE APOSTLES

God's Holy Spirit and the Unstoppable Gospel

"But you will receive power when the Holy Spirit has come upon you, and you will be my witnesses in Jerusalem and in all Judea and Samaria, and to the end of the earth." – Acts 1:8

During your first reading

Themes to track
- Actions of the Holy Spirit
- Empowerment by the Holy Sprit
- Spread of the Gospel
- Declaration of the Gospel amidst persecution
- Boldness of faith
- Guidance from God

During your second reading

Things to notice in the text
- Highlight passages referring to the Holy Spirit
- Circle "Holy Spirit"
- Mark place names and geographical locations

Chapter summaries

These are optional as they can be time consuming for the larger books. If you choose to do them, you will receive a much deeper appreciation of the book. By the end of The IBSC, you will have paraphrased the entire Bible! Go through each chapter and try to summarise it in one paragraph, using your own words; force yourself to stay big picture and capture the heart of each chapter.

After your initial readings

Setting of Acts
Author

Luke, the physician, is attributed authorship of Acts, in addition to the Gospel of Luke.

Recipient

The Gospel of Luke and the book of Acts were written to an individual named Theophilus, assumed by many to have been a Roman official.

Date and place of writing

Most scholars believe the book to have been written within Rome in 62 or 63 AD, shortly after the Gospel of Luke was written, and corresponding to Paul's Roman imprisonment. This date is given as there is no indication within the text that Paul had been martyred when the author finished his account.

Reason written

Luke gave the reason for writing to Theophilus at the beginning of his Gospel – that Theophilus might come to believe [1]. The book of Acts records the works and wonders the Lord had done through believers since sending the promised Holy Spirit. It is also suggested that the book of Acts may have been utilised as a supporting document for Paul during his trial in Rome.

Big picture
Historical background

The book of Acts details events of approximately thirty years and is an important link between the gospels and epistles. Acts gives important historical background for the epistles and is a good source to refer back to when studying the epistles.

Relevant historical people, events, and dates:
- Pentecost (Acts 2); 30-33 AD
- Conversion of Saul (Acts 9); 34 AD
- Herod Agrippa I; emperor of Rome from 37-44 AD
- Herod Agrippa I dies (Acts 12:21-33); 44 AD
- The famine is predicted (Acts 11:28); 44-48 AD
- The famine affecting the Roman world occurred during the reign of Tiberius Julius Alexander; 45-48 AD.
- Jerusalem Counsel (Acts 15:1-3); 49 AD
- Jews evicted from Rome by edict of Emperor Claudius (Acts 18:2); 49 AD
- Paul's imprisonment in Caesarea; 58-60 AD
- Paul's imprisonment in Rome; 60-62 AD
- Paul beheaded; 64-68 AD
- Burning of Rome; 64 AD

- Fall of Jerusalem; 70 AD

Character portrayal – Theophilus

Theophilus had reason to feel important as a Roman official, but he also remembered where he had come from. He rose through the ranks of soldiers serving in the Roman army. He had seen pain, suffering, and fear. Now he knew respect as he went about the city of Rome, but he could not forget his campaign days, serving on the front line as Rome pushed out its borders. There he had seen only fear or hatred in the eyes of the populace, when they had dared to meet his gaze.

Theophilus sighed. He desired peace, and the Empire had so far managed to keep this, but at what cost? Theophilus was no longer sure that he wanted the peace that Rome offered. Perhaps there was something in what the good doctor was saying about this Prince of Peace. The name "Jesus" was rippling through the entire Empire, but being a man of logic, he needed to know more. He needed to hear of the life of this man, Jesus.

Most of those around Theophilus were only interested in the rumours of how this "King of the Jews" fellow had died and reportedly been raised from the dead. In contrast, Theophilus wanted to know how Christ had lived and why His believers continued to follow Him, declaring Him to be God, the Jews' promised Messiah.

Book overview

The book of Acts gives an account on how the Holy Spirit worked during the early years of the church as the Gospel began to go out from Jerusalem. The book of Acts records very few incidences of the "spiritual gifts" (tongues, words of wisdom, etc.), being manifested. More commonly, Luke tied the presence of the Spirit to preaching the Gospel message with boldness.

The Holy Spirit emboldened believers to witness faithfully, and gave them wise words to speak before rulers and commoners alike. The unbelievers usually responded in one of two ways: they were converted to Christianity, adding to the number of believers, or they were enraged, and sought to persecute those sharing the message. Amidst persecution, the Holy Spirit gave the early believers the comfort and strength they needed to endure.

The Holy Spirit is also shown to have given them insight into God's desire and will. The Spirit manifests Himself in many different ways, but always for the glory of God, the building up of His church, and the spread of the Gospel of hope.

The book of Acts demonstrates the Gospel's power. The Gospel cannot be stopped; it will spread throughout all the earth. And yet, the book of Acts also reminds believers that persecution will come upon those who follow Christ. It shows that Christianity is not a call to an easy life, but that the fruit of the Spirit enables perseverance and boldness. Acts illustrates how ordinary people accomplish extraordinary things through God who strengthens them.

Interpreting the book of Acts
Interpretation questions

    1. Students of history may be interested in completing further research into

relevant historical background. Consider how the events through the Roman Empire would have contributed to the events in Acts and the responses of the people. Following are some research topics to get you started:

    a. Look up the Roman emperors who reigned from 30 to 70 AD. Look at what decrees they made, what significant historical events occurred during their reign, and how they treated Jews and Christians.

    b. Investigate what was happening in the city of Jerusalem. Look at the customs, the demographics of the population, and the common religions and religious practices (Acts 1-7).

    c. Look up the rights of Roman citizens compared with the rest of the population during the time of the Roman Empire (Acts 16:9-40).

    d. Explore Greek mythology and the worship of Artemis (Acts 17:16-34; 19:23-41).

    e. Investigate Jewish Law, their rights to try their people, and the limitations of their courts under Roman governance (Acts 21:27-23:11).

    f. Under Roman law, what was the significance of appealing to Caesar (Acts 25:10-12; 26:30-32)?

2. Complete a topical study on the Holy Spirit.

    a. Go back through the text and record every place where the Holy Spirit was mentioned.

    b. Draw up a table and, for each Scripture reference you found in Acts, record how the Spirit manifested, what resulted, and who was involved.

    c. Speeches account for one third of the volume of Acts. There are nine given from Paul, eight from Peter, and seven from a collection of others. Look at these speeches and comment on what the author was intending to achieve from the speech.

    d. What was their message?

    e. Who was their audience?

    f. Was the Holy Spirit mentioned and, if so, in what capacity?

3. Two books of the Bible were written so that one man (Theophilus) might believe – refer to Luke 1:-4.

    a. What does this tell you about God?

    b. What does it tell you about Luke?

    c. What does this say about Luke's approach to evangelism?

    d. Once you have considered these questions, bring it through to application by considering what this could teach you about evangelism and how believers spread the Gospel today.

Creative interpretation

1. Mark the routes of Paul's journeys on the map located at the end of this

chapter; (also downloadable from www.shannonbuchbach.com). First plot the cities on the map using encyclopaedias, bible dictionaries or the internet. After the cities are marked on your map, put the books away and trace the journey as described in the text. Use different colours for each of Paul's four journeys. The maps will become a useful resource when you study Paul's epistles. The four journeys to mark are Paul's:

    a. First missionary journey; 46-48 AD (Acts 13:1-14:26).
    b. Second missionary journey; 49-52 AD (Acts 15:36-18:22).
    c. Third missionary journey; 53-57 AD (Acts 18:23-21:10).
    d. Journey to Rome, arrest, and imprisonment; 58-62 AD (Acts 27:10-28:10).

2. The book of Acts gives an account of how ordinary people were used by God to do amazing things simply by making themselves available. Choose one of the heroes of the faith found in Acts and characterise him as a superhero.

    a. What were his attributes?
    b. What emotions did he display?
    c. Who was his audience?
    d. Was his audience appreciative of his acts?
    e. What "power" did he exhibit; for example: faith, emboldened speech, love for the poor or wisdom?

Application inspiration

The Holy Spirit in your life

- How do you view the Holy Spirit? How does your view of Him need to change or expand? How has it grown through your study of Acts?
- What testimonies do you have of the Spirit in your life?
- Are there gifts of the Spirit that you have come to resent? Are there gifts that you desire?
- For what do you need the Spirit's strength? Bring these to Him in prayer.
- Spend some time with God in prayer. Talk to the Holy Spirit about His gifts and how He has manifested Himself in your life. Ask for Him to give you boldness of speech and action to spread the Gospel message.

Map for marking Paul's journey

INTRODUCTION TO THE EPISTLES

To understand the context within which the epistles were written, one must understand a little about the cultural environment of the Roman Empire.

Rome

Rome was under Imperial rule. The emperors at the time of Christ's birth and during the age of the apostles were renowned for their vices, particularly: sexual immorality, drunkenness, cruelty, murder, and thievery. Some of them contributed to the expansion of the Empire, whilst others held festivals and sporting events to win the love of the populace, or focused on architecture and design.

Herods were locals appointed to govern over the province of Judea on behalf of the emperor. These men had to walk a fine line between pleasing the Roman officials and the Jewish populace, and were often despised by both parties.

The Empire of Rome was built upon slavery. Today, the words "slave trade" bring up images of the eighteenth and nineteenth century, and of slaves being brought from Africa, under horrific treatment, to Europe and the Americas; however, it was quite different at the time of the early church.

In Roman times, slaves were generally well-treated by their masters; they had rights to a family, received wages, and had their board and food provided. Many slaves were offered freedom after about six years of service; however, many chose to remain as slaves as they could receive a better income as slaves than as freedmen. Some slaves were freed and sponsored by their former masters to enter a trade, in which they could even rise above their former master in wealth.

Emperors of note

Claudius

Claudius reigned from 41 to 54 AD. During his reign, he banished all Jews from Rome. This became known as the Jewish dispersion of 49 AD. He is mentioned in Acts 11:28 and 18:2.

Nero

Nero reigned from 54 to 68 AD. He gave no value to human life, killing for no reason. He was a thief, lover of torture, highly sexually immoral, enjoyed sports, and fancied himself to be an artist and singer.

In 64 AD, a great fire broke out in the city of Rome and much of the city was destroyed. When the populace began to blame him for this tragedy, he shifted the blame onto the Christian populace, who were already hated for their faith. The horrors he inflicted upon Christians (and others), included: dipping them in wax, setting them on fire, and using them as living torches at his banquets.

Vespasian and Titus

Vespasian reigned from 69 to 79 AD and his son, Titus, followed from 79 to 81 AD. Vespasian began the war against Jerusalem when the Jews rebelled against Rome in 66 AD. When he took the throne, he handed over control of the war efforts to his son, Titus. It was Titus who eventually destroyed Jerusalem and the temple in 70 AD, ending the Jewish revolt.

Religious environment

Rome allowed freedom of religion, and people worshipped many gods and idols. Christians were often accused of being atheists as they worshipped only One God, had no temple, and bowed before no idols.

Emperor worship

Emperor worship arose within the Empire after the death of Augustus Caesar when a group of his loyal political supporters had him deified. Following this event, many other emperors insisted that the population worship them as gods, and commissioning idols to be made of their image. Caligula went as far as ordering the heads to be lopped off from all the statues of the gods, replacing them with sculptures of his own head.

Greek/ Roman gods

The Romans adopted the Greek gods. The gods were as man in temperament, but with immortality and power. These deities were manipulative, immoral, and unpredictable. Their worshippers sought their goodwill; however, there was no guarantee that devotion would sway the gods to favour an individual. There was also no promise of immortality for their followers. In addition to the Greek gods, worship of Egyptian and pagan gods also occurred across the Empire.

Cults

The largest cult at the time consisted of the "mystery religions". These cults grew in popularity as a result of the unforgiving Greek gods. The mystery religions promised secret knowledge and a step by step progression towards the "good god" and immortality, through the practice of secret rites and rituals. Many of the rituals included blood sacrifices, orgies, self-mutilation, ceremonial washings (often with blood), magic, and sexual acts with priests and priestesses.

The Cabirus cult was a cult in Thessalonica that taught of a coming redeemer. The cult preached on the second coming of the redeemer, causing confusion within the church as people began substituting the teachings of the cult for Christianity. It was formed out of the city's martyr god, said to once have been a young working class man who was raised again after death, becoming an immortal god.

Greek philosophy

Philosophers arose amidst the multitude of gods and idols, in order to seek a different path to enlightenment through wisdom and reason. They would gather together to discuss their philosophies on what was truth, how life should be lived, and how society should be governed.

Three major philosophies of the New Testament times are as follows:

1. *Epicureanism:* This stream of thought did not believe in an afterlife and therefore taught that one should only seek after pleasure in this world. They declared "let's eat, drink, and be merry for tomorrow we die" 1.

2. *Stoicism:* Those who held to this pool of thought taught that emotions were to be detached, one was to focus on logic, and man only lived to fulfil his duty.

3. *Greco-Roman world view:* The Greco-Roman mindset held a low view of work, which was seen as appropriate for slaves, not freemen. Those who did manual labour were looked down upon and the mind was glorified.

Gnosticism

Gnosticism has its name from the Greek word "gnosis", meaning "knowledge". It came from the combining of several belief systems and religions of the day. They believed in a "ladder system" to salvation, claiming that the good god – the Father God of Judaism and Christianity – was not interactive with man, but had created lesser gods, or "aeons", who were evil. It was one of the lesser gods, Demiurge, who was accredited the creation of man.

Gnosticism taught the separation of body from spirit (dualism). The body, and physical matter, was held to be evil, whilst the spirit was good. Two branches arose from their dualistic mindset. The first, known as asceticism, taught that because the body was evil it needed to be punished. This resulted in fasting, self-affliction, and denying oneself. The second branch, known as libertarianism, held that because the body is evil it is of no account and therefore people could do whatever their flesh desired. This led to sexual immorality, gluttony, murder, and other vices.

Gnosticism held that salvation was achieved by obtaining secret knowledge and climbing up the "rungs" of the "spiritual ladder", towards the good god. Some amongst this sect believed that Jesus was one of the lesser gods who helped man to ascend the rungs of the ladder. Gnosticism caused turmoil within the early church with false teachers entering the congregations and preaching that, on its own, faith in Jesus was not sufficient for salvation.

<u>Judaism</u>

Whilst some members of the early church struggled with beliefs brought in from their prior involvement in mystery religions and Greek philosophies, the Jewish Christians struggled with releasing the Jewish mindset, which was established on rigid laws and traditions.

One of the main issues of contention within the early church was whether circumcision was still a necessary part of entering into the people of God. In 49 AD, the Jerusalem Council was held to determine whether circumcision was necessary for the salvation of Gentile believers and resulted in the assertion that faith in Christ was all that was required for salvation [2].

Paul's missionary journeys

The final commandment that Jesus gave to His disciples while on earth was to go out into all the earth and make disciples of all nations [3]. It was Paul who took up this command, taking the Good News out into the Gentile world, and planting many of the early churches outside of Judea.

Paul's missionary journeys are recorded in the book of Acts as follows:

- First missionary journey; Acts 13:4-14:28 (46-48 AD);
- Second missionary journey; Acts 15:36-18:22 (49-52 AD);
- Third missionary journey; Acts 18:23-21:16 (53-57 AD);
- Paul's journey to Rome; Acts 27:10-28:10 (58-62 AD).

There is speculation about whether Paul completed a fourth missionary journey after an initial imprisonment in Rome.

[1] Quoted in Scripture: Luke 12:19, 1 Corinthians 15:32
[2] Acts 15:1-35
[3] Matthew 28:19-20

ROMANS

United by Righteousness under Grace

For there is no distinction between Jew and Greek; for the same Lord is Lord of all, bestowing his riches on all who call on him. For "everyone who calls on the name of the Lord will be saved." –
Romans 10:12-13

During your first reading

Themes to track

- Character of God
- Grace versus works
- Law versus faith
- Righteousness
- Unity and humility
- Who are the children of God?

During your second reading

Things to notice in the text

- Highlight the repeated words "grace", "righteousness", "faith", "law", and "sin".

Chapter summaries

These are optional as they can be time consuming for the larger books. If you choose to do them, you will receive a much deeper appreciation of the book. By the end of The IBSC, you will have paraphrased the entire Bible! Go through each chapter and try to summarise it in one paragraph, using your own words; force yourself to stay big picture and capture the heart of each chapter.

After your initial readings

Setting of Romans
<u>Author</u>
Romans was written by Apostle Paul.

<u>Recipient</u>
The book was written to the church in Rome, which consisted of both Jewish and Gentile believers.

<u>Date and place of writing</u>
Paul wrote the epistle between 55 and 58 AD whilst Paul was in Corinth.

<u>Reason written</u>
Paul penned this epistle in order to bring unity between the Jewish and Gentile believers who made up the church in Rome. He desired to establish the believers as a new people in Christ. Paul also desired the lives of the believers in Rome to become an example to those around them. He longed to see them living as witnesses to the Gospel.

Big picture
<u>Historical background</u>
The Roman church began as a predominately Jewish Christian congregation. It was founded after Pentecost (Acts 2; 30 AD) by Jews that had journeyed from Rome to Jerusalem for Pentecost (the Feast of Harvest). However, in 49 AD, Emperor Claudius expelled the Jews from Rome, at which point the Jewish Christians were forced to flee and the church in Rome became predominantly made up of Gentile believers.

As the make-up of the church changed, so did the customs within the church. The Jewish Christians had kept their customs and laws. Their focus would have remained on reading the Torah, celebrating Jewish festivals, keeping important dates on the Jewish calendar, and ensuring male babies received circumcision. In contrast, the Gentile believers had less rules and regulations, and the church became relaxed towards its pursuit of Jewish customs and ceremonies.

In 54 AD, only five years after the Jews were expelled, the new emperor, Nero, allowed the Jews to return. As the Jewish believers returned they discovered that Gentiles were now the overwhelming majority within the church. The Jewish believers responded in antagonism towards their Gentile brethren and friction arose surrounding the need to uphold Jewish customs and whether this was critical for salvation.

<u>Character portrayal – a Jewish believer antagonises his Gentile brother</u>
"You're not circumcised?" Eli exclaimed in mock surprise. "You cannot enter into God's family without being circumcised. You are no follower of Christ!"

"When did Christ ever say that I need circumcision to become part of God's kingdom?" Alexander retorted. "You Jews think yourselves so high and mighty. Well, I'll remind you that Jesus condemned the way that your Pharisees kept your laws to the letter and forgot to love. There are more important things than all your stuffy laws."

"Oh yeah? You think so, do you? Have you not heard that we are God's *chosen people*? He didn't choose your ancestors. He chose Abraham. Abraham is my father and thus I am a child of the promise. You can't claim that!"

Book overview

Grace. Grace. Grace. Grace for the Jews. Grace for the Gentiles. Grace for you. Grace made available to all mankind.

Paul aimed to build unity within the Roman church by showing what Gentile and Jewish believers had in common. All mankind has sinned, having fallen short of God's perfect standard, and is therefore deserving of God's wrath. Romans declares that neither Jews nor Gentiles can receive righteousness by their own works, but must rely on God's grace, which is accessible to everyone. The Jewish and Gentile believers had been judging one another, but Paul made it clear that God shows no partiality. Salvation is by grace working through faith, not by works, and boasting is excluded, as grace is given freely. God's mercy and grace is available to all who accept it.

Paul reprimanded the Jews and warned them not to preach Jewish traditions as a requirement for salvation. All believers have died to sin in Christ and therefore are no longer under the requirements of the Law. Hearing this released the Gentiles in the congregation of their burden. Paul also wrote that those who understood nothing is unclean of itself (such as certain foods listed in the Old Testament as unclean), should not become arrogant towards those struggling to grasp this truth, but rather support them in their faith.

Paul encouraged the congregation by proclaiming that his hope lay in Christ, who would make him perfect and holy, and raise him to glory. Paul also showed who the true children of God are: not those of the physical genealogy of Abraham, but those in Christ. Believers are to inherit God's kingdom. All of this evidence was to show that the Jews and Gentiles of the congregation were brothers in Christ, sons of God, heirs with Christ, and had been adopted into the same faith. He called them to live in harmony with one another through love, mutual up-building, and serving one another.

Paul also tackled the issue of grace abuse (continuing to sin because grace covers sin). Paul's opinion can be summed up easily: Grace abuse is stupid. Why, being freed from sin, would someone want to continue to sin? Paul saw living as a servant of love as the natural response to receiving God's grace.

The book of Romans shows that those in Christ have died to sin and thus it no longer holds power over them; Christ is now their Lord and they are slaves to righteousness. There was no grey area for Paul; the things of old are dead to those in Christ. Paul encouraged the congregation to have faith in God's grace, and spurred them on towards unity in Christ's redeeming sacrifice.

Interpreting the book of Romans
<u>Interpretation questions</u>

1. What do you learn about creation in Romans?
2. What do you see of the character of man through the book of Romans?
3. What do you see of God's character in the book of Romans?
4. In chapter 4, Paul called on Abraham as an example of righteousness by faith, not works. Read the following passages in Genesis and then compare how Abraham responded in Genesis to how Paul described the events in Romans:
    a. Genesis 15:1-6; Righteousness was attributed to Abraham because of his belief in God's promise.
    b. Genesis 16:3-4; Abraham and Sarah tried to make things happen on their own. At Sarah's instigation, Abraham had intercourse with her maid-servant, Hagar.
    c. Genesis 17:15-18; God restated His promise to Abraham, at which Abraham fell to the ground in laughter.
    d. Genesis 17:24; Twenty-nine years passed between when the promise was given (and Abraham was declared righteous) and when he was later circumcised. Keep in mind that Jewish theology saw the righteousness of Abraham as having come after his circumcision.
5. In his letter to the Romans, Paul included many quotes taken from the Old Testament.
    a. What was his reason for doing this?
    b. How would the Old Testament quotes have affected how the church in Rome received his teachings?
    c. Look up the Old Testament quotes that Paul referenced and read them in their original context. Did he use them in a similar way to the original authors of the Old Testament?
6. Read through the *Introduction to the New Testament* to gain an insight into the Jews devotion to the Law. How would the Jews have responded to Paul declaring that the Law was not sufficient for salvation, and that they were free from it?
7. Look at Paul's argument that both Jews and Gentiles are able to enter into God's family as sons and heirs.
    a. List some of his arguments for Gentile inclusion into the family of God.
    b. List his argument for Jewish inclusion.
8. Paul built unity amongst his audience by showing them how they are the same. How did Paul argue:
    a. All are the same in sin;
    b. All believers are the same in salvation, which is received through faith;
    c. All were dead, but believers are all made alive in Christ;
    d. All are chosen by God's mercy.

9. In Rome, slaves were viewed as having no moral standing.
    a. Knowing this, how would Paul calling the believers "slaves of righteousness" have affected their thinking?
    b. Would it have changed how they viewed those living as slaves in Rome?
10. Look up the dictionary definition of the words "grace", "righteousness", "faith", "law", and "sin". Then reread the text focusing on what those words mean.
    a. Did knowing the dictionary definition change how you read the passage? If so, in what way?
    b. What definition does the text give to these words?
    c. Is there a difference between the dictionary definition and the one conveyed in Romans?
11. How does Paul defend God's mercy and justice? Look at quotes from famous Christian authors and see how they define God's mercy and justice.
12. Choose one of the commands that Paul gave to the congregation in chapter 12:9-21 and look at what it means to live these out in practice. How could the believers in the church in Rome have lived out these commands?

Creative interpretation

1. Say someone has asked you to present the topic of grace, and freedom from sin, to a group of teenage believers. Write a definition for grace using the book of Romans and think of a way to explain life under slavery to sin. Keep your eye out over the next week for an illustration that may assist you in presenting the message of grace and use it to present your explanations, and Paul's message.
2. Compare Paul's message of the works of grace to that of a bank account, which has debts and credits. Draw up a "bank statement", which looks at debts as "sin", the payment of the debt, and what Christ adds to the "credit" column.
    a. Consider "debts" to be what Romans says man received through Adam and every sin that an individual commits. Comment on the debts that Paul mentions in Romans, and how every person has fallen short of God's perfect standard.
    b. Secondly, look at how the debt is cancelled. How did the old system, the sacrificial system of the Jews, cancel the debts and add "credit" to the account? How did Christ cancel the debt? The book of Romans shows that all debts (past and future) have been completely removed. Nothing was left owing from the accounts of believers.
    c. Lastly, look at the credit as what Romans says man receives through Christ.

Illustration: bank accounts

Life account of Mr Smith, before accepting Christ:

Date	Credit	Debit
Birth		Adam's sins
March 18th, 1991		Took little sister's Barbie doll and snapped off one of the arms.
May 29th, 1995		Tripped John in play ground in order to be first to the slippery slide.

Life account of Mr Smith, after accepting Christ:

Date	Credit	Debit
	Righteousness	
Past	Eternal life	Paid in full by Jesus
Present	Holy Spirit in his life	Christ
Future		

Application inspiration
Unity of believers
- How does Romans 12:1-8 affect your view of the gifts of God, and how they are to be used to build unity?
- It is easy to imagine Romans being written to the divided church of today. Believers can be quick to judge those who come from different denominations, worship in different ways or have different opinions to their own. How might the church strive towards unity using the principles seen in Romans?
- How might you need to change how you act towards others in light of chapter 14 and 15?

Grace and righteousness
- Paul's account of Abraham's life is very different to how it was recorded in Genesis. After God declared Abraham righteous he was seen by God in this light; Abraham had been given the status of righteous and it was not

removed from him despite his future actions of doubt.

- o How does knowing this affect how you respond when you make mistakes in life?
- o Are you able to look in the mirror and say: "I am righteous because of Christ's sacrifice, not my own works"?
- o What could you do to remind yourself of the truth that, in Christ, you are *righteous?*

- Do you believe that man is basically good?

- Do you ignore the wrath of God, choosing not think about it?

- To your way of thinking, is it unjust that God will exercise His wrath on sinners? If so, pray for a greater revelation of God's righteousness and justice.

- The more you understand God's grace the more you will bestow it upon others. Ask God to reveal the truth of His grace to you.

1 CORINTHIANS

Defining Unity and Love

Let all that you do be done in love. — 1 Corinthians 16:14

Themes to track
- Unity
- Love
- Living as a witness
- What is wisdom?

Things to notice in the text
- Underline important commands that Paul gave to the Corinthians.
- In different colours, place marks beside columns relating to wisdom, unity, and love.
- In chapter 12, highlight the repeated words "all", "same", and "one".

Chapter summaries

These are optional as they can be time consuming for the larger books. If you choose to do them, you will receive a much deeper appreciation of the book. By the end of The IBSC, you will have paraphrased the entire Bible! Go through each chapter and try to summarise it in one paragraph, using your own words; force yourself to stay big picture and capture the heart of each chapter.

After your initial readings

Setting of 1 Corinthians
<u>Author</u>
The epistle of 1 Corinthians was written by Apostle Paul.

<u>Recipient</u>
Paul wrote to the believers of the church in Corinth.

<u>Date and place of writing</u>
The epistle tells us that Paul was in Ephesus, see 1 Corinthians 15:32, 16:7-10, and indicates an extended stay in this city. This would mean it was written during Paul's third missionary journey; 51-56 AD.

<u>Reason written</u>
The letter was Paul's response to two letters from Corinth. Chapters 1-6 were written in response to a letter from "Chloe's people", which had raised concerns about issues within the church. Chapters 7-16 were Paul's response to a letter by the Corinthian church, in which they had evidently brought some questions before Paul.

Big picture
<u>Historical background</u>
Paul had a big job to do! He was taking on one of the ugliest churches in the New Testament. To sum it up: the Corinthian church had come out of a messed-up culture.

One of the main problems in the church was that it had been left divided by arrogance and sexual immorality. Yet before Paul could address many of the issues within the church, he had to change their world view. They would not have understood why sexual immorality was an issue needing to be addressed because they would not have known that they were being sexually immoral. The definition of love within Corinth was purely sexual. Paul had to go right back to the basics, to the point of redefining love for the Corinthians.

Much of the population of Corinth was made up of freed slaves, sailors, military personnel, and prostitutes. It was a place for sex, money, and "entertainment". This is where the phrase "to corinthianise", meaning to engage in sexual immorality, came from. Picture it as the Las Vegas, Atlantic City, Hollywood or Amsterdam of the day.

Corinth was a wealthy city, but it was characterised by vice and evil. It was a dark place. The Corinthian population valued knowledge (gnosis) and wisdom (sophia), being influenced predominantly by the Greek culture. They practiced dualism, which taught that matter (the body) was bad, and the spirit was good. There was a group of people within the church itself, called the Sophists, who pursued wisdom and practiced dualism.

The temple of Aphrodite was situated on top of a mountain, making it the highest point in Corinth, and could be seen throughout the entire city. One thousand prostitutes resided in the temple. Worship involved having sex with temple prostitutes. The male workers (priests) of the temple were eunuchs. The temple of Apollo was also located in Corinth, where worship consisted of poetry and music, prophecy, and male beauty. It was not the first time the Corinthian believers had heard about "prophecy".

Paul gave a very specific command to the congregation about head coverings, which also finds its significance within the culture. In Greek culture, a woman's hair was seen as reserved for her husband. Virgins and wives alike would wear head coverings, and the first time a husband would see his wife's hair was on their wedding night. Roman women wore head coverings to worship, but not in everyday life. Most temple prostitutes had shaved heads; whilst the prostitutes of Aphrodite wore their hair loose to identify themselves. Paul was urging the women of the congregation to show modesty in their freedom in Christ.

On top of cultural issues, the Corinthian church was seeking guidance on matters causing confusion within the church. False teachings of legalism were leading some to believe that to eat food offered to an idol was to serve that idol. There were also wrong beliefs surrounding the end times, leading to important questions, such as: "Should we marry?". The church stood divided upon all of the issues, which Paul addressed in his epistle.

Character portrayal – the prayer of a godly woman in despair

"Lord, how am I to live like this? You promised me peace and yet I have unrest in all areas of my life. I go into the town and I am accused of being no different from anyone else. They say that the church looks like them. I try to bring people to Christ and they say that our practices are like theirs. Why should they leave their gods, they ask? This saddens my heart because I know that you have brought salvation, and a freedom that they do not posses. I simply don't know how to express this to them. Will you not give me the words?

"And when I arrive home I long so much to be able to discuss these matters with my husband, but he never agrees with me. He doesn't even want to try. He tries to separate himself from me, saying he does not belong to Paul, but to Apollos. We are always fighting over doctrine and over beliefs.

"And I know that he has always done so, I used to myself, but I hate to see my husband go to the house of Aphrodite and to the priestesses. It never used to bother me, so why does it cause my heart to ache to watch as he goes to them? My heart is beginning to fill with hate for the priestesses that are no more than common prostitutes. Should I not love them and have mercy on them as you have on me? Lord, help me! I feel like I am drowning in this bitterness. I am drowning, and the church is doing no better.

"Surely you do not mean your people to be divided against one another? Jesus said that "a house divided against itself cannot stand," [1] *and these words hold true. Your church here is crumbling, God. Do you see? Do you not care? Please, merciful Lord, you must save us!"*

Book overview

The epistle of 1 Corinthians is one of the most practical letters in the Bible, dealing with real issues in the lives of the congregation. Paul was addressing specific concerns within the church when he wrote this epistle to them. Through all the vast variety of issues that Paul addressed, he consistently comes back to love and unity as the solution.

It was said in the *historical background* given above that Paul had to redefine love for them. The definition of love within Corinth was purely sexual. In the letter of 1 Corinthians, Paul showed that the love of God is not sexual. In order for them to "make love their aim" they first needed to gain a revelation of what love is. Paul showed that unity is birthed through love. Throughout the book of 1 Corinthians, Paul brought his message and instructions back to love and unity.

The epistle gave practical examples of how the church is called to walk in love. For example, Paul called them to give generously to believers in need, rebuked them from causing those still growing in appreciation of God's grace to stumble on trivial issues such as food, and showed them that love is self-sacrificing. Paul declared that, whilst they had freedom in Christ, they were not to use that freedom to hurt others in the church.

Paul also corrected their thinking, which had been rooted in the Greek mindset. Because of their dualistic beliefs, they thought that the resurrection of believers at Christ's return would be purely spiritual. This led them to fear that they had somehow missed Christ's return. The early church believed in the imminence of Christ's second coming, believing it would happen in their life time, and thus they feared it had already taken place in a spiritual realm. Paul brought in anti-Greek thinking. He reignited their hope in the resurrection and showed that God does not separate body and spirit. Paul showed that the body does matter, and therefore what they did with their bodies mattered. Paul's letter gave the Corinthian believers ample practical commands to put into practice.

Interpreting the book of 1 Corinthians
Interpretation questions

1. Read through the *historical background* given above and then read through the book a passage at a time, with the following in mind:
    a. Can you see how revolutionary Paul's ideas would have been to the believers in Corinth?
    b. Think about how the original readers may have been feeling when they received this letter.
    c. Consider how the letter may have challenged the world view of the Corinthian believers.
    d. What shifts in their world view may have needed to take place, as a result of Paul's teachings?
2. As you interpret 1 Corinthians, look at how Paul's commands and instructions have an undercurrent of living in love and unity.
    a. Explore what he said about these themes as you study each passage.
    b. Write a summary of what Paul taught them about love.
    c. Write a summary of the commands he gave them to build unity.
3. Write a few short paragraphs summing up what you have learnt through 1 Corinthians on the theme of "unity attained through love". Include a brief

commentary of how you see this theme in the world today – refer to the example theme summary below. The example has been written on the theme of "anti-Greek thinking", based on the principles given in 1 Corinthians.

4. Take notes about wisdom as Paul mentions it throughout the epistle and then write a definition describing godly wisdom.
5. What does 1 Corinthians teach about living as a witness?
6. What principles for discipleship can be taken from this book?

Example Theme Summary – Anti-Greek Thinking

Paul's letter to the Corinthian goes against many of the cultural beliefs in Corinth at that time. They were highly influenced by Greek thinking and beliefs.

Their beliefs and Paul's counter arguments:

1. *Greek-based:* Valued intellect and self-obtained knowledge. Knowledge was for the individual.

   Paul: Wisdom comes from God and is given freely to His children. God grants knowledge to strengthen and encourage the church, whilst witnessing to unbelievers. Love is greater than the knowledge, wisdom, and prophecies, which were highly valued in Greek culture.

2. *Greek-based:* Dualism (body is evil; spirit is good) led to many issues, including: libertarianism (what is done with the body does not matter), asceticism (the body must be punished), and fear that the end times had come in the spiritual realm and they had missed Christ's return.

   Paul: Resurrection of believers has not yet come; all will know, as there will be a physical transformation of the body as well as the spirit. They are not to deprive their marriage partner from sex, as the practice of asceticism was leading some to do.

3. *Greek-based:* Renowned for immorality. The temple of Aphrodite worshipped the goddess through sexual immorality, with sex seen as the ultimate expression of love and worship.

   Paul: Believers are to honour their bodies as a temple of the Holy Spirit. Love to the Greeks was about sex; the love from God is patient, kind, not envious or boastful . . . [2] Paul was showing just how great love is, and how it encompasses all that is good.

4. *Greek-based:* Served multiple gods that did not communicate with man, and mixed religions together (syncretism). Offered was food to idols.

   Paul: There is One True God. It is not a sin to eat food offered to non-existent idols, BUT only if it doesn't cause another believer to stumble, or hinder a non-believer from receiving the Gospel.

5. *Greek-based:* Women were devalued and seen as less than human. They were made by the gods as a punishment for man. In contrast, Aphrodite worshippers preached that women were created first, and held women to be superior. Some taught that there was no difference in genders.

   Paul: Gives woman value as "man's crowning glory". Paul went to Genesis to contradict the false beliefs, showing that man was created first, but both are made in God's image. Males and females are different, but of equal worth; there is no difference in value between the sexes.

Summary: Many of these beliefs and ways of thinking can still be seen in the world today: sexual immorality can be seen within most university colleges; everything must be "logical" by human standards; and the battle of the sexes continues, whilst others try to remove the difference between the genders. Paul revealed the truth nearly two thousand years ago and yet we still need it to permeate our society. Paul called the Corinthians to make love the standard, and bring light into their communities through the difference in their actions to that of the world. Today the church must be called to do the same. The church is to model true love, a love in action, to the world.

Creative interpretation

1. Write definitions for love, unity, and wisdom. First, write the definitions as the Corinthian society depicted them, and then as Paul characterised them.

2. Draw a person and think of how the body would be affected without one of its parts. Think about cooking dinner, drawing, hugging, walking, going for a job interview, and other common life tasks. Then think about how this illustration was used by Paul to illustrate the church, the different roles individuals are to play, and the need for unity.

3. In chapter 13, Paul listed attributes of love. Can you find examples of these attributes as instructed by Paul throughout his letter? For example, love is *"not arrogant or rude"* [2] can be seen in the command: *"Take care that this right of yours does not somehow become a stumbling block to the weak ... so by your knowledge this weak person is destroyed"* [3].

Application inspiration

- There are many things we look for when we choose a church.
  - List some of the attributes for which you look when choosing a church.
  - Considering your list, would you choose the church of Corinth? It is doubtful whether they would have met any of the factors on your list, but Paul still chose them.
  - Would you go to a church full of raw converts and acknowledge them as saints and mentor them?
  - Is there anyone that you have written off in judgement that you may need to come alongside in discipleship or prayer?
- In what way does your culture affect your world view? Does this affect your view of Bible study and its importance to the believer? Ask God to show you the aspects of your world view that may need to change in order to move more into alignment with a godly world view.

Of love and unity

- In which way do you see disunity within the church today or within your relationships with other believers?
- What are some areas where you need to "make love your aim"?
- What definition does your society or culture give to love? How does that differ from the definition given in 1 Corinthians? How can you live differently from your society, living out the love of God?
- Think of someone you find difficult to love. Go to the definition of love in 1 Corinthians 13 and for each attribute of love write down how you can practically love that person. For example, *"love is patient"* [2]: I am easily frustrated by a colleague who always comes asking questions. This week I will consciously choose to take the time to help that person, answering their questions and guiding them through the application to ensure they have understood.

[1] Matthew 3:25
[2] 1 Corinthians 13:4-5
[3] 1 Corinthians 8:7-13

2 CORINTHIANS

Boast in the Lord

But he said to me, "My grace is sufficient for you, for my power is made perfect in weakness."
Therefore I will boast all the more gladly of my weaknesses, so that the power of Christ may rest
upon me. For the sake of Christ, then, I am content with weaknesses, insults, hardships,
persecutions, and calamities. For when I am weak, then I am strong. – 2 Corinthians 12:9-10

During your first reading

Themes to track
- God's strength in human weakness
- Paul's defence
- Super apostles

During your second reading

Things to notice in the text
- Circle the repeated word: "boast(ing)" (or "glory" in some translations).
- Underline important commands from Paul to the Corinthians.
- Mark passages referring to the work of the Spirit.
- Mark passages referring to Christ's works.
- Highlight Old Testament quotes.
- Take note of rhetorical questions (a question to which a reply is not required). Paul uses these frequently to emphasise key points.

Chapter summaries

These are optional as they can be time consuming for the larger books. If you choose to do them, you will receive a much deeper appreciation of the book. By the end of The IBSC, you will have paraphrased the entire Bible! Go through each chapter and try to summarise it in one paragraph, using your own words; force yourself to stay big picture and capture the heart of each chapter.

After your initial readings

Setting of 2 Corinthians
<u>Author</u>
The epistle of 2 Corinthians was written by Apostle Paul.

<u>Recipient</u>
Paul wrote to the believers making up the church in Corinth.

<u>Date and place of writing</u>
Paul wrote 2 Corinthians within a year of writing 1 Corinthians and between his first visit (51 AD) and third visit (57 AD) to Corinth. Events seem to indicate a date closer to his third visit, making the time of composition around 56-57 AD whilst Paul was in Macedonia.

<u>Reason written</u>
Paul was defending himself and the Gospel message against the false accusations of "super apostles" in order to protect the church from following false doctrine. Paul was ensuring that glory was given to God, not to man. Through his words he revealed his love for them and sought to heal their relationship after a "painful visit". Paul also encouraged generosity, longing to see the church fulfil their promise to support the famine relief for the church in Jerusalem.

Big picture
<u>Historical background</u>
Please refer back to the *historical background* given for 1 Corinthians.

It is believed that Paul wrote four epistles to the Corinthians, but the first and third letters have been lost. The first letter is alluded to in 1 Corinthians 5:9, and the second in 2 Corinthians 2:1-11. It is proposed that the first letter was a call for the Corinthians to separate themselves from the ungodly culture surrounding them, and that the third letter was a "painful letter" where Paul used hard terms to speak to a straying congregation.

Understanding Corinth and its culture
Due to its location on a narrow strip of land, providing water access on both sides, Corinth was a centre of trade and industry. It was also a city offering commercialised pleasure. It was a place of money, prostitution, and "entertainment". As such, it was a wealthy city and the third largest in the Roman Empire at the time Paul wrote his epistle.

The population of Corinth consisted of local Greeks, Jews, Italians, and Roman government officials. There were also many freed slaves in the city. Influenced by Greek culture, value was placed on knowledge ("Gnosis"), and wisdom ("Sophia").

The "self", particularly the intellect, was glorified.

The Socratic Apology

The epistle of 2 Corinthians was Paul's response to his accusers. His character was being attacked by "super apostles", who sought to undermine his ministry and the Gospel he proclaimed. The church was being turned against him as false apostles declared he did not fit the world model of a leader. Through this epistle, Paul was defending his ministry, the Gospel, and his person. He modelled his argument on the Socratic Apology, which would have been well-known to his audience.

The Socratic Apology was a defence developed by Socrates in the fifth century BC following demand for teachers and philosophers to be able to defend their person. At this time, it was wrong to boast about or defend one's self. The Socratic Apology provided a culturally acceptable way for teachers to defend themselves, almost like a lawyer offering their defence.

One of the ways of formulating a defence was to "play the fool". Fools could get away with a whole lot more than an educated person would be allowed to say. Hence, Paul's boasting about his lineage; he was boasting about foolish and insignificant things and made it very clear that he was doing it as a fool. False points could be told in a way to convince people that they were true. It was not uncommon to talk about one's self in third person, as Paul did in 2 Corinthians 11:16-23 and 12:2-7.

Significantly, as Paul reached the climactic point of his speech, telling of his vision, he did not reveal a final piece of wisdom or what he saw in the heavens; instead, he boasted in his weakness because, through it, God would get the glory. Paul's highest point was that he was weak and God is strong. Through the Socratic Apology, Paul not only defended his ministry, but redefined leadership, giving a godly model for leaders.

Character portrayal – a "super apostle" boasts in possessing the attributes of a Greek teacher

"I am eloquent. My words are strong and clear. My speech will persuade you. I am obsessed with wisdom and knowledge, but I will make you work to understand what I share with you. Do not worry if you do not understand; it is my ability that you admire far more than my message. I dominate any public debate that I enter.

"I am a professional. I accept payment for my words are deep and insightful. Only amateurs and students of my trade work for free. Show me your money or I will not share my philosophies.

"The spiritual world fascinates me. I am in touch with the spiritual and supernatural realms. This is how I receive my insights. My revelations are worthy of being boasted about. I have visions that you should highly value.

"I am strong and heroic. Corinth hosts the second largest games in the Empire; did you know that? I always compete. The people admire my physical prowess. I am like one of the many Greek heroes who performed mighty deeds.

"I can offer you letters of recommendation by the handful. Be assured by these that it is worth listening to me. My message comes with authority for I trained under

Marcus, who trained under no other than the great Lucretius. I am sure you must know of Lucretius – the great Roman poet and Epicurean philosopher!

"None can fault my lineage. I am a Hebrew, an Israelite, and a son of Abraham. I come from the tribe of Benjamin. There is no mixed blood in my background! We keep the Torah, and no tax collectors will be found in our family line no matter how wide or deep you search. My uncle's brother-in-law was son to the last High Priest. I was born of a distinguished line! Now listen to my words of wisdom . . ."

Book overview

Paul wrote this letter in response to accusations that he did not fit the role or expectations of what an apostle should look like. He was not rich, physically strong or elegant of speech. He did not boast in having visions from heaven. He came against their accusations, saying he was far from being super-human – he was simply human. In his letter, Paul compared himself to an imperfect jar of clay that was entrusted with the privilege of spreading the riches of the Gospel.

Paul declared that one of the primary qualities of a good leader is being all too aware of one's own weakness. He argued that it is in weakness that God is able to work through the believer. God's strength is displayed in human weakness.

Today, weakness is often considered a problem to be solved. In this epistle, it is seen as a place for God to shine; an area for God to be glorified. God chooses weak people to reveal His glory. God's glory is revealed when He works through weak people. Being perfect does not point others to God; being weak does!

Interpreting the book of 2 Corinthians
Interpretation questions
    1. Summarise the main message of each of the following sections:
        a. Chapters 1-7, Paul explains his ministry;
        b. Chapters 8-9, Paul encourages giving; and
        c. Chapters 10-13, Paul defends his ministry.
    2. What do you learn of Paul's character from 2 Corinthians?
        a. What motivated his ministry?
        b. What does 2 Corinthians show of his heart towards the church?
        c. How did Paul's life model godly leadership principles?
        d. See more about Paul's faith journey in Galatians 1-2 and Acts from chapter 8.
        e. What do the following verses reveal about Paul: 2 Corinthians 2:17; 3:1-2; 3:5; 4:2; 4:5; 4:7; 6:12; 8:21; 10:11; 11:8; 12:15; 12:19?
    3. Having read the *character portrayal* above, consider what Paul had to say about each expectation of a teacher.
        a. What was the significance of his response for leaders within the church?
        b. How was he establishing a godly model of leadership?
        c. Does Paul's model reflect that of Christ? Find scriptural examples to support your argument.
    4. Make a list of the characteristics of the false apostles seen in 2 Corinthians.

a. What did Paul have against them?

b. How were they attacking Paul's ministry?

c. What areas did their accusations fall under (for example, money)?

d. How did they attack Paul's credentials to teach?

e. What comparisons did they give between themselves and Paul?

f. What charges did Paul bring against them?

5. Consider Paul's response to the accusations that were being made against his person.

a. How did Paul guard his work and the work of the church?

b. Why did he go to the church with his defence rather than to the super apostles?

c. What do you think Paul's motives were as he defended his ministry?

d. Was it necessary for him to make this defence?

e. Why was it important for him to remain above reproach?

f. Why was it important that the original readers saw his trustworthiness?

g. Would Paul's argument have swayed the original readers; why or why not?

6. Look at Paul's boasting in the epistle.

a. In what did Paul boast?

b. Of what would he not boast, and why?

c. What is the danger of boasting in one's strengths? Why is it wrong?

7. How would Paul's defence have affected:

a. The church;

b. The "super apostles"; and

c. The spread of the Gospel?

8. Survey what is shown about the Corinthian believers.

a. For what was the Corinthian church commended?

b. In what areas did the church need to grow? Where were they weak?

c. How did they respond to Paul's previous correspondence?

d. Had they grown since Paul's last letter?

e. Why did Paul love this church? What was his heart for them?

9. How is suffering portrayed?

a. What attitude were the Corinthian believers called to adopt?

b. Why is one's focus in trials important?

c. Of what value is affliction to one's faith?

d. How did Paul's life witness to his message?

10. Paul discussed comfort throughout the book, even as he talked of suffering.

a. From where did he draw comfort?

b. What does comfort look like, and from where does it stem?

c. How is it linked to the fellowship shared by believers?

       d. What do you learn about reliance on God?

11. What does it look like to be "in Christ"?

       a. What changes should have been evident in the life of the Corinthian believers?

       b. What points of difference did Paul make between those in Christ and those in the world?

12. To what was Paul referring through his references to aroma and fragrance; 2 Corinthians 2:14-17?

       a. Why was it important that the original readers understand that they were the fragrance of Christ?

       b. What is the significance to witnessing?

       c. Can you find (within the Gospels) occasions where Christ taught a similar message?

13. As you read through the book, you took note of Old Testament quotes.

       a. Can you find where these were quoted from in the Bible, and what they meant in their original context?

       b. How did Paul use the quote?

       c. Why would quoting the Old Testament have strengthened Paul's message?

14. Explore what is said about giving and generosity.

       a. What did Paul say about giving and generosity?

       b. Can you find other Scriptures in the Bible related to the call on believers to give?

       c. What fuels generosity?

       d. Why does Paul say it is important for the church to support each other?

       e. What is its significance to the church, as Christ's body?

Creative interpretation

1. Characterisations:

       a. According to Paul, in what would a fool boast?

       b. In two paragraphs, characterise a worldly fool using the attributes Paul put forward in 2 Corinthians.

       c. Characterise a Christian-Corinthian and a worldly-Corinthian and observe how Paul was calling his readers to be a contrast against their environment.

2. Draw a mind-map of leadership qualities, as demonstrated by Paul in 2 Corinthians. Turn to the Gospels and add what leadership qualities you see modelled by Christ.

Application inspiration

- Allow yourself to be challenged by Paul's vulnerability in 2 Corinthians. He was open to the point where he boasted in his weaknesses. Today, Paul is seen as a "super apostle": a holy man, more than ordinary, and a spiritual leader, but this is not how he was being viewed at the time he penned this

epistle.
- o Consider the strength of faith it took to record his own weakness.
- o Are you willing to make yourself vulnerable as you disciple others?
- Reflection questions to think through:
    - o Where are you weak?
    - o What weaknesses do you chose to hide? What are you afraid of other people seeing in you? What are you afraid to reveal for fear of judgement?
    - o What do you rely on to hide your weaknesses?
    - o To whose expectations are you afraid that you will not be able to live up?
    - o For which of your strengths do you fail to give God the glory?
    - o What do you need to ask God for His strength to reside over? Do you trust in His strength or your own?
- How has 2 Corinthians changed your expectations for leadership?
    - o Think about whom you look up to as leaders. Jot down a few names. What do you respect in them? Why do they make good leaders?
    - o What qualities do you attribute to a good leader?
    - o Does your list of attributes need to be modified to fit the model of Christ?

GALATIANS

Salvation in Christ alone

For freedom Christ has set us free; stand firm therefore, and do not submit again to a yoke of slavery. – Galatians 5:1

During your first reading

Themes to track

- Grace
- False teachings versus true Gospel
- Righteousness through faith, not works
- Law versus Spirit
- Life in Christ

During your second reading

Things to notice in the text

- Paul's emotions
- Highlight the repeated words "Gospel", "faith", "Law", and "justified/ justification".

Chapter summaries

These are optional as they can be time consuming for the larger books. If you choose to do them, you will receive a much deeper appreciation of the book. By the end of The IBSC, you will have paraphrased the entire Bible! Go through each chapter and try to summarise it in one paragraph, using your own words; force yourself to stay big picture and capture the heart of each chapter.

After your initial readings

Setting of Galatians
<u>Author</u>

Galatians was written by Apostle Paul.

<u>Recipient</u>

Paul wrote to the church in Galatia. Debate exists over the exact location of this church, due to the size of Galatia (part of modern day Turkey). However, there is evidence that Paul had a relationship with the church in southern Galatia, whilst it does not appear that he ever made it to the north.

<u>Date and place of writing</u>

If the epistle was written to the church in southern Galatia, this would suggest Paul wrote it shortly after his second missionary trip, prior to the Council of Jerusalem. On this basis, the book of Galatians would have been written in about 49 AD from Jerusalem.

<u>Reason written</u>

The epistle was written to combat false teachings within the church. Paul's aim was to establish the church in the truth that the Gospel of Christ is the Gospel of Grace. He wanted to ensure the Galatians knew in thought, heart, and spirit that faith in Jesus is all that is needed for salvation.

Big picture
<u>Historical background</u>

The Galatian church consisted of Jews and Gentiles. The Jews prized their Law and were proud of their Jewish traditions. During the early days of the church there was much division between Jewish and Gentile brethren as a result of Jewish laws, customs, and history. To understand the reason for this tension between the two groups, one must remember that Judaism was more than a Sunday religion; it was a way of life. The Law penetrated into every aspect of daily life.

The message of salvation through faith alone brought division between Jewish and Gentile believers. The Jews found it hard to accept that the Gentiles only had to "walk in and believe" to be received into the people of God, and children of Abraham.

Judaizers arose with the spread of the Gospel, including members of the Circumcision Party, who preached legalism. The term "Judaizer" was formed from a Latin word meaning "to be like a Jew" or "to live like a Jew". These men wanted to place Jewish customs and requirements onto the young church. Whilst Paul and the apostles taught faith alone was needed for salvations, the Judaizers opposed them, claiming that Christ alone was not enough. Judaizers taught that practice of the Law needed to continue for salvation, in addition to one's faith in Christ's saving grace. A mentality of earning salvation through works arose in many churches, and it is this legalistic mindset that Paul went against in his epistle to the Galatians.

Refer back to the *Introduction to the New Testament* for more information on why the Jews became fervent for the Law. Please see the *Introduction to the epistles* for information regarding the Circumcision Party.

Character portrayal – a divided church

"You have to be circumcised! It is in the Law!"

"A lot of things seem to be in your Law, but God gave that to you, not to us Gentiles."

"You can't be of the people of God unless you are circumcised. I think you are missing the importance of it. The travelling preacher shared this morning that it is necessary for salvation!"

"I do not believe him. The apostles say that Christ is all that we need. They say that Jesus taught that any who believes in Him shall be saved. Circumcise your family and leave me alone!"

Many such arguments were occurring in the church at Galatia and it left Paul disturbed. He was worried for his spiritual children! If he could not immediately go to them, then he would write to them and share again the message of the Gospel – only faith in Christ was needed for salvation! Christ had fulfilled the Law and His grace was sufficient.

Book overview

Galatians hits home the truth that:

Salvation **does not** = Jesus + __(works, Jewish traditions, good deeds, offerings)__

Rather:

Salvation = Jesus. Note the full stop after Jesus!

Paul wanted to make sure that the Galatians knew who they were in Christ – the righteous ones of God. He was clear that each and every member of the church could boldly declare: "I am righteous, because of what Christ did for me!" He declared that their position in Christ = RIGHTEOUS = in perfect conformity with the law! They had no role in their salvation, except to accept the free gift; the work of salvation was Christ's alone.

This message left Jewish believers asking: Why was the Law of Moses given, if not for salvation? Paul argued that the purpose of the Law was to point man to their need for a Saviour, as it revealed that no one could perfectly meet God's standards on their own. The Law formed part of God's plan of grace, but was not its fulfilment. Man is declared righteous only through the cross; Christ took man's sin upon Himself when He became the perfect sacrifice.

Paul used a courtroom analogy to help the Galatian church understand that salvation comes through grace. The Greek word for "justification" was a legal term, referring to a public declaration stating that, *based on the evidence*, a person had been declared righteous. To be "justified" under the Greek legal system was to be free, to be declared righteous.

Righteousness refers to a *perfect conformity* to the law or standard. God's standard is perfection and Paul says that, through faith in Christ, the impossible has been made possible. They had been declared by the Judge (God) to be righteous, to be free of all sin. Paul was clear that their sins were not "swept under the carpet"; the price of sin has been paid in full by Christ and now, on the basis of His evidence, believers are legally justified from all sin.

Paul anticipated a further set of questions from his audience: Could such grace be abused? Could believers use grace as an excuse to sin, because sins are forgiven? Paul covers these questions briefly in two short places: Galatians 5:13 and 6:7-8. He was possibly astounded that he needed to cover such contemplations as grace abuse at all. For Paul, Christ brought freedom from the Law, from the world, and from sin. He saw ultimate freedom as becoming a slave to Christ. In Paul's mind, the only response to God's grace was to seek God, and live for Him. The epistle to the Galatians was a call to live a life of thanksgiving before God for His saving grace.

Help with difficult passages
Cast out the slave woman and her son; Galatians 4:21-31

Paul contrasts the two sons of Abraham – Ishmael and Isaac – in order to make a huge distinction between those who are in slavery and those who are free. He was also making an inference capable of causing profound disturbance to the mindset of his Jewish audience.

Ishmael was born of Hagar, a slave. He was born of flesh (born out of an adulterous act), and would receive no inheritance. On the other hand, Isaac was born of a free woman, Abraham's wife, Sarah. He was born of a promise. God promised Abraham a son by his wife, who was past childbearing age, and that, through Abraham, all the families of the earth would be blessed. Isaac, alone, was to inherit God's promises to Abraham. This, the Jewish Christians could resonate with.

What they could not resonate with was Paul's inference that the Jews were represented by Ishmael, not Isaac. The Jews prided themselves on being children of Abraham, children of God's promise. In Galatians, Paul brought the truth that the Jews were children of Abraham – the bastard children. Paul wants his audience to see that the true people of God are those who receive His Spirit, not those of physical genealogy to Abraham. He wrote in Galatians 3:14: *"so that in Christ Jesus the blessing of Abraham might come to the Gentiles, so that we might receive the promised Spirit through faith"*.

In Paul's analogy, Hagar and her son represent the old covenant that God made with Israel, which dictated slavery to the flesh, works, and Law. It was upon Mount Sinai that God appeared to His people as a thick cloud, like smoke from a kiln. The mountain shook and trembled. It was here that God gave Moses the Ten Commandments, and confirmed His covenant with His people. His audience would have disagreed with Paul linking Mount Sinai, and then Jerusalem, to Hagar.

It is important to note how Paul differentiated his references to Jerusalem. The "present city of Jerusalem" was linked to Hagar, to slavery, and to the physical Jewish race. The "Jerusalem that is above" was linked to Sarah, to freedom, and to the spiritual people of God, saved through faith; Paul was alluding to the second covenant, the better covenant of grace.

Interpreting the book of Galatians

<u>Interpretation questions</u>

1. Paul showed great concern for the purity of the Gospel.
   a. Why was he anxious for them to stand firm in the Gospel in its pure form?
   b. Why was a modified Gospel of such repulsion to him?
   c. What implications would arise from following flawed theology?
2. Summarise Paul's argument that salvation is found in Christ alone. Consider also:
   a. How is one saved?
   b. Who can be saved?
3. Explain what Paul meant by his illustration that the Law was the guardian, until the coming of Christ and justification through faith.
   a. What was the purpose of the Law?
   b. Return to God's promises to Abraham in Genesis 12:1-3, and His covenant with Abraham in Genesis 15. How did Paul interpret the promise and covenant given to Abraham, in light of Christ's coming?
4. Consider Paul's conversion experience, used as a testimony.
   a. How did it aid his argument that one is justified by faith, not works?
   b. Why was it significant that Paul received his ministry from God and not men?
   c. How would this have strengthened his argument for the Gospel of Grace?
5. What is the dictionary meaning of the words: justification, grace, and righteousness?
6. How does the book of Galatians define justification, grace, and righteousness?
7. Why did Paul spend so little time focusing on grace-abuse (continuing to sin because, in Christ, sins are forgiven)?
8. From the epistle, what do you ascertain were the main issues in the Galatian church?
9. Consider Paul's protection of the true Gospel.
   a. Why was Paul visibly upset and astonished that the Galatians had fallen under a works mentality?
   b. How did Paul feel towards the Judaizers and the Circumcision Party?
   c. Why did he hold the Judaizers as responsible for the shift away from the true Gospel?
   d. Why did he hold the Circumcision Party as responsible for the shift away from the true Gospel?
   e. How did he hold the church as having a responsibility in

preventing a shift away from the true Gospel?

10. Consider the allegory about Sarah and Hagar.
   a. How would the illustration of Sarah and Hagar have impacted Paul's Jewish audience? How would they have responded to the allegory?
   b. How would the illustration have impacted the Gentiles amongst his readers?
   c. What would have been the significance to the early church?
   d. How would it have built unity between Jewish and Gentile believers?

11. What was Paul trying to communicate to the Galatian church regarding the issue of circumcision?
   a. What was the significance of circumcision to the Jews?
   b. Was Paul against circumcision?
   c. What implications would this have had for the Jewish Christians and their continued practice of Jewish customs and traditions?

12. How would the message of Galatians have brought unity between Jewish and Gentile believers?
   a. Remembering that Apostle Peter was the pillar of the church, what was the significance of Paul's recount of opposing Peter in the issue of Gentile believers?
   b. How would this have affected the thinking and actions of his Jewish Christian audience
   c. How would this have affected the thinking and actions of his Gentile Christian audience?

13. Explore the work of the Spirit and the call of believers.
   a. With what do servants of Christ concern themselves?
   b. In what ways does one change when living by the Spirit?
   c. How should the actions of the original readers have reflected their rebirth in Christ?
   d. What does it look like to live under the covenant of grace?

14. Consider the role of the Holy Spirit in the lives of believers.

Creative interpretation

1. Re-write the message of Galatians as a letter or e-mail to a church of today; for example, your home church. Try to capture the essential message of Paul's epistle, whilst using modern language to powerfully convey the significance of salvation coming through Christ alone.

2. Visually illustrate the message of Galatians. For example, make a mind-map, diagram, comic strip or pictorial illustration.

Application inspiration
Reflecting on grace and works

- The Galatian church was being told that the old works of the Law must be kept in order to be saved.

- o What does the church promote today, which adds to the message of salvation coming through faith in Christ? What do you tell yourself you must you do to be a good Christian? What does the church tell you that you must do?
- o Do you truly accept the Gospel message of the free gift of grace? Think about what you do to "feel" closer to God; make a list. How do you respond when someone asks you: "how are you going with God?" Things like "I haven't had a quiet time today" can be a legalistic response.
- o What is your motivation for going to church, having a quiet time or fasting?
- o What area of your spiritual life do you feel guilty if you neglect?

- Paul focused on changing beliefs before behaviour. Legalism is formed when you start with "dos" and "do nots". To put legalism in modern day terms, Max Lucado (2004) states: *"Legalism. The theology of "Jesus +". Legalists don't dismiss Christ. They trust in Christ a lot. Yet they don't trust in Christ alone."* [1]
  - o In what do you trust for salvation?
  - o Where does your confidence of God's good opinion come from: what Christ accomplished on the cross, your own "good deeds" or your Bible study and religious disciplines?

[1] Lucado, M. (2004). *It's Not About Me: Rescue From the Life We Thought Would Make Us Happy.* Thomas Nelson, Inc., Nashville, TN.

EPHESIANS

In Christ

In him we have redemption through his blood, the forgiveness of our trespasses, according to the riches of his grace, which he lavished upon us, in all wisdom and insight making known to us the mystery of his will, according to his purpose, which he set forth in Christ as a plan for the fullness of time, to unite all things in him, things in heaven and things on earth. – Ephesians 1:7-10

During your first reading

Themes to track

- Authority of Christ
- Received in Christ
- Identity in Christ
- Unity/ oneness

During your second reading

Things to notice in the text

- Highlight the repeated words "in Christ", "in Him", "in Jesus", and "in whom".
- Important time elements: before salvation and after salvation.
- Underline Paul's commands to the church in chapters 4-6.
- Circle people groups in Ephesians 5:15-6:9; "wives" form the first group, and "masters" form the last.
- Circle places and positions, such as "heavenly realms", "separate", "brought near", "above", and "under His feet".

Chapter summaries

These are optional as they can be time consuming for the larger books. If you choose to do them, you will receive a much deeper appreciation of the book. By the end of The IBSC, you will have paraphrased the entire Bible! Go through each chapter and try to summarise it in one paragraph, using your own words; force yourself to stay big picture and capture the heart of each chapter.

After your initial readings

Setting of Ephesians
<u>Author</u>
Ephesians was written by Apostle Paul.

<u>Recipient</u>
The words "in Ephesus" in Ephesians 1:1 were not part of the original text; therefore, Paul probably intended the letter for circulation between the churches in Asia Minor, rather than to the specific church in Ephesus. However, as Ephesus was an important city at this time, it would have been one of the chief places the epistle would have been read.

<u>Date and place of writing</u>
The epistle was penned during Paul's Roman imprisonment, between 60 and 61 AD.

<u>Reason written</u>
Paul was bringing enlightenment to a church living in fear of the spiritual realm, who continued to cling to their old ways of life. He was writing to encourage them with the truth of Christ's superiority, and His power to transform lives. In addition, Paul longed to see the church walk in unity, and the believers leading godly lives.

Big picture
<u>Historical background</u>
Whether you take the view that the epistle was written to churches across Asia Minor, or specifically to the church in Ephesus, the cultural background remains the same.

Religion
The people of Ephesus lived in fear of the spiritual realm. They believed that it was only through complex rituals that they could obtain forgiveness and favour. It led the church to have a work-based mentality, and insecurity towards salvation.

Magic was a part of most religions. The people sought to draw on the power of gods to influence the physical realm. Their religion was based on manipulation. Four assumptions of the people were:

1. Gods and spirits/ powers populate the heavens, the underworld, and the earth. They were believed to be a constant presence in one's everyday life.
2. There were good and bad spirits.
3. These spirits/ powers were not only present in, but had control over,

people's lives and their eternal destiny. As a result, the people were constantly seeking to appease the spirits.

4. People and situations could be influenced by evoking the help of these powerful spirit-beings. If you won their favour you went from being controlled by them, to controlling them.

Mystery religions were popular, promising eternal life through secret ceremonies. They promised forgiveness as well as physical protection. Worshippers worked themselves up into emotional orgies, believing this would bring spiritual revelation. The word "mystery" used in Ephesians is derived from the Greek word "musterion". Strong's Hebrew and Greek Dictionary (1989) defines "musterion" as: "a secret" or "mystery" [1], and links the word to religious sects using secret rites to impose silence upon their initiates [1].

Three deities were linked with the mystery religions:

1. *Artemis:* The goddess supreme in power and place, she was seen as mediator, protector or saviour. She was the mother goddess and held power over fertility.

2. *Mithra:* The lord of light, known as the light of the world, and sun god. He was the symbol of truth, justice, and loyalty, and was the gateway to eternal life. Without Mithra, one was destined to hell.

3. *Dionysus:* He was the god of ecstasy, promiscuity, and drunkenness before whom nothing was wrong or immoral. Dionysus granted protection from demons and, in the afterlife, unimaginable pleasure.

The term "heavenly places" was not a reference to heaven; it implied an unseen, celestial plane beyond the physical senses.

Gentiles and Jews

There were several walls in the Jewish temple, which acted to segregate people groups into particular courts. Only Jewish men were allowed to enter the very inner court. There was then another court for Jewish women. Gentile worshippers were restricted to the very outer court, which was situated outside the main temple area. A message on the temple gate declared: *"No foreigner may enter within the barricade which surrounds the sanctuary and enclosure. Anyone who is caught doing so will have himself to blame for his ensuring death".*

Ephesus

Ephesus was a wealthy Roman seaside city, in the present-day, small town of Selçuk, Turkey. It owed its early prosperity to its strategic location as a port sitting between two major overland trading routes. However, by New Testament times, port trading had reduced, because the River Cayster became clogged from deforestation and had in turn silted up the harbour.

The temple of Artemis brought additional trade to the city. It could be viewed as a religious bank; pilgrims coming to worship the goddess brought substantial contributions and business.

Read Acts 19, which tells about Paul's time in Ephesus. Look at what was happening: exorcisms, people being attacked by demons, witchcraft, idol worship, and money being made from the temple of Artemis.

Character portrayal – a believer's confusion and fear

The market place was filled with its usual hustle and bustle. It was difficult to steer a path through the masses. It was usually easier to wait for the tide of human bodies to sweep one to the side and then make one's way along the edges. Aelius' mind was busy in contemplation, so he subconsciously blocked out the familiar noise of trade surrounding him – hawkers, haggling, carts making their ponderous trip through the people, cheap women calling out lures, arguments over wares, and mulling animals.

The markets always reminded Aelius from whence he had come. The city was filled to the brim with idolatry, lust, and immorality. The smells of the market were, to him, the smell of corruption. And yet . . . even knowing what he knew, Aelius struggled to separate himself from the culture. He had liked the complexity of life. He had felt secure with the rituals, rites, and talismans. He had felt safe working for his salvation.

Aelius wrestled with conflicting thoughts. He strained his mind to remain focused on the truth. He knew that Christ was enough. He knew that He was secure in God. But . . . was the simplicity of Christianity really enough, when everybody else seemed to be teaching differently? The unwelcome thought cut through his mind. Was he still protected now that he was bare of amulets, charms, and magic formulas?

Aelius simply did not know where Christ stood in relation to the supernatural powers. He knew Christ was enough for salvation, but he was not sure whether He was able to protect him from the evil powers. A seed of doubt was growing in his mind. He was tempted. Tempted to go back to the blood rituals, sexual rites, magic, and emotional frenzies. Aelius was confused. He was afraid. He needed answers to the questions chasing each other around within his fear-filled mind.

Book overview

Ephesians shows that spiritual warfare equals standing boldly in faith, knowing one's identity in Christ, walking in unity, and living a godly life. Those standing in Christ stand in His authority and power. Knowing one's identify in Christ brings protection, security, and assurance of eternal life. The One to be feared is God, not demons or powers. Christ is above all things, and through Him all things hold together. This brings with it humility, knowing that it is through Christ alone that one receives salvation, not by self-righteous acts or personal striving. This common need for forgiveness, received in Christ, brings unity.

Paul argued that everyone has the same Creator, who is the Father of all mankind. God has given eternal life as inheritance to all who are in Christ, making all believers fellow citizens and fellow heirs. Paul argued that there is no partiality with God, who has broken down the dividing wall segregating Jews and Gentiles. Paul told his audience that they were all God's workmanship, formed by Him into new creations.

To illustrate his point, Paul used the image of the church being the body of Christ, joined and built together by the Spirit as a dwelling place for God. Christ is the cornerstone of unity. Each member of the body is of equal value and importance. The Spirit's gifts are given with the purpose of building up the whole. With unity, comes the need for changed living, walking in love. Believers are held to the highest standards of love and this binds them together in unity through Christ.

Paul saw the family unit as the clearest reflection of whether the church was walking in unity versus discord, and gave specific commands for each family role. He taught that unity is formed through loving as Christ loved the church, whilst submitting as the church submits to Christ. Sin is not to be glorified; it is revolting before God's eyes and should be just as revolting to His children. The Ephesian congregation was being called to imitate Christ's love, out of reverence for Him.

Interpreting the book of Ephesians
<u>Interpretation questions</u>
1. What can you infer about the original readers from Acts 19?
   a. What were the strengths and weaknesses of the church as seen from Ephesians and Acts?
   b. How did Paul encourage their strengths?
   c. How did Paul challenge them to grow?
   d. What was Paul's hope for the church?
2. How did Paul outline their identity as believers, through Ephesians 1:1-1:23?
   a. What had God done for them?
   b. What had they received in Christ?
   c. What did they obtain "in Him"?
3. What is the calling of the saints?
4. Compare the character of man after the fall versus the character of those who are in Christ.
   a. Make a table with two columns. In the first, list their "old reality" when they were dead in sin. Then, in the second column, note their "new reality" now they are alive, living as saints.
   b. How would coming to a realisation of these truths have influenced the actions of the original readers?
5. What is the position of believers in Christ?
   a. Look back at the four assumptions of the people given under historical background. State, with reference to the text, how Paul addressed each of their assumptions.
   b. The Ephesians feared spirits living in heavenly places, believing the spirits could control their daily lives. How did Paul seek to relieve these fears?
   c. What truth did Paul reveal to them about the powers in the heavenly places and about Christ?
   d. Why could the original readers be confident of their position?
6. What do you learn about Christ?
   a. What has God *already done*? What has Christ achieved?
   b. What *will He do*?
   c. What has He promised?

      d.   Who benefits from His achievements and promises?

      e.   What does Ephesians show of Christ's rule and authority?

      f.   What does it declare of His sovereignty?

7. What had the original readers already received in Christ? What did they await, hopeful of His promise?

8. What do you learn of mystery, revelation, and knowledge?

      a.   Who makes the mysteries known?

      b.   What knowledge is available, and to whom?

9. What does Ephesians reveal about the character and role of the Holy Spirit?

10. Paul's epistle, particularly in chapters 4-6 provides very practical instructions for godly living. Note the commands given to believers.

      a.   What response were the original readers called to give to the grace of Christ and what He had accomplished for them?

      b.   Would these have been hard for them, given their culture?

      c.   How would they be strengthened to walk in these commands from reading chapters 1-3?

11. The final chapters challenged the original readers to walk worthy of their calling. Draw up a table with two columns and list the "dos" and "do nots" that Paul gave to them.

12. In two-columned tables, compare the commands that Paul gave to: (a) wives versus husbands, (b) fathers versus children, and (c) slaves versus masters.

      a.   What are the implications of these commands?

      b.   How should the pairings complement each other, when each side obeys these commands?

      c.   In each pairing, who do you think was given the harder command, remembering to take the culture of the original readers into account?

13. What is said of unity?

      a.   What does unity look like?

      b.   What do all believers have in common?

      c.   How did Paul give Gentile believers confidence in their salvation?

      d.   What were some practical commands that Paul gave for unity?

      e.   How does Christ call believers to unity?

      f.   Why was it important that they walk in unity?

      g.   What does unity display to the world?

14. Consider the positions listed in Ephesians 4:11-13.

      a.   What is the purpose of each call and how do they work together?

      b.   Who dictates who gets what role?

      c.   Why is it significant that not everyone receives each title?

      d.   Which role is most important in the body (see also 1 Corinthians 12:12-27)?

15. What do you learn of Paul and his ministry?

      a.   What was the call Christ gave to him?

      b.   Where was Paul? How did he view his current circumstances?

    c. How did Paul view his imprisonment and suffering? Look for supporting scriptures that tell of Paul's times in prison and his views on suffering for the Gospel.

    d. How were the original readers feeling towards Paul's imprisonment?

Creative interpretation

1. Draw a mind map of who the original readers were "in Him".

2. To aid your understanding, think of a way to illustrate the original readers' beliefs about the spiritual realm and the "heavenly places". In your illustration, include how Christ is the highest authority and power.

3. The final chapters called the original readers to walk worthy of their calling. Draw up a table with two columns and list the "dos" and "do nots" that Paul gave to them.

4. On a poster, categorise the commands Paul gave, giving each category a picture. For example, a command under the heading "speech" could be Ephesians 4:29: *"Let no corrupting talk come out of your mouths, but only such as is good for building up, as fits the occasion, that it may give grace to those who hear"*, which you might illustrate with a picture of a mouth.

Application inspiration

- Consider the table of "dos" and "do nots" you created during interpretation.
  - Which of these do you struggle with? Give specific examples of situations where you commonly fall into one of the "do nots".
  - How can you actively change your behavioural response?
  - Choose a "do" to focus on. List five ways you can walk out this "do" over the next month. Focus on this "do" rather than the "do not" with which you struggle.
  - In light of this list, consider the television shows that you watch, the topics of conversation you introduce with friends, the way you respond when you arrive home at night, the time you give to your children, how you relate to those at church, and how you live as a witness at work.
- Reflect on what Christ has done for you:
  - Read some of His teachings from the parables recorded in the Gospels.
  - Give Him glory and know that you are safe in Him.
  - Build up your identity in Christ by stating out loud what you have "in Him".

Looking at unity

- Consider unity in the church today.
  - How do you create unity in your church?

- o Describe some of the different roles you see people taking on in your church and why each is important.
- o Is there someone with whom you need to build unity?
- What "walls" still act as divides in society, today? Think of race, education, and religion as a starting point.
  - o How do you see segregation show itself in different countries?
  - o What about in your own community?
  - o Where are they seen in your church?
  - o How can you take God's love through these walls? How can you help break down these walls and spread the Gospel message that all who believe in Christ, and call on His name, shall be saved?

[1] Strong, James, S.T.D., LL.D., (1989). *Strong's Hebrew and Greek Dictionaries, e-Sword*, Ver. 9.7.2, Dictionary, G3466.

PHILIPPIANS

Unity through Humility

So if there is any encouragement in Christ, any comfort from love, any participation in the Spirit, any affection and sympathy, complete my joy by being of the same mind, having the same love, being in full accord and of one mind. – Philippians 2:1-2

During your first reading

Themes to track
- Unity through humility
- Joy in suffering
- Witnessing through persecution

During your second reading

Things to notice in the text
- Highlight words relating to unity: "all", "same (mind)", "one", "like-minded", and "together".
- Mark the repeated words "joy" and "rejoicing".
- Underline the commands Paul gave to the Philippians.

Chapter summaries
These are optional as they can be time consuming for the larger books. If you choose to do them, you will receive a much deeper appreciation of the book. By the end of The IBSC, you will have paraphrased the entire Bible! Go through each chapter and try to summarise it in one paragraph, using your own words; force yourself to stay big picture and capture the heart of each chapter.

After your initial readings

Setting of Philippians

<u>Author</u>

Philippians was written by Apostle Paul.

<u>Recipient</u>

The epistle was written to the church in Philippi.

<u>Date and place of writing</u>

Given the length of Paul's imprisonment, it seems that Paul wrote this epistle during his time in Rome. There is debate regarding whether Paul was imprisoned in Rome once or twice. The first imprisonment is dated between 60 and 62 AD with a possible second imprisonment between 63 and 66 AD. Therefore, the letter can be dated between the years of 60 and 66 AD.

<u>Reason written</u>

Paul desired to thank the church for their support and assistance in meeting his practical needs, particularly during his imprisonment. They had supported his ministry and he was grateful for their contribution. However, more than this, he desired them to grow in maturity of faith. It was his aim to encourage them onwards in faith in the face of the persecution that came to those who believed in Christ. Paul wanted them to know that the joy of Christ is not related to circumstances. There also seem to have been issues of disunity and pride within the church that needed to be addressed.

Big picture

<u>Historical background</u>

The city of Philippi

Philippi, a city of eastern Macedonia between the rivers Strymon and Nestos, was established by Philipp II of Macedonia in 356 BC, and became a Roman colony in 42 BC. The ruins of the city are located in the modern-day region of East Macedonia and Thrace, Greece. Philippi's position was a strategic location allowing for control of the route between Amphipolis and Neapolis, and its position between the two rivers favoured it with fertile soil. Gold mines to the north of the city contributed to the wealth of Macedonia.

Culture of Rome, Philippi, and the church

The colonies of Rome were governed by Roman officials. Rome ensured the loyalty of its colonies by settling retired soldiers in the cities, giving the soldiers land as a reward for service. The soldiers brought with them Roman dress, titles, and culture.

Philippi was the first place Paul preached in Europe on his second missionary journey, in around 50 AD. His first visit to the city is recorded in Acts 16:12-40. Apostle Luke was a native of Philippi and, as a physician, he would have been educated at the city's famous medical school and associated with the guild of physicians. From the account given in Acts, it appears that Luke remained behind after Paul left Philippi in order to aid the young church.

The believers in the Philippian church were of a predominately Gentile population, including Roman citizens. The Philippi Christians were proud of their Roman citizenship; it was a privilege to be a Roman as they received special rights, such as fair trial and different taxes. The words "manner of life" (also translated as "conversation") used by Paul in Philippians 1:27 come from the same Greek word as "citizen" (Strong, J, 1989) [1].

The Romans did not understand Christianity's teaching on the coming Kingdom of God, and came to believe that Christians were threatening the Empire. The Romans were further confused by the church's respect for Roman law, and utterly baffled that Christianity taught that there was only One God.

Romans had a diversity of religious beliefs

Rome held naturalistic beliefs, holding that the Law of Nature reigned over the universe, rather than a Sovereign God. Greek influence over Roman culture led to the fusing of native deities with the Greek pantheon. They also practiced worship of state, or Caesar-worship, where the spirit of Rome was worshipped, and the emperor was viewed as a god. Romans allowed for many religions and gods, and could not grasp the church's message of there being One True God.

Higher classes of society viewed death as final and mocked preaching of the resurrection, whilst longing for longevity. The lower classes engaged in superstitions and animalistic beliefs (that humans are no different in nature to animals, with neither having a spirit). People sought fulfilment from philosophy, magic, and foreign rites. Judaism was a "licensed" religion, giving Christianity a degree of early freedom as it was viewed as a sect of Judaism. Crucifixion was judged as a curse by the Jews; refer to Deuteronomy 21:23.

Character portrayal – Paul in prison

Paul's thoughts turned again to his fellow workers in Philippi and he thanked God for them. Their support and love had encouraged his spirit many times over the past ten or so years. He longed to be among them again and he was confident that God would grant him his desire. Even though he longed to see them, he considered it a privilege to be in chains for his beliefs as Christ the Lord Himself had suffered, counting it no cost to break the dividing wall of hostility between God and man.

Paul followed the example of Christ, walking in humility of spirit, willing to suffer in order to bring others into the Kingdom of God. Considering the members of Caesar's household, he saw many that had come to salvation during his time in chains and he praised the Lord for them. Nevertheless, he prayed that God would grant his desire to return to Philippi and strengthen that beloved congregation.

Love was welling up within him for the Philippians and so, needing an outlet, he called for Timothy to bring him parchment. The pair then sat and composed a letter of encouragement to strengthen the hearts of the believers in Philippi and urge them towards unity in the faith.

Book overview

Whilst studying this book, it is necessary to keep in mind that Paul was in prison. He was suffering because of his faith, and yet he maintained an upbeat and encouraging vibe in his letter. The love he had for the Philippians is clearly shown in the opening paragraphs and throughout the epistle. Because of this love, Paul boldly declared that he was willing to continue in this life, where he had known many pains and sorrows, because he knew that they were still in need of his leadership to grow in maturity as believers.

Paul showed that he was well pleased with the Philippian church and desired them to grow further. He made himself an example by declaring: *"not that I have already reached this goal or have already become perfect"*[2]. The fact that he addressed deacons in their congregation, and thanked them for their gifts, shows that leadership had been established and that they were seeking to live out their faith and support Paul to continue the spread of the Gospel.

Paul sought to build a united church through inclusive language, seen by the repeated words "all", "one", and "same" – there was no place for pride because Christ alone saves. Their society was one that valued what an individual earned as well as the privileges they had from the Roman government, yet Paul proclaimed that everything they were in the world was as nothing compared to knowing Christ and what He had done for them. He wanted them to stop looking at themselves and adopt his mindset. Paul challenged them to walk in unity and to foster the humility of Christ.

Interpreting the book of Philippians

Interpretation questions

1. Explore what Paul says of joy and suffering.
    a. What does the repetition of the words "joy" and "rejoicing" within the letter suggest was on Paul's mind when thinking of the Philippians?
    b. How can one have joy in the midst of persecution and hard times? It may be helpful to compare the meaning of joy to that of happiness in order to distinguish between the two words.
    c. Why was it important for the Philippians to hear that they could have joy in the midst of pain, distress, and trials?
2. Look at Paul's character and life.
    a. How was Paul energised?
    b. What can be said of his character and the focus of his mind?
    c. What did he view as his purpose on earth? What did he see as his call?
    d. What do you learn of how he discipled his followers?
    e. What do you see of his heart for the Philippians? What was his prayer and desire for them?
3. Consider Paul's character amidst suffering.
    a. How did he find hope in his circumstances (imprisonment)?

    b. What was Paul's focus in prison? In what other ways could he have responded to his time in prison?

    c. What results had come from his imprisonment?

    d. How did he use his circumstances to encourage the original readers in Philippians 1:27-30?

    e. How did Paul view suffering for the Gospel?

4. What is the significance of persecution with respect to spreading the Gospel?

5. Investigate the call of the church to stand united.

    a. What does unity of faith look like?

    b. What commands did Paul give to build unity within the church?

    c. How would living in humility have brought the Philippian church together?

    d. How would serving each other have led to unity within their church?

6. Read Philippians 2:5-16 again as well as Philippians 3:2-11. Paul wrote of how Christ lived a humble life, a lowly one in the eyes of the world, and yet will receive all glory. Paul, on the other hand, had all that the world valued, but he now counted it as nothing.

    a. What would it mean for the Philippian congregation to have the same attitude as Christ?

    b. How would their culture have viewed them if they began to live this way?

    c. Is it wrong to take pride in one's societal status?

    d. From what was Paul calling the Philippians to gain their identity?

7. Consider Timothy and Epaphroditus.

    a. What is seen of Timothy's character?

    b. What do you learn of Epaphroditus?

    c. How did Paul view these men?

    d. How did Paul desire the original readers to view them?

    e. How were the original readers to treat them if they came to Philippi?

8. What do you learn of Christ?

    a. What do you see of His rule and authority?

    b. What does this reveal about His sovereignty?

9. Compare Paul's statement in Philippians 3:1-14 with his defence in 2 Corinthians 3-5,11-12.

    a. What is the significance of earthly titles and acclaim in the Kingdom of God?

    b. From where did Paul obtain his identity?

    c. In Paul's eyes, what was the most valuable thing to obtain in life?

10. What does it mean to work out one's salvation with fear and trembling?

    a. Was Paul saying that there is more to learn about being saved?

    b. What do the following passages say on the requirements for salvation: John 3:16-17; Romans 5:9-11; Romans 8:14-17; 2

Corinthians 5:17-21; Galatians 3?
c. Now consider what is said of the process of sanctification (becoming more Christ-like) in: Romans 6:11-14,22; Romans 12:1-2; 1 Corinthians 6:20; 2 Corinthians 6:16-7:1; Galatians 5:16-26.
11. Consider Philippians 3:13-14:
a. What lies behind?
b. What lies ahead?
c. What is the prize?
12. Consider Philippians 4:8-9 and then contemplate:
a. What is true?
b. What is honourable?
c. What is just?
d. What is pure?
e. What is lovely?
f. What is commendable?
g. What is excellent?
h. What is worthy of praise?
i. What did they learn from Paul's example?
13. Give attention to what is shown of the Philippian believers.
a. What had the Philippians done for Paul?
b. What may have fuelled their giving?
c. What motivated their love for Paul?
d. What was their response to his imprisonment?

Creative interpretation
1. Write a definition for humility using references from the text.
2. Create a story around Paul's sufferings.
a. Expand upon the sufferings noted in Scripture such as in 2 Corinthians 11:23-33 and Acts 14:11-19.
b. Given what Paul endured for the Gospel, consider why he felt the trials and hardships worthwhile, and how the love of Christ propelled him to give his life to his call.
c. Consider what he had given up and what he received.

Application inspiration
- How do you respond to trials?
  o Do you keep preaching in persecution or does it effectively shut your mouth? How does the message of Philippians embolden you to rejoice in suffering?
  o Are you able to count it joy when you face trials?
  o Do you need to ask God to strengthen you, and change your focus, in these times?
- Make a list to compare the following two sets of values.
  o What is regarded to be of greatest worth – sporting abilities, book

smarts, looks, successful career, university degree, musical abilities, wealth, fame, family – in your culture; compared with
- o What is of greatest worth to God?
- Ask yourself: "What does humility (servanthood) look like to me?"
  - o How can you live out humility?
  - o What practical steps can you take to put the needs of others before your own?
  - o Think of acts of service you can do in your home, for your family, this week.

[1] Strong, James, S.T.D., LL.D., (1989). *Strong's Hebrew and Greek Dictionaries, e-Sword*, Ver. 9.7.2, Dictionary, G4176.

[2] Philippians 3:12

COLOSSIANS

Christ is sufficient for Salvation

For in him the whole fullness of deity dwells bodily, and you have been filled in him, who is the head of all rule and authority. – Colossians 2:9-10

During your first reading

Themes to track
- Christ is the fullness of God
- Christ is sufficient
- Serving God with thankfulness
- Christian living

During your second reading

Things to notice in the text
- Mark the repeated words "all", and "full (fullness/ fully)".
- What Christ has done; look for "in/ through/ by Him (Christ)".
- Circle who (people/classifications/names): "holy", "beloved", "Paul", "prisoner" . . .
- Underline where (places/ positions): "Colossae", "prison", "heaven", "earth", "things above".

Chapter summaries
These are optional as they can be time consuming for the larger books. If you choose to do them, you will receive a much deeper appreciation of the book. By the end of The IBSC, you will have paraphrased the entire Bible! Go through each chapter and try to summarise it in one paragraph, using your own words; force yourself to stay big picture and capture the heart of each chapter.

After your initial readings

Setting of Colossians
<u>Author</u>
Colossians was written by Apostle Paul.

<u>Recipient</u>
Paul wrote to the church in Colossae.

<u>Date and place of writing</u>
It is seen in the epistle that Paul was in prison and it appears, from the names listed, that it was the same time and place as those from which he wrote the book of Philemon. The two main options are: from Jerusalem/ Caesarea (58-60 AD; see Acts 21-26) or from Rome (60-62 AD; see Acts 27-28). Paul was under house arrest when in Rome, which makes the later date the more likely option as he appears to have had some degree of freedom at the time of writing the epistle, with people coming and going from his home.

<u>Reason written</u>
Paul wrote this letter to the Colossians to correct heresies arising in the church from wrong beliefs, flowing from their cultural mind-set. His language throughout the letter is one of loving encouragement, telling them that Christian living comes as a response to the Gospel message.

Big picture
<u>Historical background</u>
Paul's language within his letter to the Colossian church shows that they had a solid faith in Christ, and hope in the Gospel. They were a church that seemed to desire spiritual growth, but were being held back by wrong beliefs. Their incorrect thinking flowed from Greek philosophy, Jewish Law, and the teachings of the mystery religions that their culture had adopted. Paul was writing in order to correct their philosophy and align it with the truth of the Gospel message.

The Colossians believed in a spiritual ladder with spiritual beings holding different positions of authority along the ladder. At the top of the ladder was the first god, the father god. This god was deemed good, but was not interactive with man. He gave birth to lesser gods (aeons), who were not perfect, and it was these lesser gods who interacted with man. The Colossians believed that it was Demiurge, one of the lesser gods, who created the imperfect world. This created a belief that there was a gap between man and the good god.

Colossians shows that the only way to God is through faith in Jesus Christ. Grasping at rungs of the ladder, and trying to climb to God is foolish as the ladder is destined to fall, and yet this is what the original readers were attempting to do. In order to ascend this spiritual ladder, the Colossians believed that the elemental spirits could influence them, and thus these beings were believed to hold the destiny of men. The Colossians feared these unseen beings. They began worshipping the lesser gods and angles, believing these lesser spirits would grant secret knowledge and enable them to climb the "spiritual ladder" towards the good god. It should be noted that there is no evidence that Jews took up the worship of angels, and this seems to have been a local religious practice in Colossae.

The church also struggled with Gnosticism (from the Greek word "Gnosis", meaning knowledge). They saw the physical/ material world as evil and the spiritual world as good; this is known as dualism, the separating of body and spirit. Within this mindset, secret knowledge was again seen as the key to salvation.

Dualism resulted in one of two responses: asceticism or libertarianism. Those walking in asceticism believed that the flesh must be punished, which led to self-mutilation, even to the point where they could no longer feel the pain. They believed that, by punishing the evil flesh, they would be brought closer to the good god. On the other hand, those walking in libertarianism believed that, because only the soul was divine and immortal, the body, which was earthly, was of no consequence and they could therefore do what they wanted with their bodies, without consequence.

Because of this dualistic mindset, the church had come to believe that, as Christ came to earth as a physical being, He could not be perfect and therefore was not fully God. They had come to see Jesus as one of the intermediary beings, who filled the gap in the ladder between man and the good god. Christ was seen as a lesser god among the angels, and not equal to the father god.

Not seeing Christ as fully God in turn led the Colossian believers to undervalue the work of Christ, as they strove to reach the fullness of God on their own. They did not trust that Jesus alone was enough to receive salvation, gain protection from the spirits or become children of God. They did not believe they were spiritual enough and so fell under the worship of angels, rules and regulations, and dualism. This was furthered by false teachers in the church who began claiming they had gained special revelations of knowledge that were not from Scripture. This led the church members to try and earn their way to salvation.

See also the *historical background* given for 1 Timothy in relation to gnosticism and false teachings.

Character portrayal – a believer throwing off involvement in the mystery religions

Violent images swirled in Attilia's head. She could still smell the blood of the sacrifice that had hung heavily in the air during her initiation ceremony. She was repulsed as memories of self-mutilation, frenzied cries, and yowling animals flicked across her minds' eye – all of which were common sights in the mystery religion sects of Colossae. And to think she had been part of it!

Dwelling on Paul's letter, Attilia knew both freedom and fear. Her emotions and mind told her that she must keep pursuing knowledge for salvation, but her spirit confirmed the truth of Paul's words: Christ was enough! In her Beloved Saviour was all the wisdom and knowledge needed for salvation. It was time she stopped seeking after things of no worth.

"*Lord,*" Attilia prayed, "*free me of this bondage to earthly things: to sexual immorality, impurity, passion, evil desire, and idolatry. Release me to live as you call us to: with a compassionate heart, kindness, humility, meekness, and patience. Help me to truly know that I am chosen, holy, and beloved of you."*

Book overview

In his letter to the Colossians, Paul emphasised two critical elements of the faith: first, that Jesus is fully God and, secondly, that believers have attained the fullness of God through Him. The moment believers accept His free gift of grace, made attainable through Jesus, they become righteous before God. They are holy and blameless in the eyes of God. The message Paul made was clear: God rules supreme and Christ is sufficient. Jesus is fully sufficient to bring them into holiness. Christ is shown to be fully God and Head over all rule and authority. This includes the spiritual realm, the Jewish Law, and even over death.

Paul was saying to the Colossians: "You don't need to climb a spiritual ladder to reach God!" He showed them that they were seeking to reach God in the wrong way. They had been lessening the value of what Christ had done for them. Paul set Jesus on every rung of their ladder. The Colossians could get off the ladder and relax in Christ. They did not have to practice self-harm to grow closer to God. Christ was shown to be the One that has the power to bring people into the kingdom; not angels, spirits or any other being. Paul also showed that what they did in the physical mattered in the eyes of God.

Paul's message proclaimed that Christ is before all, above all, and Creator of all; He is the only means of salvation. Paul wanted the church to move away from rules and regulations, which were holding them captive, and into the freedom of grace. Paul showed that the appropriate response of believers should be praise and thanksgiving towards God. He was telling them to leave the world behind and walk in the peace and love of the Spirit.

Interpreting the book of Colossians
Interpretation questions
1. Jesus is Paul's focus in this epistle. So, from the text:
    a.   Who is Jesus?
    b.   How did Paul describe Christ?
    c.   What had Christ done for the Colossians? (This is also the focus of *creative interpretation* for this book).
2. Look at the meaning of "all" and "fullness". What would Paul's message convey to the readers, who did not believe that Christ's work on the cross was sufficient to bring them to God?
3. How did Paul counter each of the following *wrong* beliefs, to lead the Colossians to the truth? Their *wrong* beliefs about Jesus included that:
    a.   He delivered them from sin, but not from the cosmic powers;
    b.   He was one of the angels;
    c.   He was not truly God.
4. Consider Paul's call to be thankful of heart.
    a.   What does it mean to be thankful, always?
    b.   How were the Colossians to show their thankfulness to God?
    c.   How would this have looked in practice?

      d. What actions may the Colossians have been challenged to undertake in response to the epistle?
5. Paul commands them to "think on things above".
      a. On what things from above were they to focus their thoughts?
      b. What would this mean to the Colossian readers?
      c. How does focusing on things above protect one from falling back into the things of earth?
6. What motivated Paul to spread the Gospel?
7. What were some of Paul's desires for the Colossian church?

Creative interpretation
1. Make a mind map to display what is seen of Christ and His character throughout the book.
2. On another page, mind map who Paul declared the Colossians to be "in Christ".

Application inspiration

Take time to soak in the message of Colossians. Reflect upon it. The message of this book should become a lifestyle. Live a godly life out of thankfulness and put the ways of the world aside. Trust God to bring this change in your life as you focus on Him and your identity in Him.

Know that:

- Christ IS SUFFICIENT
- Salvation = Christ. (Full stop!)

Know your identity in Christ: Who are you? What has He done for you? Write out who you are in Christ. Place this list in a prominent place for the next week; for example, on the back of your bedroom door.

Reflection questions
- Consider who Christ is:
  - Do you see Him as fully sufficient in your life?
  - Do you need to step off the ladder – be it of works, idols, etc.?
  - What of the world do you need to shed?
- How has your culture influenced your Christianity? What does it mean to you to be "spiritual enough"? What does it look like to accept that Jesus is enough for you?
- For what have you been ungrateful? What has taken replaced thankfulness for His gift?
- Why are you doing the things you do? Are you serving Him through your actions?
- Look through the list in Colossians 3:5-10. Ask the Holy Spirit to bring conviction if there are any of these you need to work on. Remember that guilt, shame, and condemnation are NOT the same as conviction! Trust God to bring the change within your heart.

- Meditate on the list in Colossians 3:12-17. Consider how you can practically walk these out in your family, at work, and at church over the next fortnight.

1 THESSALONIANS

Stay strong in your Faith

For God has not destined us for wrath, but to obtain salvation through our Lord Jesus Christ, who died for us so that whether we are awake or asleep we might live with him. Therefore encourage one another and build one another up, just as you are doing. – 1 Thessalonians 5:9-11

During your first reading

Themes to track
- Hope
- Faith
- Suffering/ persecution
- Second coming

During your second reading

Things to notice in the text
- Emotions
- Paul's relationship with the church
- Who (names/ people); for example, "brothers", "imitators", "apostles".
- Christ's return/ day of the Lord
- Instructions for the church

Chapter summaries

These are optional as they can be time consuming for the larger books. If you choose to do them, you will receive a much deeper appreciation of the book. By the end of The IBSC, you will have paraphrased the entire Bible! Go through each chapter and try to summarise it in one paragraph, using your own words; force yourself to stay big picture and capture the heart of each chapter.

After your initial readings

Setting of 1 Thessalonians
<u>Author</u>

1 Thessalonians was written by Apostle Paul.

<u>Recipient</u>

Paul wrote to the church in Thessalonica, which consisted of Greek and Jewish believers.

<u>Date and place of writing</u>

Acts 18 and 19 tell of Paul's missionary journeys and the movement of Timothy. Using these to determine time frames, it is likely that Paul wrote this letter between 50 and 51 AD from Corinth.

<u>Reason written</u>

Paul wrote this letter to affirm the Thessalonian church and to encourage them to persevere during a time of suffering. Wrong beliefs were circulating in regards to Christ's return and Paul wanted to teach them the roots of their wrong beliefs, and establish the church in the truth. It was a letter of encouragement calling them to stand firm in their faith and live holy lives as they wait in hope for the second coming of Christ.

Big picture
<u>Historical background</u>

Paul was fleeing persecution when he first visited Thessalonica and brought the Gospel to them and the church was founded amidst harassment from Jews. The Jews raised questions regarding Paul's motives and conduct; some of these accusations included that Paul was a heretic, deceiver, religious adventurer, and a victimiser of the ignorant. The Thessalonians continued to cling to their faith in Christ despite the suffering they endured for their beliefs.

It is clear that the church had a sound faith in Christ and that Paul loved them dearly. Nevertheless, they were still undergoing the process of growth and sanctification as God weaned them from their worldly mindset. Believers had brought their previous beliefs and practices with them when they converted to Christianity and as a result the church was struggling with sexual immorality. For example, sex and sexual practices were part of the worship of the other cults and religions of the time, and therefore the sanctity of the marriage bed was a foreign concept for the Thessalonian believers.

In addition, the Thessalonian church had come out of a culture fascinated by the end times. Many in the church were living in confusion, and even fear, of Christ's return because of false teachings that had arisen surrounding this anticipated event. A cult had also sprung up, known as the Cabirus cult, which caused further confusion within the church about the time of Christ's return. Cabirus was the city's founding deity. It is believed that he was god to manual labourers, having been a young worker who died unjustly, and then returned as god to bless those who had supported him. Some theologians have hypothosised that this deity was being integrated with the message of Christianity.

Character portrayal – Paul's first visit to Thessalonica[1]

"And Paul went in, as was his custom, and on three Sabbath days he reasoned with them from the Scriptures, explaining and proving that it was necessary for the Christ to suffer and to rise from the dead, and saying, "This Jesus, whom I proclaim to you, is the Christ."

"And some of them were persuaded and joined Paul and Silas, as did a great many of the devout Greeks and not a few of the leading women. But the Jews were jealous, and taking some wicked men of the rabble, they formed a mob, set the city in an uproar, and attacked the house of Jason, seeking to bring them out to the crowd. And when they could not find them, they dragged Jason and some of the brothers before the city authorities, shouting, "These men who have turned the world upside down have come here also, and Jason has received them, and they are all acting against the decrees of Caesar, saying that there is another king, Jesus."

"And the people and the city authorities were disturbed when they heard these things. And when they had taken money as security from Jason and the rest, they let them go.

"The brothers immediately sent Paul and Silas away by night to Berea, and when they arrived they went into the Jewish synagogue."

Book overview

1 Thessalonians encourages a persecuted church to continue to shine their light out for others to see despite their own personal suffering. This light was faith in their salvation and their hope for eternal life. The book is focused on faith and hope; faith to endure the present day, living in holiness; and hope for tomorrow, as they awaited Jesus' second coming and the Kingdom of God.

Paul's message was: "Christ is coming, and no one knows when, so be ready". Paul wanted this dearly loved church to live holy and blameless lives, looking forward to eternity. He encouraged them by reaffirming the big picture: their current persecution was temporal, and they could have hope for the eternal Kingdom of God. Paul wanted to put their minds at ease surrounding the second coming and give them a proper perspective on eternity.

Paul also wanted them to continue to welcome the work of the Holy Spirit in their lives. Paul called them to live lives worthy of imitation as they disciple other believers. They were also called to be witnesses in their society through the example set by their lives. Paul was encouraging a church, strong in their faith, to continue to grow in Christ and be transformed by the truth of the Gospel.

Interpreting the book of 1 Thessalonians

Interpretation questions

1. Why did Paul recount his initial stay with the Thessalonians and the attitude they held when they first received the Gospel?
2. How did Paul view the believers in Thessalonica?
   a. What illustrations did he use to illustrate his relationship with them?

    b. What emotions did he display towards them?

    c. What do you think fostered the feelings Paul had for the Thessalonians?

3. Consider Paul's original readers:

    a. What might have been some of the issues within the Thessalonian church (internal issues) from what Paul writes in 1 Thessalonians 4:1-12 and 5:12-22?

    b. What might have been some of the issues for believers living in Thessalonica (external issues) from what Paul writes in 1 Thessalonians 4:1-12 and 5:12-22?

    c. Conversely, what did Paul commend the church for in 1 Thessalonians 1:2-10 and 3:6-9?

    d. What were the strengths of the church?

4. What response was Paul seeking from his readers?

    a. What commands and instructions did he give to them?

    b. How did he use encouragement to add further passion to their faith, and strengthen them amidst persecution?

5. What does 1 Thessalonians reveal about discipleship? Consider what Christ, Paul and the Thessalonians exemplify of discipleship.

6. What do you learn about hope from this letter?

7. What is the correlation (connection) between faith and hope as shown in 1 Thessalonians?

8. What do you learn of the Holy Spirit through this letter, and how He equips believers in their faith?

9. Think on the illustrations that Paul used surrounding the second coming ("thief", "labour pains", etc.).

    a. Look at each illustration as is, if taken literally.

    b. How was Paul using the illustration in the context of his message?

10. What did Paul convey about the following:

    a. Eternity;

    b. Living with an eternal focus; and

    c. Jesus' second coming?

<u>Creative interpretation</u>

1. Pay attention to the words "like" and "as a" throughout the letter, marking them as you read. Look at the illustrations that Paul was using to portray his message to the Thessalonians.

    a. What picture comes to mind as you read the illustration?

    b. What message was Paul trying to portray to his readers?

    c. How would the illustration have strengthened his message?

Application inspiration

- Would you live differently if you knew the date of Christ's return; why or why not?

- How does it affect your life when you do not know a fact about God?
- What have you learnt about living as a witness through this book? How can you apply it to your life this week?
    - Will it be washing up dishes of work mates after lunch break?
    - Could you take a meal to a neighbour who is going through a hard time?
    - Is there someone you feel compelled to befriend, whom others have avoided or who has been stigmatised?
- What have you learnt about living as a disciple-maker for Christ through 1 Thessalonians? How can you apply it to your life this week?
    - Will you offer to lead a Bible study at church?
    - Do you need to be faithful with the preparation for a ministry in which you are already involved?
    - Do you need to stay longer after the Sunday service to engage in fellowship with your fellow church members?

[1] Acts 17:2-10

2 THESSALONIANS

Day of Christ's Return

Now concerning the coming of our Lord Jesus Christ and our being gathered together to him, we ask you, brothers, not to be quickly shaken in mind or alarmed, either by a spirit or a spoken word, or a letter seeming to be from us, to the effect that the day of the Lord has come. – 2 Thessalonians 2:1-2

During your first reading

Themes to track
- Day of the Lord/ Christ's return
- Suffering and persecution
- Prayer for the persecuted

During your second reading

Things to notice in the text
- Day of the Lord
- Prayers
- Commands
- Who (names): "Man of lawlessness", "Satan", "busy bodies", etc.

Chapter summaries

These are optional as they can be time consuming for the larger books. If you choose to do them, you will receive a much deeper appreciation of the book. By the end of The IBSC, you will have paraphrased the entire Bible! Go through each chapter and try to summarise it in one paragraph, using your own words; force yourself to stay big picture and capture the heart of each chapter.

After your initial readings

Setting of 2 Thessalonians
<u>Author</u>
The epistle of 2 Thessalonians was written by Apostle Paul.

<u>Recipient</u>
The epistle was written to the church of the Thessalonians.

<u>Date and place of writing</u>
It is believed that this second epistle was written very close on the heels of Paul's first epistle to the Thessalonians. The books could have been sent as close as two weeks apart and no further than a year, making the date between 50 and 51 AD. It was probably sent whilst Paul, Timothy, and Silas were still in Corinth.

<u>Reason written</u>
Paul wrote this second epistle to the Thessalonians in order to ease their minds regarding Christ's return. He also rebuked the idle, commanding and encouraging them to do good works and live fruitfully. In addition, Paul offered them encouragement, reminding them that their current persecution was temporal, and God's wrath will come upon the persecutors of His church.

Big picture
<u>Historical background</u>
Paul had already written to the church in Thessalonica about Christ's second coming (1 Thessalonians); however, an unknown event must have occurred between the two letters that made them waver from the reassurance he offered them in his first letter.

The church was still young and inexperienced, which had left them uncertain of the authority they held in Christ. The early church was also affected by false teachings, which left congregations in confusion and fear. Believing they had missed His return, they feared that they were about to suffer the tribulation of God's judgement.

Paul also addressed idleness within the church, as some of the original readers had become idle in anticipation of the end times. These members of the church had become reliant on others to provide for their needs. Another causal factor towards idleness was the Greco-Roman world view, out of which some of the Christians had come. The Greco-Roman world view held work in low opinion, believing it was for slaves to complete, not freemen. They looked down upon those who did manual labour whilst they glorified the mind. Paul used himself as an example of working for one's needs, rather than burdening others.

Refer to 1 Thessalonians' *historical background* for information regarding Thessalonian culture and the religious background of the city.

<u>Character portrayal – confusion in the church</u>

"There was another prophet; come to proclaim the end days are upon us," the thin, tall man shivered. "Those of us remaining are forgotten. It seems our faith was in vain."

"Stop your foolishness, Adir!" Raakel replied. "Paul spoke truth. I feel it in my spirit. When was the last time you prayed to God, and sought the Comforter?"

"Why would He reply, if He has already judged the faithful?"

Raakel walked away in disgust. Paul's letter had come mere months ago and already the church had lost its way. The same fear and confusion was back. Many of his fellow followers of Christ believed the words of divisive men, rather than seeking the Spirit of Truth. Others of the body were falling to idleness, assured of their salvation, and ready for the Kingdom of God to appear any day. Raakel could see the decay in their worship and devotion, but could do nothing to call them back to Paul's words.

Book overview

Paul's heart for the Thessalonians is seen in his first epistle to them. In 2 Thessalonians, Paul's discipleship is seen as he uprooted unsound doctrine and replaced it with truth. He offered the church encouragement to endure their suffering, corrected their wrong beliefs, and gave them instructions for godly living. Paul condemned attitudes of idleness, firmly establishing that God calls believers to live fruitfully at all times. He also reassured the body of Christ that Christ's return would be clearly marked by events that must precede it.

These events surrounding Christ's return centre around a rebellion by the Son of Destruction. Paul stated that the Son of Destruction, or Man of Lawlessness, will be released by the activity of Satan. However, this should not cause fear in the hearts of believers because Christ, by His mere breath and appearance, will kill the Lawless One.

When Christ comes, He will bring righteous judgement upon the earth. He will come from heaven in vengeance upon the disbelieving and disobedient. Those who do not believe are condemned and will suffer eternal separation from God, but believers are justified before Him, having been sanctified by the Spirit and His truth. His saints will glorify Him and be declared worthy of the kingdom. Believers have no need to fear the second coming. They will not miss it and they will not face the vengeance of the Lord. Instead, believers have been declared worthy, and are to live to praise and glorify God.

Help with difficult passages
Man of Lawlessness; 2 Thessalonians 2:1-12

Remember to always start interpretation by looking at what you can observe from the text! Here are some observations that can be made about the Man of Lawlessness:

- Son of destruction;
- Is revealed;
- Opposes and exalts himself over every so called god;

- Proclaims to be God;
- Seats himself in God's temple;
- He is restrained (by something or someone), and will become unrestrained;
- Mystery of lawlessness is already at work;
- Jesus will overthrow him by a mere breath;
- Comes by the activity of Satan;
- Displays power and false signs and wonders.

Common suggestions as to who the Man of Lawlessness is/ was, include:

- *Antiochus Epiphanes*: In 186 BC, he desecrated the temple of Jerusalem by dedicating it to Zeus and sacrificing a pig (an unclean animal by Jewish Law), on the altar. He sat upon the Temple Seat and proclaimed himself to be a god.
- *Caius Caligula*: Emperor of Rome 37-41 AD. He ordered a statue of himself erected in the temple of Jerusalem; however, he died suddenly and his commands were not completed.
- *Nero*: Emperor of Rome 54-68 AD. Committed atrocities against the church. Christians suffered extreme persecution under his reign.
- *Titus*: Emperor of Rome 79-81 AD. Destroyed the temple of Jerusalem in 70 AD, commanding the army of his father, Emperor Vespasian.

Remember the purpose for which Paul was writing this letter. He was calling the Thessalonians back to the truth. He was preparing them for these events so that fear would not overtake them and cause them to fall away from God when the events occurred. The passage would have been reassuring to the original readers as they saw that Jesus would destroy the Man of Lawlessness without effort. There would not even be a fight. In 2 Thessalonians 2:13, Paul went on to remind them that they were chosen of God, and saved through the Spirit of Truth; they had no need to fear.

What and who is holding the Man of Lawlessness back; 2 Thessalonians 2:7

There is only speculation as to what and whom this verse refers. Here are some of the options:

What:

- The Roman Empire, as it brought order and control;
- The principle of law and order;
- Proclamation of the Gospel;
- Power of God;
- Presence of the church or until every tribe and nation has heard the Good News (the missions movement);
- Force of evil; or
- False prophecy.

He:

- Emperor of Rome;
- Political leaders;

- God, Himself;
- Holy Spirit;
- Satan; or
- False prophets.

Remember not to get caught in the details. Know that something will happen before the end times, but *Christ will conquer*!

Interpreting the book of 2 Thessalonians

Interpretation questions

1. What is seen of God's judgement and justice in 2 Thessalonians?
2. What other attributes do you see of God through the book?
3. Looking at the end times and Christ's return:
    a. What is seen of the day of the Lord/ Christ's return?
    b. What are some of the events that Paul listed must come before Christ's return?
    c. How would Paul's letter have encouraged the original reader that they had not missed Christ's return?
    d. How would knowing the things that had to come before His return have encouraged or strengthened their faith amidst persecution?
4. What role does the Holy Spirit play in the lives and sanctification of believers? What else do you learn about the Holy Spirit in this letter?
5. What is the call placed on believers, as given by Paul in 2 Thessalonians? To what actions should this call lead?
6. How would this letter have been an encouragement to the Thessalonians as they suffered persecution and trials for their faith? How did Paul seek to comfort them?
7. How did Paul combat false doctrine through the book? How did he waylay the false beliefs that the church held?
8. What was the significance of Paul's prayers for the original readers?
    a. What did he convey through the prayers?
    b. How did he strengthen and encourage the church through these prayers?
9. What commands and instructions were given to the Thessalonian church for godly living?
10. Why were the original readers being tempted to idleness? How did Paul spur them on to live fruitful and godly lives?

Creative interpretation

1. Write a summary on the day of the Lord.
    a. What do you learn of it in 1 and 2 Thessalonians?
    b. What did Jesus tell about the coming kingdom and the day of His return, as recorded in the Gospels?
    c. If you have completed the study on the prophets, consider what

you learnt about the great day of the Lord during the ongoing prophet's assignment.

2. Using the content of 2 Thessalonians, write a sermon to a church of today encouraging them to stand firm amidst trials. Make it relevant to the type of persecution current believers' face. Try to bring comfort through your teaching, as Paul did to the Thessalonians by addressing their fears and strengthening them in the truth.

Application inspiration

Suffering and persecution

- Do you see suffering as character building?
- Does your faith waver when hard times come?
- How can you embed yourself in the truth and take comfort in your salvation?
- How do you pray for those facing persecution during intercession times? Model a time of intercession on the prayers Paul said for the Thessalonians.

The end times

- Do you see God's judgement as just?
- What were your views about the end times before studying this book? Did they change?
- How can you live well, looking towards eternity?

Idleness

- Are you prone to idleness? Is there an area of life in which you fall into laziness? How might you remedy this?
- Where is the balance between idleness and working oneself to the bone?
- How does this book affect the view you have towards working with diligence?

1 TIMOTHY

Sound Doctrine leads to Godly Living

I hope to come to you soon, but I am writing these things to you so that, if I delay, you may know how one ought to behave in the household of God, which is the church of the living God, a pillar and buttress of the truth. – 1 Timothy 3:14-15

During your first reading

Themes to track
- Sound doctrine
- False teaching
- Church leadership
- Godly living

During your second reading

Things to notice in the text
- Underline commands
- Mark contrasts; for example, "but", "rather".
- Highlight who is being addressed, for example: "deacons", "older men", "widows".
- Underline references to wrong teachings, for example: "taught by demons", "myths".

Chapter summaries
These are optional as they can be time consuming for the larger books. If you choose to do them, you will receive a much deeper appreciation of the book. By the end of The IBSC, you will have paraphrased the entire Bible! Go through each chapter and try to summarise it in one paragraph, using your own words; force

yourself to stay big picture and capture the heart of each chapter.

After your initial readings

Setting of 1Timothy
<u>Author</u>
The epistle of 1 Timothy was written by Apostle Paul.

<u>Recipient</u>
Paul wrote the letter to Timothy who was like a son to him.

<u>Date and place of writing</u>
Paul wrote the letter from within Macedonia, whilst seeking to get back to Ephesus. There has some conjecture of when it was written. Many scholars believe that Paul completed a fourth missionary journey after his first Roman imprisonment. Such a proposal would match the events and locations mentioned in the book. This would date 1 Timothy between 63 and 65 AD.

<u>Reason written</u>
1 Timothy was written as an instructional and mentoring letter to Timothy, in order to warn against false teachers, and instruct him in how to deal with trouble makers. Paul also gave directions to help Timothy select church leaders. He defined godly conduct for Timothy, men, women, slaves, and the rich in the church. He gave further instructions relating to caring for the needy and warned against a love of money.

Big picture
<u>Historical background</u>
Ephesus (where Timothy was ministering)
Ephesus was a Roman seaside city between two major overland trade routes. By New Testament times, trade via the harbour had declined due to clogging of the river with topsoil following extensive deforestation for timber, charcoal, and to create grazing land. The city contained a theatre, baths, gymnasiums, and many impressive buildings. It was home to the temple of Artemis, which brought important additional trade to the city. At this time in the Roman Empire, business transactions took place in temples, and trade guilds were established to seek protection and favour from the gods.

There is conjecture regarding how the city initially came to be established. One belief is that it was an Amazon city, built in its location for its proximity to the birth place of the mother goddess of earth. This goddess was adopted by the Greeks and took on the characteristics of Artemis. In the temple existed an artefact of Artemis said to have come directly from Zeus (Acts 19:35).

Refer to the following verse references for background relating to the Ephesian church, to which Timothy was ministering:
- Ephesians 4:14; 4:22-23; 4:30-31; 5:3-4;

- Acts 19;
- Revelation 2:1-7.

See the *historical background* given for Ephesians for more information.

Gnosticism and false teachings

The false teachers that were disrupting the early church combined Greek philosophy, false religions, and Christianity. Their beliefs contained a dualistic mindset, with the body being seen as evil and only the spirit as good. Teachings against marriage and the eating of certain foods are examples of the false teachings that emanated from their dualistic mindset.

The false teachers taught that the god who created matter was not a good god, believing that a good god cannot create evil. They believed that a good god created emanations of himself, called aeons, and that the final gods of these emanations were evil; it was a progression from good to evil. Combining the above belief with Judaism and Christianity, they taught that the evil aeon took knowledge to Adam and Eve. They also believed that women were the medium of knowledge, and men could get this knowledge by having sex with a woman. For example, the wife to Noah was considered to have been the medium of knowledge to him.

These false teachers further confused the church by teaching that the God of Israel was the evil god who created the world, and the serpent rebelled and gave woman and man knowledge. The serpent was a hero in their beliefs and so, to them, sin was not a problem. They declared that the way to get past sin was to gain knowledge. To them, salvation was all about knowledge. One act of sex (as a man with a woman) passed them through another aeon, and thus brought them a step closer to the good god; it was like climbing a "spiritual ladder".

By these teachings, the false teachers were attacking the very nature and character of God and this false teaching was coming from within the church! They would quote from Scripture to support their teaching, but subtly changed the meaning of the scriptures quoted. They also changed the teachings of Jesus. The false teachers were preaching distortions of the truth to a vulnerable, young church.

Character portrayal - who was Timothy?

Timothy was the son of a Gentile father and Jewish Christian mother. He probably converted to Christianity under Paul and became one of Paul's closest associates. He was given important responsibilities over stewarding young churches founded by Paul. Timothy was an active evangelist and his strongest traits were sensitivity, loyalty, and affection. Paul commended Timothy to the Philippians on these traits. Warnings to be strong[1] suggest that he suffered fearfulness[2] and perhaps youthful lusts[3]. Paul's love for him is clear. Timothy was viewed by Paul in the light of a beloved son.

Book overview

The epistle of 1 Timothy shows that godly living requires a firm foundation in sound doctrine. Without knowledge and understanding of the truth, one will fall into ungodliness. Godly living flows from following sound doctrine and believers must be active in their pursuit of the truth. Paul likened it to training the body; you must put the effort in to see the fruits of righteousness. This change comes through the grace, mercy, and faith of Christ, but believers also have an active role – they must remain planted firmly in the truth.

The epistle of 1 Timothy was written as an instructional letter to a young man of God who was given the leadership of a young church. Paul encouraged Timothy to continue in godliness, and gave instructions for strengthening the church.

The epistle teaches that godly living involves the pursuit of kingdom qualities: love, faith, righteousness, godliness, steadfastness, and gentleness. A godly life is quiet, dignified, self-controlled, and peaceful. The observable fruits are unity of speech, modesty of dress, hospitality, humility, gentleness, the raising of godly families, and not loving money. A church walking in godliness will care for those in need, such as the widows, elderly, and people with disabilities. The body will be rich in good works, display generosity, and set their hope on God to provide for their practical needs. They will intercede on behalf of all. The individual in the body will take responsibility to care for the needs of others, and their security will rest in God. Godly living is shown to be valuable in every way.

Interpreting the book of 1Timothy
<u>Interpretation questions</u>
1. Consider the character of Timothy:
    a. What do you glean about Timothy's faith from the epistle?
    b. What do you learn of his call?
    c. What does Paul desire from Timothy?
    d. List the commands that Paul gave to him and the principles behind the commands.
2. Where was Timothy?
3. What was occurring in Ephesus – inside and outside of the church? Look up additional Scripture references relating to the city and the church in that city.
4. How did Paul use his testimony to bring instruction in godly living?
5. Consider the commands that Paul gave to the church. Be sure to consider historical background when considering these commands.
    a. What commands were given to the church? What should be guarded against?
    b. What was occurring in the congregation that led Paul to give these commands?
    c. How was Paul moving them towards godly living?
    d. How could you rewrite these commands to be relevant in the church today, considering the differences between the cultures?
6. What was Paul's main focus for himself? What was Paul's hope and prayer for the church?
7. What importance did Paul give to teaching and discipleship?
    a. How did Paul combat false teaching?

   b. What do you learn about the process of discipleship?
   c. How was Timothy to bring this about within the Ephesian church?
8. Who is a good leader by Paul's standard?
   a. List some characteristics of leadership, as seen in 1 Timothy.
   b. What is not important when choosing a leader?
9. What do you learn of God and His character?

Creative interpretation
   1. Write character references for each of the people groups that Paul mentions: younger women, older men, widows, slaves, etc. For example, write a description of a young woman living in obedience to Paul's commands; how would she live?
   2. Why are false teachings and wrong doctrine so dangerous to the church? From 1 Timothy, write two to three paragraphs summarising the dangers associated with false teachings and how the church can fight against them.

Application inspiration

- Spend time meditating on, and journaling about, what godly living looks like. Commit to living out the doctrine of grace. Consider:
  o How can the church protect its members and establish them in the truth?
  o What will you do to cling to the truth?
  o Will you allow your brothers and sisters to be pulled away from the truth?
- Reflect on the needy in today's society.
  o Who are those in need?
  o What about the people who are needy, but lazy?
  o What should your response be to the needy? What should be the church's response?
  o When you give, do you point the glory to yourself or to God?
  o Do you teach those in need to rely on God and seek Him to be the Provider of their needs?

[1] 2 Timothy 2:1
[2] 1 Colossians 16:10-11, 2 Timothy 1:7
[3] 2 Timothy 2:22

THE INDUCTIVE BIBLE STUDY COMPANION

2 TIMOTHY

Paul's last letter = one of discipleship

As for you, always be sober-minded, endure suffering, do the work of an evangelist, fulfil your ministry. – 2 Timothy 4:5

During your first reading

Themes to track
- Suffering for the Gospel
- Eternal perspective
- Preaching the Gospel
- Discipleship/ godly leadership
- Fulfilling one's call

During your second reading

Things to notice in the text
- Lists, for example: 2 Timothy 3:1-5 gives a list of what many people will be doing in the last days.
- Commands and the emotion in which they were written.
- Figures of speech, for example: illustrations, similes, and metaphors.

Chapter summaries

These are optional as they can be time consuming for the larger books. If you choose to do them, you will receive a much deeper appreciation of the book. By the end of The IBSC, you will have paraphrased the entire Bible! Go through each chapter and try to summarise it in one paragraph, using your own words; force yourself to stay big picture and capture the heart of each chapter.

After your initial readings

Setting of 2 Timothy
<u>Author</u>

The epistle of 2 Timothy was written by Apostle Paul.

<u>Recipient</u>

Paul wrote the letter to Timothy who was like a son to him.

<u>Date and place of writing</u>

The epistle was written in the last year of Paul's life, during his Roman imprisonment. There is uncertainty whether Paul was released from his first Roman imprisonment (recorded in Acts), conducted another missionary journey, and then was rearrested and killed in Rome. Because of this uncertainty, the book is dated between 63 and 67 AD.

<u>Reason written</u>

Paul saw his death approaching and wanted to encourage Timothy, and give him final instructions. Paul wrote of his life as an example for Timothy to follow – to proclaim the Gospel, resting in the assurance of eternal life, and not focusing on one's physical surroundings. Paul, in the face of false teachings in Asia, and his own imminent death, urged Timothy to always be sober-minded, endure suffering, do the work of an evangelist, and fulfil his ministry. He wished to encourage Timothy to persevere in the faith.

Big picture
<u>Historical background</u>

Refer back to the *historical background* given for 1 Timothy.

Paul's situation

Paul was in jail as he wrote to Timothy. It was his third (or fourth) imprisonment. The text conveys that this was his letter of goodbye; he was about to be martyred for his faith.

Remember the number of times Paul had been beaten, and the other trials he had endured for his faith. Many of the persecutions he suffered are recorded in the books of Acts and 2 Corinthians. As he wrote this letter he was in a physically challenging situation. His final imprisonment would have been a very different environment to the freedom he had known during his previous house-arrests. It was likely that he was confined in an underground Roman Tullianum – a stone, cold prison, where prisoners were held whilst awaiting trial or the death penalty.

Timothy's background

Read Acts 14, referring to Timothy's home city. When Paul and Barnabas healed a man crippled from birth, the people attributed them with god-like status. We read in Acts 14:20-21 that these same people, who would have worshipped them as gods, stoned them after the Jews raised the people to violence. Acts 14:8-19 gives insight to the spiritual atmosphere of the city where Timothy grew up – for example, there was a temple of Zeus right at the city's gates – and yet 2 Timothy 3 shows that Timothy was raised in the Jewish faith, being acquainted with Scripture from his youth. He was raised in a godly home amidst an ungodly society.

Beliefs regarding the end times

Remember the people in Paul's time believed themselves to be in the "last days"; the references to the last days relate to what will happen between Christ's resurrection and His return. He has won victory, but believers wait in an "age of tension" until the coming fullness of the Kingdom of God.

Paul also commanded him to *"avoid such people"* [1], indicating that the people referred to in chapter 3 were already there, and not just to be expected in the last days. When Paul gave negative examples in this letter he was not referring to unbelievers, but primarily to people within the church, who were disrupting the congregation with false teachings.

Character portrayal – Paul in prison

His body aching from past pains, Paul looked around his stone, cold prison cell. He had known great abundance since his conversion, but he had also known deprivation, of which this was the worst. And yet his heart was not defeated and his head refused to be bowed. The visit from Onesiphorus had been timely in restoring his spirits. Yes, his time was running out on earth, but glory awaited him with Christ. Now he was suffering, but still he would rejoice!

A sense of urgency was coursing through his old veins and frail body. There was work to be done for the Gospel. He had fought the good fight, but his time in the boxing ring had not yet come to an end. As he sat pondering his ministry, the face of young Timothy entered his mind and a faint smile lessened the severity of his expression.

Young Timothy, who was strong of personality, yet with a disposition that led him towards self-doubt. How he longed to see his dear friend, nay, his dear son, just one more time! He longed to assure himself that God's work in Timothy's life would continue. Timothy had already proven himself loyal to the call on his life, and faithful to the teachings of his mentor. The young man conducted himself in all godliness, and was faithful, patient, and steadfast. He was proven in trials and persecution. If Timothy could hold to the truth, then he would not fall under fear, but would remain strong in his leadership. Paul wanted to assure himself that Timothy would hold to the knowledge that, in Christ, he had a spirit of power, love, and self-control.

Paul would not let fear of death creep unbidden into his heart at this late hour! Not whilst there were hours left in the day that could be spent serving the One True God! Timothy must be encouraged not to count suffering, or even death, as signs of weakness. Timothy must be encouraged to push on in the faith so that he would remain faithful to the end!

"Lord Jesus, grant me one last meeting with Timothy before you take me to be with you. And if this is not your will, then let this letter at least bring to him the words he needs in order to remain

faithful in his service to you and your Gospel . . ."

Paul pulled forward the last few sheets of parchment Onesiphorus had brought to him, even as he continued to assure himself that Timothy would persevere in godly living as he had done from youth.

Book overview

The book of 2 Timothy gives believers encouragement to endure persecutions in the hope of their eternal calling. It is a call to live lives focused on proclaiming the truth.

Paul was a prisoner for Christ, suffering for the Gospel, as he penned this letter. However, because he was assured of his place in Christ, he was not ashamed of His suffering, despite his culture, which viewed such suffering as shameful.

Paul started his letter by thanking God as he remembered Timothy, who was constantly in his prayers. This theme is seen throughout the book as Paul reminisced of his journey with Timothy, which had involved friendship, fellowship, and mentorship.

It seems that Timothy was coming under some fear in his leadership, but Paul wrote to remind him that, in Christ, they had a spirit of power, love, and self-control. Paul encouraged Timothy to continue in the beliefs he had learnt from Paul and through study of the Scripture. Paul charged him to be ready to preach the Word at all times and commended his young disciple for his loyalty, having followed Paul's teaching, conduct, aim in life, faith, patience, love, and steadfastness in persecutions.

Paul saw members of the church swerving from the truth, saying that the resurrection had already happened, and who, by doing so, were causing their brethren distress. He was clear on the folly of those who were preaching false teaching, and forcibly told of the danger such people pose to the church. He warned caution towards the false teachers, and wisdom in dealing with them. Despite the false teaching in Asia, and despite the lies being proclaimed, Paul knew that the truth would endure. The letter called Timothy to remember the Gospel, to remember Christ, and to rightly handle the truth.

Interpreting the book of 2 Timothy

Interpretation questions

    1. Where was Paul as he wrote the epistle to Timothy?
        a. How did he view his circumstances?
        b. What emotions would he likely have been experiencing?
        c. Why was he conveying these to Timothy?
    2. From all the people to whom Paul could have written he chose Timothy.
        a. Why Timothy?
        b. Who was Timothy to Paul?
        c. How did Paul feel towards him?
        d. What commands did he give to Timothy, and why?
    3. Look at the character of Timothy.
        a. What do you learn of him through 2 Timothy?
        b. How does this build on what you saw of him in 1 Timothy?

   c. What gifts had he been given?
   d. What was his ministry/ call?
   e. With what might he have been struggling?
   f. Also consider what you learn of him in: Acts 16:1; Acts 16:3; 1 Corinthians 4:17; 1 Corinthians 16:10; Philippians 2:22; 1 Thessalonians 3:2; Hebrews 13:23.

4. How do you think Timothy felt towards Paul?
   a. How do you think he would have responded emotionally to this letter?
   b. What may have changed in his actions, or life, as a response to the letter?

5. Three positive examples were given in a row at the beginning of chapter 2.
   a. What were these images depicting?
   b. Through them, what was Paul illustrating to Timothy?
   c. What was their message?
   d. Also consider 2 Timothy 4:7.

6. Consider the conditional statements (if x, then y) in chapter 2:11-13.
   a. How do these relate to the significance of choice?
   b. Notice that the last is a statement of fact, regarding God's character. What does this show of God contrasted with man?

7. When looking at the verses relating to the last days, see also:
   a. Acts 2:17/ Joel 2:28
   b. Hebrews 1:2
   c. 1 John 2:8
   d. 2 Peter 3:3

8. How did the church in Asia respond to Paul's imprisonment?
   a. Why do you believe they responded in this way?
   b. How should they have responded?
   c. What motivated Paul to endure these sufferings?

9. Who are "the elect" referred to in 2 Timothy?

10. Contrast the list of qualities portraying ungodly character to the list of qualities portraying righteousness.

11. What role does Scripture play in the Christian walk?

12. What do you learn of Christ through 2 Timothy?

13. What do you learn of the Holy Spirit?

14. What is shown of Paul's relationship with God?

15. What was Paul's primary focus?

16. What do you learn of discipleship through this book?

17. How did Paul convey principles of godly living to his disciples?

Creative interpretation

1. Depict a scene at the church in Ephesus, considering a few different characters who might have been present, from the commands and lists that Paul gave in 2 Timothy.

2. Write a few paragraphs on Timothy's reaction to receiving the letter from

Paul. Consider his thoughts, feelings, and actions.

3. Summarise what you learn in 2 Timothy of enduring hardship and persecution, clinging to the hope of eternal life.

Application inspiration

Personal reflection questions

- Allow Paul's life to bring a challenge to your own. Ask:
  o How can I become more effective for heaven in this life?
  o How do I want to live my life on a daily basis?
  o When I am at the end of my life, what do I want to look back and see?
  o What do I want my legacy to be? How will I be remembered?
  o Daily choices matter. How will I live my life today, in order to complete the task that God has given me to do?

- Consider your call. Consider what God has entrusted into your care. Consider:
  o What has God spoken to me?
  o What have I done with it?
  o In what areas am I weak? In what areas do I struggle with sin?
  o What hinders my faithfulness to God and His commands?
  o Ask the Holy Spirit to bring illumination and revelation.

The last days

- What wrong teaching about the last days have you heard preached at church, by the media, and in society?
- Why is it important to go back to Scripture when hearing contentious teachings?
- How do wrong teachings cause confusion in the body? Why are they disruptive to the church of Christ?

[1] 2 Timothy 3:5

TITUS

Godly living & Sound doctrine

For the grace of God has appeared, bringing salvation for all people, training us to renounce ungodliness and worldly passions, and to live self-controlled, upright, and godly lives in the present age, waiting for our blessed hope, the appearing of the glory of our great God and Savior Jesus Christ, who gave himself for us to redeem us from all lawlessness and to purify for himself a people for his own possession who are zealous for good works. – Titus 2:11-14

During your first reading

Themes to track
- Sound doctrine
- Teaching
- Leadership
- Godly living through grace

During your second reading

Things to notice in the text
- Mark who (people/ groups); for example: "elders", "Cretans", "circumcision party", "older women".
- Underline instructions and commands.
- Mark lists, for example: Titus 1:6 lists the attributes of an elder.

Chapter summaries
These are optional as they can be time consuming for the larger books. If you choose to do them, you will receive a much deeper appreciation of the book. By the end of The IBSC, you will have paraphrased the entire Bible! Go through each chapter and try to summarise it in one paragraph, using your own words; force yourself to stay big picture and capture the heart of each chapter.

After your initial readings

Setting of Titus
<u>Author</u>

Titus was written by Apostle Paul.

<u>Recipient</u>

Titus was the primary recipient of the letter, but it would also have been read out to the church congregations of the Island of Crete.

<u>Date and place of writing</u>

Some scholars argue that the letter was written during one of Paul's imprisonments, but this option becomes less probable since the text declares that he hoped to winter in Nicopolis. The book shows that Paul left Titus behind in Crete, but the book of Acts does not describe a situation with Paul and Titus together in Crete. Other epistles suggest that Paul was released from his first Roman imprisonment (recorded in Acts 27-28) around 62 AD. It is therefore likely that Titus was written from Nicopolis (Titus 3:12) between 62 and 67 AD.

<u>Reason written</u>

Paul wrote to Titus to encourage him in his leadership and ministry. Paul also desired to see godly leadership, and the teaching of sound doctrine, established in the Cretan church, and to ensure that the people were living godly lives.

Big picture
<u>Historical background</u>
What is known of Titus

Titus appears to have been an uncircumcised believer [1]. He was a close associate of Paul, a good pastor, and showed genuine pastoral concern for those under his discipleship [2].

Crete and the Cretans

In Greek mythology, Mt Ida, located on the Island of Crete, was the birth place of Zeus, who was the head of the Greek gods. Cretans were worshippers of Zeus and their name for him was "saviour". The word "Saviour" appears by percentage of words in the book more than any other book of the Bible. Zeus was known for being a liar. When Paul wrote to Titus: *"God, who never lies"* [3], he was distinguishing the True God from the mythological Zeus. Paul wanted to separate Zeus and his attributes from the True God in the minds of the Cretan congregation. Paul was reinforcing to the original readers that Jesus is the True Saviour of man.

Paul's quote: *"Cretans are always liars, evil beasts, lazy gluttons"* [4], is attributed to Epimenides, a philosopher-poet and prophet, from the poem "Cretica". The poem was a song to Zeus, declaring him immortal, despite the claims of those in Crete that Zeus was mortal. Epimenides is believed to have lived during the sixth century BC.

Cretans were present on the day of Pentecost [5] and Paul's first visit (without Titus) is recorded in Acts 27.

What was the Circumcision Party?

The Circumcision Party was a contingent of Jews that followed Paul around in his ministry, contradicting Paul's teachings on circumcision. Paul taught that Christ alone was sufficient for salvation, whereas the Circumcision Party said that, because circumcision was the sign of the covenant Christ fulfilled, it was a necessary part of salvation. Paul declared in Romans 2:29 that circumcision, under the new covenant of grace, was a spiritual circumcision of man's heart. The Circumcision Party was not concerned about Paul's teachings on Christ, but rather on maintaining the Jewish practice of male circumcision.

Character portrayal – Titus ponders Paul's letter

Titus sat with Paul's letter in his hand, bent forward over his writing desk to think over Paul's instructions. The church would meet tomorrow, and he would read Paul's latest letter to the congregation. It had been several weeks since he last stirred from home and, after reading the letter out in his home congregation, Titus knew he would need to journey to each town and spend time with the different congregations to read Paul's letter to them, establish elders, and see that they were walking in the truth.

His mind had already begun filtering through the men of his congregation and a few likely candidates for elders had come to mind. Added to the charge to appoint elders, Titus needed to bring teaching to the different groups within the churches. Perhaps he could ask old Esther to help with the teaching of the women; she was a devoted daughter of God and Titus felt confident he could trust her with the duty.

Titus continued reviewing the men and women he knew in the congregations across the towns of Crete long into the night, considering his next actions for the discipleship and growth of the community of believers living on the island.

Book overview

The book of Titus deals with leadership issues within the church of Crete. Titus had been left in Crete to establish church leadership, and Paul was encouraging him to fulfil this charge. Paul gave Titus guidelines regarding how to select godly men to serve as church elders and overseers. The future of the Cretan church had been entrusted to Titus.

The book also gives instructions on how the wider congregation of believers were to live. Paul sought to establish the church in grace and knowledge of the truth, knowing that the fruit of these things would be godly lives. The people were reminded that they were saved through grace, and Paul used this as an encouragement to give grace to those who still did not know the Lord. Paul wanted to ensure the congregation continued in the knowledge that it is the Holy Spirit who is responsible for continued transformation and renewal in the lives of believers.

The book of Titus is one of discipleship for leaders and congregations. It shows that sound doctrine leads to godly deeds and encourages vigilance against those who would distort the truth.

Interpreting the book of Titus
<u>Interpretation questions</u>
1. Consider Paul's instructions for the appointing of elders and overseers.
    a. What attributes were listed for a church elder?
    b. What attributes were listed for a church overseer?
    c. What should they not be like?
    d. What might these lists imply about the culture in Crete, and within the Cretan church?
    e. Are these lists relevant to the church today? Why or why not?
2. For what were the people of Crete renowned?
3. What was the emotional climate of the letter to Titus?
4. What were Paul's commands for the congregation?
    a. Why were they being called to live this way?
    b. To what would such characteristics lead?
5. Make a table listing the attributes of the Cretan church. Comment on their strengths and weaknesses, which can be seen from what Paul was challenging them to improve, and for what he encouraged them.
6. Make contrasting lists looking at "good deeds" and "ungodly deeds" identified in the book. Similarly, make contrasting lists of "worldly characteristics" and "godly living".
7. What is said of the Circumcision Party?
    a. Why was Paul against them?
    b. Why were they dangerous to the church?
    c. How were they disrupting the church and Paul's ministry? (You can also use in your answer information gained from Paul's other letters where the Circumcision Party comes up, such as Galatians).
    d. What commands did Paul give to Titus regarding the Circumcision Party?
8. What were Paul's instructions for Titus' teachings? Why was it necessary for Paul to emphasise these?
9. How were the Cretans charged to live towards those outside the church, and for what purpose?
    a. What was the significance of this charge, coming straight after Paul reminded them of how they came to salvation and who they were before they came to be in Christ?
    b. What are the implications for evangelism?
10. How does Titus contrast evangelism (ministry to unbelievers) with that of discipleship (ministry to believers)?

<u>Creative interpretation</u>
1. Research further information on the history of Crete as the mythological birthplace of Zeus. Write a story on how Zeus differs to Christ as saviour, showing how much better Christ the True Saviour is to Zeus. Be sure to include the reasons for Christ's superiority, and use the book of Titus to

support your story's argument.

2. Draw a picture representing what the family life of a godly elder should look like. You could also depict the characteristics Paul wanted to see from individual groups within the church, as listed in Titus 2.

Application inspiration

- Using your lists of "good deeds" and "ungodly deeds" from your interpretation, write down/ say how :-
  - o Politicians living out the ungodly deed would affect the governing of your nation.
  - o Government would be affected if all politicians lived according to the list of godly deeds.
- After seeing these two extremes, think of the difference a single Christian could make if living out the godly principles within government.
- What areas cause division amongst the church today (just as you saw that issues regarding circumcision, Jewish myths, arguments, and so on were dividing the church in Crete)? What is one small step that you could do to break this divide? For example, could you invite a few people over for coffee from you church with whom you do not usually interact, in order to help build unity?
- The Circumcision Party was teaching that the people needed laws and works to be saved. Ask God to reveal any works that you may be putting above His grace.

---

[1] Galatians 2:3
[2] 2 Corinthians 8:16-17; 8:23; 12:18
[3] Titus 1:2
[4] Titus 1:12
[5] Acts 2

PHILEMON

Appeal for Onesimus

I appeal to you for my child, Onesimus, whose father I became in my imprisonment. – Philemon
1:10

During your first reading

Themes to track

- True forgiveness
- Reconciliation within the church
- Cost of being a Christian
- Brotherly love

During your second reading

Things to notice in the text

- Character of Philemon
- Character of Onesimus
- Character of Paul
- Highlight emotions and emotional passages.
- Mark connectives, for example: "for", "so that", "because".

Chapter summaries

These are optional as they can be time consuming for the larger books. If you choose to do them, you will receive a much deeper appreciation of the book. By the end of The IBSC, you will have paraphrased the entire Bible! Go through each chapter and try to summarise it in one paragraph, using your own words; force yourself to stay big picture and capture the heart of each chapter.

After your initial readings

Setting of Philemon
<u>Author</u>
Philemon was written by Apostle Paul.

<u>Recipient</u>
The book was primarily written to Philemon, but also named are: Apphia, Archippus, and the church that met in Philemon's house. From comparing the names given in the book of Philemon to those in Colossians, it is likely that the *"church in [Philemon's] house"*[1] was a reference to the Colossian church.

<u>Date and place of writing</u>
Paul was in prison at the time he penned this letter. Theologians disagree regarding the exact date the book was written as there are three known incidences of Paul being in prison. However, it seems that it was written sometime between 55 AD (imprisoned in Ephesus) and 58-62 AD (imprisoned in Rome). Considering the book suggests that he was under house arrest and experiencing some degree of freedom in daily life, with the evidence in Acts 28:30-31, it is likely that it was written during his Roman imprisonment, around 60-62 AD.

<u>Reason written</u>
The book was written as an appeal to Philemon, asking him to extend grace and forgiveness towards Onesimus, who was his runaway slave. Paul sought to reconcile Onesimus to his owner, Philemon, and to encourage the Colossian congregation to welcome Onesimus back into their midst as a brother.

Big picture
<u>Historical background</u>
It is very important to step away from the modern-day view of slavery when interpreting the book of Philemon in order to see it through the eyes of those in the Colossian church. Slavery was a part of Roman culture, and their economy was dependent upon it. This is not to say that it was right, but it needs to be remembered that slavery was the norm. Slaves were common, but expensive, and because they were expensive, they were usually well treated by their masters.

However, Roman laws regarding slaves that ran away were extremely harsh because the Roman Empire was built upon slavery. Not only could the runaway slave be put to death, but all the slaves of that household could be executed as punishment. Consequences also existed for those who harboured runaway slaves. Paul would have been liable for the time Onesimus was with him and required to pay back, in value, the work that Onesimus would have completed for Philemon during the time of his absence.

The Empire could not risk an uprising from amongst the slaves – as ninety percent of the population in the city of Rome were slaves, freemen were severely outnumbered. That is why the punishment for running away was death; it ensured the survival of the Empire by protecting the survival of their economy.

Character portrayal – Onesimus returns home

Onesimus quivered as he approached the end of his journey back to Colossae. He knew that he went with all the protection Paul could give him, but he also knew that it was more than within Philemon's rights to put him to death for having escaped.

Onesimus could not pin-point the reason why he had run away – he had known it to be wrong; Philemon had been a fair master, nay, a kind one even; and the title of "slave" had never irked him. He had entered slavery as the result of unpaid debts, and that decision had saved him from greater trials. Whatever the reason had been, the fact remained that he had escaped and found his way to Rome. There he had become desperate. He had nowhere to go to find honest work, and his stomach had grown hungry.

Thank the Lord that he had heard whispers of Paul being imprisoned in that very city! Onesimus had sought Paul out, remembering the stern yet loving follower of Christ, whom his master respected. He had been certain that he would be received by Paul, and so he had been. He worked hard for Paul, and Paul, in turn, saw that his physical needs were met. Over time, a love had formed between them, and Onesimus had come to know the Lord. Onesimus served Paul as a loyal son, and Paul had discipled Onesimus in the ways of the Lord.

A time had come when Paul had felt called to send him back to his master. Paul had discussed it with him and, though his heart was fearful, Onesimus knew it was the right thing to do. As he breathed in the dust of the road, Onesimus prayed for God's protection over himself, God's wisdom to fall upon Philemon, and God's favour to be bestowed upon Paul, who had brought him to Christ and eternal salvation.

Book overview

Paul dearly loved Onesimus and was determined to do all that was possible to protect him as he returned to his master. If Paul had not written this letter, Onesimus would probably have been severely punished or even killed, as this was the culturally acceptable way of treating a run-away slave.

Whilst the outcome of Onesimus' return home remains unknown, the principles of Paul's letter remain. Paul sought to bring forgiveness and reconciliation between two children of God. He was showing that worldly rank and status are not significant in the Kingdom of God, and that the ways of love ask a higher personal cost than the ways of the world. It may have cost Philemon his pride and status to forgive Oneimus, but it was what love demanded.

Interpreting the book of Philemon
Interpretation questions

1. Paul calls Onesimus his child, whose father he became in prison.
   a. What did he mean by this term?
   b. What does it convey of his relationship with Onesimus?
   c. What motive might have compelled him to call Onesimus his

child in this letter?

2. Why was Paul sending Onesimus back, even when he said he wanted to keep him with him (Philemon 1:13-14), and knowing his life was at stake?

3. How could Onesimus be a slave of Philemon, if Philemon was the leader of the church and slavery is wrong? Use the information given in *historical background* to help form your answer.

4. In light of what you know about slavery at the time Paul penned this letter, how might Philemon have felt when Onesimus arrived bearing Paul's letter?

5. Why did Paul not command Philemon to welcome Onesimus back into his household?

6. Why do you believe that Paul did not directly seek to abolish slavery within the church?

7. Remember that Paul addressed his epistle to Philemon, Apphia, Archippus, and the church. Why did Paul write the letter not only to Philemon, but to the whole church in his house?

8. Look at how Paul tells Philemon to treat Onesimus: *"welcome him as you would welcome me"* [2].

   a. How would Philemon have welcomed Paul?

   b. What were the implications of these instructions?

   c. Do you think that Philemon would have been popular in his community if he had followed through with such a command? How may have his fellow slave-owners responded if he welcomed Onesimus as a brother?

   d. How may have following Paul's command affected Philemon's household, and other households within the church?

9. What does this letter show about Paul's style of mentoring churches and believers?

10. What does the book show about the call for the church to walk in forgiveness and love towards one another?

Creative interpretation

1. Try and put yourself in the shoes of each of the main characters: Paul, Onesimus, Philemon, and the Colossian church.

   a. Picture how they would have felt before this letter was sent, and upon receipt of the letter.

   b. Write a short paragraph for each of these four groups expressing how they felt – the mix of emotions, the wrestling with decisions, and the way they looked at the other people in the situation.

   c. Write each of their names at the top of a blank page and then search through magazines for words or pictures that express these emotions.

Application inspiration

- Who did you most identify with in the story: Paul, Onesimus, Philemon or the church?

- o Write a story, in character, and discuss the character's feelings surrounding the situation of Onesimus' return.
- o Underneath, write why you relate to the character and how their circumstances or emotions resonate with your current circumstances.

- Is there anyone that you need to forgive? Is there anyone in your church that you need to accept and welcome into your heart as a brother or sister in Christ?
- With whom do you need to walk out true repentance? How will you practically seek reconciliation with this person? It might be over a small matter within your home or a greater matter that has stewed in your heart over many years.

[1] Philemon 1:2
[2] Philemon 1:17

HEBREWS

Supremacy of Christ brings Hope

Therefore he had to be made like his brothers in every respect, so that he might become a merciful and faithful high priest in the service of God, to make propitiation for the sins of the people. For because he himself has suffered when tempted, he is able to help those who are being tempted. –
Hebrews 2:17-18

During your first reading

Themes to track
- Superiority of Christ/ Jesus is greater
- Endurance in suffering
- Confidence in Christ

During your second reading

Things to notice in the text
- Mark comparisons: "better than", "greater", "superior", "old", "new".
- Circle repeated words: "priest", "rest", "faith, "covenant"/ "Law".
- Underline commands: "do not . . .", "make every effort . . .", "encourage . . ."
- Underline promises: "will receive . . .", ". . . will all know me".

Chapter summaries
These are optional as they can be time consuming for the larger books. If you choose to do them, you will receive a much deeper appreciation of the book. By the end of The IBSC, you will have paraphrased the entire Bible! Go through each chapter and try to summarise it in one paragraph, using your own words; force yourself to stay big picture and capture the heart of each chapter.

After your initial readings

Setting of Hebrews

The setting of Hebrews remains largely unknown. Outlined below are some of the more accepted arguments for its authorship, audience, date written, and place of writing.

Author

In modern times, Paul has become a more accepted candidate for author; however, the letter is not of his style, and he claims authorship in all his other epistles. Paul also claimed first-hand revelation of Christ (Galatians 1:12) whereas the author of Hebrews was a second-hand hearer of the Gospel (Hebrews 2:3). More evidence exists for Silas as author (although it is unknown whether he possessed adequate Jewish background), Apollos (shown in Acts to have great biblical knowledge, plus he knew Timothy and Paul), or Priscilla aided by her husband, Aquila (they were Jews and the book of Acts records that they came from Italy when Claudius commanded the Jews to leave Rome).

The authorship argument for this book is still summed up best by Origen, the Alexandrian church father who died about 255 AD. He said: *"But who it was that really wrote the epistle, God only knows."*

Recipient

The most accepted argument is that it was written to the church in Rome given that: there is a greeting for them from Italians living abroad, Timothy was known in Rome, the Roman church had a Jewish Christian population, and historical events in Rome match the focus of the author's exhortation to his audience.

Date and place of writing

If the Roman church is taken as the recipient, then it was likely written after the persecution under Claudius between 49 and 54 AD (Hebrews 10:32-34) and before the temple was destroyed in 70 AD (Hebrews 8-10). It was likely written as persecutions began under Nero's reign, but before they intensified (Hebrews 12:4), narrowing the date range to between 64 and 65 AD.

Because we do not know who wrote the book it is nearly impossible to make a guess at where it was written. Hebrews 13:24 reads as if it was written from Rome; however, *"those who come from Italy"* is generally interpreted to mean that natives of Italy, who are now living away from Italy, were sending their greetings back to those still in Italy. This fits with the Jewish population having dispersed throughout the Empire during Claudius' reign.

Reason written

Hebrews was written as a warning to Jewish Christians not to submit to the temptation to turn back to Judaism, which would have protected them from persecution during the reign of Nero (see *historical background*). The author encouraged his audience to stand firm in the promises of Christ, who is the fulfilment of both God's promise to Abraham and the Law of Moses.

Big picture
Historical background
Religion and the Jewish Audience

Angels held an elevated rank in the eyes of the people. They were worshipped in many cults and the Rabbis (at that time in history) taught that it was the angels who brought the Law to Moses.

The Jewish Christian audience was wrapped in an identity established from five essential components of the Law:

1. *Priesthood:* The priests acted as mediators between God and His people.
2. *Tabernacle:* After the fall, the tabernacle became God's dwelling place with man. God is a holy God and cannot abide with sinful people. To enter the tabernacle, worshippers needed to go through cleaning rituals, which provided the needed purification.
3. *Sacrificial system:* The means of atoning for their sins. Sin is costly and requires the shedding of blood. The sacrificial system showed the Jews that sin has a price. To be restored in relationship with God, the individual had to bring, and kill, an animal, which was a financial burden upon their family.
4. *Feasts and celebrations:* The Jewish feasts and festivals called the people to remember what God had done for them. The Jewish calendar of religious events held a strong role in forming their identity as a nation.
5. *Consequences:* The old covenant taught that actions have consequences. There were blessings for obedience and curses for disobedience.

Important dates in the church of Rome:

- *30 AD:*
  The church of Rome was founded at Pentecost (Acts 2). It began primarily as a Jewish population of believers, who would have placed continued focus on circumcision, reading the Torah, and keeping Jewish festivals, dates, and celebrations.

- *49 AD:*
  Emperor Claudius expelled the Jews from Rome, who dispersed into the greater Empire. As a result, Gentiles went from being the minority within the church of Rome, to the overwhelming majority. The church completely changed shape as it became a Gentile church, with rules, regulations and Jewish practices slipping away.

- *54 AD:*
  The new emperor, Nero, allowed the Jews to return and placed them under legal protection. Conflict between Gentile believers and the returning Jewish Christians saw separate churches forming.

- *64 AD:*
  Before the rise of Emperor Nero, the Roman government had been on

friendly terms with Christians. However, succumbing to excess and plunging into immorality, Nero speedily used up the riches of the treasury and began stealing from nobles. He also rid himself of his best advisors. On the 18th of July, 64 AD, a great fire began in the city of Rome. Out of the fourteen regions of the city, seven were completely destroyed, and four were partially burned. To divert suspicion from himself, Emperor Nero turned the blame onto the Christians. From then on, persecution of believers spiralled to greater heights of torture. This included wrapping them in animal skins and feeding them to dogs, crucifixion, and making them into human torches to light the emperor's feast. Remember that the majority of scholars believe Hebrews was written as the Neronain persecution was beginning, but before Nero's truly horrendous acts of cruelty.

Character portrayal – temptation to return to Judaism

Matthew has returned to his family, Markus reflected. His family had accepted him home. He could not believe that Matthew would betray the body of Christ in such a way! It was attractive, of course: to be embraced by one's mother and father again as one back from the dead. Markus' own parents had held a funeral for him when he turned to Christ, and he had been forced to leave behind his earthly possessions. Those first few months were days of trial as he relied on hand outs from the brethren until he was able to re-establish himself in the business world, finding employment helping a fellow believer in his cloth business.

And now, Emperor Nero was turning eyes onto Christians as scapegoats. Markus knew that the Roman populace feared an uprising from the church because they professed a coming kingdom, other than that of Rome. The fellowship of communion was also believed to be a cannibalistic practice. The misconceptions saddened Markus. They were so far from the truth!

Markus knew that some believers had laughed at the populace's wrong assumptions when they first became known, but everyone was too scared to laugh now. More and more Jewish believers were returning to their former ways in order to protect themselves, their families, and their earthly possessions. Markus clung to Christ, and the hope he had in Him, but he feared what choice he would make if faced with renouncing Christ or being burnt alive as a human torch at one of the emperor's dinner parties.

Book overview

Jewish believers in Rome experienced persecution under Claudius, and were now facing greater horrors under Nero. However, the Jewish Christians in Rome had a way out that their Gentile brethren did not have – they could go back to Judaism, and receive the Emperor's legal protection. This is all they had to do to protect their families, possessions, and lives – they just had to go back to their old way of life – except that the cost was renouncing Christ. They would not be allowed back into the synagogues without denying Jesus. The Jewish believers of Rome had a special temptation to deny Christ.

The author made a case for Christ, and the covenant He brought in, by comparing Him to things of old for the Jews. Hebrews shows that Christ is the great High Priest and the only acceptable sacrifice for sin. Jesus is shown to be superior to the angels and to the prophets, who were revered by the Jews. He is greater than all the heroes of the Jewish faith, for it was in Him that these very heroes had set their hopes. Christ has become the minister of a more excellent covenant.

Christ and the new covenant are shown to be superior in all ways to the old covenant. His priesthood is superior to the Levitical priesthood, for He was without sin, whereas the priests had to atone for their sins and those of the people. Not only is He shown to be High Priest, He was also the greater sacrifice; sanctification through His blood does not need to be repeated continually as sacrifices were under the old covenant. Christ died once, for all.

The original readers were given hope to endure persecutions in the truth that Christ has inherited an eternal kingdom that is still to come, and believers are welcomed into this kingdom. He is the High Priest forever and will bring believers into the inner sanctuary, into the very presence of the Father. The promise of old was for physical rest, tempting to the readers, but Christ came to give spiritual rest, which is worth one's perseverance. He is holy, innocent, unstained, separated from sinners, perfect forever, and exalted above the heavens. He died once, for all sin. Jesus is the Founder and Perfector of the Faith.

The original readers were exhorted not to turn back to their old lives in Judaism, but move forward with endurance and faithfulness for Jesus is superior.

Help with difficult passages

[Christ] perfect through suffering – Hebrews 2:10

The Greek word used is "teleioo", which means to "consummate, fulfil, or be completed" (Strong, J., 1989)[1]. We know that Christ was perfect, without sin, and the author confirms this in 4:15. So the author was not referring to one who had sin being made holy, but rather that God's plan was perfected, or made complete, through Christ's victory on the cross. The plan was perfected and finished because of what He suffered.

Is it possible to lose one's salvation? – Hebrews 6:4-6

When interpreting this passage, look at the verses before and after it (study the passage in its context). The author had been talking about leaving the elementary teachings of faith to push forward into maturity. Immediately after this passage, the author referred to them as "beloved", the only time in Hebrews where this term is used. It does not seem likely that he was driving them towards fear of their eternal position, but rather trying to encourage them not to go back to the old ways in Judaism, for what they had in Christ was so much better.

Always consider what the passage would mean to the original readers before you try to fit it into a modern theology. The author was urging them not to go back to Judaism. The original readers were left with a choice to renounce Christ (and return to a protected life in Judaism for them and their families), or cling to the hope they had in Christ (and face persecution in this life).

For those who want to go deeper into doctrinal beliefs, you can consider the two main theologies that people hold in light of the security of salvation.

1. The first is that of eternal salvation: once saved, always saved. Those approaching the passage with this view point will say that the author is speaking hypothetically (not that it can happen, but if it could), or that the passage is not referring to believers, but to those standing on the edge of conversion.

2. The second theological standpoint is that of apostasy: a believer rejecting Christ. Those approaching the passage with this view point may say viewpoint may say that believers who fall away cannot return to Christ's salvation if they maintain their rejection of Him, or alternatively, that believers who fall away cannot return to Christ's salvation (although this is to limit Christ's work on the cross).

Interpreting the book of Hebrews

Interpretation questions

1. Who is Christ, as revealed in Hebrews?
    a. What names were used for Him? What do these names indicate about His character, nature, and relationship in the Holy Trinity?
    b. Where is Christ's position with regard to authority?
    c. What has Christ accomplished?
    d. How did the author testify to His deity?

2. Discuss how Hebrews shows Christ to be greater than angels, the prophets, Moses (a patriarch of the faith), Joshua (who brought the Israelites physical rest), the Levitical priesthood, and the sacrificial system, and how He brought a greater covenant.
    a. Why was it important for the original readers that the author demonstrate Christ's superiority to each of these beings, people, and systems?
    b. Why did the author choose to compare Christ to this list?
    c. How would the original readers, if swayed by the author's argument, receive courage to persevere through the knowledge of Christ's superiority over these individuals and groups?

3. What do you learn of the Father in Hebrews?
    a. What is revealed of His nature through His actions?
    b. What do you learn of His interaction in the Holy Trinity?

4. What do you learn of the Holy Spirit in Hebrews?
    a. What do you learn of His interaction with the Father and the Son?
    b. How is He active in the lives of believers?

5. What is said of salvation?
    a. What is said of the position of believers before God, in Christ?
    b. Why would the message of salvation have given confidence to the Jews in the congregation?
    c. In his message, why did the author emphasise the confidence believers can have in Christ?

  d. How would a focus on eternal salvation have encouraged the original readers to endure through hardships and persecutions?

6. What is the role of a High Priest? Refer back to Leviticus for background, especially Leviticus 16 and 21:1-22:16.

7. See Exodus 38:21 and 40:9-15 to learn of the perpetual nature of the Levitical priesthood. Read of Melchizedek in Genesis 14 and Psalm 110. Then consider:

  a. Who was Melchizedek?

  b. What did the author say about with the idea of Christ being of the order of Melchizedek?

  c. What does the author relate of Melchizedek and his background in Hebrews? What else can you discover about Melchizedek through Genesis 14 and Psalm 110? How does this correlate to Christ and His life?

  d. Why was the author using him to compare the old priesthood to a new order of which Christ is the High Priest?

  e. What argument did the author make for Christ being a superior High Priest of the order of Melchizedek?

  f. Note that Melchizedek was both a priest of the Most High God and a king, whereas a Levitical priest could not be made king. How would this be significant to the author's argument that Christ is High Priest and King?

8. The author of Hebrews was arguing for a new covenant, which Christ brought in. Consider:

  a. How did the Law, sacrificial system (including the priesthood, atoning sacrifices, and tabernacle), and old covenant foreshadow the coming of Christ?

  b. What is the connection between the Law and the priesthood?

  c. In what ways is the Law of Christ better than the Law that was given to Moses?

9. Look at the new covenant:

  a. What is required of man?

  b. What is God's part in the covenant?

  c. What are the promises of the covenant?

10. What is the significance of faith in the life of a believer? What is the significance of faith to enduring through persecution?

11. What is said of hope, and how does it relate to rest?

  a. Why did the author focus on the promised rest for God's people?

  b. Why would this have enabled the original readers to remain steadfast in their faith?

12. How was Christ held up as an example for the original readers to persevere in suffering?

13. What is said of obedience, suffering, and reward through the book of Hebrews? Note also whether the anticipated rewards and expected trials are of a temporary nature (to be expected in this life time) or eternal

nature (belonging to the eternal kingdom of Christ).

14. Consider the intended recipients of this letter:
    a. What were the original readers praised for by the author?
    b. What were the congregation's strengths?
    c. Can you list some of their weaknesses, where the author desired to see growth?
    d. What role were the original readers called to play in each other's lives?
    e. How would the letter of Hebrews have impacted the daily lives of the original readers? What should have been their response to the letter?

15. Hebrews was written to encourage a persecuted church to remain firm in their faith. Consider:
    a. How were the original readers called to confidence in Christ?
    b. For what reasons were they called to remain firm in faith in the face of persecution?
    c. What warnings were given against turning back to Judaism?
    d. Why was Judaism appealing to them?
    e. What made Christ worth paying the cost?
    f. Consider what the original readers would have faced in the aftermath of the great fire in Rome.

<u>Creative interpretation</u>

1. Design illustrations, which represent Christ's superiority to: angels, the prophets, Moses, Joshua, the Levitical priesthood, and the sacrificial system.

2. Rule up a two columned table to use for comparison between the old system of Judaism, and the new system under Christ. Choose one colour to denote what is similar in both columns (the old a shadow of the new) and another colour to denote what is different in the second column (the new being better than the old). Symbolise each heading with a graphic design. In the table, compare and contrast:
    a. The Law of Moses to the Law of Christ;
    b. The old covenant with the new covenant;
    c. The earthly tabernacle with heaven;
    d. By Law or by oath (in the appointing of priests); and
    e. The Levitical priesthood to Christ as High Priest.

Application inspiration
Reflect upon Christ and His sacrifice

- Do you accept Christ as your High Priest and King?
- Do you believe that He is the only atoning sacrifice that can save you from condemnation for your sins?
- Do you treat Christ's sacrifice lightly or value His sacrifice above all else?

- Is your hope in Christ?

Consider faith and endurance

- Would you suffer for your faith, clinging to Christ?
- Do you believe Christ is worth the cost of following Him? Are you prepared to follow Him even to death, disability or social ostracism?
- Is He worth more than anything else in your life, including: family, friends, financial security, possessions or the life of your children?
- What would you not be willing to sacrifice for Christ? Think of your career, your family, the opinion of your friends, your house, your car, and your country. As you think on these, consider whether you could part with them if God so asked you. What does your heart shy away from giving up?

Establishing an eternal focus

- Do you have an eternal perspective or are you focused on temporal circumstances?
- Is your assurance and confidence in your eternal inheritance and what you will receive when Christ returns?
- What is hindering you from fixing both eyes on Jesus?
- Do you see suffering as an opportunity to be taught by God?
- What persecution or trial are you currently enduring? Ask Christ to give you strength to persevere.
- Meditate on Hebrews 12:1-2.

[1] Strong, James, S.T.D., LL.D., (1989). *Strong's Hebrew and Greek Dictionaries, e-Sword*, Ver. 9.7.2, Dictionary, G5048.

JAMES

Faith in Action

But the one who looks into the perfect law, the law of liberty, and perseveres, being no hearer who forgets but a doer who acts, he will be blessed in his doing. – James 1:25

During your first reading

Themes to track
- Faith
- Obedience
- Tongue/ speech
- Rich/ poor
- Wisdom

During your second reading

Things to notice in the text
- Highlight passages according to their theme, marking the side column of your Bible.

Chapter summaries

These are optional as they can be time consuming for the larger books. If you choose to do them, you will receive a much deeper appreciation of the book. By the end of The IBSC, you will have paraphrased the entire Bible! Go through each chapter and try to summarise it in one paragraph, using your own words; force yourself to stay big picture and capture the heart of each chapter.

After your initial readings

Setting of James

Author

James, the brother of Jesus, is traditionally credited as the author of this book.

Recipient

Different views exist regarding who was referred to as the "twelve tribes of the dispersion". Given the time the book was written, it is probable that James was writing to the Jewish Christians who left Palestine due to persecution.

Date and place of writing

If authorship is attributed to James, the brother of Jesus, then the epistle would have been written between 45 and 62 AD from Jerusalem.

Reason written

James desired to challenge his readers, calling them to remove partiality, jealousy, and evil words from their lives. He encouraged them to walk in wisdom and remain steadfast in trials. He was calling them to be doers of the Word, and not merely preachers or hearers of it. James' purpose was to spur them on to works of love, which would display their faith to the world.

Big picture

Historical background

Wisdom in Jewish culture

The original readers were of Jewish heritage. In contrast to the beliefs of the Greeks and Romans, the Jews did not necessarily link wisdom to intellect or acquired worldly-knowledge. The Jews knew that it was to be earnestly sought through prayer and that it was given by God. Wisdom literature in the Old Testament was not seen as philosophical but primarily practical, and in the book of James wisdom again calls for practical application.

Whilst wisdom was not necessarily linked to intellect, the position of a teacher was still highly respected in the Jewish community. Incentives for going into teaching included: being held in high honour, getting to travel, and being assured of receiving the best hospitality wherever one went.

The original readers

It is believed that the "twelve tribes of the dispersion" referred to the Jewish Christians who fled from Jerusalem, scattering after the stoning of Stephen [1]. These believers dispersed into the greater Empire.

These Jewish Christians fled from Jerusalem to escape persecution, but more trials followed them. They were suffering from famine and persecution at the time James penned his epistle. The persecution appears to have been internal, coming from the rich in their community, who were exploiting the poor. In addition to facing famine and persecution, they had the everyday trials of a new environment, including the emotional strain of building new lives amongst strangers.

James, the brother of Jesus

Having ridiculed Jesus before the resurrection[2], he was converted after Christ's death[3], and remained in Jerusalem with his mother, brothers, and the disciples[4]. We know that he was still in Jerusalem in about 37/38AD[5], and was the leader of the church in Jerusalem[6]. He was a great choice for leader, as church tradition universally holds that he was respected by non-believing Jews as well as believers, and was known as James the Just. He advocated respect of the Jewish laws, but did not hold Gentile believers to them.

Character portrayal – James as he wrote the letter

With his brother's words echoing in his ears, James penned the letter to those who had fled from Jerusalem to escape persecution. His heart continued to be burdened for those Jewish believers that had left the congregation to find safety outside the city walls. He had heard of the internal strife occurring amongst them and he longed to encourage them towards righteousness.

Had they not heard the words His brother spoke about the woman who was considered great, not because she gave great wealth, but because, out of her poverty, she gave all she had to live on 7? He pondered in frustration. How could they continue to look down upon the poor in their midst when Jesus had elevated the poor so highly? Faith was not declared by one's worldly possessions, but in obedience to the Word of God. They needed to be jarred out of their complacence! When would they see that their faith called them to action?

Returning to the page before him, James' hand displayed the urgency he felt for the message contained in his letter as his pen hurried across the paper. He prayed fervently that the words he wrote would take root in their hearts and compel them to action.

Book overview

The message of the book is two-fold: faith in action, and faith for action. James declared that faith requires an active response. Faith without works is meaningless; it becomes an empty religion. The world will judge God and Christianity by the deeds and words of believers, not their knowledge of right and wrong or their beliefs. This is why he says they should have no need of oaths; the world should know from their past actions that the "yes" of believers' means "yes" and their "no" means "no".

It is not the old Law that he was calling them to uphold. James was calling the original readers to obey the new Law, given by Christ. They were now under the Law of Liberty (Law of Freedom), which required them to walk in love – love God and love one another, fulfilling Christ's commandments. He told them that living under the Law of Love required them to live out the words of Christ. He warned them not to fall back under the old Law of transgression, which led to death. James desired to spur his audience on to steadfast obedience to the Word. James wanted them to focus on the eternal reward, which would bring an end to their trials and sufferings.

Interpreting the book of James

<u>Interpretation questions</u>

1. Consider how James opened the book.
    a. Why call himself a servant, rather than the brother of Christ?
    b. What does this tell you about his character?
2. James used an illustration of looking into a mirror in passage 1:22-25.
    a. Picture the scene that he described.
    b. What does the image mean?
    c. What message did James want his readers to take away from that image?
    d. How should the original readers have responded?
3. James addressed a division between the rich and poor, which existed within the church.
    a. What makes one rich? What makes one poor?
    b. Why were the church members allowing worldly status to cause division amongst them?
    c. How did James address the issue?
    d. What argument was made for unity?
    e. Within the church, how were members of different social classes to live towards each other?
    f. James did not say "if" they met trials, but "when". He made it clear that they needed to expect suffering.
    g. How would this have affected the mind-set of the original readers?
    h. What words of advice did James offer them, which would help them when these trials came?
    i. How were the readers to endure the persecution?
    j. How were the readers to respond during times of famine?
    k. Where is James' message supported elsewhere in Scripture? Can you find other Bible passages relating to endurance and suffering?
4. How did James define one who is wise? What shows that a person has wisdom?
5. Write definitions for the words listed in James 3:14-16, which led to disorder and every vile practice.
6. Write definitions for the words listed in James 3:17, which result in a harvest of righteousness, sown in peace.
7. What does obedience look like, according to James?
8. If faith is lived out by action, what were some of the actions that James was calling the readers to do?
9. For each of the following themes, write two paragraphs about what the book of James teaches:
    a. Faith;
    b. Obedience;
    c. Tongue/ speech;
    d. Rich/ poor;

e. Wisdom.

Creative interpretation

1. Draw up a flow chart of James' view on how sin progresses from thought/temptation to action (see James 1:12-15).
    a. Who is responsible for the sins an individual commits?
    b. Consider Ezekiel 18 in completing your answer.
2. In Romans 3:28, Paul wrote *". . . one is justified by faith apart from works of the law"*. Questions to ponder:
    a. How does this correspond with the assertion in James 2:24 that *". . .a person is justified by works and not by faith alone"*?
    b. How can two seemingly contradictory statements fit in the same faith? Consider the reason each author was writing, and the wider message of the book.
    c. Dig deeper into this question by looking at other scriptures that discuss the correlation between faith and works. Write a couple of paragraphs about your findings.

Application inspiration

Creative application

- Carry a small mirror around with you this week to remind yourself that the Word of God should impact what you do in daily life. When you look in the mirror and see your hair is messy, you put a comb through it; what you see affects what you do. Let the mirror remind you this week that what you read in the Word should also affect your daily actions.

Faith in action

- The book of James is a book of application. It is a very practical book. It does not allow one to just listen; it requires a response. What will be your manifestation of faith?
- Who are the needy around you? Whose needs could you meet? Think of one person that you can help today.
- James addressed the division between poor and rich in the church.
    o Who are you putting at a distance?
    o Is there a divide in your community or within your church? What is the nature of the segregation? What is one practical step that you can do to help heal the divide?
- When do you let your tongue run away from you? In what setting do you need to rein it back? Is it at school, work or with family, or perhaps in the sporting environment?
- What trial are you going through at this time? Can you trust God to give you the wisdom you need to endure it?

[1] Acts 11:19
[2] Matthew 12:46-59 and John 7:1-8
[3] 1Corinthians 15:7
[4] Acts 1:14
[5] Galatians 1:19
[6] Act 12:1-3,17; Acts 15 (v13-21); and Acts 21:17-26
[7] Mark 12:41-44

1 PETER

Hope to Endure Persecution

Therefore let those who suffer according to God's will entrust their souls to a faithful Creator while doing good. – 1 Peter 4:19

During your first reading

Themes to track
- Suffering and endurance
- Eternal perspective
- Submission/ lifestyle
- Example of Christ

During your second reading

Things to notice in the text
- Mark passages relating to suffering.
- Mark passages relating to endurance/ hope in Christ.

Chapter summaries

These are optional as they can be time consuming for the larger books. If you choose to do them, you will receive a much deeper appreciation of the book. By the end of The IBSC, you will have paraphrased the entire Bible! Go through each chapter and try to summarise it in one paragraph, using your own words; force yourself to stay big picture and capture the heart of each chapter.

After your initial readings

Setting of 1 Peter

Author

The epistle of 1 Peter was written by Apostle Peter.

Recipient

Peter wrote to five provinces in northern, central, and western Asia: Pontus, Galatia, Cappadocia, Asia, and Bithynia. These congregations consisted of Gentile believers, and the Jewish believers who dispersed through the wider reaches of the Empire when exiled from Rome in 49 AD.

Date and place of writing

The epistle was written in the early 60s AD, before Christian persecution began under Emperor Nero. It is believed that Peter wrote the epistle from Rome, where he was later martyred between 64 and 68 AD.

Reason written

Peter was calling the church to endure their present suffering by focusing on the hope that they had in Christ, and their inheritance in the eternal Kingdom of God.

Big picture

Historical background

Peter was writing to believers who were being persecuted for their faith, although their lives were not yet under threat. It appears that the persecution was a local outburst against Christians, rather than government-ordained. Accusations were made against them for certain practices of the faith. For example, the early Christians were accused of being cannibals due to the taking of communion.

At the time this book was written, false teachers were spreading heresies throughout Asia Minor as they mixed Gospel truths with Jewish laws, Greek customs, and false religions.

Character portrayal – an allegory on 1 Peter 2:25-26

The sheep had been grazing in the fields, but one by one they were straying from the flock. Those left were being tantalised by the sight of the tall grass higher up the slopes, which appeared so fresh and green. They could see their brothers and sisters, who had already strayed, getting plump and fat on the richer grass. What they could not see from below was the mishaps that happened to those who left the safety of the flock. Some were taken by wolves; others injured themselves when they stumbled into holes, breaking bones. The sheep had not wanted to stay by the Shepherd, and they did not know their Owner who oversaw their care and so, over time, the flock scattered.

The Shepherd had not forgotten about His sheep. He longed for them, and grieved the loss of so many. He spent many hours calling after the sheep gone astray, and even pursued them up the treacherous terrain of the mountain slopes. He fought the wolves that sought to harm them, and brought them back to the safety of the fold. However, some of the sheep had forgotten Him and would not come at the sound of His voice. They refused to come back. Some of these even ran further afield, taking fright at the sound of His voice.

Nevertheless, many did respond to His call and were brought back to the fold. They were fed on choice grain, and had lush grass to eat and rest upon. And still, the better promise was yet to come. There would come a time free of dangers and strife, when they could roam outside the enclosed pastures in safety. For now, however, there remained many things to fear in the world outside.

The sheep of the fold watched their Shepherd and He guided them by His voice. They helped Him to call back other sheep to the fold, adding their voices to His own in an entreaty to their brethren. Wolves would still come and rove around the enclosure, but the sheep rested in the knowledge that their Shepherd had saved them and would not let them be taken by wolves, bears or any other threat in the world. They were safe in His care.

Book overview

The epistle of 1 Peter points the way to how one can endure through suffering. In his letter, Peter showed his readers that they needed an eternal perspective in order to maintain their faith in the face of persecution, trials, and sorrows. Peter called them to live in holiness, imitating Christ who set the example of how to live out God's will in the face of suffering. Peter reminded his readers again and again that they had been redeemed.

Christ's example on earth was one of servanthood, humility, and love, in the face of persecution. He was rejected by man and became the sacrifice for all. Peter asked his audience: "If Christ suffered, should not believers also expect to face times of trial, since they are not greater than Christ?" Christ held firm in suffering, and it is by looking to Him, and the reason for which He chose to suffer, that enables believers to hold firm to their faith, amidst times of hardship. These hardships are not limited to facing death or brutality for the Gospel, but also include things such as slander or rejection. Suffering for Christ does not bring shame, but glory, which will come at Christ's return. In light of eternity, believers can persevere through trials, entrusting their souls to God.

Furthermore, Peter wrote that believers are called to submit to both the just and unjust who sit in authority above them. This is what would bring glory to God — living differently to the world and not retaliating against those who persecuted them for their faith. Not only could the original readers be encouraged by Christ's example in suffering, but they could also gain encouragement to endure through the example of fellow believers, also enduring suffering for their faith. Believers have a hope of eternal glory with Christ, and having this eternal perspective, they are enabled to endure until Christ returns.

Interpreting the epistle of 1 Peter

Interpretation questions

1. What can be ascertained from 1 Peter about the trials and sufferings that the original readers were facing? For example, 1 Peter 2:18 suggests that some believers were suffering at the hands of their earthly masters.

2. Make a list of the commands that Peter gave to assist the original readers to endure persecution, holding to their faith.

   a. Look at the practical instructions for godliness, such as: "*Show hospitality . . . without grumbling*" [1].

   b. What did Peter teach them about holiness?

   c. How was he calling them to live?

   d. Having listed Peter's practical instructions for godliness, write a definition for what it looks like to live in godliness.

3. Complete a brief summary (one to two paragraphs) on each of the following themes:

   a. Holiness (1 Peter 1:1-2:12);

   b. Submission (1 Peter 2:13-3:12);

   c. Suffering (1 Peter 3:13-5:14).

4. Read Mark 8:29-33 and 14:27-31,66-72.

   a. How did Peter view suffering during the years of Christ's earthly ministry?

   b. What stance did he hold at the time he wrote this epistle?

   c. Comment on how Peter's view of suffering had changed, and what may have brought the change.

5. Discuss the characteristics of Christ that Peter proclaimed through the use of analogies in this epistle. Old Testament references may be helpful in gaining a wider context for the analogies. Consider the following:

   a. "Christ, a lamb without blemish, or defect" (1 Peter 1:19);

   b. Christ, "a living Stone"(1 Peter 2:4);

   c. "Shepherd and Overseer of your souls" (1 Peter 2:25);

   d. "Chief Shepherd" (1 Peter 5:4).

Creative interpretation

1. Find a place that is quiet for you. Make it a place away from the distractions of others, and the call of undone chores. Perhaps in your room with soft music playing in the background or a quiet spot in the garden, local park or a café. When in that special place, reflect on the following passages, and journal about the insights that come to you:

   a. 1 Peter 2:9-10;

   b. 1 Peter 2:23-25;

   c. 1 Peter 3:8-14;

   d. 1 Peter 4:1-2;

   e. 1 Peter 4:12-14.

Application inspiration
Living with an eternal perspective

- Suffering and persecution played a foundational role in the early church. It is also one of the primary themes within the New Testament. How do you, or how could you, live as a testimony to Christ in the midst of suffering for your faith?
- Peter called the original readers to look to eternity.
  - Why do many believers spend so much time on earth trying to make their lives comfortable?
  - Is your time spent focusing on this life, and making yourself comfortable now, or are you focused on eternity?
  - Are you seeking to live in obedience, with your eyes fixed on Jesus regardless of where this will lead you?
- How do you evaluate your life – in light of what you have now or looking to eternity, and the promise that give you hope?

Reflection questions for 1 Peter 2:13-17

- What does obeying this command look like when laws are unjust or governments are persecuting their people?
- What role should those within their country fulfil, in order to bring justice?
- What role should believers outside these countries play?
- Do believers have a role in politics?

Fun applications

- Buy a sweet and sour lollipop or sweetie.
  - Do not chew it, but continue sucking on it, enduring the initial sourness.
  - Reflect on the bitter things that life can bring your way. Hold on to the thought of the sweetness that is coming.
  - Persevere until you get to the sweetness at the end. Reflect on the coming glory of the Lord in which you will partake.
- If you can find a copy of it, read the novel: "Hinds' Feet on High Places," by Hannah Hurnard. It is worth the read! The book takes its title from Habakkuk 3:19: *"The Lord God is my strength, and he will make my feet like hinds' feet, and he will make me to walk upon mine high places."*

[1] 1 Peter 4:9

2 PETER

Be vigilant awaiting Christ's return

You therefore, beloved, knowing this beforehand, take care that you are not carried away with the error of lawless people and lose your own stability. But grow in the grace and knowledge of our Lord and Savior Jesus Christ. To him be the glory both now and to the day of eternity. Amen. – 2 Peter 3:17-18

The epistles of 2 Peter and Jude are very similar in theme and content. It is believed that the author of whichever of the two was written second drew on the letter by the other author for content. For this reason, it is beneficial to study the books in partnership.

During your first reading

Themes to track
- False prophets
- Christ's second coming

During your second reading

Things to notice in the text
- Highlight words of comparison: "like", "better than", "worse off", "more", "less".
- Make time elements: "last days", "day of judgement", "day of the Lord".

Chapter summaries
These are optional as they can be time consuming for the larger books. If you choose to do them, you will receive a much deeper appreciation of the book. By the end of The IBSC, you will have paraphrased the entire Bible! Go through each chapter and try to summarise it in one paragraph, using your own words; force yourself to stay big picture and capture the heart of each chapter.

After your initial readings

Setting of 2 Peter
Author

Many modern scholars do not believe that Apostle Peter was the author of 2 Peter due to discrepancies in writing style with that of 1 Peter. However, given the internal information contained in the book, indicating the author to have been an eye witness to the life of Christ, and that Peter is mentioned by name, it is reasonable to credit the book to Apostle Peter.

Recipient

If 1 Peter was the letter alluded to in chapter 3, then 2 Peter was written to be read in various congregations across Pontus, Galatia, Cappadocia, Asia, and Bithynia.

Date and place of writing

Apostle Peter was martyred in Rome between 64 and 68 AD. It is therefore likely that he wrote this epistle from Rome, just prior to his death.

Reason written

Peter wrote to encourage the congregations to cling to the hope they had in Christ, and live godly lives whilst awaiting Christ's return. Peter was reassuring them that they had not missed His second coming, and warning the church to be on guard against false teachers.

Big picture
Historical background

The book of 2 Peter presents as a testament, which was a well-known and easily identifiable literary form. It was written as a farewell discourse of one about to die.

At the time the book was written, false prophets were scoffing at the belief that Christ was still to return. They thought that if Jesus was going to return, He should have done so already. They were mocking believers and Christ because He had not come. There was also mounting concern within the churches because He had not returned. Jewish belief held that living a religious life would speed up the (first) coming of the Christ. The belief through the time of New Testament writing was that the end was near, and Christ's return was imminent.

The false teachers were also beginning to add Gnostic concepts to the teachings of the church. Gnosticism taught the separation of body from spirit (dualism); the body, and physical matter, was held to be evil, whilst the spirit was good. Two main false teachings being spread were:

- *Antinomianism:* teaching that one is free from the moral obligations of the Law, since faith alone is necessary for salvation.
- *Libertarianism:* they believed that only the soul is divine and immortal, and that the body is merely earth-bound. As a result, they thought that they could do what they liked in the flesh, without spiritual consequences attached.

442

<u>Character portrayal – believers listening to a false teacher</u>

Stephan felt uneasy as he listened to the words of the teacher, and yet he could not help but be drawn to them. The teacher seemed to know what he was saying, but something was niggling at Stephan's spirit. He continued to listen attentively to the teacher as he tried to discern what was true.

The teacher continued in greasy words, speaking boldly to those who would listen to him: "Ah brothers, you know that I travel from town to town, teaching the truth of God to those who will listen, and must rely on the hospitality of the people as I do. I do this for the love of our God for God has saved our souls from death. We receive life through our Lord who has rescued us. Why do you remain bound by laws and regulations when your souls have been freed?

"The body is merely earthly," he continued. "It is the soul that will live on. This body, this flesh – it is temporary. Why worry about a body that will not endure? We are free from the confines that those around you allow to be placed upon themselves by other men. It is not God that puts these laws upon man, but other men. You are free from them. The body makes its desires known to us. These desires are not wrong. They are natural, and God has freed us to indulge our flesh and experience the pleasures of earth before our souls are saved and brought into eternal life . . ."

Stephan was overwhelmed by fear. He longed to embrace the words of the teacher and was drawn in like one mesmerised, and yet – he also had a growing urgency to break free from the mass gathered in the public square. His body told him to stay, but his spirit was ill at ease, pulling at his mind. Finally, he turned and began making his way from amidst the crowd. Pushing and weaving, he broke free of the press of bodies and felt like he could breathe again.

Hurrying away, he went in search of a quiet place to think, where he could go before God. He had been encouraged to pursue the Lord and to ask questions of Him by Peter, during the apostle's last visit. That was what he determined to do now, and after he had brought it before God, he would also seek wisdom from his church elder.

<u>Book overview</u>

Peter declared that the way to stay safe is to keep growing. The moment you stop growing you are in danger. Growing in faith, and holding to hope in Christ's return, provides protection against false teachers. Wrong doctrine can lead believers astray; therefore, such teachers need to be actively resisted. The means of resistance is continual strengthening of one's faith. Christ's return should be awaited with eager expectation and believers should live holy, godly lives, in light of the great inheritance they will receive.

Peter also made the point that, just because God is waiting, does not mean He is weak. That Christ has not yet returned reveals His longing for all people to reach the place of repentance and forgiveness. Yet as He continues to wait, it hurts Him because more tragedies are happening in the world, and to His people. It is not His weakness, but His mercy, that holds Him back from bringing His kingdom in all the fullness of its glory.

Interpreting the epistle of 2 Peter

<u>Interpretation questions</u>

1. Peter did not start his letter by listing the attributes of the false teachers that he was writing to warn the churches against. Rather, in 2 Peter 1:5-8, he wrote down a list of qualities that his readers should have been seeking to attain.
    a. Why begin this way?
    b. What was the significance?
    c. What response was he seeking from his audience?

2. What commands did Peter give to his readers?
    a. What might these convey of the strengths and weaknesses of the congregations?
    b. How did Peter want them to live?

3. 2 Peter 1:5-8 lists characteristics of holiness: faith, virtue (goodness), knowledge, self-control, steadfastness, godliness, brotherly affection, and love.
    a. Of what does each of these attributes consist? Write a definition for each characteristic.
    b. What might each look like in practice? Give examples of how you could actively live out each characteristic.
    c. What further attributes did Peter call the church to focus on?
    d. How would pursing these attributes have protected them against false teachers and wrong doctrine?

4. What do you learn of God's character in the book of 2 Peter?

5. Note the contrasts of people – the faithful versus the ungodly:
    a. Noah preserved, contrasted with a generation judged (Genesis 17).
    b. Lot preserved, whilst Sodom and Gomorrah perished (Genesis 18-19).
    c. What was Peter communicating to the original readers in 2 Peter 2:4-7?

6. Peter challenged his readers not to become impatient as they awaited Christ's return.
    a. What advice did Peter give to them about waiting for Christ's return?
    b. What was conveyed of the temporal and what of the eternal?
    c. What information did Peter provide regarding the nature of Christ's second coming?
    d. How were they called to live in light of His coming return?

<u>Creative interpretation</u>

1. Using the information and descriptions provided by Peter, write a character summary for the false prophets. Verses 2:1-3, 10-13 will be particularly helpful, but do not forget to look through the rest of Peter's letter for references to the false teachers. Consider:

a. Who were the false prophets?
b. What were they teaching?
c. What made them dangerous to the congregations to whom Peter was writing?

Application inspiration

- Remember the teachings of Galatians on the fruits of the Spirit; it is the Spirit that brings the fruit, not effort on the believer's part. How may you seek the attributes Peter lists in 2 Peter 1:5-8, whilst trusting God to bring the change into your life?
- The epistle of 2 Peter talks about growing in Christ, growing in faith, resisting false teachers, and hoping for Christ's second coming. False teachers are everywhere in today's society and they are leading people astray. This book is about resisting these teachers, and looking forward to His return. How can you apply this message in your life and within your community?
- The epistle of 2 Peter gives wise counsel about how to deal with false teachers. Today's church often struggles to know what to do with false teachers, and is often uncertain about how to deal with heretics. This book brings wisdom to address unsound teaching.
  - How would you respond to someone who brought incorrect teachings before the church?
  - Try to think of specific scenarios. For example, how would you respond to a youth at church seeking God and yet holding what you believe to be wrong theologies, compared with a Jehovah's witnesses at your door, or a press-release in the media?
- Challenge what is taught by the world and by believers to ensure it lines up with Scripture. Hold the Scripture as the only secure reference.

Questions for reflection
- If you knew Christ was coming tomorrow would you live differently?
- What would you change?
- In what ways are you compromising godliness?

1 JOHN

Abide in His Love, knowing you are Saved

Whoever confesses that Jesus is the Son of God, God abides in him, and he in God. So we have come to know and to believe the love that God has for us. God is love, and whoever abides in love abides in God, and God abides in him. – 1 John 4:15-16

During your first reading

Themes to track

- Love
- Abide (in God)
- Obedience
- "Know" (who you are, what Christ has done, and that you are in Him)

During your second reading

Things to notice in the text

- Mark the following repeated words:
  - "Light" and "dark"
  - "Truth" and "error/ lie"
  - "Sin" and "righteousness"
  - "Child of God" and "child of devil"
- Underline commands that John gave to the churches.
- Mark repeated words: "love" and "heart".
- Mark the names of God, for example: "Spirit", "Holy One", "Father".

Chapter summaries

These are optional as they can be time consuming for the larger books. If you choose to do them, you will receive a much deeper appreciation of the book. By the

end of The IBSC, you will have paraphrased the entire Bible! Go through each chapter and try to summarise it in one paragraph, using your own words; force yourself to stay big picture and capture the heart of each chapter.

After your initial readings

Setting of 1 John
<u>Author</u>
The epistle is ascribed to Apostle John.

<u>Recipient</u>
The epistle of 1 John was intended to be circulated to a number of churches throughout Asia Minor, including the churches in Ephesus, Smyrna, Pergamum, Thyatira, Sardis, Philadelphia, and Laodicea.

<u>Date and place of writing</u>
The epistle was written between 80 and 90 AD from Ephesus.

<u>Reason written</u>
The reason John wrote his letter can be derived from looking at the following verses:

- 1 John 1:4 – John desired their joy to be made complete;
- 1 John 2:1 – He wanted them to cease walking in sin;
- 1 John 2:26 – The letter was to bring the truth, as protection against false teachers; and
- 1 John 5:13 – John wrote in order that they might believe in the name of the Son of God. John assured them that they already knew the truth, and desired that they continue to live in light of it.

Big picture
<u>Historical background</u>
Historical background is very important to understanding 1 John!

John was not trying to make his readers insecure in their relationship with God. This epistle would have brought surety of faith and security to the original readers, and would have helped them to distinguish truth from lies. John's repeated use of the word "know" emphasises that they were able to know the truth, and indeed did know the truth.

This epistle was necessary to combat doubt and confusion, which had entered into the churches throughout Asia Minor as a result of false teachers. These teachers preached that they had the Spirit of God, denied Jesus was the Christ, and claimed that they were sinless.

There were three main beliefs of Gnosticism that the original readers were struggling to lay aside, even though they had been enlightened by the truth. John sought to bring truth against the lies. <u>These wrong beliefs,</u> with John's responses, were:

1. *To rise in spirituality you must gain secret, hidden knowledge.*
   Those who had secret knowledge were considered superior. The false teachers would claim "I am in the light," but they were loveless and proud. In contrast, John proclaimed that God is light and you are in the light if you are living faith out in action.
2. *Dualism, which taught that the spirit was good and that physical matter was evil.*
   Dualism led either to asceticism (punishing the flesh as evil), or libertarianism (the flesh does not matter, so you can do whatever you please with your body). John showed that Jesus is the propitiation for sin; they do not have to punish the body to rid it of sin. He also stated that *"no one born of God makes a practice of sinning"*[1]; they were not to keep on sinning, because God cares about their lifestyle.
3. *Rejection of the incarnation of Christ (that Jesus was 100% God, whilst also 100% man).*
   John made it clear from the start of the epistle that Christ was there in the beginning, and repeats throughout the book: "Son, Jesus Christ" and "Father and Son". John emphasised the deity of Christ.

Refer to the *Introduction to the epistles* for more information about Gnosticism.

<u>Character portrayal – prayer of a once confused believer having heard the truth</u>
"Thank you, Lord! Thank you, Lord! Praise Him!

"Bring me to complete understanding of this truth, bring me into your light. I've been walking in conformity to lies and deceit. Enable me to break free of these chains that have held me back; chains that proclaimed the knowledge of Christ was not sufficient, that the cross wasn't sufficient, and that I needed secret knowledge for my salvation.

"I thank you that you have freed me from the hold of sin and brought me into the covenant of love. No more fear, and no more condemnation! This knowledge is too good to keep to myself, as the false teachers claim we must do with the secret knowledge. I pray that my enthusiasm will not wain. Let me boldly declare the truth of Christ!"

<u>Book overview</u>
John began by reminding the original readers that they knew Jesus (who was from the beginning and is always), and the Father (through His Son). God had not kept this knowledge secret. John wrote that they might be assured of the eternal life they had received through the Son of God. Jesus was enough for their salvation. Jesus had brought them understanding; He had revealed all they needed; they did not need to seek more knowledge to obtain salvation because they had already been given all they needed for it.

The epistle also testifies that the original readers could be assured that the Holy Spirit abided in them. Their love of God, and love for the children of God, was the proof that they abided in Him. Likewise, observing the actions of others would reveal to them who was walking with God, not in the ways of the world. Those who know God no longer abide in sin, but abide in the God of love.

John cautioned them to be careful to remain in the truth. Living in the world, they were not to return to living of the world. They were established in the Spirit. The

Spirit would bring them knowledge of what was of God, and what was not. As believers, they needed to walk in confidence for they were in Him, and in the truth. They knew how to love because Jesus had given them the example. John wanted this knowledge to result in practical love within the church. John's heart was that they abide with one another in love. This is the best form of evangelism because it shows God's love to the world, through His children.

Interpreting the epistle of 1 John

<u>Interpretation questions</u>

1. How did John feel towards the original readers, the churches throughout Asia Minor?
2. What were John's main concerns for the original readers?
3. Consider John's audience.
   a. Were the original readers believers?
   b. Who were their teachers?
   c. What weaknesses within the church was John addressing?
   d. What were their strengths?
4. How does one remain in Christ, and their anointing?
5. What is the hope of believers?
6. What do you learn of the Holy Trinity – of the Father, Son, and Holy Spirit?
7. Who are the "antichrists", in the context of 1 John?
8. What does 1 John teach about sin?
   a. How does this compare to the teachings of Christ and the epistles of Paul?
   b. What is the sin that leads to death? Look back at the Gospels. Did Christ speak of such a sin? What point was John trying to make?
9. What do you learn of the process of sanctification (the process of becoming more like Christ)?
10. What is said of the world and those who are of it?
    a. What can believers expect from the world?
    b. What causes separation from the world?
11. What is love, as defined by 1 John?
    a. What are its actions?
    b. How does it show itself?
12. John gave the saints ways by which they could know that they were of the truth.
    a. What were these ways?
    b. How could the saints remain assured of the truth?

<u>Creative interpretation</u>

1. Note down key verses from 1 John, which relate to each of the following contrasts:
   a. Light versus dark;
   b. Truth versus error/ lie;

    c. Sin versus righteousness;

    d. Child of God versus child of the devil.

Once you have recorded the relevant passages, write one to two short paragraphs summarising what John taught about each of the contrasts.

2. Summarise what John taught about the following themes, and how they build upon each other:

    a. You know God

      i. Walk in the Light (1 John 1:1-2:17);

      ii. Remain in the Truth you know (1 John 2:18-2:29).

    b. Abide in Him

      i. Know love and truth (1 John 3:1-4:6);

      ii. God's love (1 John 4:7-5:5);

      iii. Confidence in Christ (1 John 5:6-5:21).

Application inspiration

Consider the love of God

- Ponder God's character. God is love. Think about what this means and what it implies.
- What is love in the eyes of the world? What does God say is love?
- John knew he was loved by God. He knew he was the one that Jesus loved. Do you know that you are the one Jesus loves? Refer to:
  - John 13:34-35
  - John 14:15
  - John 14:21
  - John 14:24
  - John 15:4
  - John 15:10
  - John 15:12-13
  - John 15:16

Reflection questions

Take time to ponder on these questions. Ask God to bring revelation.

- Does your life show a difference to the world?
- Are you living a life of righteousness? Are you allowing God to expand your view of righteousness?
- Do you invite God's conviction?
- Where have you become numb to sin?
- What do you do, even though you know God abhors it?
- What idols are coming before God in your life?
- Are there people with whom you need to seek reconciliation? Pray about what the first step of reconciliation should be, and then act upon it.
- Reflect on the following quote (Barclay 2002, p. 74): *"The object of the apostle in writing was not to communicate fresh knowledge, but to bring into active and decisive*

use the knowledge which his readers possessed.' The greatest Christian defence is simply to remember what we know. What we need is not new truth, but for the truth which we already know to become active and effective in our lives" [2].

[1] 1 John 3:9

[2] Barclay, W. (2002). The New Daily Study Bible: The Letters of John and Jude, 3rd edition. Westminster John Knox Press, Kentucky.

2 JOHN

Hospitality with Caution

And this is love, that we walk according to his commandments; this is the commandment, just as you have heard from the beginning, so that you should walk in it. For many deceivers have gone out into the world, those who do not confess the coming of Jesus Christ in the flesh. Such a one is the deceiver and the antichrist. – 2 John 1:6-7

During your first reading

Themes to track
- Hospitality
- Truth and love
- False teaching

During your second reading

Things to notice in the text
- Mark the words: "truth" and "love".
- Underline commandments given by John to his readers.

Chapter summaries

These are optional as they can be time consuming for the larger books. If you choose to do them, you will receive a much deeper appreciation of the book. By the end of The IBSC, you will have paraphrased the entire Bible! Go through each chapter and try to summarise it in one paragraph, using your own words; force yourself to stay big picture and capture the heart of each chapter.

After your initial readings

Setting of 2 John

<u>Author</u>

The epistle is ascribed to Apostle John.

<u>Recipient</u>

The epistle was probably written to a church within Asia Minor; however, some theologians contend that it was written to an individual lady and her children. See *historical background* below for more information.

<u>Date and place of writing</u>

The epistle of 2 John was written between 80 and 90 AD from Ephesus.

<u>Reason written</u>

John did not false teachers welcomed into the church through the extension of customary hospitality. He warned the church to abide in the commandments and teachings they had heard from the beginning, walking in love and truth.

Big picture

<u>Historical background</u>

The setting of 2 John is very similar to that of 1 John; refer to the *historical background* given for 1 John for information regarding three main beliefs characterising Gnosticism, which were causing confusion within the early church.

The original readers were struggling with false teachers who saw themselves as superior to "ordinary" Christians. These teachers were claiming they were sinless and denying Christ. Their teaching was spreading confusion within the church and believers were beginning to doubt themselves, wondering if they truly knew everything needed for salvation. However, their cultural practice of hospitality did not enable them to turn these false teachers from their homes.

Hospitality in Jewish culture

There are different expectations regarding receiving guests today than there were at the time of the early church. Back then, the guests (who were often strangers), were given an opportunity to share during meals; it was an open ticket for the guest to preach. Travelling teachers were quickly received because the people desired to hear their messages. They were invited into homes, provided with food, and given the gift of accommodation. Welcoming a teacher into one's home was a sign that you supported and blessed their teaching. John reflects this in both 2 and 3 John when he speaks of the host becoming part of the guest's ministry just by offering the teacher hospitality.

Hospitality was part of life; it was normal to receive strangers. The church was already established at this time. The gathering of believers occurred in people's homes, hence the term "home churches". The travelling teachers would know where the church would be meeting, and these people would be welcomed by the church. False teachers were going to these same congregations and were getting the opportunity to preach (we see references in many of Paul's letters that he was being followed in his travels by these false teachers). The number of false teachers was growing, and thus their message was spreading, bringing lies into the church.

Who were the original readers of 2 John?

We see the epistle addressed to "the elect lady" and her children. So, was this an actual woman, or was it symbolic of a church congregation? Here are some differing opinions:

1. Some believe it was written to a real lady and her children, whom John knew very well. The family would have been one with influence over a church. John was writing to encourage her to continue in love and truth, and to be wary of the false teachers.
2. Other scholars think that the elect lady was leading the church, and the children refer to the congregational members.
3. The third option is that the lady was a symbol of the church, and the children were representative of the congregational members.

Remember that the message of 1 John remains the same regardless of which of the above you think most likely to have been John's intended audience.

Character portrayal – a family of the church applies the message of John's letter

"Father, a man has come into town! A teacher, Father!"

"Now, there, Mary, hold up. What is he proclaiming to teach?"

"He was teaching in the market square on the light of Christ. He said that Jesus was a man who shed the light of God, and that he walked in the footsteps of Elijah."

Peter could see the light in Mary's eyes as she spoke. His daughter had been captured by the traveller's words. "Walked in Elijah's footsteps? That is not what the apostles proclaim. What else did he say?"

"That another will come, the Messiah, and save us from sin if we remain true to our customs; we must cling to the good heritage that the Lord Almighty gave to us."

"He proclaims Christ in the flesh, but not that He was the Son of God. Mary, I do not want you listening to such a man again."

"Ruth's father approves of him, Father. He invited the man to dinner, and rest."

Peter was concerned. "Bring me my cloak, Mary. I must remind Timothy of John's commandment. I would have thought he would be more cautious. My ruling does not change; you are not to listen to the man."

"Yes, Papa," she replied, submissively.

Book overview

The epistles of 2 and 3 John contrast two different types of people: those who come to teach truth, and those who bring falsehood. To John, hospitality was more than it is made out to be today, where it is often viewed as just the provision of a meal or a bed. The book of 1 John conveys the message that the readers took part in the work of those they hosted.

John was writing to warn his readers not to welcome the false teachers with hospitality. This command was not against showing travellers compassion, but to offer hospitality in that time was to support the message they preached. Try to remember that hospitality went beyond just giving them a meal; to accept a teacher into one's home was to accept the message they brought. This was dangerous for the young church of God!

John wanted to equip them to recognise false teachers by the message they shared, and hold fast to the Gospel that they had been taught since the beginning. He encouraged the church to walk in love and truth, but also with wisdom and discernment.

Interpreting the epistle of 2 John
Interpretation questions

1. If you think the lady was an individual:
    a. What was Apostle John's concern for the "elect lady"?
    b. What might her position have been within the church or in her city?
    c. What does this imply about the position of women in the church?
    d. How do you believe she was connected to John?
    e. What did John wish to see from the elect lady and her children?
2. If it was to a church, what were John's instructions to the congregation? Were they to apply these instructions to outsiders, church members or both?
3. Consider John's concern regarding the false teachers:
    a. What were the false teachers saying?
    b. Why were these travelling teachers dangerous to believers?
    c. Why would John command the readers not to take false teachers into their homes?
    d. What was John afraid would happen if the elect lady/ church offered hospitality to the false teachers?
4. Look at John's call for the readers to walk in Christ's commands:
    a. What commands did John emphasise?
    b. How would the readers apply these commands practically?
    c. How did the command to love fit with John's command to be cautious with hospitality?
5. How would this letter have affected their practice of hospitality? How might the original readers have reacted, knowing their cultural standpoint on hospitality?
6. Where else in the Bible is hospitality mentioned? Does this add to, balance or change your interpretation of the message of 1 John? If so, how?
7. Why did John emphasise truth and love? What was the significance to the original readers, in their circumstances?
8. Walking in love and truth:
    a. What does it mean to walk in the truth?
    b. What does it mean to love a person in truth?

c. How is truth held in contrast to the false teachings?

Creative interpretation

1. Study 2 John with 3 John. Write a summary of the principles of hospitality that can be gathered from these books. Make sure to include observations from the text, and then carry it into an application for today.

Application inspiration

Hospitality

- Consider what hospitality is truly.
- Where does John's letter leave one today in regard to offering hospitality? Consider:
  - o What were the principles that John was giving his readers?
  - o Should you slam the door in the face of anyone who is not a believer? What would that look like in terms of evangelism?
  - o How can you apply the principles found in 2 John to your practice of hospitality?
- To whom should you offer hospitality?
- How can you show hospitality? Is there a young adults' group, new family or missionary at your church that you could host for a meal?

Hospitality and false teaching

- Do you have friends or acquaintances who lead you to walk contrary to your beliefs? How will you respond to these friends in a way that will love them, but also protect your faith?
- Be careful of those who preach false doctrine.
  - o How will you avoid being swayed by falsehood?
  - o Are there television programs or movies that you watch where the message is not reinforcing God's ways?
  - o What music do you listen to? Is it sound for your ears to hear?
- Another very relevant consideration regarding hospitality today is for parents:
  - o When you have friends over who are not Christians, do you ensure your children have a foundation in the truth?
  - o How much do you know about what they are taught at school?
  - o Are you anchoring them in knowledge of the truth at home?
  - o Do you read them Bible stories and teach them to study the Word, as appropriate to their age?

3 JOHN

Hospitality in Love

Beloved, do not imitate evil but imitate good. Whoever does good is from God; whoever does evil has not seen God. – 3 John 1:11

During your first reading

Themes to track
- Hospitality
- Truth and love
- Pride

During your second reading

Things to notice in the text
- Emotion and praise
- Names and people
- Contrasts of people

Chapter summaries
These are optional as they can be time consuming for the larger books. If you choose to do them, you will receive a much deeper appreciation of the book. By the end of The IBSC, you will have paraphrased the entire Bible! Go through each chapter and try to summarise it in one paragraph, using your own words; force yourself to stay big picture and capture the heart of each chapter.

After your initial readings

Setting of 3 John
Author

The epistle is ascribed to Apostle John.

Recipient

The epistle of 3 John was written to Gaius, who was an individual member of a church congregation, in which John was an elder.

Date and place of writing

The epistle was written between 80 and 90 AD from Ephesus.

Reason written

The epistle of 3 John was written to encourage the welcoming of visiting brothers, working for the truth. John praised Gaius' hospitality and spurred him to continue the practice. The letter was also a warning against following the example of Diotrephes, who was not practising hospitality or walking in love. In contrast, Demetrius is presented as a good example to follow.

Big picture
Historical background

Refer to *historical background* in 2 John for information on the Jewish practice of hospitality.

The epistle of 2 John was written concerning false teachers entering the church. The epistle of 3 John refers to the true teachers, and was written to encourage Gaius to continue his support of such men.

To whom was John writing?

Gaius was a common Roman name. There are three other people named Gaius' mentioned in the New Testament:

1. Gaius of Corinth (Romans 16:23 and 1 Corinthians 1:14);
2. Gaius from Macedonia (Acts 29:29); and
3. Gaius of Derbe (Acts 20:4-5).

The Gaius referred to in 3 John could be one of the above or an entirely different individual.

Character portrayal – Gaius' guests report to John

"Dear John, our beloved brother and fellow worker in Christ.

"We take great joy in writing to you of the love we have received from our brother Gaius. He welcomed us into his home and has been a great support to us, as well as to the preaching of the Gospel in this area. We found his hospitality to be all that you assured us we would receive from him.

"Not all the brothers in the church show such concern for our needs and well-being. It saddens us to share that there is one man, by the name Diotrephes, who appears to stir up the church against visiting brethren. It seems that his struggle is against pride. He thinks more highly of his person than he should, and is unwilling to receive correction. It is with sorrow that I say he has also caused some within the church to close their doors to travellers such as ourselves, doing so out of fear of him.

"We continue in our work as you have instructed. We hope and fervently pray that you will be able to join us here soon. Whilst we eagerly await your coming, we stand in prayer over you. Greet our brothers and sisters in Ephesus."

Book overview

John was motivated by love and the truth. He found joy when he heard that believers were walking in the ways of truth and love. In 3 John, hospitality is shown as one way in which believers can join together as a body and become fellow workers for the truth. 3 John indicates that hospitality flows as the natural response to abiding in the truth and obeying Christ's command to love one another; it is a sign that one abides in the teaching of God.

It was John's joy to hear that Gaius was being shown faithful to Christ's command to love, by his deeds towards other believers. Gaius was praised for his efforts on behalf of believers he did not know. It was these believers who testified to John of Gaius' hospitality. John stated that these brethren were worthy of the church's hospitality, unlike the false teachers who were the focus of 2 John.

True teachers go out for the sake of Christ's name, to spread the Good News. Supporting such believers makes the church co-workers of the travelling teachers, striving together for the Word of God. John encouraged Gaius to continue his support of godly men who spread the true Gospel.

Interpreting the Epistle of 3 John
Interpretation questions

1. List the names that John uses in reference to Gaius. What do these tell you about John's relationship with him?
2. Read *historical background* from 2 John, and then consider what hospitality meant to the original readers. Consider John's message in his second and third epistles.
   a. To whom should hospitality be extended?
   b. What purpose does this serve for the church?
3. How did Gaius show love? How was he contrasted with Diotrephes?
4. Consider John's mention of Diotrephes.
   a. What fault did John find in Diotrephes? How was he acting wrongly, and what made it wrong?
   b. How was he affecting the church?
   c. What do you think was Diotrephes' role in the church?
5. List some of the fruits of pride as seen in 3 John. What else does Scripture say on pride? Can you find references from elsewhere in the Bible?
6. Consider John's mention of Demetrius.

     a. Who might Demetrius have been?

     b. Why might John be singling him out in the epistle?

7. What did John hope to achieve from this epistle?

8. What instructions did John give to Gaius?

9. How would Gaius have been encouraged by this letter? What effect would it have had on his actions?

<u>Creative interpretation</u>

1. Study 3 John with 2 John, and write a summary of the principles of hospitality that they convey. Make sure to include observations from the text, as well as your interpretation, and bring it to an application for today. In addition, consider, based on these two epistles, when should hospitality be extended, and when should it be withheld?

Application inspiration

Consider how true hospitality is shown

- How was showing hospitality displayed in your home growing up? How is it practiced in your current home?

- How does your practice of hospitality compare to how it was shown in the first century AD?

- In what way could you increase your hospitality to be more than a dinner or cup of coffee? Could you write a letter of encouragement down for each guest before they arrive or pray over them before they leave?

- How might you encourage discussion of the Gospel at your dinner table?

To whom do you extend hospitality?

- Consider inviting your church youth group over to your house and spoil them with a delicious dessert.

- Perhaps you would like to initiate an evening Bible Study at your house where you provide dinner for those who attend?

- Could you support missionaries by giving them a retreat at your home when back from service? Granny flats are perfect for such retreats. If you are already doing this, think about how could you extend it beyond giving them a place to sleep and some food? Maybe you could seek to draw out their stories and what God is teaching them. This is a double blessing: it blesses them and yourself!

JUDE

False teachers & Christ's return

Beloved, although I was very eager to write to you about our common salvation, I found it necessary to write appealing to you to contend for the faith that was once for all delivered to the saints. – Jude 1:3

Jude and 2 Peter are very similar, with seventy-five percent of the content of Jude contained in 2 Peter. It is believed that the author of whichever of the two was written second drew on the letter by the other author, for content. For this reason, it is beneficial to study the books in partnership.

During your first reading

Themes to track
- False teachers
- Day of Christ's return

During your second reading

Things to notice in the text
- What is said of unbelievers and believers
- Mark time elements

Chapter summaries

These are optional as they can be time consuming for the larger books. If you choose to do them, you will receive a much deeper appreciation of the book. By the end of The IBSC, you will have paraphrased the entire Bible! Go through each chapter and try to summarise it in one paragraph, using your own words; force yourself to stay big picture and capture the heart of each chapter.

After your initial readings

Setting of Jude
Author

The internal evidence supports that the book of Jude was written by Judas, the brother of James and Jesus.

Recipient

The specific congregation the letter was written to remains unknown; however, it can be seen that it was written for believers.

Date and place of writing

Both Jude and 2 Peter are dated in the 60s AD, prior to Peter's death, which is dated between 64 and 68 AD. It is unknown which letter was written first. The epistle of Jude was written from an unidentified location.

Reason written

Jude was written to spur the readers to contend for their faith against false teachers. The author was entreating them to remain firm in their hope for Christ's second coming by establishing themselves in the love of God.

Big picture
Historical background

At the time the book was written, false prophets were scoffing at the belief that Christ was still to return. They thought that, if Jesus was going to return, He should have done so already. They were mocking believers and mocking Christ, because He had not come. There was also mounting concern within the churches because He had not returned. Jewish belief held that living a religious life would speed up the (first) coming of the Christ. The belief through the time of New Testament writing was that the end was near, and Christ's return was imminent.

The false teachers were also beginning to add Gnostic concepts to the teachings of the church. Gnosticism taught the separation of body from spirit (dualism); the body, and physical matter, was held to be evil, whilst the spirit was good. Two main false teachings being spread were:

- *Antinomianism:* teaching that one is free from the moral obligations of the Law, since faith alone is necessary for salvation.
- *Libertarianism:* they believed that only the soul is divine and immortal, and that the body is merely earth-bound. As a result, they thought that they could do what they liked in the flesh, without spiritual consequences attached.

Character portrayal – Jude's righteous anger

Jude was besieged with fury as he thought of the false teachings being circulated throughout the churches. He could hardly credit that such teaching had taken root within the church. He was less harsh in his condemnation of those outside the church, who disrupted believers, because they did not know the truth. However for teachers within the church to be leading their brethren astray . . . it made his blood boil!

Jude gritted his teeth together, even as his hands balled in to fists. He cried out in his frustration, releasing a sound of anguish. Before God, he prayed:

"Lord, protect your young church. Let not your children be swept up by waves of falsehood onto hidden reefs, to be destroyed. Keep them safe in the truth. Strengthen them to pursue your righteousness. Do not let them turn to the lustful and sinful ways of the flesh, believing the lie that such actions are meaningless. Show them that you do care what they do in their physical bodies. Reveal to them that you are a God over all things; spiritual and physical, there is no separation.

"Root out the false teachers and send them fleeing before your righteous anger. Whip them out of your churches. And have mercy upon those whom they have led astray. Bring your confused sheep back into safe pastures."

Book overview

Jude lists the qualities of false teachers so that the original readers could identify them. This list served as a warning to remain firm against the deceit of such people, whose end would be condemnation and judgement. In contrast, the original readers could be encouraged by the promise of eternal life. The readers were told to resist false teachings by focusing on growing in Christ-likeness and keeping an eternal perspective.

Believers are called to stand firm as a congregation against false teachings, and to place their hope in the second coming of the Lord Jesus Christ. Jesus is the Perfector of the Faith, and He will come again in glory and power to execute judgement on all – convicting the ungodly and bringing believers into the eternal Kingdom of God.

Believers have the Holy Spirit as God's gift and "down-payment" of the promise of eternal life. The Holy Spirit protects believers and keeps them safely in the love of God. Prayer is powerful and through prayer, Christians remain firm in their faith.

Help with difficult passages
Michael not blaspheming Satan; Jude 1:9

Deuteronomy 34:6 states that Moses was buried by God and no one knows the place of burial. Jewish tradition held that when Moses died, they relied on the Lord to lay him to rest, and so God sent Archangel Michael to bury him. Satan tried to stop him, but Michael won. Whilst victorious, Michael did not blaspheme against the devil. This tradition comes from the "Assumption of Moses", a Jewish apocryphal book. "Apocrypha" means "secretive" or "hidden". Apocryphal books were excluded from the Bible as these books were deemed not to stand on the same level of authority as Scripture and doubts remain over the authenticity of some of the books.

Interpreting the epistle of Jude
Interpretation questions

    1. Draw up a two-columned table.

        a. On one side, list the characteristics of the ungodly identified in

Jude.
   b. On the other side, write a list of the attributes Jude called his readers to pursue.
2. Consider the false teachers that Jude was warning against.
   a. What may have been motivating the false teachers?
   b. How could they be distinguished amongst the faithful in the congregation?
   c. What was false about their teachings or deeds?
   d. Why would Jude give such a detailed description of the ungodly in the congregation?
   e. How may the ungodly people have come to be in the congregation? How did they go unnoticed?
3. Jude uses imagery in Jude 1:12-13 to describe the ungodly people in the congregation.
   a. What feelings or pictures do his examples bring to your mind?
   b. What characteristics was he describing through these images?
4. What was Jude communicating to the original readers through verses 2:4-7? You may wish to explore Old Testament references. Note the contrasts of people (people who were faithful versus the ungodly):
   a. Korah rebelled against Moses and Aaron (Numbers 16);
   b. Balaam wanted to go against the children of Israel (Numbers 22-24).
5. Jude was writing with a sense of urgency. Why was he impassioned about the need for them to contend for the faith?
6. What is the difference between the people listed in Jude 1:4-16 and Jude 1:22-23? Why did Jude only want mercy shown to the second group?
7. What does the book reveal about the day of Christ's return?
8. What was Jude's intention in mentioning the incident between Archangel Michael and Satan?
9. What connection did Jude make between Jewish traditions and the situation of the congregation?
10. To what response was Jude calling the original readers? How did he wish for them to respond to this letter?
11. Jude gave commands that demanded an active response. He used words such as: building, praying, keep, and waiting. What does this imply about the process of sanctification that believers go through?

Creative interpretation
   1. Look up information about hidden reefs. Explore what makes them dangerous and what sailors do to avoid them.
      a. How could this relate to the church to whom Jude was writing?
      b. What would the metaphor have meant to the readers, in their situation?
      c. What warning should they have taken from it?

Application inspiration

- Continue to seek a deeper relationship with the Holy Spirit.
- God's will is that no one will perish. In light of this, consider:
  - Are you jealous about your faith?
  - Are you willing to risk rejection to proclaim the coming Kingdom of God?
  - Are you praying for those in your life (family, friends, neighbours, and workmates) who do not know the Lord or do not have an established relationship with Him?
  - Do you show mercy to those within the church who stumble? Have you been helping them up to renewed faith or pushing them out of fellowship with believers?
  - Think of one person within your church whose faith you could encourage this week.

REVELATION

Christ Victorious

"Behold, I am coming soon, bringing my recompense with me, to repay everyone for what he has done. I am the Alpha and the Omega, the first and the last, the beginning and the end." Blessed are those who wash their robes, so that they may have the right to the tree of life and that they may enter the city by the gates. – Revelation 22:12-14

Note: Do not miss the beauty of this book by carrying in preconceived thoughts or ideas to your study of it. Many people have been burdened with undue fear towards this book. Others do not wish to study it because they have been told it is too difficult to understand. There are some debated passages in Revelation, but overall it is a book of encouragement and hope for the people of God. It should bring excitement, joy, anticipation, and peace to the hearts of Christians. Enjoy it!

During your first reading

Themes to track
- Worthiness of the Lamb
- God's judgement and mercy
- God's justice and wrath
- Kingdom of God – triumphant and victorious
- Praise and worship
- Enduring persecution

During your second reading

Things to notice in the text
- Underline the promises of God, for example: "I will . . ." statements.
- Mark beside passages that convey an aspect of God's character.
- Mark beside passages that relate to one of the themes. Choose a different

colour or symbol for each theme.
- Notice the contrast between:
    o Those whose names are written in the book of life, and those whose names are not;
    o Those who bear the mark of the Lamb, and those who bear the mark of the beast;
    o The saints, and those who spilt the blood of the saints.

Chapter summaries

These are optional as they can be time consuming for the larger books. If you choose to do them, you will receive a much deeper appreciation of the book. By the end of The IBSC, you will have paraphrased the entire Bible! Go through each chapter and try to summarise it in one paragraph, using your own words; force yourself to stay big picture and capture the heart of each chapter.

After your initial readings

Setting of Revelation
Author

Revelation was penned by Apostle John, but the words and message were given to him by Christ Jesus.

Recipient

Revelation was written to the churches of Ephesus, Smyrna, Pergamum, Thyatira, Sardis, Philadelphia, and Laodicea.

Date and place of writing

John wrote Revelation at the end of the first century AD; around 81-96 AD from the Island of Patmos.

Reason written

God told John to write down his revelation, and so he did! Jesus was bringing encouragement to His early church, which was facing tribulation and persecution. It was a significant time in the church's history with John, the last remaining apostle, drawing close to the end of his life.

Big picture
Historical background
  1. Ephesus

Ephesus, near present-day Selçuk in Izmir Province, Turkey, was the foremost city in Asia Minor and boasted the temple of the Greek goddess, Artemis. As well as worshipping Greek gods, many people practiced magic arts and were involved in the mystery religions. It had a large colony of Jews and is thought to have been the home of Apostle John, during his old age, before being exiled to the Island of Patmos.

The church in this city was probably founded by Pricilla, Aquila, and Paul. The

Nicolaitans, who practiced pagan worship and immorality, opposed the church. By the time Revelation was written, the church had successfully persevered through false teachers, but had sadly lost its "first love".

For further information see *historical background* from the book of Ephesians.

2. Smyrna

Located at a strategic point on the Aegean coast, Smyrna was a natural port and successful in sea trade. It was situated in modern Turkey's providence of Izmir. Under the Roman Empire it became famous for beautiful buildings, and was a centre of education. Smyrna became the hub of emperor worship from 23 AD, and also had temples to the Greek god, Zeus, and the Phrygian goddess, Cybele. The Gospel probably reached Smyrna at an early date. The Smyrnean church suffered from persecution at the hands of the Jews as well as poverty.

3. Pergamum

Pergamum, in modern-day Mysia, Turkey, was the official capital of the province of Asia and was accessible via the river Caicus by small sea craft. The first temple of the imperial cult was built there in 29 BC in honour of Rome and Caesar Augustus. It was a centre of worship for four great pagan gods: Zeus, Athena, Dionysus, and Asclepios. The church in Pergamum was founded as Paul's teaching spread from Ephesus.

4. Thyatira

Thyatira, the modern Turkish city of Ak-Hissar, occupied an important position on the Roman road system, strategically situated on the main road between Laodicea and Pergamum. Never a large city, it was, nevertheless, a thriving manufacturing centre, and every tradesman was required to be a member of an organised guild. Meetings of the trade guilds were tied up with acts of pagan worship and immorality. Apart from trade, the city was part of the imperial post road linking Italy, Greece, and Asia Minor to Egypt.

5. Sardis

One of oldest and most important cities in Asia Minor, Sardis was located in modern Sart, in Turkey's Manisa Province. In early times, it was a wealthy city, but lost its prominence after being destroyed by an earthquake in 17 AD. Although subsequently rebuilt, the city never regained its former status. The church was probably founded as Paul preached in Ephesus.

6. Philadelphia

Philadelphia, the modern city of Alaşehir in the Manisa Province of Turkey, was also destroyed by an earthquake in 17 AD and was rebuilt. It gained commercial prosperity and was a wine-growing district. The city became known as "Little Athens" for its beautiful buildings and temples.

The church was probably founded as Paul ministered in Ephesus. It remained steadfast and loyal to the Gospel amidst persecution. Some believe that the "synagogue of Satan" that Christ mentioned in Revelation was a reference to the temple of Zeus in Philadelphia; however, Jesus also mentioned that the members of the synagogue claimed to be Jews, making it more likely that He was referring to the Jewish synagogue, who denounced Christ and Christianity.

7. Laodicea

Laodicea is located in the modern-day Turkish province of Denizli. It lay on an important crossroad and was surrounded by fertile land. The city had no permanent water supply and therefore had to pipe water from hot springs, which arrived lukewarm – hence the illustration used in Revelation. Laodicea was made rich from industry, banking, and commerce. The city was probably reached by the Gospel at an early time. Laodicea had a large Jewish population.

Character portrayal – Laodicean believer

"Oh Father, I come to you with a sorrowful heart! We have been proud of our wealth in Laodicea. Break our hearts that seek riches for ourselves. Draw us back to you. May we repent and cry out to you. May your Spirit come back into our church, touching lives and transforming hearts.

"All my wealth . . . I cast it aside. What good is it to have storehouses filled with gold, and yet not know you? What will wealth get me in the next life? How many times have we heard the apostles preach your command not to store up treasures on earth, where moth and rust destroy and where thieves break in and steal [1], but that is exactly what I have done.

"I give all I have to you. Show me where I am to use my wealth for your kingdom. All I have and all I am belong to you. I am yours; heart, body, mind, and soul. Refine me; make me to see. Grant me your eternal riches and treasure that will not fade. Lord, I kneel before you in repentance! Once again, ignite my passion for the Gospel. Let my life be lived as a song of praise to you."

With Jacob's heartfelt confession came a wave of peace and the knowledge of forgiveness. God would not condemn him for his sins. Christ had died to save him. It was by grace alone that he would receive the crown of life. He asked the Lord to add fuel to the fire within him. He did not want it to die down – not for fear that he would miss out on a heavenly paradise, but because he knew what God had done for him, a sinner. Whilst God demanded everything, he knew that the Lord was worth everything and more.

Getting to his feet, he disdained the beauty within his house with inner columns of polished stones, lifelike statues, and exquisitely detailed carvings. It was time he gave to his neighbours, who were in need. He would not wait a moment longer. Praising the Lord with a heart of thanksgiving, he went into the streets to show God's love to others.

Book overview

Christ's revelation came to a persecuted church, asking: "Where is God in the midst of our sufferings?" They watched loved ones die for their faith, and feared for their safety. They were in need of encouragement and strengthening. Christ essentially said to them: "Worship me because I am worthy of your life, and I am worthy of your death". It was a message of comfort and hope.

Remember that John knew what it meant to suffer for his faith; he saw Jesus die, he was literally thrown into a boiling pot of oil, he witnessed the growing persecution against the church, and saw Christians tortured for their faith. And yet, he saw this revelation as a message that would bring hope and encouragement to believers throughout Asia Minor. Do not forget that John was worshipping God for the message of this book.

Revelation was foremost a message of hope. Yes, there are some graphic images in Revelation, but for the believers who read Revelation it should bring with it comfort and a desire to evangelise. The revelation was to bring hope, comfort, and a desire to praise God through hardships. It is such a beautiful picture of what believers have awaiting them. And who is the painter? God; God was the One who brought this message of hope to His church.

Revelation declares the truth that Jesus wins, and so do His saints! Jesus was a faithful witness, which can also be translated as "martyr" (Strong, J, 1989)[2]. He suffered; He was the first born of the dead; killed, He rose victorious over death, and paved the way for the saints whose names are written in the Book of Life. Jesus is victorious, and believers achieve victory in Christ. He is the conquering Lamb. He is the hope of the church.

Help with difficult passages
Stick to the big picture when studying Revelation!

There is a wealth of theology based very loosely on single verses pulled out of context from Revelation. There is also much disagreement among respected theologians on the meaning of specific passages. Do not let this daunt you when studying the book.

Remember the big picture and the reason why Christ gave this revelation to the churches. It was to bring them comfort, and strengthen them to remain steadfast in their faith amidst persecution. Similarly, it should bring comfort, peace, hope, and joy to all believers who soak in its message.

Do not forget context when studying Revelation!

This book references other scriptures and therefore cannot be read in isolation. It is beneficial to study the Old Testament prior to studying the book of Revelation. Think of this book as a retelling of the same story, which is told throughout Scripture, simply put into a 3-dimentional movie. Much of the content in this book is not new information!

In Revelation, you will find fresh views of visions from the Old Testament. For example, the woman Jezebel is referred to in Revelation 2:20. Jezebel can be found in 1 Kings 16-21 and 2 Kings 9 as the evil queen who sought to destroy the Israelites and kill God's prophets. She led the people into idolatry and worship of the false god, Baal. This brought abominable practices, including child sacrifices and sexual immorality, into the land of Israel. It was a dark and evil time. From the Old Testament reference to Jezebel, it can be supposed that the church in Thyatira was also tolerating sexual immorality and idol worship (similar to Corinth).

Help with imagery

- The common interpretation of number symbolism in the Bible is as follows:
  - o The number 3 is symbolic of divine perfection.
  - o The number 6 is given to be the number of man, short of perfection (seven), and evil.
  - o The number 7 is symbolic of perfection and fullness, and is often considered as referring to spiritual perfection.
  - o The number 10 symbolises completion or completeness of order.
  - o The number 12 is also symbolic for completion, and is often considered to refer to governmental perfection.
- 7 lampstands = 7 churches (Revelation 1:11, 20)
- 7 stars = angels of the seven churches (Revelation 1:20)
  - o This is interpreted as either literal angels protecting the churches or the elders of the seven churches. The root word from Greek is "aggelos" means "messenger", and can refer to an angel or church pastor (Strong, J, 1989)[3].
- 7 lamps of fire burning before the throne = 7 spirits of God (Revelation 4:5)
  - o This is gathered to be the seven characteristics of God, by reference to Isaiah 11:2, which says: *"And the Spirit of the LORD shall rest upon him, the Spirit of wisdom and understanding, the Spirit of counsel and might, the Spirit of knowledge and the fear of the LORD".*
  - o Seven lampstands are equated with the Holy Spirit as in Zechariah 4:2-6.
- 7 horns (Revelation 5:6)
  - o Elsewhere in Scripture, horns are associated with power. See 1 Kings 22:11 (false prophets); Ezekiel 34:21; Daniel 8:3-4; Zechariah 1:18-21.
  - o Revelation 5:6 declares the seven horns to be the seven spirits of God sent out into all the earth.
- 7 eyes (Revelation 5:6)
  - o Seven eyes are also mentioned in Zechariah 3:7-4:14; however, their exact meaning in Revelation 5:6 remains unclear. Zechariah 4:10 appears to be referring to the all-knowing character of God who sees all that happens throughout the world.
  - o Revelation 5:6 declares them to be the seven spirits of God sent out into all the earth.
- Four living creatures, with eyes in front and in back; 6 wings; like lion, like ox, like man, like flying eagle (Revelation 4:5-11)
  - o There was a Rabbinic teaching at this time, saying: *"the mightiest among birds is the eagle, the mightiest among domesticated animals is the ox, the mightiest amongst beasts is the lion, and the mightiest of all is man".*
  - o The most accepted interpretation is that all creation worships the

Lord (because this would make sense to the original readers). The best of everything worships Him and the centre of all worship is God.

- o The sealed 144,000 (Revelation 7, 14, 21)
- o This number is thought to represent: 12x12x10x10x10. Remembering that there were twelve tribes of Israel (representing the people of God), and that the numbers ten and twelve are both symbolic of perfection, it is thought that this number represents the complete number of God's chosen people – all the people who will come to salvation in Christ, and enter into His kingdom.

- 7 trumpets (Revelation 8)
  - o In the Old Testament, trumpets heralded war. At the mentioning of trumpets, the original reader would be preparing to see war and battle described.
- The number of the beast is 666 (Revelation 13)
  - o Keep the original readers in mind. They saw the number 6 as symbolic of evil, short of perfection. So seeing the number 666 would have them thinking: "evil, evil, evil".
- Prostitution, adultery, and sexual immorality were used throughout the Old Testament to represent the idolatry of God's people against Him.
- To the original readers, Babylon represented evil. In their minds, it would be associated with persecution, and the nation that led the people of God into exile. It was also seen as a nation of sexual immorality and idolatry, which led into sin. At the time of writing, Rome was often called "Babylon" by the Jews.

Interpreting the book of Revelation

Notes: Remember to stay big picture when interpreting the book of Revelation! Pray for the Holy Spirit to help you lay down all of your pre-conceived ideas about the book and see what it would have meant to the original readers, the seven churches listed in the revelation.

The interpretation of a great portion of this book is not yet known, because God has not chosen to reveal it, but most of this REALLY does not matter! Do not get hung up on images or small details. Stay big picture! Consider what is knowable, and why Christ gave this revelation to the seven churches.

Interpretation questions
1. Who bore witness to the prophecy? Why was it important that John made it clear that the revelation was not his own?
2. How does Christ portray Himself throughout the revelation?
   a. List all the ways He described Himself and which of His names He revealed. What do they show of His character and attributes?
   b. Why did Christ come to the earth?
   c. What example did He set for believers?

      d. What has He achieved?

      e. Did He overcome?

      f. What position does He hold?

3. For each of the seven churches, identify the following from Christ's messages to them:

      a. Christ's character;

      b. Christ's commendation: "I know . . .";

      c. Christ's complaint: "I know . . .";

      d. Christ's challenge;

      e. Christ's threat; and

      f. Christ's covenant promise – each church was given a promise of eternal life, if they overcame.

4. After you have identified each segment of Christ's message, note how you believe each church would feel receiving the message.

      a. Consider what the church's response may have been, as well as how individuals within the church might have reacted.

      b. Would this have changed their view of Christ? If so, in what way?

5. Which of the churches do you believe Christ came down hardest upon?

      a. What was His complaint against them?

      b. What is the implication of His sternness upon the faults of this specific church? What does this show about attitudes of the heart?

      c. Can you find other scriptures to support what you discover?

6. Remember that, in Bible study, accurate interpretation of an individual passage is gained through the context of the book and the entirety of Scripture. Discover where else in Scripture the following images, people, and items can be found. Please note that electronic Bibles are useful tools when seeking specific scripture references; refer to *Additional study resources* for a few popular ones. Find additional scriptural references for the following images:

      a. Lamb (used throughout Revelation);

      b. Lampstand (Revelation 1:12-13,20; 2:1; 11:14);

      c. Sword (Revelation 1:16; 2:12,16; 19:15,21);

      d. Balak and Balaam (Revelation 2:14);

      e. Key of David (Revelation 3:7);

      f. Lion (Revelation 5:5);

      g. Jerusalem (Revelation 3:12; 21:2,10);

      h. Bowl of incense (Revelation 5:8; 8:3-5);

      i. Plagues (Revelation 9:18-19; 15-16; 18:4,8; 22:18);

      j. Two olive trees and Two lampstands (Revelation 11:4-14);

      k. Sodom and Egypt (Revelation 11:8);

      l. Firstfruits (Revelation 14:4);

      m. Babylon (Revelation 14:8; 16:19; 17:5; 18:2,10,21);

      n. Sickle, reap, harvest, winepress of wrath (Revelation 14:14-20; 19:15);

      o. Bowl of wrath (Revelation 16);

     p. Bride (Revelation19:7; 21:2,9,17);

     q. Water/ river of life (Revelation 21:6; 22:1,17).

7. Consider Apostle John:
     a. How would John have felt as he received the revelation?
     b. What was his response?
     c. Would it have changed the way he worshipped the Lord or how he ministered to the churches?

8. How would Revelation have helped the original readers, being persecuted for their beliefs, to remain firm in their faith? Consider:
     a. What was heavier: their fears or God's glory and worthiness?
     b. How would Christ's revelation have helped them to choose endurance, rather than turning back to worldly comforts, when faced with opposition and persecution?
     c. Consider the mentioning of the bowls of incense (the prayers of the saints), and note why God's acknowledgement of these would have been meaningful to the original readers. See Philippians 1:21-25.
     d. What traits were encouraged in the original readers?
     e. What character attributes of the saints were commended?
     f. What are the rewards promised in Revelation for those who "overcome"?

9. According to what is seen in Revelation, why is Christ worthy of praise?
     a. How is He worshipped?
     b. Why is He glorified?
     c. Is He glorified through His sacrifice, His victory or both?

10. How was the throne room of God described in Revelation? Look at the background information given above under *Help with imagery* pertaining to the four living creatures.

11. Remember that the original readers were facing death and torture for their beliefs. In light of this, what was the significance of God saying, from the beginning: "I am worthy of your worship; all of creation will sing my praise"?

12. Consider the contrasting images of the Lion of the Tribe of Judah and the Lamb that was Slain:
     a. Think on the imagery.
     b. Where else in Scripture has Christ been described as a lion or lamb?
     c. Where else does Scripture show power coming from suffering?
     d. How would this have encouraged the original readers to persevere?

13. What is learnt of heaven, the "new Jerusalem"?

14. What is learnt of the "great day of the Lord"?
     a. How does this fit with other scriptures regarding Christ's return?
     b. What is the significance of John not being able to record what he saw of the mighty angel in Revelation 10:1-7?

15. The scroll with 7 seals (Revelation 5:1-9:21)
    a. Stay big picture when looking at the seals. Consider the result of opening each seal. What events on earth were the scrolls depicting? How have these been seen throughout history in the way men act towards one another?
    b. What did the four horsemen bring? What would this have represented to the original readers?
    c. What is the implication for the saints, as seen upon the opening of the fifth scroll? How would this have encouraged endurance and given hope to the original readers?
    d. What does the sixth seal show regarding the result of the wrath of the Lamb coming on the great day? What do you learn of Christ's return in this passage?
    e. To the original reader, the seventh seal would have depicted their entering into the very presence of God, an image of heaven, and the end to the chaos and destruction around them. How would this have impacted them, given their current situation of turmoil? How would reflecting on the complete peace to come have helped them to endure – would it have helped them to endure?

16. The 144,000 sealed, and those marked (Revelation 7 and 14:1-13)
    a. Read all of Revelation 7. In light of Revelation 7:9-10, do you believe that 144,000 is a literal number, the total number of those who will receive salvation?
    b. Notice that God's chosen are the first marked (chapter 7), before those of the beast are marked (chapter 14). Is this significant; why or why not?
    c. What was the significance to the original readers of hearing of those sealed by the Lamb, just after Christ told of the six seals of judgement? What was God communicating to the churches?
    d. Recall that the number twelve is symbolic of completion and the twelve tribes represented the people of God. Also remember that adultery in the Old Testament was used to describe Israel's idolatry against God.

17. The 7 trumpets (Revelation 8:1-9:21)
    a. The seven trumpets follow a similar pattern to the seven seals; the first six were depictions of God's coming wrath and judgement on mankind. The seven trumpets can be seen to depict nature's judgement against man.
    b. What is the significance of only a third being destroyed, damaged or affected in the first four, and sixth, trumpet sounds, and that there was a timeframe placed on the affliction coming from the fifth trumpet? Look at verses 20-21 for a hint. What was God's goal in these disasters? Was He sending random judgement or did it have a purpose? What does this show of God's heart towards man and His mercy?

      c. Compare the plagues coming with the sixth trumpet to the plagues of Egypt. What would this have meant to the original readers?

      d. The seventh trumpet signals the coming of the Kingdom of God. How would John and the original readers have felt at this? What will happen on this day, as seen in this passage?

18. The scroll to eat (Revelation 10)

      a. Compare this command to the one given to Ezekiel in Ezekiel 3.

      b. The scroll describes the Gospel message: bitter to those of the world, but sweet news to believers. Where else in Scripture are there similar comparisons about faith bringing a different perspective to the world? Would this encourage the readers to proclaim their faith; why or why not?

19. Two olive trees and two lampstands (Revelation 11:1-14)

      a. What is the significance of them being dressed in sackcloth?

      b. In verse 3, they are seen to be two witnesses sent to the earth, which were killed by the world. Notice what will come upon those who did harm to these witnesses.

      c. How would the original readers have felt as they read of the death of these witnesses?

      d. How would the original readers have felt when they heard of God calling the witnesses to life again?

      e. How would this have encouraged the readers to live as witnesses to Christ, and the Gospel?

20. The woman and the dragon (Revelation 12:1-13:1a) There is much debate surrounding the dragon (and the beasts). If you do not come to a decided opinion that is okay! Remember to look at what the image was depicting, and how it would have been interpreted by the original readers. Look at what they cause (destruction, harm, leading others astray), their involvement with the saints and with man, and their end. Stay big picture.

      a. Who did the dragon represent? (Common views include Satan or King Herod).

      b. Consider the vulnerability of a woman in childbirth. Christ was vulnerable coming to earth as a helpless babe. What does this scene show of God's sovereignty, power, and protection? What does it show of the will of God versus the will of Satan? Who is in control? Who is almighty?

      c. Who fought in the battle? Who had the victory? How does salvation come? Through whom does it come? Who has the authority? Who is the accuser?

      d. Who are the woman's offspring? What happens to them?

      e. How would this passage encourage those watching friends and relatives being martyred? See John 16:33.

21. A beast out of the sea and the earth (Revelation 13:1b-18)

As mentioned above, it is okay not to take a decisive standpoint with the theology surrounding the beast, or its number 666, or other controversial details in Revelation. Stay big picture! Look at the context of the whole passage and its core message about God, the saints, and those against God. Consider what it meant to the original readers.

    a.   Who worshipped the beast, and what caused them to follow it? Who was the beast against? What was the attitude of the beast and its worshippers towards God?

    b.   What is the significance of the beast of the earth being like a lamb in appearance, but speaking like a dragon? What attribute might this represent?

    c.   How are the saints called to respond?

    d.   What two sides are depicted by the two marks? Who is safe from the mark of the beast? What does this show about assurance of salvation?

    e.   How would Revelation 13:8 and 14:1-5 reassure the original readers that they had been distinctly marked as separate to those marked by the beast?

    f.   Find other scriptural verses that would encourage believers to know that those in Christ are safe. Consider Revelation 15:2.

22. Eternal Gospel (Revelation 14:6-13)

See these passages as a continuation of Revelation 13:1b-18. The beast of the earth marked those who were not in Christ. The Lamb has marked His own, and the Father's name is written on their foreheads.

    a.   To whom is the eternal Gospel proclaimed? What should be their response?

    b.   What will befall those belonging to the beast?

    c.   How should the saints respond? Why should the saints find hope and reason to endure, from hearing that those of the beast will face the wrath of God?

23. The wrath of God (Revelation 14:14-16:21)

    a.   Notice the contrast of the two harvests. The first harvest is ripe, but the type of harvest is not specified; the second harvest is of grapes and is thrown into the winepress. Who belongs to the first harvest and who to the second? Who is God separating in the harvests? How would this have encouraged the original readers?

    b.   What is the significance of the interlude in Revelation 15:2-4? What would this convey to the original readers? Also consider whom the plagues fall upon in Revelation 16:2.

    c.   Who conquerors and who is defeated? What is the response of those who are victorious? What happens to the beast, dragon, false prophet, Babylon, and the kingdom of the beast?

    d.   What do you learn of God's character, the wrath of God, and His judgement? What should man's response be to the coming judgement? What was the response of the saints? Compare this with the response of those who bear the mark of the beast.

e. Consider the phrase "they did not repent" in Revelation 16:9, repeated in Revelation 16:11. What does this show of God's desire for those currently walking contrary to His ways?

f. When will Christ bring final judgement upon the earth? Also consider: Matthew 4:42-44; 1 Thessalonians 5:1-5; 2 Peter 3:10-13.

24. The fall of Babylon (Revelation 17:1-19:10)

a. Consider the imagery used in these chapters. How was the great prostitute described? What emotions are raised by the description? How would the persecuted churches have felt as they listened to this imagery?

b. What is the limit of the beast's authority? Notice the comparison to Christ: Christ "was and *is* and is to come", whereas the beast "once was, now *is not* and yet will come". For how long will the beast come?

c. What sins were brought against Babylon?

d. Who will bring the prostitute to ruin? Who placed this purpose in their hearts? What does this show of God's sovereignty?

e. What are the various responses to the fall of Babylon, the fall of the great prostitute? What happens to the earth? What does the angel proclaim? How are the saints looked after? How do the kings and merchants respond? What is the response of those in heaven?

f. How would these chapters hearten the believers being persecuted for testifying to Christ? Would it have increased their trust in God?

g. What is the significance in relation to attaining assurance of faith?

h. Who is invited to the wedding feast of Christ? What is the wedding feast? Who are those that are blessed? How do you suppose the original readers would have responded?

25. Judgement of Satan and the dead (Revelation 19:11-20:15) There are many views surrounding this passage; about the time frames, and whether it should be interpreted literally or symbolically. Nevertheless, it is enough to reflect on the big picture: who conquers, who is dictating the time frames, what happens to the saints, and what end does Satan face? In addition, consider what it would have meant to the original readers.

a. What do you learn of Christ, the Judge? What do you learn of how He rules as King? What is His purpose for coming out of heaven and down to the earth?

b. Where are His followers shown to be? Who is on which side of the two battling armies? What would this have conveyed to the original readers?

c. Who should the original readers fear? Which is heavier: God's worthiness or their fear of persecution in the current life?

    d. What do you see of the worthiness of God? Is He worth dying for?

    e. Who is being judged? Why are they unworthy of the Lamb?

    f. Contrast the wedding feast of the Lamb to the great supper of God.

    g. What is the significance of Satan's power being shown to be limited? Why is he bound? Who is dictating the amount of time?

    h. Notice that there are multiple books; those whose names are in the Book of Life will receive the new Jerusalem, but those who are not in the Book of Life will be judged by what was written of their deeds in the other books, and then thrown into the lake of fire. How would the original readers have responded to this? What does this show of God's grace and mercy? What is the significance regarding the works of the saints? What does it tell of salvation? Go back to Romans 3:21-28 and Ephesians 1:7-10.

26. Everything made new (Revelation 21-22)

    a. Where will God dwell? How would the original readers respond to this promise?

    b. What other promises are given in these final chapters, and what is their significance to believers?

    c. What will no longer exist? Why will the temple no longer be needed?

    d. Consider the following, and what they reveal of God's heart towards mankind:

        i. Read Genesis 1 and 2. Read John 1:1,11. Compare these verses to the vision received by John in Revelation 21 and 22. The Bible starts with God walking with man and ends in the same way.

        ii. To the original readers, the repetition of the number twelve would symbolise the people of God. To them, the city would be communicating that God's city is His people; His dwelling place is with His people.

    e. Take time pondering on this vision and the details within it.

Creative interpretation

1. Explore what Scripture says about the end times and Christ's second coming. Remember not to enter into your study with preconceived ideas, holding to popular theologies, but rather, seek what is said by Scripture.

    a. What does Revelation reveal about the end times and what remains uncertain?

    b. Where else is Christ's return discussed in Scripture? Compare these verses with what you have learnt through Revelation.

2. Write a summary on worship as seen through the book of Revelation. Include how God is worshipped through Revelation, why He is worthy of worship, why this revelation would have lead the original readers to

worship Him, and why worship should be the response of today's believers to the message of Revelation.

3. Look at the following repetitions in Revelation:
   a. Write a summary about the judgement of God based on the following passages:
      i. Revelation 6:1-8:1 – the seven seals (man judging man);
      ii. Revelation 8:6-15:19 – the seven trumpets (creation judging man);
      iii. Revelation 15-16 – the seven bowls (God judging man).
   b. Write a summary about the final battle based on the following passages. Be sure to include who is on which side, and what happens to the armies.
      i. Revelation 16: 12-20 – the battle of Armageddon;
      ii. Revelation 17-18 – judgement of the great prostitute;
      iii. Revelation 19:19-21 – judgement of the beast and false prophet;
      iv. Revelation 20:7-15 – judgement on Satan and those whose names are not in the Book of Life.

Application inspiration

- Ponder on Revelation 21:3-4, which reveals God's desire for intimacy with man.
- Journal through the following questions:
  o What were your feelings about the end times before beginning your study of Revelation? How has this book changed or added to what you feel and believe?
  o What impacted you the most during your study of Revelation? How will this affect you in daily life?
  o How has this book impacted your view of persecution and the need for endurance as Christ's servant? Do you really believe that God is worthy of your life? Do you value Him as worth more than anything else in your life? See Romans 8:24-39.
  o Do you live in light of Christ's victory? Do you underestimate the power of the cross, the resurrection, and the authority and power of God? Do you live a life of victory, knowing that Satan has been bound (he has power, but God's people overcome with Christ)? See also Ephesians 1:18-23 and 2:4-10.
  o How has this book affected your view of God and your worship of Him?

[1] Matthew 6:19-20

[2] Strong, James, S.T.D., LL.D., (1989). *Strong's Hebrew and Greek Dictionaries*, e-*Sword*, Ver. 9.7.2, Dictionary, G3144.

[3] Strong, James, S.T.D., LL.D., (1989). *Strong's Hebrew and Greek Dictionaries, e-Sword*, Ver. 9.7.2, Dictionary, G32.

GLOSSARY OF TERMS

Age of the apostles

The "age of the apostles" was the period of time after Christ's ascension, during which His disciples spread the Good News of the kingdom out from Judah into the world. Its beginning was marked by the coming of the promised Holy Spirit on the day of Pentecost.

Allegories

An allegory is a type of analogy, as are metaphors and similes. Allegories use story form, telling of something known, to symbolically represent a deeper meaning, intangible concept or depict a message. For example, Hosea's life became an allegory for God's relationship with the people of Israel.

Analogies

An analogy uses two things with common features to make one of them easier to understand; allegories, metaphors and similes are all types of analogies.

Antinomianism

Antinomianism is the false teaching that, since faith alone is necessary for salvation, one is free from the moral obligations of the Law. It was prevalent during the age of the apostles.

Apostasy

Apostasy refers to a person falling away from the truth. An apostate is one who has renounced their former religious beliefs and faith, and now walks in opposition to them.

Asceticism

Asceticism was one of two streams of belief arising from dualism. Dualism taught a separation of body from spirit, with the body being evil and the spirit, good. Asceticism held that the flesh had to be punished for its evil. Those practicing asceticism inflicted physical punishment upon their bodies believing this would bring them closer to God; this resulted in fasting, self-affliction, and denying of themselves.

Atonement

Atonement refers to making amends for wrong. To atone for one's sin is to pay the price of the sin. Atoning results in forgiveness, reconciliation, and cleansing.

Cabirus cult

The Cabirus cult was a cult in Thessalonica that taught of a coming redeemer. The cult caused confusion within the church by preaching on the second coming, and people began substituting Christianity for the teachings of the cult.

Canaan

Canaan was the land promised to the Israelites, the Promised Land. Before Israel conquered the land, it consisted of many small kingdoms. The land of Canaan was entered in 1406 BC and divided among the twelve tribes of Israel.

Canaanites

The Canaanites were the original inhabitants of the land of Canaan, whom the Israelites forced out when they conquered the Promised Land. Unfaithful to God's commands, the people of Israel did not rid the land of all its original inhabitants, and these remaining people led the Israelites into sin against God.

Day of the Lord

The "day of the Lord", seen in many books of the prophets, primarily referred to the coming judgement of God upon the physical nation of Israel (Northern Kingdom of Israel), and Judah (southern kingdom of Israel), which was seen when these nations were taken into exile. Israel went into exile in 722 BC, at the hands of the Assyrians, and Judah, in 586 BC, at the hands of the Babylonians.

Dualism

Dualism was a common body of belief in the age of the apostles. Dualism held that the body (physical matter) was evil and the spirit, good. This led to either libertarianism (what is done with the body does not matter, so indulge the flesh), or asceticism (the body must be punished). Dualistic beliefs also caused fear in the early church, with a belief circulating that the end times had come in the spiritual realm and they had missed Christ's return.

Divided Kingdom (of Israel)

The kingdom of Israel divided after the death of King Solomon, during the reign of his son, Rehoboam, in 931 BC. The southern tribes of Judah and Benjamin remained loyal to Rehoboam, despite the hard yoke he put on the people, and became known as the southern kingdom of Judah. The remaining tribes rebelled against the king and chose Jeroboam as their ruler, as God had foretold; they became known as the Northern Kingdom of Israel.

Edom

The nation of Edom was founded by the descendants of Esau, who was the son of Isaac and the elder twin brother of Jacob. In Numbers 20, Edom refused to allow their brothers, the Israelites, to pass through their land on the Israelites' way to the Promised Land. The judgement of Edom was prophesied in the book of Obadiah. The land of Edom forms part of modern-day Jordan.

Enacted symbols

Sometimes the prophets were called to use physical actions to visually illustrate God's message. For example, Ezekiel 4:1-5:17 records God's commands to Ezekiel to act out different elements of the final siege against Jerusalem.

Ephraim

Ephraim was the second son of Joseph and founded one of the tribes of Israel. The term "Ephraim" is also used in the prophets to represent the people of the Northern Kingdom of Israel.

Epicureanism

Epicureanism was a popular school of philosophy during the age of the apostles. This stream of thought did not believe in an afterlife and therefore taught that one should only seek after pleasure in this world.

Epistles

Epistles are letters. The epistles in the Bible are the letters written to the early churches; for example, 1 John.

Gnostic/ gnosticism

Gnosticism has its name from the Greek word "gnosis", meaning "knowledge", and taught the separation of body from spirit (dualism). It came from the combining of several belief systems and religions of the early first century AD. Some in this sect believed that Jesus was one of the lesser gods who helped man to climb up a "spiritual ladder" to the "good god (father god)".

Gnosticism caused turmoil within the early church with false teachers entering the congregations and preaching that, on its own, faith in Jesus was not sufficient for salvation.

Great day of the Lord

The "great day of the Lord", seen in many books of the prophets, primarily referred to the final judgement of man, which will occur at Christ's return. It will bring in the fullness of the Kingdom of God.

Greco-Roman world view

The Greco-Roman mindset held a low view of work, which was seen as appropriate for slaves, not freemen. Those who did manual labour were looked down upon and the mind was glorified.

Greek philosophy

In New Testament times, philosophers arose amidst the multitude of gods and idols to seek out a different path to enlightenment through wisdom and reason. They would gather together to discuss their philosophies on what was truth, how life should be lived, and how society should be governed.

Hellenists

Alexander the Great conquered the known world and began the process of hellenisation, compelling captive peoples to adopt Greek culture, language, and religion. The Hellenists were Jews who adopted the Greek culture and language (but not religion). They mostly lived outside of Judea, and because they lost their ability to speak Hebrew, the Old Testament was translated into Greek, and this translation was known as the Septuagint.

Israel

During the years of the United Kingdom of Israel (1043-931 BC), Israel refers to the united nation of Israel, made up of the twelve tribes of Israel in the Promised Land. After the kingdom divided in 931 BC, the Northern Kingdom became known as Israel, and consisted of ten of the tribes of Israel (the tribes of Benjamin and Judah became the southern kingdom of Judah).

Judges

During the time of the judges (approximately 1406-1043 BC), God was King over His people. A cyclical pattern emerged during this time, where the people broke God's commandments, came under attack from surrounding nations as a result of their disobedience, and then cried out to God in repentance. God, in His mercy, would send judges to save the people from their enemies. Thirteen of these judges were recorded in the book of Judges. They were ordinary men and women with flawed characters, who were used by God to His glory.

Judah

Judah was the fourth son of Jacob and Leah, and founded one of the tribes of Israel. Of the twelve tribes of Israel, Judah and Benjamin were the only two who remained loyal to King Rehoboam when the kingdom of Israel divided in 931 BC. Judah became the name of the southern kingdom of Judah, consisting of the tribes of Benjamin and Judah.

Lament

Laments are passionate displays of grief. The prophets were given God's heart for the people, which was a bitter sweet blessing for they had to watch as God's judgement fell upon the nation as a result of the people's rebellion. The most famous lament is recorded in Lamentations and is attributed to the prophet, Jeremiah.

Libertarianism

Libertarianism was one of two streams of thought arising from dualistic beliefs. Dualism taught a separation of body from spirit, with the body being evil and the spirit, good. Libertarianism held that, as only the soul was divine and immortal, one could do as one pleased with the body, which was earthly. Followers of libertarianism thought that they could gratify the desires of the flesh without spiritual consequences attached; this led to sexual immorality, gluttony, murder, and other vices.

Major Prophets

The books of the Major Prophets are: Isaiah, Jeremiah, Ezekiel, and Daniel. The terms "minor" and "major" are not indicative of the importance of the books; rather, they refer to the length of the books.

Minor Prophets

The books of the Minor Prophets are: Hosea, Joel, Amos, Obadiah, Jonah, Micah, Nahum, Habakkuk, Zephaniah, Haggai, Zechariah, and Malachi. The terms "minor" and "major" are not indicative of the importance of the books; rather, they refer to the length of the books.

Mount Zion

See "Zion".

Mystery religions

The largest group of cults existing during the age of the apostles was known by the general term "mystery religions". These cults grew in popularity as a result of the unforgiving Greek gods. The mystery religions promised secret knowledge (that was needed to progress step by step towards the "good god"), and immortality (through the practice of secret rites and rituals). Many of the rituals included blood sacrifices, orgies, self-mutilation, ceremonial washings (often with blood), magic, and sexual acts with priests and priestesses.

Northern Kingdom of Israel

See "Divided Kingdom" and "Israel".

Oracles

Oracles were the predictions given to the Israelites and surrounding nations. They either gave predictions of God's coming judgement, for the sins of the nation or promises of restoration, giving hope to the people of Israel.

Original hearers

In the IBSC, the term "original hearers" denotes the people who were present when the events recorded in any given book took place. For example, original hearers of the parables of Christ included the Pharisees, the crowds, and His disciples.

Original readers

In the IBSC, the term "original readers" denotes the people who were the intended recipients of any given book of the Bible. For example, the original readers of the Gospel of Mark were those of the church in Rome between 64 and 69 AD. The original readers are also referred to as the "recipient" in the IBSC.

Parity covenant

A parity covenant was a common covenant in Old Testament times, in which a covenant was made between equals.

Pharisees

The Pharisees were the dominant sect within Judaism. They were responsible for the creation of the oral law, teaching the laws to the people, and ensuring that the Law was kept. The Pharisees set themselves apart for the keeping of the Law, promising to keep every single law, both of Moses and the oral traditions. Teaching and worship mainly occurred within synagogues, rather than the temple.

Polytheism

Polytheism is the belief in multiple gods. For example, the Greek culture was polytheistic, with a pantheon of gods.

Royal grant

A royal grant was a common covenant in the time of the Old Testament, in which a covenant was sworn between two individuals of unequal rank (a king to a servant). It was an unconditional covenant, as opposed to the Suzerain-Vassal covenant, which was conditional. With a royal grant, the king promised to do something for one of his servants without any action being required on the part of the servant.

Sadducees

The Sadducees were a sect within Judaism. In opposition to the Pharisees, the Sadducees held that only the laws recorded in the Pentateuch were God-inspired laws. They also rejected the existence of an afterlife, and did not believe in angels or demons. Where the Pharisees looked to the religious practices of the people, the Sadducees focused on politics and obtaining power.

Samaria

Samaria was the capital of the Northern Kingdom of Israel. In Scripture, the name "Samaria" is often used to represent the northern kingdom, after the kingdom of Israel divided in 931 BC. When the Northern Kingdom went into exile at the hands of the Assyrians, few Israelites were left in the north. These remaining Israelites mixed with the displaced people planted in their land by the Assyrians, and so, by New Testament times, the Samaritans had mixed Jewish and pagan ancestry. They worshipped God, but only accepted the Law of Moses, not the oral traditions of the Pharisees. Because of their differences in religious practices to mainstream

Judaism, they were despised by the Jews.

Sanhedrin

This was the ruling body of the Jews that advised the Chief Priest. The Romans gave some self-governing rights to the Jewish people, and these matters were managed by the Sanhedrin, which was made up of both Pharisees and Sadducees. The Chief Priest no longer had to be a descendant of Aaron (as the Law required), but was appointed by Herod.

Scribes

The Scribes worked out the oral law and determined the interpretation of Old Testament law. For example, the law that no burden should be carried on the Sabbath gave rise to an oral law, which stipulated that a "burden" was equal to the lifting of any food weighing more than a dried fig.

Second coming of Christ

The time of Christ's return is unknown; however, His return is promised. The second coming of Christ will see the completion of God's redemptive plan for mankind. At the time of His return, which will be both physical and spiritual, unbelievers will be judged and believers will be rewarded. Christ will bring the Kingdom of God in full.

Stoicism

Stoicism was a popular school of philosophy during the age of the apostles. This stream of thought taught that emotions were to be detached, one was to focus on logic, and man only lived to fulfil his duty.

Suzerain/ Vassal covenant

The Suzerain/ Vassal covenant was a common covenant in the time of the Old Testament, in which a covenant was made between a greater kingdom, or king (Suzerain), and a lesser kingdom, or king (Vassal). Vassals were usually in a position that left them with no choice about whether or not they would enter into the proposed covenant, such as following defeat in battle.

United Kingdom (of Israel)

Israel began its days with God as its King. However, after three hundred and sixty-three years in the Promised Land, they asked for a human king in order to be like the surrounding nations. The United Kingdom refers to the time in which all the tribes of Israel were united under a single king. Kings of the United Kingdom were King Saul, King David, and King Solomon. The years of the United Kingdom were approximately 1043 to 931 BC.

Visions

God gave the prophets visual images and pictures to represent His messages. For example, Ezekiel 1:5-28 depicts Ezekiel's vision of the four living creatures and the wheel within a wheel.

World view

Everyone, and every culture, has a "world view". A world view is the way in which someone's beliefs and experience shape the way they view and evaluate the world and universe.

Zealots

The Zealots were Jewish extremists determined to have no foreign ruler over the Jewish people. They openly rebelled against Roman governance, for example: by refusing to pay taxes to Caesar. It was the Zealots who stirred the people up to revolt during the war against Rome, from 66-70 AD, which ultimately led to the fall of Jerusalem and the destruction of the temple.

Zion

Mount Zion was a mountain near Jerusalem. On Mount Zion was a strong fortress, which was taken by King David and became known as the City of David. The words "Mount Zion" are sometimes used to represent Jerusalem, and they became representative of the Kingdom of God, of heaven.

REFERENCES

Please note that the information in this book comes as an amalgamation of my previous study, teaching and research. As a result, it is impossible to list all resources that have been accessed throughout the years. However, I have endeavoured to include in *Additional study resources* some of my favourite study tools, information sources, and faith resources.

Introduction to the New Testament
  [1] 2 Chronicles 7:1
  [2] Ezra 6

Introduction to the Epistles
  [1] Matthew 28:19-20
  [2] Quoted in Scripture: Luke 12:19, 1 Corinthians 15:32
  [3] Acts 15:1-35

Genesis
  [1] Paraphrase of Genesis 25:23-32

Numbers
  [1] Hebrews 9:13-14

Deuteronomy
  [1] Deuteronomy 31:6
  [2] Deuteronomy 31:7
  [3] Deuteronomy 31:23

Judges
  [1] Hosea 2:2-4; Scripture taken from The Message. Copyright © 1993, 1994, 1995, 1996, 2000, 2001, 2002. Used by permission of NavPress Publishing Group.
  [2] Hosea 2:7; Scripture taken from The Message. Copyright © 1993, 1994, 1995, 1996, 2000, 2001, 2002. Used by permission of NavPress Publishing Group.

[3] Hosea 2:10-11; Scripture taken from The Message. Copyright © 1993, 1994, 1995, 1996, 2000, 2001, 2002. Used by permission of NavPress Publishing Group.

[4] Hosea 2:14-16; Scripture taken from The Message. Copyright © 1993, 1994, 1995, 1996, 2000, 2001, 2002. Used by permission of NavPress Publishing Group.

[5] Hosea 2:19-20; Scripture taken from The Message. Copyright © 1993, 1994, 1995, 1996, 2000, 2001, 2002. Used by permission of NavPress Publishing Group.

1 & 2 Samuel
[1] 1 Samuel 8:4-6
[2] 1 Samuel 8:7-9

Esther
[1] Esther 4:14

Job
[1] Job 32:6

Ecclesiastes
[1] Ecclesiastes 12:13
[2] Ecclesiastes 12:13

Isaiah
[1] Isaiah 29:1-4
[2] Isaiah 29:5-6
[3] Isaiah 43:1-7
[4] Isaiah 61:1-4

Lamentations
[1] Lamentations 2:20; Scripture taken from The Message. Copyright © 1993, 1994, 1995, 1996, 2000, 2001, 2002. Used by permission of NavPress Publishing Group.

[2] Lamentations 4:4-5; Scripture taken from The Message. Copyright © 1993, 1994, 1995, 1996, 2000, 2001, 2002. Used by permission of NavPress Publishing Group.

[3] Lamentations 4:9-10; Scripture taken from The Message. Copyright © 1993, 1994, 1995, 1996, 2000, 2001, 2002. Used by permission of NavPress Publishing Group.

Daniel
[1] Daniel 3:16-18
[2] Smith, R. (2004). *Daniel: Chapter 11; handout of the School of Biblical Studies Department.*
[3] Matthew 12:14-17

Hosea
[1] Hosea 6:1

Amos
[1] 2 Kings 14:25
[2] Amos 6:13; 1 Chronicles 5:17
[3] Amos 3:15-4:1
[4] 1 Kings 12:28-29

Jonah
[1] Author's interpretation and paraphrase of Jonah 4:1-11

Micah
[1] Based on 2 Kings 18-20

Nahum
[1] Isaiah 10:13-14

Habakkuk
[1] Strong, James, S.T.D., LL.D., (1989). *Strong's Hebrew and Greek Dictionaries*, *e-Sword*, Ver. 9.7.2, Dictionary, H2265.
[2] Habakkuk 3:17-19 (The Message)

Matthew
[1] Matthew 19:29-30

Luke
[1] Tractate Berachot, Chapter 6, *Tosefta 26*
[2] Luke 5:31-32

John
[1] John 14:7-9
[2] John 6:35
[3] John8:12
[4] John 8:58
[5] John 10:7-10
[6] John 10:11-15
[7] John 11:25-26
[k] John 13:13
[9] John14:6
[10] John 15:1-5

Acts
[1] Luke 1:3-4

1 Corinthians
[1] Matthew 3:25

[2] 1 Corinthians 13:4-5
[3] 1 Corinthians 8:7-13

Galatians
[1] Lucado, M. (2004). *It's Not About Me: Rescue From the Life We Thought Would Make Us Happy.* Thomas Nelson, Inc., Nashville, TN.

Ephesians
[1] Strong, James, S.T.D., LL.D., (1989). *Strong's Hebrew and Greek Dictionaries, e-Sword,* Ver. 9.7.2, Dictionary, G3466.

Philippians
[1] Strong, James, S.T.D., LL.D., (1989). *Strong's Hebrew and Greek Dictionaries, e-Sword,* Ver. 9.7.2, Dictionary, G4176.
[2] Philippians 3:12

1 Timothy
[1] 2 Timothy 2:1
[2] 1 Colossians 16:10-11, 2 Timothy 1:7
[3] 2 Timothy 2:22

2 Timothy
[1] 2 Timothy 3:5

Titus
[1] Galatians 2:3
[2] 2 Corinthians 8:16-17; 8:23; 12:18
[3] Titus 1:2
[4] Titus 1:12

Philemon
[1] Philemon 1:2
[2] Philemon 1:17

Hebrews
[1] Strong, James, S.T.D., LL.D., (1989). *Strong's Hebrew and Greek Dictionaries, e-Sword,* Ver. 9.7.2, Dictionary, G5048.

James
[1] Acts 11:19
[2] Matthew 12:46-59 and John 7:1-8
[3] 1Corinthians 15:7
[4] Acts 1:14
[5] Galatians 1:19
[6] Act 12:1-3,17; Acts 15 (v13-21); and Acts 21:17-26

[7] Mark 12:41-44

1 Peter
  [1] 1 Peter 4:9

1 John
  [1] 1 John 3:9
  [2] Barclay, W. (2002). *The New Daily Study Bible: The Letters of John and Jude*, 3rd edition. Westminster John Knox Press, Kentucky.

Revelation
  [1] Matthew 6:19-20
  [2] Strong, James, S.T.D., LL.D., (1989). *Strong's Hebrew and Greek Dictionaries, e-Sword*, Ver. 9.7.2, Dictionary, G3144.
  [3] Strong, James, S.T.D., LL.D., (1989). *Strong's Hebrew and Greek Dictionaries, e-Sword*, Ver. 9.7.2, Dictionary, G32.

ADDITIONAL STUDY RESOURCES

The following resources may be helpful to your study; this is by no means an exclusive or exhaustive list. Some are sources offering further background information; some will assist you with cross referencing or interpreting the text; and others will provide you with narrative that helps you to get into the shoes of the original readers, and thus expand your ability to picture what is happening at that time of history when you read the Bible.

Bible dictionaries
A Bible dictionary is a handy resource to have beside you as you study. They hold a wealth of historical background to dig deeper into the text. A few well-known Bible dictionaries include:
1. *Holman Illustrated Bible Dictionary*; produced by Holman Bible Publishers.
2. *Nelson's New Illustrated Bible Dictionary*; edited by Youngblood, R., Bruce, E., and Harrison, K.
3. *The New Unger's Bible Dictionary*; edited by Unger, M.
4. *Zondervan Pictorial Bible Dictionary*; edited by Tenney, M.

Bible encyclopaedias
Bible encyclopaedias go into more detail than Bible dictionaries. A couple of well-known Bible encyclopaedias are as follows:
1. *The International Standard Bible Encyclopaedia*; 4 volume set; edited by Bromiley, G.
2. *The Zondervan Encyclopedia of the Bible*; 5 volume set; edited by Tenney, M., and Silva, M.

Listed below are a couple of Bible encyclopaedias that focus specifically on prophecy. Do not take these as a final authority, as the interpretation of many prophecies remains contested amongst theologians; however, they are useful guides.
1. *Dictionary of Biblical Prophecy and End Times*; by Hays, D., Duvall, S., and Pate, M.
2. *Encyclopaedia of Biblical Prophecy*; by Payne, B.

Bible maps

Maps are useful study tools, which enable you to visualise distances, places, and journeys discussed in the Bible. Here are a few options:

1. *Atlas of the Bible, an illustrated guide to the Holy Land*; produced by The Reader's Digest Association
2. *Bible Atlas – Access Foundation*; edited by Zaine Ridling
3. *Holman Book of Biblical Charts, Maps, and Reconstructions*; edited by Marsha Ellis Smit.
4. *Nelson's Complete Book of Bible Maps and Charts*; produced by Thomas Nelson Publishers.
5. *Then and Now Bible Maps* are a series of pamphlets containing Biblical maps produced by Rose Publishing Inc. They show key Biblical landmarks with current-day nations depicted in an overlay of red.

Electronic Bibles and resources

Electronic dictionaries allow fast searches of particular verses and words; they are a handy tool when cross referencing scriptures and themes between books in the Bible. Electronic resources allow instant access to large volumes of information. Here are a few:

1. *Studylight* has a range of study resources and tools. You can access it at: http://www.studylight.org/
2. *Bible Gateway* allows you to search multiple translations of the Bible as well as explore additional resources, such as dictionaries and commentaries. You can access it at: http://www.biblegateway.com/
3. *Bible Study Tools* contains commentaries, encyclopaedias, dictionaries, and parallel Bibles. It can be accessed at: http://www.biblestudytools.com/
4. *E-sword* is a free, downloadable electronic Bible. It has many free translations as well as additional tools such as dictionaries and commentaries. You can download it at: http://www.e-sword.net/
5. You will also find additional study resources and topical posts on the *author's website*: http://www.ShannonBuchbach.com

Bible commentaries

Try not to rely too heavily on commentaries, especially when you are starting out. The Bible is a treasure to be explored! Try coming to your own conclusions, interpreting Scripture on the basis of the historical background, before going to Bible commentaries. After considering the text and forming an opinion, Bible commentaries are a great resource to bring in different perspectives to then consider. It is a good idea to consult several at a time because they will often present different views on the difficult passages. A couple of popular commentaries are:

1. *Adam Clarke's Commentary on the Bible*; by Adam Clarke (1715-1832).
2. *NIV Bible Study Commentary*; by Sailhamer, J.
3. *Matthew Henrys Commentary on the Whole Bible*; by Henry, M.
4. *Tyndale Old Testament Commentaries*; various authors.

Bible study resources

1. *How to Read the Bible for all its Worth, a guide to understanding the Bible*; by Gordon Fee and Douglas Stuart
2. *Strong's Exhaustive Concordance of the Bible*; by James Strong
3. *Vine's Expository Dictionary of New Testament Words*; by William Vine

Works of fiction

The following list contains some of my favourite fictional reads that are either set in Biblical times or offer encouragement in one's faith. They are:

1. *A.D.Chronicles series*; by Bodie and Brock Thoene
2. *Ben-Hur: A Tale of the Christ*; by Lew Wallace
3. *Hinds' Feet on High Places*; Hannah Hurnard
4. *Mark of the Lion series*; by Francine Rivers
5. *Redeeming Love*; by Francine Rivers
6. *The Fifth Testament*; by Ernest A. Gray
7. *The Pilgrim's Progress*; by John Bunyan
8. The author has released a faith novel entitled *A Walk through Winter*, and is currently working on her second *Mosaic of Shattered Crystal*.

ABOUT THE AUTHOR

Originally from Australia, Shannon now lives in the Central Drakensberg region of South Africa with her husband. She studied Occupational Therapy at the *University of Queensland* and worked in this profession before entering the mission field in 2008. She completed the School of Biblical Studies with *Youth with a Mission* in 2010 and has since worked with Christian organisations in East Africa and Southern Africa, teaching Inductive Bible Study. In 2014, Shannon pioneered a Bible school in Rwanda with Youth with a Mission's Kigali base. She has also authored several study booklets for the *Shan Project*.

Shannon is passionate about seeing the Word of God lived out for community transformation, holding to the teaching of James 1:22-27: "*But be doers of the word, and not hearers only, deceiving yourselves. For if anyone is a hearer of the word and not a doer, he is like a man who looks intently at his natural face in a mirror. For he looks at himself and goes away and at once forgets what he was like. But the one who looks into the perfect law, the law of liberty, and perseveres, being no hearer who forgets but a doer who acts, he will be blessed in his doing. If anyone thinks he is religious and does not bridle his tongue but deceives his heart, this person's religion is worthless. Religion that is pure and undefiled before God, the Father, is this: to visit orphans and widows in their affliction, and to keep oneself unstained from the world.*"

From this passion, Shannon co-founded the NGO *Redefined Ministries International* in 2011. Redefined Ministries continues its community development work in Mahagi Territory, Democratic Republic of Congo; Shannon completes administrative work for them from home, visiting as often as she can. She authored *Congolese Grandpa; A Life of War, Work and Worship* to raise funds for this work, and awareness of life for many Congolese. Additionally, she has written a number of contemporary Christian novels.

You can read more about Shannon and her works on her webpage: www.ShannonBuchbach.com.